WAGE DETERMINATION AND INCOMES POLICY IN OPEN ECONOMIES

WAGE DETERMINATION AND INCOMES POLICY IN OPEN ECONOMIES

By
Anne Romanis Braun

INTERNATIONAL MONETARY FUND
WASHINGTON, D. C. 1986

Library of Congress Cataloging-in-Publication Data

Braun, Anne Romanis.
Wage determination and incomes policy in open economies.

Bibliography: p.
1. Wages—Government policy—Europe. 2. Wage-price policy—Europe. I. International Monetary Fund. II. Title.
HD5014.B7 1986 331.2'94 86-10414
ISBN 0-939934-75-2

Price: US$18.50

For S.B.

CONTENTS

Part III. Wage Bargaining Institutions, Incomes Policy, and Demand Management Since the 1960s

Part IV. Conclusions

PREFACE

This volume deals with the nature of wage determination and the problem of securing an economically appropriate development of money incomes in an open industrial economy under a fixed or a flexible exchange rate system. Several chapters focus on the scope for incomes policy as an adjunct to fiscal and monetary policy.

Throughout the volume, the industrial countries are defined as the 14 closely integrated economies of Austria, Belgium-Luxembourg, Canada, Denmark, France, the Federal Republic of Germany, Italy, Japan, the Netherlands, Norway, Sweden, Switzerland, the United Kingdom, and the United States. Finland and Australia are not included in the group because their export composition, and; in Australia's case, the protected home market, set them outside the framework of the analysis. They are, however, referred to when their experience is of particular interest.

The book consists of four parts. Part I (Chapters 1–3) comprises a historical survey and an evaluation of industrial countries' experience with incomes policy since World War II. Parts II and III supplement this account with studies of price and wage determination and the scope for incomes policy in practice and theory, and with case studies of wage bargaining institutions and incomes policies in seven countries during the 1970s and early 1980s. Conclusions concerning the experience with incomes policy are to be found in Chapters 2, 3, 4, and 10. Part IV presents an unorthodox account of the process of price and wage determination in the industrial economies and its apparent implications for economic management over the medium term.

In Part II, Chapter 4 comprises an account of the nature of cost inflation in industrial countries and of the role of incomes policy under fixed exchange rates in the 1960s. Chapter 5 examines the reasons for the growing ineffectiveness of national demand management and incomes policies and the progressive failure of the fixed exchange rate system during the late 1960s and early 1970s. Chapter 6 describes the revolution in economic theory during the 1970s. It compares the currently accepted view of wage and price determination based on general equilibrium theory—in which there can be little case for incomes policy—with Keynes's account of wage bargaining, and with the description of the wage determination process in industrial countries in Chapter 4. Chapter 7 treats the related issue of the relation between demand expansion and real output growth under imperfect competition. Chapter 8 considers the case for indexation of wages in theory and practice, and includes a brief account of recent experience with an indexation-based incomes policy in Australia.

The case studies in Part III provide a closer look at the nature of wage bargaining and the recourse to incomes policy, illustrating the differing problems encountered under changeable exchange rates during the 1970s and the early 1980s. Chapter 9 comprises studies of four large economies—the United Kingdom, Japan, the Federal Republic of Germany, and Canada. Chapter 10 comprises studies of three small economies—Austria, the Netherlands, and Norway. The chapter closes with some general observations on the experience of these three countries, the United Kingdom, and Canada with incomes policy during this period.

In conclusion, Part IV sets out a summary account of the determination of prices and wages, of unemployment and concealed unemployment, and of productivity growth in open economies characterized by marked differences in the ease of entry to sectors of large-scale and small-scale production. It outlines the influence of the different wage bargaining characteristics of the 14 industrial economies within this framework and suggests how those differences came about. Part IV ends with a brief consideration of the policy implications of this view of the industrial world economy and its relevance to the current problems of the industrial countries.

Much of the book was written while I was working in the Research Department of the Fund. Several chapters have previously been published in *Staff Papers* and elsewhere or circulated as internal Fund papers. Chapters 6 and 9–11 were written especially for this volume. The opinions expressed throughout are those of the author and should not be interpreted to represent the views of the Fund.

I am indebted to J.J. Polak and the late J. Marcus Fleming for directing me to this extraordinarily interesting field of economics and permitting me to pursue that interest in numerous studies, and I am grateful to Sir E.H. Phelps Brown, Professor John Dunlop, Dr. J.E. Isaac, and Christopher Saunders for their expert help and encouragement.

In preparing these studies, I have benefited from access to Fund documents, and from the comments and expertise of many Fund colleagues. I cannot possibly mention all those who have helped me over the years, but I must express an especial debt to Marcus Fleming's penetrating comments, and thanks for the assistance and comments I have received from Victor Argy, Eckhard Brehmer, Benedicte Christensen, Jouko Hauvonen, William Hemphill, Michael Kucynski, Harilaos Vittas, and the late William H. White, and for assistance from the late Martin Loftus, Anne Salda, and Barbara Perry of the Joint Library.

My special thanks are due to the Director of the External Relations Department, Azizali F. Mohammed, to Norman K. Humphreys, Chief Editor, who suggested this project, and to Esha Ray and Elin Knotter of the Editorial Division, for whom my admiration is unbounded. Esha Ray carried out the monumental task of preparing the text and footnotes of Chapters 1 through 10 with extraordinary thoroughness and efficiency, and bore the tribulations of updating with unfailing good humor. Elin Knotter finalized Chapters 9 and 10 and prepared Chapter 11 for publication with similar thoroughness and was responsible for seeing the entire text set up in print. I am grateful to Phyllis Lake and Lina Turnbull for typing my handwritten drafts. I am also indebted to the staff of the Fund's Graphics Section for their work in the production of this book.

Part I
A Survey of the Use of Incomes Policy Since World War II

1

What Incomes Policy Is and When It Has Been Used

The term "incomes policy" is commonly employed to cover specific measures aimed at restraining the rate at which money incomes increase, by curbing the exploitation of market power by business and labor, professional, or other groups. Incomes policy is thus an adjunct to fiscal and monetary policy. Its purpose is to moderate the rate at which prices and costs tend to rise when the level of aggregate demand and employment is not so high as to force up prices and wages by creating scarcities or to provoke a balance of payments crisis.[1]

The need for incomes policy arises when it appears that a tolerable degree of price stability cannot be achieved by reducing the level of demand, or that it can be achieved only at an unacceptably high cost in terms of unemployment, loss of real output, and interference with growth. Hence, incomes policy is often presented as a means of improving the trade-off between unemployment and price stability.

Incomes policy is sometimes defined as deliberate intervention by the government in the process of price formation for labor and products aimed at preventing pretax money incomes from rising faster than the growth of national income in real terms. It is desirable, however, also to include concerted efforts to this end made by private sector organizations, on a nationwide basis, without direct government intervention. Under systems of coordinated national wage bargaining, the central labor and employers' organizations are faced with the need to work out an incomes policy, since they are generally

[1]This chapter is largely based on Braun (1975).

obliged to relate their decisions to the overall economic situation and outlook. Hence such systems may be as effective in ensuring a reasonable rate of increase in money incomes as a policy directly involving the government.[2]

Incomes policy as here defined is essentially an anti-inflationary device. It should not be interpreted to cover the whole range of policy with respect to incomes. Policies concerned with income distribution per se, such as measures to reduce the inequality of incomes, to eliminate very low wages, or to reduce poverty by social welfare legislation, are not comprehended by the term. In practice, however, such measures are often adopted along with an incomes policy, because the labor organizations regard measures to improve the position of lower-paid workers as a prerequisite for their cooperation in an incomes policy. "Indeed, one of the general comments on the experience of incomes policy in Western Europe is that it has been impossible to evade the distributional aspect of even the simplest kind of incomes policy."[3]

The term incomes policy is sometimes used in the other sense. In particular, its French equivalent *(politique des revenus)* has meant policy with respect to the distribution of income in the course of development. In France, during the 1950s and early 1960s, the formulation of such a policy involved discussions between the representatives of the different interest groups in the process of preparing the medium-term Economic Plans.[4] Similar discussions have taken place in connection with the drawing up of five-year plans in the Netherlands, with coordinated bargaining in Austria, and with centralized wage bargaining or combined wage settlements in Norway.

The specific objectives and methods of incomes policy differ greatly with the institutional and political characteristics of the countries where it is implemented. The wide variety of measures applied may be grouped under the following headings:

(1) Short-term intervention by means of "freezes" or temporary controls to prevent wages or prices from rising. Such measures are often applied in the hope that if increases can be avoided temporarily, conditions later may be more conducive to restraint so that the increases may be moderated or prevented; or the measures may be specifically aimed at checking the development of inflationary price expectations.

---

[2]Saunders (1971, p. 332). See also Economic Commission for Europe (1967, Chapter 1, p. 2).

[3]Blackaby (1971, p. 41), referring to the introduction to the ECE Survey (see footnote 2).

[4]Massé (1964); International Monetary Fund (1964, p. 120); and Hayward (1966).

(2) Efforts to inform public opinion by investigating price and wage increases, setting up advisory bodies, or other means, so as to promote agreement on the need for moderation of pay claims if inflation is to be avoided and establish a consensus on what is an appropriate rate of increase in wages and salaries. The aim is to bring the force of public opinion to bear as a curb on wage and price increases. This objective involves the formulation of a more or less explicit "guideline" for wage and salary increases and of concomitant ideas concerning pricing behavior, profit margins, and the share of nonwage incomes in national income.

(3) Mandatory, or voluntary, implementation of guidelines for wages and salaries, with or without measures of price control or profit restraint.

(4) Tax-based incomes policies (that would impose tax penalties for firms or employee groups exceeding a prescribed "norm" for wage increases or grant tax breaks to those settling for smaller increases) have been advocated as an alternative to administratively enforced wage guidelines, especially in economies characterized by decentralized wage bargaining, such as the United States and Canada.

(5) Measures aimed at restraining cost pressures in specific sectors such as construction, basic industries, public services, and rental housing through provisions for investigation of price or wage decisions, for prior notification or approval of price increases, or for approval of wage settlements.

(6) Operation of a coordinated system of wage and salary determination (often covering farm incomes as well), with or without direct government involvement, as in Austria, the Netherlands, and the Scandinavian countries; or through compulsory arbitration procedures for wages and salaries, as in Australia and New Zealand.[5]

(7) Indexation provisions of two kinds were adopted as a form of incomes policy in the context of accelerating inflation during the 1970s.

(a) Indexation of wages and salaries by means of price escalator clauses was seen as a means of preventing expectations of higher inflation from inducing further acceleration of wage and price increases. It could thereby serve to lessen the unemployment and loss of output associated with measures to bring down the rate of monetary expansion.

---

[5] A high degree of coordination in wage fixing applied throughout much of the postwar period in the countries mentioned and at times in Belgium and Ireland. See Blanpain (1971) and Browne (1965).

(b) Indexation adjustment of progressive taxes to correct for inflation-induced increases in tax liability was sometimes adopted in order to avoid "tax-push" efforts by wage and salary earners seeking to compensate for the effect of rising taxes in reducing *real* take-home pay by securing larger nominal wage increases. Alternatively, discretionary tax adjustments were proposed as a means of moderating wage pressures in the face of external price shocks or following a devaluation by allowing the authorities to increase the share of disposable income in gross earnings at those times. Under centralized systems of income determination involving the government, reductions in direct taxes were often granted in return for moderate wage increases in the "frame" settlement between the employers' and union organizations. This strategy was actively pursued in Norway and the Netherlands, where rising revenue from taxes on oil or natural gas provided an exceptional opportunity for reducing other taxes.

(8) Longer-term measures falling under the heading "institutional engineering." These include, for example, improved facilities for mediation and arbitration of disputes, provision for sanctions against unofficial strikes or for mandatory "cooling-off" periods; measures to reduce the scope of disputes concerning employer, employee, and union prerogatives; clarification of the legal status and duration of wage contracts, simplification of wage structures, systems of payment, etc.; reorganization of the union structure to avoid disputes about membership coverage, to simplify wage bargaining, and to lessen tendencies for interreaction of wage claims, causing a wage/wage spiral; and labor market policies to improve mobility or to provide retraining facilities in order to lessen the tendency for wages to rise at a time of considerable unemployment in some regions or among some categories of workers.

The objectives, general approach, and specific measures of incomes policy adopted at various times have differed greatly as a result of the very different circumstances in which incomes policy has been implemented. One can distinguish four main periods of widespread recourse to incomes policy since 1945, each with a particular character:

(1) The period soon after World War II when incomes policies were adopted during reconstruction in a fragmented and distorted industrial economy.

(2) The early 1960s when incomes policies were implemented with full employment policies and macroeconomic demand management generally was consistent with the fixed exchange rate system.

(3) The Viet Nam war era of the late 1960s and early 1970s when incomes policies were utilized in the context of destabilizing mac-

roeconomic policies and strains within the international payments system.

(4) The period after 1973 when incomes policies were adopted in the aftermath of excessive monetary expansion, the breakup of the fixed exchange rate system, and the oil price increase and were implemented in a confused environment of sharp swings in national policies, uncertain exchange rate policies, and structural changes required by the higher cost of energy and real exchange rate adjustments. Although there was a general shift away from incomes policies during the late 1970s, a few countries (notably the Netherlands and Australia) implemented incomes policies in the early 1980s.

With the sole exception of the early 1960s, all the instances of widespread recourse to incomes policy occurred in response to severe disequilibrium and malfunctioning of the international payments system. The coincidence of recourse to incomes policy at particular periods strongly suggests that, contrary to appearances, the need for incomes policy often arose because of international factors rather than because of an autonomous increase in the "pushfulness" of wage bargaining and pricing behavior within individual economies. That is to say, such changes in behavior may represent a response to the supranational economic conjuncture rather than an autonomous factor in generating inflationary pressure. It is a running theme of this book that the drastic worsening of inflationary pressures in the 1970s was produced by the combination of inflationary policies with secular factors that tended to increase the market power of enterprises and organized labor; thus contrary to the widely held opinion, rising inflation was not principally due to increased rigidities in the labor market and a worsened functioning of the wage bargaining system.

With the resurgence of neoclassical economics and the widespread recourse to monetarist policies of restraint, incomes policy fell into disfavor at the end of the 1970s. However, a renewed interest in incomes policies has arisen in the mid-1980s, with the growing realization, once again, of a need for deliberate measures to influence the determination of nominal incomes as one element in a consistent set of national macroeconomic policies.

2

Incomes Policy Under Full Employment Policies and Fixed Exchange Rates

After World War II, incomes policies were applied in a number of European countries in a context of scarcities of goods and critical shortages of foreign exchange. Economic policies then involved a considerable element of direct compulsion.[1]

Policies of the Late 1940s and Early 1950s

Centralized control over wage and salary decisions was enforced in several countries (the Netherlands, Norway, and Sweden) and coordinated wages policies were adopted in Austria and the United Kingdom against the background of widespread controls and restrictions. These included measures such as direction of labor into essential employment, rationing, allocation of materials, price and rent controls, dividends restraint, and excess profits taxation.[2]

Wages policy was implemented through central organizations of the labor unions and employers' associations or by joint institutions set up to formulate and coordinate policy during the Great Depression or created as a result of clandestine wartime cooperation. Wage restraint was accepted by wage earners as necessary in the short run to ensure an equitable

---

[1]This chapter is a slightly revised version of Braun (1975, pp. 4–28).

[2]Policies during this period are described in Sturmthal (1957); Roberts (1958); Marris (1961); Edelman and Fleming (1965); David C. Smith (1966); and Economic Commission for Europe (1967, Chapter 4). See also Skånland (1964) on Norway; Johnston (1962) on Sweden; Markmann (1964) on the Federal Republic of Germany; Pedersen (1964) and Hoffmeyer (1964) on Denmark; and Zoeteweij (1955), Pedersen (1957), and Windmuller (1969) on the Netherlands.

distribution of the strictly limited resources available for consumption and as useful in the longer run as a means to promote increased employment opportunities and higher living standards by fostering industrial expansion and greater import capacity. Popular support was conditioned by the existence of a stringent and highly "visible" balance of payments constraint, in the shortage of "hard" currency to pay for essential imports. Furthermore, the bargaining power of wage earners was circumscribed by the prevalence of considerable unemployment and of underemployment in agriculture and distribution, as well as by fear of a recurrence of the heavy unemployment experienced before the war. In all the countries mentioned, the implementation of incomes policies was aided by the development of a considerable consensus on economic policy objectives during and immediately after the war, and the cooperation of the unions was facilitated by their close ties with the socialist or coalition governments then in power. The experience of "wages policy" associated with rationing and controls tending to protect real wages promoted popular acceptance of the case for intervention to secure an "equitable" development of incomes. At its simplest, this was taken to mean that all wages and salaries should go up more or less in line and that extreme disparity of income distribution should be curbed by taxation. All these countries returned repeatedly to the quest for an "equitable" incomes policy in inflationary circumstances.

Countries in which the political situation was not conducive to the adoption of comprehensive policies along these lines experienced severe inflation. One consequence of this was the adoption of widespread indexation of wages in France and Italy and the reinforcement of existing wage indexation in Belgium and Luxembourg.[3] In France and Italy, an extensive wartime system of price controls continued to be enforced in the immediate postwar period.[4] In the Federal Republic of Germany, nominal wages were kept at wartime levels, but real wages depended on differential rations, the provision of housing, and so forth. The French and the Italian authorities subsequently developed a weapon for influencing the pricing behavior of large enterprises through their control over sources of external financing. In both countries, the power of producers or distributors to raise prices was a more important cause of inflation than cost pressures originating in union wage claims in the private sector

[3]See Chapter 8. Indexation was also customary in the Scandinavian countries other than Sweden in the context of centralized wage bargaining.

[4]Hackett (1963); Dessau (1963); Organization for Economic Cooperation and Development (1964); and Giugni (1965).

because the unions' power to negotiate wage increases was limited and the employers combined to resist the development of collective bargaining.

In countries where supply conditions were comparatively normal and the need to strengthen the country's balance of payments position was absent, as in the United States, Canada, and Belgium, explicit incomes policies were not adopted. In the United States, wage pressures were somewhat moderated by tightening labor legislation (especially through the provision for injunctions against strikes and legally imposed cooling-off periods under the Taft-Hartley Act).[5] Controls were imposed during the Korean war period.

The violent upsurge of commodity prices in 1950 caused by the conflict undid efforts to ensure wage and price restraint. Subsequently, cost pressures lessened as primary product prices fell back sharply and industrial capacity in Western Europe and Japan was restored. Restraints on the free working of the market economy were gradually removed, and interest in incomes policy subsided, except in countries still facing severe balance of payments difficulties. The systems instituted in the Netherlands[6] and Austria[7] after 1945 proved their usefulness in the balance of payments crises experienced late in the 1950s. In the United Kingdom[8] and Sweden,[9] the problem of incomes policy continued to attract considerable attention because of the tendency for labor costs to rise more rapidly than in other countries with a lower degree of utilization of labor. In Sweden, the system of centralized wage bargaining, which has been characterized as a "private incomes policy," was developed during this period. In France, the basic price control legislation of 1945 remained in force, with modifications, throughout the 1950s and early 1960s, and the Government was able to reimpose control at any time. The 1950s were characterized by alternating periods of liberalization and stiffening of price controls.[10]

---

[5]Marris (1961, pp. 451–89).

[6]Roberts (1958, pp. 118–34); Economic Commission for Europe (1967, Chapter 4); Pen (1964); Barbash (1972, pp. 61–80); Bhatia and Bouter (1961); and Windmuller (1969). See also Chapter 10.

[7]Economic Commission for Europe (1967, Chapter 4); Spitäller (1973); and Robinson (1973, pp. 14–22).

[8]Knowles (1962); Economic Commission for Europe (1967, Chapter 4); and David C. Smith (1968a).

[9]Johnston (1962); Mouly (1967); Anderman (1967); Lindbeck (1972a); Barbash (1972, pp. 5–41); and Brehmer and Bradford (1974).

[10]Successive price freezes in 1952, 1954, 1956, and 1957 were followed by a progressive easing of controls that lasted until 1964. Organization for Economic Cooperation and Development (1964, pp. 59–62).

Policies of the Early 1960s

When output and employment began to rise after the 1958 slowdown, there was a widespread revival of interest in incomes policy. Attention was concentrated on voluntary measures aimed at moderating the rate of increase of prices, and more especially of wages, by influencing the climate of opinion and the attitude of partners in wage bargaining.[11] Such measures were intended to aid in (1) securing the cooperation of employers and trade unions in limiting inflationary pressures by appropriate wage and price decisions; (2) educating those concerned with such decisions on the "public interest" aspect of avoiding inflationary repercussions and mobilizing the forces of public opinion against undue increases in wages, salaries, and profits; and (3) establishing or strengthening specific checks and balances to reduce cost pressures in particular areas of the economy.

Productivity Guidelines

The productivity guideline (also called guidepost, guiding light, or gearing) came into prominence in the early 1960s. "The proposition that prices will be stable so long as aggregate factor incomes increase no faster than the total volume of output ... passed out of economics into public relations" and this was "further simplified into the proposition that, to avoid a general price increase, average pay per employed worker should not increase faster than average productivity per employed worker."[12]

"Norms" based on this principle were widely adopted with two basically different aims. In the Netherlands, Norway, Sweden, and the United Kingdom, the basic aim was to prevent pay rising faster than productivity in order to avoid loss of competitive power vis-à-vis countries in which industrial prices were under only slight upward pressure, such as the United States, the Federal Republic of Germany,

---

[11] "For the present purpose, incomes policy is taken to mean the effort to acquire a degree of direct collective control over the level and structure of the remuneration of labour and capital and over the distribution of the national income to households and enterprises.... The phrase 'collective' rather than 'government' control is used because it is taken as a reasonable assumption for western European societies that the decisions will remain, essentially, in the private sector and that governments, even if they hold certain compulsory powers, must influence primary incomes mainly by guidance and persuasion of managements, workers and their representative organizations; in practice, in particular for wages and salaries, it is the policies adopted by these collective organizations which must be the instruments of incomes policy." Economic Commission for Europe (1967, Chapter 1, p. 2).

[12] Economic Commission for Europe (1967, Chapter 1, p. 5). See also United Kingdom, Council on Prices, Productivity and Incomes (1961, pp. 25–29).

Japan, and Italy. In the Netherlands, this aim was not altogether appropriate, because Dutch wages were by then well below those in neighboring countries and strong upward pressures were beginning to be experienced for that reason, weakening the entire system of coordinated wage fixing.[13] In some of the second group of countries, notably in the Federal Republic of Germany and the United States, the aim was to reconcile fuller utilization of manpower resources with the high priority accorded to price stability by the electorate.[14] That is, the object was to forestall price increases as full employment was more nearly realized.[15] In either case, wage restraint could plausibly be presented to the wage earners as necessary for maintaining full employment in a world in which there were strong pressures for price stability.

Exceptional Conditions Favoring Price Stability

Price stability was a not unrealistic goal during the late 1950s and early 1960s, when prices of internationally traded goods were not increasing, largely as a result of exceptional factors.[16] While primary product prices were tending to decline, export prices for manufactures were virtually stable. There were two main reasons for this. One was that a number of countries were still in the position of having considerable underutilization of the labor force (allowing for excess manpower in low-productivity agricultural and services sectors) and were expanding industrial employment under the stimulus of export-led growth, in some cases aided by highly favorable exchange rates at the going level of wages (e.g., the Federal Republic of Germany, Italy, Japan, the Netherlands, and Norway). The second reason was that in the United States, the Administration of President Eisenhower placed a high priority on price stability. Unemployment there was increasing, and, despite subsequent measures, remained quite high until the mid-1960s.[17]

---

[13]Kervyn de Lettenhove (1965). See also Chapter 10.

[14]The highly influential framework of guidelines in the *Economic Report of the President* for 1962 clearly relates to a situation of less than full employment, as it refers to industries in which there is usually an excess of manpower. United States, *Economic Report of the President* (1962).

[15]Policies during this period are described in the Economic Commission for Europe (1967, Chapter 4). See also Pen (1963) and (1964) and Flanagan, Soskice, and Ulman (1983) on the Netherlands; Johnston (1963) and Faxén (1964) on Sweden; Phelps Brown (1971a) and Isaac (1972) on Australia; and Dunlop (1966), Sheahan (1967), and Ackley (1972a and 1972b) on the United States.

[16]See Chapter 5.

[17]Lindbeck (1972b, pp. 307–308), and Johnson (1972a, p. 319).

The maintenance of price stability in industrial countries was, of course, facilitated by the gradual improvement in the terms of trade over most of the 1950s and 1960s. Declining prices for basic commodities make it possible for the aggregate level of prices not to increase even if wages and salaries are rising somewhat faster than productivity and profit margins are maintained. Alternatively, price stability can be achieved and real wages can rise in line with productivity, even though some shift to profits is taking place. Of particular importance for countries that are heavily dependent on imported food and raw materials is the fact that declining primary product prices may make it possible to stabilize the cost of living, even though unit labor costs and prices of many industrial goods and services are rising. Thus, the effect of specific large wage increases in inducing further increases to compensate for the resulting rise in the cost of living can be avoided. This suggests that even the stabilization of primary product prices would make it more difficult to avoid price inflation, while rapidly rising commodity prices would tend to provoke an accelerating rate of inflation.

Purpose of Incomes Policies

The goal of incomes policy during this period was essentially to modify the working of the existing system, with the least possible interference with the market mechanism, by strengthening underlying forces of competition, which, it was presumed, could be revived or brought into play. In most countries, interest centered on moderating wage increases rather than on limiting price increases directly because prices in general were relatively stable. In the light of recent experience, it was not implausible to suggest that if unit labor costs were prevented from rising, prices could be stabilized by aggregate demand policies. Indeed, in some countries declines in profit margins were actually seen as posing a risk that private investment would decline, and hence that the expansion of employment opportunities would be reduced. However, it seemed more feasible to restrain increases in pay rather than increases in prices because of the smaller number of decisions involved. Formal collective bargaining was still the predominant factor in wage and salary determination; hence, the rate of increase was effectively decided by a manageable number of bargaining units, with changes occurring relatively infrequently—rarely more than once a year. Therefore, the Economic Commission for Europe was of the opinion that "no great administrative apparatus is required. Even the imposition of statutory control [on collective wage settlements] would not prove too overwhelming an administrative task." On the other hand, it was generally believed that "the number of significant price fixers is too large for control through a few organizations or a small administrative machine."[18]

Within a few years this view had been reversed in the light of changing circumstances, and by 1971 the Organization for Economic Cooperation and Development (OECD) was expressing the opinion that "basically, it is apparent that incomes are, in many countries, less amenable to institutionalised systems [of control] than prices."[19]

Under fixed exchange rates, the scope for implementing an incomes policy with good prospects of public support was strongest in two very different situations: (1) where the tendencies to cost inflation in the economy were relatively moderate compared with other countries but the incentive to maintain that advantage was strong owing to a desire to provide more employment opportunities and shift labor out of disguised unemployment in low-productivity sectors; and (2) where the tendencies to cost inflation were strong, and a weak balance of payments position threatened to require a devaluation.

The motivation for union support of wage moderation was liable to be drastically weakened (1) if governments deliberately adopted restrictive demand policies aimed at keeping down wage increases by raising unemployment, or (2) if efforts at moderating wage increases coincided with a strong balance of payments position. The weakening of the motivation for wage restraint in these two situations was an important influence on wage bargaining attitudes and outcomes in the late 1960s and early 1970s.

Policies of the Late 1960s and Early 1970s

In the mid-1960s, stronger incomes policies were implemented by countries faced with severe balance of payments problems. Thus, the U.K. Government established a mandatory policy in 1965 in an effort to avoid devaluation, taking legal powers to prohibit or postpone increases in pay and prices,[20] and Finland instituted a comprehensive national incomes policy after devaluing the markka in 1967.[21]

---

[18]Economic Commission for Europe (1967, Chapter 1, p. 12).

[19]Organization for Economic Cooperation and Development (1971b, p. 36)

[20]Fels (1972, Chapter 3); David C. Smith (1968a); Economic Commission for Europe (1967, Chapter 4, pp. 17–20); Organization for Economic Cooperation and Development (1970, pp. 86–88); Ulman and Flanagan (1971, pp. 17–23); Blackaby (1971); Balfour (1972); Hunter (1973); Mitchell (1972); Roberts and Rothwell (1972); Jones (1973); and Clegg (1972).

[21]Organization for Economic Cooperation and Development (1970, pp. 79–80), and Derek Robinson (1973, pp. 22–33).

Increased Resort to Direct Intervention

Many countries again resorted to direct intervention in price and wage setting in an attempt to curb the marked acceleration of inflation at the end of the 1960s. Canada set up an independent Prices and Incomes Commission, which sought to organize a comprehensive package of income restraint; although the unions opposed the approval for wage guidelines, large businesses undertook to limit price increases in 1970.[22] Several small countries with a tradition of incomes policy—Denmark, Finland, the Netherlands, Norway, and also Ireland—implemented price and/or wage freezes, took steps to prolong wage agreements, and adopted other measures[23] in an attempt to curb a marked acceleration of the rate of price increase. In an astonishing *volte face* President Nixon imposed a 90-day freeze of all wages, prices, and profits at the time of the de facto devaluation of the dollar in August 1971. Incomes policies of varying forms continued to be applied in the United States until the spring of 1974.[24] Elsewhere, except in the United Kingdom, recourse to incomes policies lessened after 1971, but price restraints again became widespread during 1973. (See Chart 1.) In the United Kingdom, the Conservative Government adopted stringent incomes policy measures late in 1972, both to suppress the consequences of a runaway monetary expansion that followed a liberalization of controls on the banking system and to counter the sharp deterioration in the wage bargaining climate after the passing of the Industrial Relations Act in 1971. A 90-day freeze of prices and incomes at the end of 1972 was followed by six months of strict control in Stage II, and by some easing in Stage III, when the disastrous threshold agreements were introduced.[25]

Changed Context for Incomes Policy

The increased emphasis on controlling prices during this period reflected changes in the context in which incomes policies were

[22] Berger (1973).

[23] Derek Robinson (1973, pp. 37–41); Ulman and Flanagan (1971, pp. 48–87 and 116–46). See also Brunot (1974) on price policies in France and Kasper (1972) and Giersch (1971) on developments in the Federal Republic of Germany.

[24] The experience of the United Kingdom and the reports of the Prices and Incomes Board had a considerable influence on the measures adopted in the United States. For details of the U.S. stabilization program during the period August 15, 1971 to April 30, 1974, see United States, Cost of Living Council, *Economic Stabilization Program Quarterly Reports*, 1971–74. See also Bosworth (1972) and (1974); Doeringer (1972); Weber (1973); Dunlop (1974a) and (1974b); Hamilton (1974); Mitchell and Weber (1974); and Pencavel (1981).

[25] See Chapter 9.

Chart 1. Selected OECD Countries: Calendar of Direct Action on Prices and Incomes, 1970–73

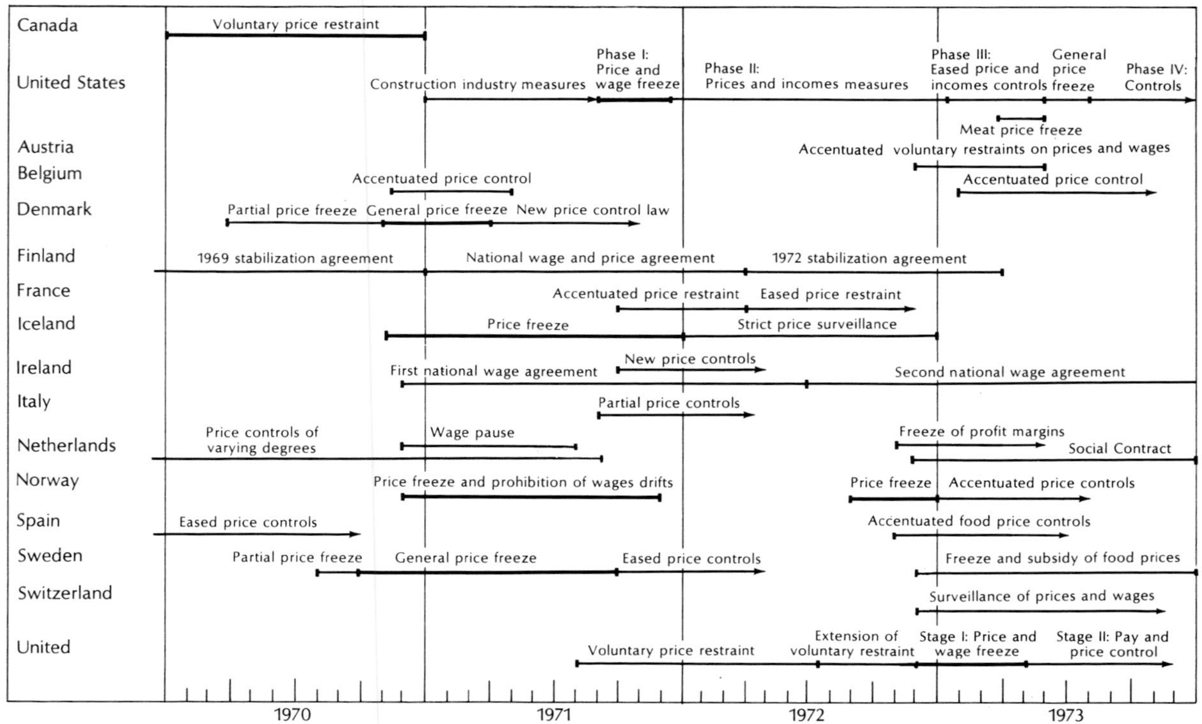

Source: Organization for Economic Cooperation and Development, *Economic Outlook*, July 1973, p. 24.

implemented. First, and most important, in the inflationary world situation (not altogether unlike the situation at the time of the Korean conflict), it could no longer be assumed that the general level of prices within an economy could be stabilized if the average unit labor cost was prevented from rising. It became impossible to specify a guideline for wages and salaries without allowing for the effect of rising prices abroad. Second, under full employment conditions, changes in pay had ceased to be so strongly determined by formal collective bargaining on a national basis and wage bargaining no longer appeared to be more amenable to restraint than pricing decisions. Third, the events of 1968 in France affected the climate for wage decisions, strengthening the aggressiveness of labor and making employers' organizations and governments elsewhere in Europe unwilling to risk provoking a similar confrontation by policies that curbed wages rather than prices.[26] Fourth, evidence was emerging that expectations about future price increases were a major determinant of union wage claims. If prices could be stabilized (or their rate of increase reduced), then wage demands could probably be moderated. Under these circumstances, a government commitment to try to control the cost of living was essential in order to win the support of trade unions for a prices and incomes policy.

After mid-1968, external influences ceased to be a factor restraining the rate of price increase and became strongly inflationary. For countries other than the United States, the major factor was the change in the U.S. situation as the result of the acceleration of the Viet Nam war and the incurring of large budget deficits.[27] However, the effects of this change were enhanced because it coincided with a cyclical upturn in Europe and Japan and occurred at a time of pronounced secular change in the climate and practice of wage bargaining in many countries outside North America. Because of these latter factors, the sharp rise in U.S. demand for imported manufactures, especially durable goods, and the steep rise in raw material prices had a stronger and swifter impact on the level of prices and wages in the other industrial countries than would have occurred in the late 1950s or early 1960s. The weakening of monetary restraint by heavy inflows of capital, induced by exchange rate speculation and encouraged at times by interest rate differentials, also was important in strengthening the upward pressure on costs and prices (see Chapter 5, pp. 116–21). As a result of these developments outside the

[26]Giugni (1971); and Sellier (1971). See also Chapter 5, pp. 120–21.
[27]Johnson (1972a, pp. 310–11).

United States, the restraining influence of foreign price movements on price and wage increases in the United States was also lessened.

Shift of Wage Bargaining Power

Meanwhile, a vitally important change in wage determination was taking place with the shift of bargaining power from the union headquarters to workers at the plant level.[28] This shift, which represented a factor of fundamental importance for the implementation of incomes policy, was apparent during the late 1960s in nearly all the Western European countries, except the United Kingdom, where it had occurred earlier. The change was less significant in North America and Japan, where collective bargaining has traditionally taken place between unions and particular enterprises.

Most authorities agree that the shift in bargaining power came about in part because workers were less afraid of losing their jobs and therefore were more inclined to strike (or to work to rule) at the plant level.[29] Another important factor was the dissatisfaction of wage earners with union policies of moderation in wage bargaining.[30] Moreover, the change in the attitude of wage earners was conditioned by the changed situation of the enterprise in an economy where the authorities had successfully fulfilled a commitment to maintain a low level of unemployment for a number of years. This context justified a belief that the enterprise would concede wage increases because it had the "capacity to pay" higher wages without necessarily losing business (thereby reducing employment). (If the firm is a large producer and "price leader," it may be ready to concede wage increases and raise prices because other firms are likely to raise their prices in line when it does so, especially if their scope for expanding output is restricted by the difficulty of hiring much additional labor; or a firm may do so simply because it knows that, under full employment conditions, other firms are, or soon will be, subject to similar wage pressures.)[31]

Disillusion with Incomes Policy

At the beginning of the 1970s, there was a tendency to write off attempts at incomes policy as a failure. This was, perhaps, natural, since incomes policies had broken down or had been abandoned in the

---

[28]Albeda (1971); Reichel (1971); Delamotte (1971); and Giugni (1971).

[29]Phelps Brown (1971a, p. 11); and Marris (1972, pp. 304–305).

[30]Wildcat strikes in the United Kingdom, France, Italy, the Federal Republic of Germany, Sweden, and elsewhere were sometimes directed against the central union negotiators as well as against the employers. Ulman and Flanagan (1971, pp. 236–37).

[31]See Chapter 4, pp. 63–68.

United Kingdom, Canada, Finland, the Netherlands, and the United States. In the Scandinavian countries, coordinated wage fixing continued only in the face of extreme tensions, while national wage fixing under compulsory arbitration had virtually collapsed in New Zealand[32] and seemed to be evolving into something more similar to collective bargaining in Australia.[33]

The disillusion was partly due, however, to judging the policies by inappropriate standards. Thus Ulman and Flanagan, for instance, concluded that "incomes policy, to generalize from the experience of the countries studied . . . has not been very successful." In their opinion, the accumulated experience of countries suggested that "in none of the variations so far turned up has incomes policy succeeded in its *fundamental objective, as stated, of making full employment consistent with a reasonable degree of price stability*."[34] However, that objective is not likely to be attainable in an open economy at full employment under fixed exchange rates unless the external situation is one of stable or falling prices. In an inflationary external environment, what Johnson referred to as the basic fallacy of incomes policy philosophy, the closed economy assumption, becomes clear.[35] One must conclude, therefore, that the late 1960s and beginning of the 1970s was an exceptionally unpropitious period for incomes policy if its success is to be judged by this criterion.

Strengthening International Transmission of Inflation from 1945 to 1973

It is important to recognize the implications for incomes policy of the growing "openness" of the industrial economies. The influence of international conditions on national wage developments should be seen as increasing progressively from the end of World War II until the adoption of flexible exchange rates in 1973.[36]

Increasing Openness of Industrial Countries

During the immediate postwar period, the international market was fractured by high tariffs and direct controls imposed by most industrial countries: imports of nonessentials were severely limited

---

[32]New Zealand Monetary and Economic Council (1971).

[33]Isaac (1972) and Braun (1974).

[34]Ulman and Flanagan (1971, p. 216, italics added).

[35]Johnson (1972c).

[36]The impact of the increasing integration of the industrial countries and of other factors in intensifying the national authorities' difficulty in controlling inflation after the mid-1960s is discussed in Chapter 5.

and much trade was carried out under bilateral agreements. Thus, for the time being, wage decisions were largely insulated from the influence of current price developments abroad, and, in this regard, the world consisted of virtually closed economies.

As long as the industrial economies approximated "closed economies," measures to limit the rise in wages and salaries in any one country were likely to be effective in checking price increases. If wages and salaries rose no more than average productivity, aggregate money demand was prevented from rising much faster than real output, provided that the authorities avoided large budget deficits or excessive credit expansion[37] and the average level of prices and profit markups was likely to be maintained. When trade barriers were reduced, the influence of international prices on price movements within the national markets was at first comparatively slight because national markets were not fully penetrated by foreign products and because domestic producers were not conscious of, or capable of, quickly seizing export opportunities.

During the early 1950s, conditions were conducive to the rapid development of a high-productivity export sector in countries where the lack of investment during World War II and destruction of the capital stock had created abnormal possibilities of raising output per worker by new investment, while there were also exceptional constraints on wage claims in the form of abnormally heavy unemployment, the inflow of refugees, and the wartime suppression of the unions in some countries. At the exchange rates prevailing after the devaluations in 1949, unit wage costs in industries utilizing new, technically advanced equipment were very low in relation to world market prices set in dollar terms. High profit margins on exports permitted continuing heavy investment and the expansion of high-productivity, capital-intensive industries dependent on export sales.

The second phase of strong interest in incomes policy in the early 1960s occurred during a period of strengthening competition in the international market for manufactures resulting from a number of causes. These included the coming into production of much new capacity in Western Europe and the Far East; the liberalization of direct controls and tariff reductions and the initiation of the European Economic Community (EEC) that encouraged efforts of firms within the area to enlarge their markets and of foreign concerns to establish

[37] In the immediate postwar years, however, there was an exceptional complicating factor in the form of large pent-up liquid personal savings in some countries, notably the United Kingdom and the United States.

themselves within the area. "Collusive" pricing behavior was limited by the struggle to acquire dominant positions in the markets that had been newly opened up. Easy labor market conditions and the still relatively weak collective bargaining position of recently organized or reorganized labor unions were conducive to price competition in many countries, notably the Federal Republic of Germany, Japan, and Italy. As the scale of exports from these areas grew, their price competitiveness became an increasingly important factor in restraining price increases in other centers of production.

During the late 1950s and early 1960s, wage movements over a widening "open" sector of each economy came to be directly influenced by demand conditions and price movements in international markets. As long as substantial unemployment, underemployment in agriculture and distribution, and weak organization and bargaining power of labor existed in some important industrial countries, the growing integration of the world market was a factor tending to curb inflationary pressures in other industrial countries.

The relatively weak forces of cost-push in certain countries led to a tendency for their currencies to become, or remain, undervalued, and for those of other industrial countries to be overvalued. For some considerable period, therefore, the regime of fixed exchange rates enabled certain countries, which gave a high priority to price stability and shunned expansionary budgetary and monetary policy, to raise the level of employment under the stimulus of favorable exchange rates. At the same time, those countries that accorded a lower priority to price stability and were prepared to protect the level of employment by expansionary financial policies were both shielded from inflationary repercussions and prevented from applying unduly expansionary policies by the rise in net imports associated with expansionary policies. The balance of payments constraint on these economies was not oppressive, however, as long as the production, income, and imports of the former group, and of the industrial world in general, were expanding rapidly.[38]

Declining Effectiveness of Demand Management

With the absorption of unemployed and underemployed manpower and the strengthening of cost-push forces in the former group of countries, the integration of the industrial economies ceased to have an important moderating influence on the rate of inflation in most industrial countries. By the late 1960s, the general economic setting

[38]Romanis (Braun) (1965).

had changed, following the maintenance of a high degree of manpower utilization throughout the industrial countries for some years and with the adaptation of pricing behavior and wage bargaining institutions and practices to the expectation that full employment would be more or less continuously maintained. Less strong competition now prevailed in the international market under generalized full employment and stronger unionization.[39] Consequently, there was a greater likelihood that a temporary increase in the pressure of demand for certain industrial goods, or a raising of prices by producers in a major economy affected by inflationary pressures, would be reflected in a generalized price rise in the international market, which, in turn, would lead to an upward movement of costs in the open sectors of most economies (under the combined influence of external pricing conditions and domestic cost-push forces).

In a world of fixed exchange rates and confident expectations of the maintenance of full employment in the industrial countries, employers in the open sector will tend to judge the "room" for wage increases by the growth of productivity and the movement of prices for their products in the international market; that is to say, the movement of prices for competing foreign products in export markets and in the domestic market. Enterprises with access to export markets and exposed to foreign competition in the domestic market would be unlikely to cut back prices in that market when domestic demand was restrained by the authorities, if export markets were buoyant. Foreign enterprises competing in the domestic market also would have little incentive to initiate price reductions *because* demand in a single market was weak, although they would most probably match price reductions initiated by domestic producers, or by other exporters to the market, in order to protect their share of the market (which represents an asset acquired by investment in advertising, sales organization, and management time). The likelihood of this occurring would be a deterrent to price reductions. In effect, oligopolistic pricing behavior would now be liable to extend over the area of the international market.

Under these conditions, measures of demand restraint in any one country, with the exception of the United States,[40] would have only a slight impact on price and wage developments in the open sector of the

[39] Firms will generally be disinclined to charge prices that are much below the going rate, or to keep down prices when other producers are raising prices, unless they can foresee being able to expand output and employment considerably without causing the existing level of wage rates to rise.

[40] Because of its larger size, the United States is a more important component of the international market than any other industrial country, and a less open economy.

economy. That effect would be dispersed over the much wider area of the international market in the form of some easing of demand and intensification of competition between suppliers that would tend to restrain the rate of price increase to a minor degree. Given the existence of powerful labor unions in the open sector, easier conditions in the domestic labor market would be unlikely to have a marked effect in reducing the size of wage claims or in altering firms' response to such wage claims if prices in the international market were foreseen to be increasing. That result might only be attainable if the exchange rate was allowed to appreciate.

With fixed exchange rates and integrated markets, measures of monetary and fiscal restraint implemented in the face of strong international demand conditions impinged mainly on the sheltered sector, in areas such as construction, public utilities, domestic transportation, local and central government, and public services. However, the power of the authorities to restrain wage and price increases in the "sheltered" sector had also weakened in many countries by the late 1960s, as a consequence of the strengthening of the bargaining power of wage earners with the absorption of underemployment and the establishment of more powerful labor unions in these fields. The difficulty of restraining wage and price increases in the sheltered sectors intensified when prices in international markets and industrial wages began to rise more rapidly under the impact of strongly expansionary policies in the United States and the Federal Republic of Germany.

Scandinavian Model of Wage Determination

The ultimate tendency for all wages to move upward in line with wages in the high-productivity growth open sector in the small economy where the whole labor force is organized in a strongly coordinated union movement and wage bargaining is dominated by the powerful organizations of the open sectors was exemplified in the Scandinavian model of wage determination.[41]

The model suggested that under strongly coordinated wage bargaining, wages in the "exposed" sector should rise approximately in line with the increase in labor productivity in that sector *plus* the increase in world market prices for its products, in order to leave the exposed industries "reasonably competitive."[42] (In other words, employers should resist wage claims that would require larger price

[41] Aukrust (1970); Edgren, Faxén, and Odhner (1969); and Lindbeck (1972a).

[42] Aukrust (1970, p. 38).

increases than were occurring in the world market prices if their existing percentage markups for depreciation and profits were to be maintained. The reasoning was apparently that enterprises needed to maintain the existing markups to be sure of maintaining their competitiveness (by investment, promotion efforts, etc.) vis-à-vis foreign concerns that were presumed to be following the same rule.) Wages would then increase at much the same rate in the sheltered sector, and since average profit margins there tended to be maintained, the rate of price increase would be determined by the rise in world market prices for the exposed sector and the difference between the rate of productivity growth in the two sectors.

The model illustrates the incompatibility of price stability with income distribution goals involving the maintenance of both the share of wages in income generated in the open sector and the relative levels of wages in the two sectors. Such goals clearly imply the likelihood of substantial domestic price inflation should world prices for industrial products rise strongly. Although the published versions of the model appeared as late as 1969 or 1970, when the presumed external constraint on the exposed sector had greatly weakened with strong demand conditions and rising prices for durable goods in world markets, they contain almost no reference to this danger and are permeated by the idea that the exposed industries are facing stiff price competition.[43]

Causes of Strong Wage Pressure in Late 1960s and Early 1970s

When prices are rising quite rapidly in the international market, domestic restraint will soon disturb the relative level of wages and salaries in the open and sheltered sectors. Mounting pressures for catching up with pay in the open sector and militant action in key industries and services then are liable to result in large wage increases, provoking a round of cost-push apparently originating in the sheltered sector. Furthermore, after a period of restrictive financial policies, housing shortages and inadequacies of basic urban services and social infrastructure are likely to produce a relaxation of monetary and budgetary restraint.

The wage explosions of 1968–70 and strong wage pressure of the early 1970s should thus be seen as largely the result of the exceptionally strong demand conditions in the international market that prevailed in 1968–69 and again in 1972–73. The first occurred as a

---

[43] For example, Aukrust (1970, p. 8), "If their costs increase, they must sustain the whole effect in the form of reduced profits."

result of the coincidence of a resurgence of the conflict in Viet Nam and excess demand conditions in the United States with a cyclical upturn in Western Europe and Japan; the second as a consequence of expansionary measures implemented in almost all industrial countries late in 1971 and early in 1972 reversing previous measures to restrain demand and curb price increases.[44] During the early 1970s, large wage increases in the open sector of these economies had more effect than hitherto in inducing similar wage claims in other sectors, owing to the secular change in the bargaining position of wage earners referred to earlier. Measures of demand restraint impinging most heavily on sheltered sectors could only temporarily contain pressures for matching wage increases there, often at the cost of subsequent unrest and eventual large percentage increases, which in turn generated higher expectations concerning possible rates of wage increase throughout the economy.[45]

Case for Exchange Rate Adjustments

In these circumstances, national authorities faced a choice, provided that a balance of payments deficit was not a critical constraint. They could maintain a fixed rate of exchange and accept the tendency for wages throughout the economy to rise at a rate approaching the rise in per capita productivity in the open sector *plus* the rate of price increase for industrial products in the international market, this implying a substantially higher rate of increase in the general level of prices within the economy. Or, they could seek to maintain domestic price stability by absorbing the "room" for wage increases in the open sector in excess of the average rise in per capita productivity within the economy by allowing the exchange rate to appreciate.[46]

The problem of intractable worldwide inflation might have been mitigated or avoided if the industrial countries—other than the United

---

[44]See the analysis of the aggregate experience of 1965–74 of industrial countries in Chapter 5.

[45]"Britain provides a very clear example of this. Attempts to restrain wage movements in the public sector (a sheltered sector) between 1971–72 eventually resulted in a coal miners' stoppage (1972) which was settled by the awarding of a 25 per cent wage increase. This resulted in a general increase in the level of wage settlements during 1972 and in November of that year the Government was forced to introduce a statutory wage freeze followed by a gradual relaxation. The relaxation was more freely applied in the 'open' sectors of the economy than in the sheltered sectors. Attempts to prevent wage increases in this sector matching the 'open' sector again led to a coal miners' stoppage (1974) and the end of statutory wage restraint." (Professor B. C. Roberts in correspondence with the author.)

[46]As was proposed by the independent Council of Economic Advisors in the Federal Republic of Germany in 1965 (see Chapter 8).

States—had agreed upon a joint appreciation of their currencies vis-à-vis the U.S. dollar in 1969.[47] Many influences, however, worked against such a solution. These included the opposition of powerful interests in the open sectors of the economies, the unwillingness of deficit countries to weaken their balance of payments position vis-à-vis the United States, and the reluctance of central banks to see a reduction in the real value of their international reserve holdings.

Opposing Views of the Need for Incomes Policy

The problem of stabilization in an open economy was the subject of intense controversy at the beginning of the 1970s. Growing awareness of the inflationary impact of international conditions led to calls for measures to control the growth of international liquidity and thus enforce greater discipline through the balance of payments constraint or for the use of exchange rate appreciation as a weapon against "imported inflation." Although incomes policies were implemented in several countries, a growing number of monetarist economists dismissed the need for such policies on the grounds that inflation was a purely monetary phenomenon, caused by laxity of control over the world money supply and was "not a matter of various political and sociological problems, even though in many individual countries these factors may be deduced as an explanation of the particular sequence of events or mechanism."[48] They held that inflation itself was not a serious economic problem requiring to be corrected, except insofar as a faster-than-average rate of inflation produced a balance of payments deficit. That problem could be solved by flexible exchange rates.

Context for Incomes Policies in Early 1970s

The argument that the rate of inflation was not necessarily a matter of concern rested on the belief that "the institutional mechanisms of a society based on freedom of choice and competition will, if the system of contract is reasonably flexible and inflation not too erratic, act to bring about the elimination of major inflationary injustices"[49] *once* the rate of inflation is correctly anticipated. That happy situation did not apply however in the late 1960s. As the monetarists themselves

[47] See Johnson (1969). For further discussion of the issues involved in securing exchange rate adjustments, see Chapter 5.

[48] Johnson (1972a, p. 311).

[49] Johnson (1972b, p. 24).

emphasized, in the initial phase the rate of inflation is likely to be held down by "the persistence of belief in the stability of prices"; for a period thereafter, the rate of inflation will be enhanced by "the effects of growing belief in the continuance of inflation in reducing the demand for real balances."[50] In this instance, the change in the climate of expectations occurred at the same time as the institutional changes conducive to stronger and more generalized inflation that have been described earlier in this chapter. Given levels of employment were now associated with higher rates of increase in prices and money incomes, which, if not validated by the monetary authorities, were liable to give rise quickly to marked problems of unemployment in particular sectors of the economy.[51] Thus, it had become more difficult for the monetary authorities in many countries to enforce restraint. Consequently, the incentive to alter the exchange rate, or to permit it to vary as a means of protecting the economy from inflationary pressures abroad, had strengthened by the time that the first realignment of rates took place under the Smithsonian agreement at the end of 1971 and the incentive persisted until the fixed rate system was abandoned in 1973.

Use of Incomes Policies

Two somewhat different uses of incomes policy were envisaged in the early 1970s, depending on the time-horizon involved.[52] In North America especially, incomes policy was regarded as an essentially short-term weapon, involving temporary intervention by the government aimed at forestalling or reversing increasingly inflationary price expectations. Inflation was treated, by economists at least, as an economic phenomenon, arising from such causes as the lagged effect of mistakes in fiscal management or the impact of external price movements, or from special factors (such as the rise in oil prices and exceptional wheat exports) that may impinge on the generally satisfactory working of a neoclassical competitive economy. In many European countries, however, cost inflation was seen not as the outcome of efforts to ward off the effect of rising prices on real income but rather as an essentially political phenomenon, provoked by the deliberate attempts of various organized groups to secure a larger share of the national income. Hence, as Saunders pointed out: "It is evident that incomes policy cannot be regarded simply as an

---

[50]Johnson (1967, pp. 124–25).
[51]Braun (1971, pp. 63–65).
[52]Ulman and Flanagan (1971, p. 217).

instrument of economic management, short-term or long-term, on the same plane as monetary policy. It is political, in the widest sense."[53]

If rapid inflation represents the means of resolving the competing claims of different groups to real income while avoiding open political conflict (at least for the time being), the antidote of an incomes policy must encompass deliberate efforts to devise and to utilize institutions for working out a compromise between the competing claims of the various income groups. The case for indexation of both wages and financial claims was also put forward in this connection. Wage indexation was advocated as a means of assuring protection of real income in the face of price increases and as a means of ensuring a deceleration of nominal wage increases when inflation moderated under the influence of easier demand conditions and greater stability in commodity markets. Financial indexation was advocated as a means of protecting borrowers from the risk of having to pay much higher real interest rates should the rate of price increase slow down but nominal interest rates not be adjusted downward.[54]

Results of Incomes Policies Under Fixed Exchange Rates

This account has shown that with the exception of the early 1960s, all the episodes of widespread reliance on incomes policies occurred in response to severe disequilibrium and malfunctioning of the international payments system.

The incomes policies of the late 1940s and early 1950s were implemented in the context of the fragmentation of the international economy and the destruction of productive capital by World War II. They were a response to abnormal scarcities and the need to allocate essentials, and they represented part of a general situation in which economic incentives had been largely superseded by physical controls. The policies adopted were considered equitable. They evoked strong popular support both because they protected the level of real wages and because they provided a "quiet life" in which the effort of struggling to stay ahead of other groups or individuals via wage bargaining, changing jobs, and so forth was largely obviated. Something of this latter situation prevails under effectively coordinated wage bargaining, as at times achieved in the Scandinavian countries, Austria, the Netherlands, and the Federal Republic of Germany; and

[53]Saunders (1971, p. 352).

[54]Ulman and Flanagan (1971, pp. 255–56); and White (1976). Isaac (1973) also emphasized the need to adjust progressive income tax schedules for inflation (see p. 253).

it is an important reason why union members as a whole will support such a system so long as specific groups do not secure very large and visible increases via wage drift or plant bargaining.

The rather modest incomes policies of the early 1960s represented an honest endeavor to cope with the problems of cost inflation in a free market international system at close to full employment, in a setting of sensible national macroeconomic policies and a functioning, coordinated international monetary system. Incomes policy was rightly treated as an adjunct to fiscal and monetary policies, not as a substitute for—or a determinant of—such policies.

The early 1960s saw such helpful developments as the widespread acceptance of the concept of productivity-based guidelines (which was best expounded in the United States); the practice of tripartite bargaining in connection with budget planning (as carried out in Norway, de facto but not explicitly in Sweden, and less successfully in Denmark and Finland); the start of "concerted action" in the Federal Republic of Germany; and the establishment of the Prices and Incomes Board in the United Kingdom. All these institutional arrangements served the purpose of informing the public of the scope for real income increases and of the direction of government policies. The Prices and Incomes Board added greatly to the knowledge of how the economy worked at the microlevel, identifying areas where competition could be strengthened or productivity increased. It also served a useful purpose of "ombudsman" to which specific issues could be referred for cool and objective study. During this period, there were also genuine efforts in the United Kingdom to secure a more coordinated wage bargaining system by union amalgamations and by a strengthening of the employers' organizations.[55]

Like any tool, incomes policy can be used constructively or negatively—or merely flourished as a theatrical prop. In the late 1960s and early 1970s, it was essentially employed as the means to suppress the consequences of unsound and conflicting national macroeconomic policies.

A large number of econometric studies have attempted to measure the results achieved by incomes policy in moderating the rate of price and wage increases by comparing the rate of change during periods when the policy was or was not applied.[56] While these analyses have been valuable in advancing economists' knowledge by quantifying the behavior of prices and wages over the whole economy, few if any of the

[55]See Romanis (Braun) (1966).

[56]See, for example, the 1970 study by Lipsey and Parkin, to which the criticisms made here are particularly applicable, Eckstein and Brinner (1972), Perry (1973), and Ball (1971).

studies can be treated as a reliable measure of the results achieved by incomes policy. Most of the aggregative models employed are not able to capture all the other influences affecting the rate of price (or wage) change sufficiently well to justify the interpretation that the difference in the observed relationship with explanatory variables during "policy-on" and "policy-off" periods solely reflects the influence of the incomes policy. In many cases, too little attention has been paid to the way in which shortcomings of the wage and price series used affect the results. Furthermore, the brief historical account given here suggests that an econometric assessment of countries' experience of inflation would need to consider the effects of changes in the organizational framework and industrial structure within the country and of changes in the degree of integration with the international market, in causing the basic price and wage equations to change over time.

Some general conclusions can be drawn here concerning the usefulness of incomes policy during the period covered in this chapter. It seems clear that, despite breakdowns, failures, and even at times perverse effects in worsening the inflationary climate and enhancing the rate of increase in prices and wages, incomes policy in its various manifestations was a valuable instrument for the economic authorities at certain times. In a number of European countries, incomes policy contributed to the attainment of full employment and to the maintenance of relative price stability for lengthy periods, facilitating the achievement of a high rate of investment and consequent rapid rise in productivity and real income and aiding in the maintenance of political stability. In many other instances, incomes policy provided a temporary measure of restraint through price and wage freezes or controls, provisions for justification of particular increases, or even merely by a well-timed effort to influence public opinion. There were occasions, however, when the temporary success in holding down increases resulted in a buildup of pressures, producing an upsurge of inflation when the policy was lifted (or collapsed).[57]

Commentators agree that the impressive performance of the Netherlands economy in terms of rapid growth despite limited natural resources, reasonable price stability, and low cyclical and structural unemployment represents an achievement of democratic economic planning to which the successful implementation of wage and price

[57] For a general review of the results achieved by incomes policy in particular countries up to 1973, see especially, Roberts (1958); Edelman and Fleming (1965); David C. Smith (1966); Turner and Zoeteweij (1966); Economic Commission for Europe (1967); Organization for Economic Cooperation and Development (1970); Ulman and Flanagan (1971); and Fels (1972).

policies contributed greatly up until 1963. Even in subsequent years, management of the economy was made easier, in times of crisis, by the possibility of reactivating the institutions and the legal powers to control prices and wages still left to the Government.

For more than a decade after 1956, the Swedish system of centralized national wage bargaining, with carefully specified provisions for arbitration in cases where agreement could not be reached, constituted an important element in the realization of the policy goals of minimal unemployment, moderate price inflation, rapid growth of productivity, rising real income, and greater equality of income distribution, especially through the provision of pension benefits and health insurance. In Norway, incomes policy based on similarly centralized bargaining but with more direct participation by the Government in the process, enabled the authorities to keep the rate of unemployment generally below the European average and to secure steady and rapid economic growth.[58] The experience of Denmark and Finland, however, shows that centralized wage bargaining in itself is no panacea for inflation, if conditions for achieving a consensus favoring moderation of claims are lacking.

The results achieved by wage and price controls in the United States in the early 1970s are the subject of controversy between the proponents and opponents of government intervention. It is generally agreed that the controls had a significant effect in restraining wage increases in particular sectors, notably construction and health care[59] and that the measures had an effect in reducing the average rate of inflation during 1971 and 1972, although the extent of the reduction is uncertain because the rate of inflation was already declining when controls began.[60] In 1973, when controls were first relaxed and then intensified and when the increase in prices was more than twice as large as in 1972, the Council of Economic Advisers found it more difficult to believe that they had a significant effect in reducing the rate

[58]Organization for Economic Cooperation and Development (1971a).

[59]United States, *Economic Report of the President* (1974, pp. 101–102); and Dunlop (1974b, pp. 462–63).

[60]The purpose of the controls was described in United States, *Economic Report of the President* (1973), as being to reduce the risk that the rate of inflation would rise again and to increase the probability of a further decline, so as to enable the Government to follow a more expansionary policy (p. 53); it concluded that the controls had made a "very significant contribution" in this respect during 1971 and 1972 (p. 62). "The fact of the controls, plus their initial success, had reduced inflationary expectations, held down total spending, restrained the tendency to boost wages and prices, and permitted output to rise more rapidly than it would otherwise have done" (United States, *Economic Report of the President* (1974), p. 99).

of inflation.[61] The faster rise in prices was, however, due mainly to sharp increases for food, fuel, and primary commodities that were not subject to control. The Administration was reluctant to claim that controls had an effect in moderating wage increases during 1973; but first-year increases in wages and fringe benefits under major collective bargaining settlements were actually smaller in 1973 than in 1972.[62] In the opinion of Dunlop, then Director of the Cost of Living Council, "the existence of controls in place also significantly restrained inflation when the international price surge developed from the [oil] embargo in the last quarter of 1973. . . . The impact more generally on wages and prices was of a small but perceptible order."[63]

In Dunlop's view, wage restraint cannot be concerned exclusively with holding down the current rate of increase in compensation. "Wage stabilization is also concerned with changes in the structure of collective bargaining, in the development of voluntary dispute settling machinery, in encouraging the joint study and introduction of new technology and changes in work rules, in the development of new sources of wage and benefit data for the parties, and a host of other activities which over the long run will improve the quality of collective bargaining and create a less inflation-prone sector of the economy. . . . In my experience a better job of short-term restraint can in fact be accomplished if the stabilization agency is genuinely assisting the parties in a particular industry or sector to approach systematically problems which they previously have ignored or patched up temporarily."[64]

The role of labor market structure in determining the feasibility and effectiveness of incomes policy as a continuing instrument can hardly be overemphasized. The existence of strong central federations, or of representative organizations including labor unions and employers, was a major factor in making possible the consistent implementation of wage and price policy for lengthy periods in the Netherlands and the Scandinavian countries. In Australia and New Zealand, the compulsory arbitration system provided a similar factor of continuity. In countries where such institutions did not exist—notably, the United Kingdom—it proved difficult to maintain a consistent course in the pursuit of price and wage stability. Thus, although incomes policies in the United Kingdom were distinguished by their inventive use of new

---

[61] United States, *Economic Report of the President* (1974).

[62] The average increase, excluding increases resulting from cost of living escalator adjustments, was 7.1 compared with 8.5 in 1972 and 13.1 in 1971 and 1970 (Dunlop (1974b, p. 466)).

[63] Dunlop (1974a, p. 10).

[64] Dunlop (1974a, p. 19).

institutions and devices, the results achieved in total were disappointing. Proposals for major institutional changes dominated discussions of incomes policy in the United Kingdom during the late 1960s and early 1970s.[65]

Not surprisingly, the direct results of incomes policy in restraining the rate of wage and price increases were more apparent in the early postwar period than in later years, when the forces making for the international transmission of inflation had become more powerful. The fact that incomes policies in the late 1960s and early 1970s had little apparent effect in moderating the current rate of inflation does not however preclude the possibility that measures commanding some degree of popular support nevertheless had an effect in lessening the buildup of inflationary expectations and conflicts. In some countries, the whole climate of income determination worsened dramatically after efforts to achieve an incomes policy were abandoned; this does not always seem to have been the result of pent-up pressures accumulated while the price and wage policies were in force. It would appear that the long-run benefit derived from popularly supported measures of incomes policy consists not only of the moderation of the rate of inflation that may be achieved but also of the contribution that the existence of the policy can make to the smoother working of the political and economic system.

---

[65]Phelps Brown's 1972 proposals for a "workable incomes policy," for example, were intended to "improve on the present system of collective bargaining so as to provide means of pay-fixing that will do more to meet" such requirements as the avoidance of cost inflation; equity for the individual employee and a say in fixing his own terms of employment; the adjustment of differentials in accordance with the job requirements; and adjustment of the broader pay structure in accordance with macroeconomic and social considerations. See Phelps Brown (1972, pp. 31–32).

3

Incomes Policy After the Inflationary Crisis of 1973

The problem of ensuring mutually consistent and tenable national policies that would provide a stable noninflationary environment for investment and trade and promote confident expectations concerning prospective demand, prices, and exchange rates remained unsolved at the time of the shift to managed floating in 1973. By the end of the year, the commodity boom, sharply accelerating domestic inflation rates, and the shock of the oil price increase had created general recognition of the urgent need for stabilization measures, even in the countries most committed to maintaining full employment. The case for restraint was underlined by the increasing attention now given to expectations as a crucial factor in determining price and wage behavior. The belief that moderating inflation was essentially a problem of reducing inflationary expectations, encouraged the view that if only a substantial measure of price stability could be regained *by whatever means*, a lasting reduction in inflation would be facilitated.[1]

New Setting for Incomes Policy

The context for incomes policies differed from that of the 1960s, in that the need was to bring down very rapid rates of inflation, not to forestall rapid inflation before it took hold, and because policies were applied in a new exchange rate setting, the characteristics of which were far from clear. The experience of double-digit price inflation in many countries during 1973–74 or 1973–75 rendered the immediate problems of

[1]This chapter is a revised version of Braun (1978). Parts of this paper are reproduced in Addison (1981) without attribution.

demand management more intractable by exacerbating the political climate and intensifying industrial and social conflict as various groups struggled to protect their standard of living. Effective demand management policies became more difficult to achieve in countries where government majorities were reduced or existing coalitions became unworkable. In several cases, political parties that had not held office for many years came to power. Thus, inexperienced policymakers were faced with the need to implement a new set of policies in exceptionally difficult circumstances.

The inflationary experience of the early 1970s had two other important consequences that seriously affected the functioning of certain economies: namely, the rapid spread of indexation provisions and the occurrence of severe fiscal drag in countries relying on progressive taxes on personal incomes and company profits. Those countries that depended mainly on proportional indirect taxes, such as value-added tax (VAT), for revenue had an advantage in this respect since the real burden of these taxes was unaffected by the rate of inflation.

As rapid inflation took hold, there was increased recourse to explicit (or implicit) escalation of wages and salaries for changes in the cost of living between wage negotiations in a number of countries, notably Canada, France, the Netherlands, and the United Kingdom (under the "threshold agreements"). In countries where indexation was already widespread, for example, Belgium and Italy, further protection was demanded if existing compensation for price increases was incomplete or was based on a price index with limited coverage. Indexation of pensions and social security benefits became general.[2]

Incomes policies were widely adopted as a short-term strategy to aid in bringing down inflation rates more quickly and smoothly than would otherwise be possible. In the prevailing circumstances, the case for direct intervention in the process of nominal income determination rested not only on the need to supplement conventional macroeconomic policies in checking the inflationary spiral but also on the need to lessen the divisive effects of the sudden worsening of the economic environment.

The problem of achieving a general reduction in rates of inflation was complicated by the widely differing positions in which industrial economies found themselves at the end of 1973. Weaker economies were confronted by huge current account deficits, a recent experience

[2]The theoretical issues concerning the indexation of wages and its impact on the working of the economy are explored in Chapter 8, "Indexation of Wages: A Monetarist Prescription."

of much-above-average rates of inflation, and the prospect of continuing higher-than-average inflation owing to institutional arrangements for the maintenance of real incomes by the formal or de facto indexation of wages and social benefits and a marked potential for industrial unrest. Imbalances on current account and the disparity of recent (and continuing) rates of inflation created a need for further exchange rate adjustments. However, following the oil price increase, few countries were prepared to let the exchange rate move freely downward. Governments that could allow the rate to move without fear of enhancing domestic inflation adopted a flexible exchange rate strategy. Others, if they were able to do so, adopted policies to maintain the rate either explicitly or implicitly, impelled by the desire to curb inflation and by the fear of possible "vicious circle" effects and spiraling inflation, stemming from depreciation and the impact of the oil price increase.

Consequences of Widespread Indexation

The widespread use of price escalation clauses in contracts (and particularly in wage settlements) had the effect of reinforcing the momentum of inflation, making it more difficult to bring down the rate of inflation by restrictive monetary policy. It also exposed the economy to a swift and automatic acceleration of inflation as a consequence of the oil price shock.

Indexation was inappropriate in the context of the sudden worsening of the terms of trade and the need to adjust the balance of payments by an increased transfer of resources. Countries in which there was relatively little indexation, such as the Federal Republic of Germany, Japan, Sweden, Canada, and the United States (see Tables 1 and 2), were less exposed than others to a sharp rise in nominal incomes and an ongoing momentum of nominal income increases, stemming directly from the commodity price boom and oil price rise of 1973. Hence, the authorities could, if they chose, enforce a sharp deceleration of monetary growth and nominal expenditure, with the likelihood of less severe effects on output, profits, and employment than in a highly indexed country. Where explicit or implicit indexation was pervasive (in Belgium, Denmark, France,[3] Italy, the Netherlands,

[3]Automatic adjustment of wages other than the minimum wage (*salaire minimum interprofessionnel de croissance—SMIC*) for price changes was forbidden by law in France, but an increasing proportion of collective agreements provided for de facto indexation by the inclusion of a clause calling for renegotiation in the event of a marked rise in prices, or by guaranteeing an additional increase in wages if the rise in prices exceeded that foreseen at the time of the settlement.

Table 1. Factors Conditioning Countries' Vulnerability to Shock of External Price Increases in 1973

	Current Account Balance, 1973[1] *(Percent of GNP)* (1)	Degree of Wages Indexation[2] (2)	Vulnerability of Tax System to Inflation[3] (3)	Measure of Vulnerability Under (1)–(3) (4)
Least vulnerable group: flexible exchange rates				
Germany, Fed. Rep. of	1.94	Slight	Slight	0
Switzerland	0.95	Considerable	Slight	½
Japan	0.02	Slight	Slight	½
United States	0.01	Moderate	Slight	½
More vulnerable group: maintaining exchange rates				
Canada[4]	0.68	Moderate	Moderate	1
Austria	−0.02	Moderate	Slight	1
Norway[5]	−1.43	Moderate	Moderate	1
Sweden	2.84	Slight	Marked	1
France	−0.02	Considerable	Slight	1
Netherlands	2.65	Considerable	Moderate	1½
Belgium	3.25	Considerable	Moderate	1½
Denmark[6]	−2.61	Considerable	Marked	3
Most vulnerable group: flexible exchange rates				
Italy	−0.83	Considerable	Slight	2
United Kingdom	−0.65	Considerable	Marked	3

Sources: See footnotes below.

[1]Current account excluding official transfers as a percentage of gross national product (GNP). Data derived from International Monetary Fund, *International Financial Statistics*, various issues.

[2]Evaluation based on Table 8 in Chapter 8.

[3]See Table 2.

[4]Rate was effectively supported vis-à-vis the U.S. dollar by interest rate policy.

[5]Medium-term balance of payments prospects favorable because of oil resources. Effect of wages indexation and progressivity of taxes mitigated by coordinated income bargaining between the economic groups and the Government.

[6]Although the Danish krone was pegged to the deutsche mark, Denmark belonged in the most vulnerable group.

Table 2. Vulnerability to Inflation-Induced Increases in Tax Liability in 1973

Degrees of Vulnerability	Effect of: Progressivity of personal income taxes[1] (1)		Dependence on direct rather than indirect taxes[2] (2)		Percentage ratio of direct taxes to GNP (3)		Ranking by combination of (1), (2), and (3) (4)
Highly vulnerable	Sweden	2.51	Japan	31	Denmark	26.2	Denmark
	Denmark	2.14	United States	27	Sweden	19.3	Sweden
	United Kingdom	1.82	Canada	24	Canada	15.5	United Kingdom
	Norway	0.01[3]	Denmark	22	Netherlands	15.1	
			Switzerland	20			
			Sweden	18			
Moderately vulnerable	Canada	0.77[4]	United Kingdom	14	Norway	13.5	Norway
	Netherlands	0.66	Netherlands	11	Belgium	13.1	Canada
	Belgium	1.02	Germany, Fed. Rep. of	9	United Kingdom	13.1	Netherlands
	Austria	0.41	Belgium	8	Germany, Fed. Rep. of	12.9	Belgium
					United States	12.5	
					Switzerland	10.5	
					Japan	10.4	
					Austria	10.2	
Less vulnerable	Germany, Fed. Rep. of	0.52	Norway	−8	France	6.2	Germany, Fed. Rep. of
	United States	0.53	Austria	−10	Italy	5.6	Austria
	Switzerland	0.51	Italy	−15			Switzerland
	Japan	−0.47[5]	France	−17			United States
	Italy	1.27[6]					Japan
	France	0.21					France
							Italy

Sources: Statistical data based on Organization for Economic Cooperation and Development, *Revenue Statistics of OECD Member Countries*, 1965–73 and 1965–74.

[1]Figures show change in percentage ratio of personal income tax to GNP from 1973 to 1974.

[2]Figures show excess of direct taxes on income and profits over indirect taxes on goods and services as a percentage of total tax receipts.

[3]Effect offset by discretionary tax changes.

[4]Automatic adjustment of tax schedules began in 1974 but was implemented with a lag of over 15 months.

[5]Decline due to discretionary tax reduction.

[6]Increase due to tax reforms.

Norway, and the United Kingdom—while the threshold agreements applied), governments were generally disinclined to implement deflationary monetary policies, yet were unwilling to allow the exchange rate to depreciate if that could be avoided since it would expose the economy to the risk of accelerating inflation. Almost all these countries experienced a severe worsening of the competitive position at the going exchange rate over the next few years. Efforts to mitigate the effect of indexation constituted a major element of incomes policy.

Fiscal Drag

The increasing real burden of progressive taxes was important in exacerbating the impact of rapid inflation. Rapid inflation vitiates the fundamental premise of progressive tax rates based on *nominal* income, that a higher nominal income represents a higher real income, on which it is equitable to charge a higher rate of tax. Moreover, taxes unadjusted for inflation are conceptually inconsistent with provisions for indexation of nominal incomes to protect real incomes.

Measures to alleviate the effect of fiscal drag in intensifying wage pressures formed an integral part of incomes policies in a number of countries. The problems raised by the distortion of conventional measures of profits and corporate incomes by inflation were not less complex. The real burden of corporate income tax rates was increased if depreciation was calculated on the basis of historical costs and if windfall profits resulting from the rise in price of inventories were included in taxable profits. Furthermore, the resulting high level of recorded profits tended to raise wage claims.[4] The industrial countries generally avoided the revaluation of business accounts (which has been widely adopted in developing countries that have experienced rapid inflation) in favor of tax relief by means of provisions such as accelerated depreciation, investment allowances, and special treatment of inventories.[5] In addition, widespread employment-related payments by governments to enterprises, remission of social security charges for new employees, and so forth, served to offset part of the increasing tax burden on enterprises in a politically acceptable manner.

In countries relying on steeply progressive income taxes (notably in the United Kingdom, the Scandinavian countries, and the Netherlands), rapid increases in wages under the impetus of sharply rising

---

[4]It is beyond the scope of this book to deal with these issues and their solution in different countries. See Lent (1975). See also Aaron (1976), especially the chapters by George E. Lent, Sidney Davidson and Roman L. Weil, and Martin J. Bailey.

[5]See Irwin (1976).

consumer prices led to unplanned increases in tax liability and resulted in a marked rise in the share of gross personal income taken in taxes.[6] Even countries that had already implemented some form of indexation of tax brackets and allowances, such as Canada and Denmark, did not escape this effect since the system of adjustment had been designed to counter the cumulative effect of creeping inflation, *not* the effect of a sudden inflationary shock, and adjustments for the effect of inflation were made with a lag of about 15 months or longer.[7] The unlegislated rise in already high tax rates had severe repercussions in intensifying wage pressures and political conflict, in lessening constraint on real public expenditure, and in rendering budgetary outcomes less predictable. In some cases, for example, in Canada and the Netherlands in 1973 and Denmark in 1974, the rise was associated with large budgetary surpluses having a severe deflationary impact on the economy, which created political pressure for the adoption of expansionary policies. In other cases, rising revenue encouraged unplanned increases in real public expenditure, with such consequences as lax control over spending and weak constraint on increases in wages, salaries, and pensions in the public sector and a tolerant attitude toward large increases in social security benefits, which tended to intensify inflationary cost pressures throughout the economy.[8] In general, the unforeseen rise in tax liability made it more difficult to bring down the rate of inflation and, in some cases, increased the difficulty of maintaining employment and investment in the open sector of the economy.

In Scandinavian countries, wage and salary earners accustomed to indexation guaranteeing real wage increases now found that with larger nominal increases, the combined effect of indexation and direct taxes was to reduce their real disposable income. The much increased tax liability of some groups greatly intensified the difficulty of reaching coordinated wage agreements in Denmark and Sweden. In the Netherlands and the United Kingdom, employees who had recently secured cost of living protection found the benefit largely offset by their

[6]A striking illustration is the Australian case. "During the 1974–1975 year Australian personal income tax collections rose by 1.9% for every 1.0% increase in salaries and wages. On the basis of a 20% rate of inflation in 1974–1975, a taxpayer on average weekly earnings in 1974–1975 needed to increase his gross income by 29.8% to maintain a constant real income after tax." Irwin (1976).

[7]For a description of problems of adjusting direct taxes see Tanzi (1976) and Organization for Economic Cooperation and Development (1976).

[8]Sharp increases in income tax revenue did not serve to finance a *planned* expansion of real public expenditure obviating the need for *planned* tax increases.

increased liability to taxes.[9] Tax push was an important factor contributing to the rapid rise in nominal incomes in the Netherlands in 1973–74 and to the wage explosion in the United Kingdom in early 1975.[10]

The effect of progressive tax scales in reducing differentials in disposable income between skilled and unskilled workers, between blue collar and white collar workers, and between recipients of untaxed unemployment and social security benefits and the employed wage earner became highly divisive issues in industrial relations and national politics, especially in the Netherlands, Sweden, Denmark, and the United Kingdom. The level of direct taxes was a major issue in political crises in Denmark and the Netherlands.

Demand Policies and Recourse to Incomes Policy Measures

When considering the incomes policies pursued after 1973, three groups of countries need to be distinguished according to their vulnerability to continuing inflation (see Table 1).

The first group, consisting of countries least exposed to continuing inflation under the impact of the oil price increase, comprised the three largest economies and Switzerland. The second group, consisting of countries which, though more exposed to continuing inflation, could seek to maintain the exchange rate, comprised France and five small open economies closely integrated with the Federal Republic of Germany, which chose to peg on the deutsche mark as a means of restraining domestic price movements.

The third group, consisting of countries in the grip of surging inflation and highly exposed to continuing inflation, where the possibility of avoiding further depreciation was virtually excluded,

---

[9]In the United Kingdom, the number of people paying income tax actually rose by 25 percent in three years. A further distortion of the tax system came about because revenue from indirect taxes on expenditure did not keep pace with inflation as a large proportion of indirect tax revenue was derived not from ad valorem taxes (VAT, turnover taxes, etc.) but from excise duties, stamp taxes, etc., levied as fixed *nominal* charges that were not increased in line with prices. The share in total revenue of indirect taxes on expenditure fell from 39 percent to 27 percent between the beginning of the 1970s and 1976–77, while that of direct taxes and social security contributions rose from 53 percent to 63 percent. The lowering of the real income threshold for direct taxes led to anomalies such as the fact that taxes were payable on wages and other incomes below the level of tax-free weekly payments to the unemployed. See United Kingdom, Treasury (1977).

[10]See Chapter 10 and Chapter 9, respectively.

comprised Denmark,[11] Italy, and the United Kingdom. The possibility of adopting a restrictive policy stance was ruled out in the United Kingdom by the mandate under which the Labour Government had come to power in 1974, and in Denmark and Italy by the existence of fragile coalition governments.

The authorities of the first group of countries were under less constraint than others in implementing restrictive policies. This was so because of the greater tolerance of unemployment in Japan and the United States than in Western Europe, and because in Germany and Switzerland the rise in unemployment was alleviated by the departure of about a million foreign workers. None of these countries adopted incomes policies in the years immediately after 1973.

The prospects for moderating inflation by restrictive measures were relatively favorable in the first group for several reasons, namely,

(1) the greater effectiveness of domestic policy in larger, less open, economies than in smaller economies;

(2) the well-developed international capital markets of the United States, the Federal Republic of Germany, and Switzerland, which meant that the authorities of these countries were well placed to strengthen the exchange rate and the terms of trade by keeping interest rates high and attracting large inflows from the oil producing countries;[12] and

(3) the comparative unimportance of wage indexation (except in Switzerland, where its impact was mitigated by appreciation) and the presence, especially in Japan, of institutional factors[13] ensuring greater flexibility of wage costs than in other industrial countries.[14]

The countries in the second group that pegged on the deutsche mark hoped to benefit from Germany's success in achieving a moderate rate of increase in labor costs and prices. By doing so they imposed a powerful curb on price increases in the open sector, thereby strengthening market forces of restraint in the highly organized industrial sector. In most cases, the maintenance of the pegged rate acted as a constraint on monetary policy. It also provided a strong rationale for deliberate policies aimed at moderating price and wage increases. The case for incomes policy in these countries remained

---

[11] Although the Danish krone was pegged to the deutsche mark, Denmark belonged in the most vulnerable group as Table 1 shows.

[12] This did not, however, apply to Japan, where the exchange rate fell sharply at the time of the oil crisis and was maintained at a lower level thereafter.

[13] Chapter 9 provides an account of the labor market characteristics that lessened the need for incomes policy in the Federal Republic of Germany and Japan.

[14] In the United States, the strength of ongoing cost-push forces was moderated at the time by the influence on wage bargaining of the 1971 wage/price controls that were in the process of being phased out.

much the same as under the fixed rate system.[15] All these countries, except Sweden, implemented some incomes policy measures after 1973. The United Kingdom also made very extensive use of income policies in an effort to slow down the very rapid rate of inflation and avoid further depreciation.[16]

While restoration of price stability was the principal goal of policy in the Netherlands and Belgium, the maintenance of high employment was the primary objective in Austria and the three Scandinavian countries, in France until 1976, and in Canada until mid-1975. Austria, Denmark, Norway, and the Netherlands consistently, or repeatedly, implemented comprehensive incomes policies during the 1970s.[17] Canada adopted a comprehensive anti-inflation program during 1975–78,[18] which was aimed at checking a rapid acceleration of wage increases, especially in the public sector. Belgium applied temporary measures to protect the balance of payments in 1976. After leaving the joint exchange rate float in September 1976, France imposed a price freeze, temporarily lowered value-added taxes, and undertook measures to halt the acceleration of wage increases and to prevent a continuing depreciation. In Sweden, tentative moves toward a voluntary policy of wage and price restraint were ruled out by the fall of the social democratic government, but a moderate wage settlement was achieved after the devaluation of the krona in 1977.

Results Achieved by Mid-1970s

By 1976, the rate of wage increase had been brought down to single-digit figures in all of the first group of countries, except Japan, and also in Austria and the Netherlands (Table 3). In the latter countries, this outcome had been realized under the influence of an appreciation in line with the deutsche mark, supported by incomes policy measures. The other countries that chose the hard currency option had higher rates of wage increase and were increasingly exposed to rising unemployment in the open sector and to difficulty in maintaining the exchange rate. Where the maintenance of full employment commanded a high political priority, governments used expansionary budgets and specific intervention measures (such as wage subsidies and incentives for early retirement) to hold down unemployment and sought to offset pressures on the exchange rate arising from a

[15]See Chapter 4.

[16]See Chapter 9.

[17]The policies applied in Austria, the Netherlands, and Norway are described in Chapter 10. Developments in Denmark are described in Chapter 8, pp. 197–99.

[18]See Chapter 9.

Table 3. Industrial Countries: Nature of Policies and Results Achieved, 1973–76

	Change in Real Domestic Demand[1]	Current Account Balance, 1973[2]	Exchange Rate Strategy[3]	Changes from 1973 to 1976[1]			Wage Increase, 1976[7]	Incomes Policy
				Effective exchange rate[4]	Current account[5]	Unemployment[6]		
Main emphasis on price stability[8]								
Germany, Fed. Rep. of (0.0)	3.0	++	FL*	10.8	. . .	+(L)[9]	9.6	None
Switzerland (0.5)	−9.5	++	FL	33.5	+	+(L)[9]	1.7	None
United States (0.5)	1.8	. . .	FL	6.6	. . .	+(M)	7.9	None[10]
Netherlands (1.5)	4.5	++	HC	9.6	. . .	+(L)	8.5	Price controls, wages policy
Belgium (1.5)	5.5	++	HC	2.4	—	+(M)	11.1	Price surveillance; wages policy, 1976
Main emphasis on maintaining employment[8]								
Canada (1.0)	12.3	+	FL[11]	3.9	—	+(H)	13.8	Wage and price controls, 1975–78
Austria (1.0)	6.8	. . .	HC	13.2	—	. . .(L)	9.0	Social partnership; price controls
France (1.0)	7.8	. . .	HC-FL	−2.5	—	+(L–M)	14.5	Price and wages policy, late 1976

Sweden (1.0)	11.2	+ +	HC	5.4	—	. . . (L)	17.9	None
Norway (1.0)	21.0	—	HC	10.7	—	. . . (L)	18.0	Combined income settlements
Denmark (3.0)	1.7	—	HC	6.6	—	+ + (L)	12.4	Price controls, wages policy
Main emphasis on strengthening current account[8]								
United Kingdom (3.0)	−3.0	—	FL	−24.2	. . .	+ (L–M)	16.7	Price controls, wage constraint
Italy (2.0)	1.5	—	FL	−28.9	. . .	. . . (M)	21.1	None
Japan (0.5)	3.5	. . .	FL	−4.2	+	. . . (M)	12.6	None

Sources: International Monetary Fund, *International Financial Statistics* and *Balance of Payments Yearbook*, and Organization for Economic Cooperation and Development, *Monthly Bulletin of Statistics* and *OECD Economic Surveys*, various issues.

[1]Percentage changes.

[2]Based on figures given in Table 1, Column 1. Current account position indicated as follows: + + = very large surplus; + = large surplus; . . . = slight imbalance; and — = large deficit.

[3]FL = flexible exchange rate; FL* = flexible rate except vis-à-vis countries following hard currency option; and HC = hard currency option.

[4]Changes in effective exchange rates calculated from the Fund's multilateral exchange rate model (MERM).

[5]Change in current account indicated as follows: + = marked improvement; . . . = slight change; and — = marked deterioration.

[6]Change in unemployment rate indicated as follows: + + = very marked increase; + = marked increase; and . . . = slight change. Unemployment level in 1973 indicated as follows: (L) = low; (L–M) = low to moderate; (M) = moderate; and (H) = high.

[7]Increase in average hourly earnings in manufacturing.

[8]Figures in parentheses show vulnerability to external price shock in 1973 as indicated in Table 1, Column 4.

[9]Including unemployment of repatriated foreign workers.

[10]Price/wage controls of 1971 were phased out in 1973–74.

[11]Exchange rate effectively maintained vis-à-vis the U.S. dollar until 1975.

weakening balance of payments position, by interest rate policy and/or heavy official borrowing abroad. Those countries that had an initially strong external position (Austria and Sweden), or especially favorable circumstances for maintaining high employment and for financing the external deficit (the Netherlands and Norway), were able to maintain the pegged exchange rate and avoid a marked increase in unemployment.

There had, however, been little adjustment of current account imbalances. Of the five countries that were heavily in surplus in 1973, the Federal Republic of Germany, Switzerland, and the Netherlands still had very large surpluses in 1976 and 1977, as did Japan. The four countries that were heavily in deficit in 1973—Denmark, Norway, the United Kingdom, and Italy—had similar, or even larger, deficits as a proportion of gross national product (GNP) in 1976. Belgium, Sweden, Canada, and France had moved into substantial deficit by 1976, and Austria and the United States were also heavily in deficit in 1977.

Table 3 shows that of the five countries that made price stability their primary goal, four—the Federal Republic of Germany, Switzerland, the United States, and the Netherlands—had achieved a moderation of wage increases by 1976 at the cost of substantial underutilization of capacity and a marked increase in unemployment (largely outside their national boundaries, however, in the case of Germany and Switzerland). A broadly similar outcome was realized in Canada by 1977, with the help of wage and price controls; the rise in unemployment and the deterioration in the current account were, however, aggravated by the appreciation of the Canadian dollar vis-à-vis the U.S. dollar during 1976.[19] The Netherlands, which was more vulnerable to the inflationary shock than Germany and Switzerland, but which benefited from rising receipts from natural gas production, implemented price-wage policies throughout the period after 1973 and was able to maintain a somewhat lower rate of unemployment. Belgium, which was also vulnerable owing to the prevalence of indexation, failed to secure a corresponding moderation of wage increases and experienced a marked deterioration of the current account *and* a very high level of unemployment. The Belgian authorities enforced a temporary incomes policy during the last nine months of 1976 to prevent a further loss of competitiveness.

The six countries that placed the main emphasis on supporting employment all suffered a marked weakening of the current account position by 1976 or 1977 but had different experience in limiting

[19] See Chapter 9.

unemployment. While Austria, Norway, and Sweden maintained very low percentages, unemployment rose substantially in France and reached a high level in Denmark and Canada.[20] In the three former countries, the low level of unemployment reflected the maintenance of the high level of consumer demand and was influenced by retraining programs and by efforts to induce employers to retain labor. In Norway, high employment was associated both with strong private investment, encouraged by the favorable prospects of the economy as oil production increased, and with rising real consumption promoted by budgetary policies. The policy of maintaining employment with a pegged exchange rate was appropriate for Norway, which could afford to incur large current account deficits, and not inappropriate for Austria, owing to its initially favorable competitive position and its success in limiting cost inflation.[21] The policy mix need not have been inappropriate for Sweden, given its strong initial current account position, if excessive cost increases and a disproportionately rapid expansion of domestic demand had been avoided.

France abandoned the pegged exchange rate when it became clearly inappropriate and did not experience such a rapid cost inflation and weakening of the current account as Sweden, or such a marked worsening of the current account and severe rise in unemployment as Denmark. In Denmark, direct measures to support employment were comparatively unimportant, and measures to support consumption mainly resulted in increased imports.

It is doubtful whether the hard currency strategy adopted by Denmark and the pegging of the krone at its existing level relative to the deutsche mark in 1973 was consistent with the maintenance of the low level of unemployment, given the already unfavorable competitive position; or whether the large wage increases provided for in the imposed wage settlement for 1975–76 were compatible with the maintenance of the pegged rate. The very marked worsening of the current account was also partly due to the policy of stimulating private consumption by a temporary reduction of indirect taxes in the hope of raising employment quickly, which instead prompted a sharp rise in imports. The adverse effects were compounded because the stimulus to consumption coincided with an unforeseen rise in real disposable incomes following the introduction of new income tax schedules.

[20]It should be noted that the less marked increase in unemployment in Austria—and also in Japan and Italy—was aided by the larger size of the family business sector in terms of employment than in most other industrial countries, which facilitated the absorption of unemployed persons in non-wage employment.

[21]See Chapter 10.

In Canada, the Anti-Inflation Program apparently achieved its purpose of slowing down wage increases over the three years covered, although the intended deceleration of increases in the consumer price index was not realized, largely owing to fluctuations in food prices. The initial impact of the Program in restraining price increases was reinforced by the appreciation of the exchange rate during 1976, when a very marked disparity developed between interest rates in Canada and the United States. The appreciation compounded the loss of competitiveness in relation to the United States owing to the unfavorable development of relative costs.[22]

The United Kingdom and Italy, the two countries that experienced marked depreciations after 1973, had secured slight reductions in their 1973 current account deficits by 1976. The United Kingdom was more successful than Italy in moderating the rise in hourly wages in manufacturing by 1976 and achieved a marked further deceleration during the first three quarters of 1977, although at the cost of a substantial rise in unemployment. In Italy, open unemployment had risen only moderately, in part because a larger proportion of the work force had been absorbed in agricultural and other small family enterprises. While real wages fell sharply in the United Kingdom during 1976–77, real gross wages were more or less maintained in large-scale enterprises in Italy. However, heavy tax and social security charges payable by wage earners and employers, together with the unions' enforcement of indexation and improvements in hours and conditions of work in the organized sectors, created profitable possibilities for evasion by small-scale enterprises and promoted a rising share of employment in such undertakings.

The combination of voluntary wage restraint and statutory controls on prices, profit margins, and dividends in the United Kingdom, together with the eventual enforcement of stringent restraint in the public sector, succeeded in curbing the rate of wage inflation during Phase II (mid-1976 to mid-1977).[23] The unions' agreement to stiff wage restraint in the guideline for Phase II was influenced by the moderation of price increases resulting from the maintenance of a nearly stable, and therefore increasingly overvalued, effective exchange rate for six months of Phase I. However, the delay in adjusting the rate—in late 1976 rather than in 1975—intensified the pressure on industrial profits, weakening business confidence and worsening the climate for investment during Phase II and adding to the rise in

[22]See Chapter 9.
[23]See Chapter 9.

unemployment. The sharp depreciation increased the difficulty of securing the unions' continued agreement to the policy of wage moderation after Phase II ended.

The Problem of Stabilization in an Open Economy

It is difficult to draw general conclusions concerning the experience with incomes policies in the years after 1973, because the results achieved depended far more on the appropriateness and consistency of the mix of monetary and fiscal policies and the exchange rate regimes adopted than on the efficacy of the incomes policy measures themselves. However, study of the context in which the policies were implemented brings into focus certain common problems of economic management in the industrial countries during this period.

An erratic and protracted process of international adjustment after the inflationary disturbances of the early 1970s took place during the latter part of the decade. Because of the widely differing inflation rates experienced in 1973, it was virtually certain that rates of cost inflation would continue to diverge over the next year or two, since the rate at which domestic costs tend to increase is strongly conditioned—over periods of a year or two—by lagged effects of past developments.[24] (Such effects include the influence of past rates of monetary expansion and price increase in determining inflation expectations; wage increases already provided for under long-term contracts or indexation provisions and the "demonstration effect" of recent wage settlements; and other factors such as official interventions in fixing minimum wages, "tax push," and so forth.) As a result, a high rate of domestic cost increase will not respond immediately, even to stringent demand restraint or foreign competition and rising unemployment. Hence, there was, in effect, some differing minimum attainable rate of domestic cost increase in each country in 1973, given its existing institutions and political context.

It was desirable that nominal exchange rates should continue to adjust in order to prevent growing disparities in relative costs during the process of stabilization that would tend to bring about undesired and persisting changes in the distribution of industrial employment and investment between countries, and also in order to avoid delayed corrections that would tend to precipitate renewed price inflation in the devaluing countries and possibly check real growth in the appreciating countries. It was not desirable therefore that countries should adopt policies tending to brake inflation, or to sustain activity,

[24]See Chapter 7.

by promoting a marked overvaluation, or undervaluation, of the real exchange rate. Lack of appropriate exchange rate adjustment was bound to create increasing uncertainty, with repercussions on business confidence and the willingness to invest or to respond aggressively to apparent opportunities for expansion.

Need for Dual Objective for Prices and the Real Exchange Rate

In the open industrial economy subject to faster-than-average inflation, the authorities need to have a dual objective for stabilization policy: restoring stability of the general level of prices and costs, while at the same time avoiding a marked and sustained rise in the relative level of wages and other factor costs at going exchange rates, such as to have damaging effects on future development of the real economy. A country that has an uncompetitive level of wage costs for any sustained period tends to fall behind other countries in the replacement of plant and equipment and the adoption of new techniques, to experience a contraction of its share in world industrial output, and to cease to participate in rapidly expanding, mass export industries (such as chemicals, computers, automobiles, machine tools, and electronics). Unfavorable job opportunities encourage a drain of skilled manpower. Hence, the authorities have to seek a balance between the aims of stabilizing the general price level and stabilizing the relative level of domestic factor costs vis-à-vis competing countries via the exchange rate. It is in this latter connection that the need for incomes policy measures arises most clearly.

Under a flexible exchange rate regime, a strongly contractionary monetary policy aimed at restoring domestic price stability will tend to promote an appreciation of the exchange rate by affecting capital flows. It is likely to exert a powerful influence on the movement of the general level of prices without having a commensurate effect in slowing down the rise in factor costs.[25] This is so because the

[25] "A monetary contraction will in the first instance induce a sharp appreciation in the spot rate and thereby cause domestic commodities to become overpriced relative to foreign goods. This applies across the board to all traded goods and therefore will immediately exert a deflationary effect on the traded goods sector. Thus, even in the absence of any interest response of aggregate demand, monetary policy does exert a strong effect on the demand for domestic output by inducing international price differentials and therefore substitution effects. While this avenue will speed up the real effects of monetary policy, it will also imply that it will tend to be *quite transitory*. The international price connection will exert strong pressure on the prices of traded goods and will cause changes in money to be more rapidly matched by changes in prices." Dornbusch (1977, p. 259, italics added).

"law of one price" applies more strongly to output prices than to factor costs in the short to medium run. Monetary policy may therefore succeed in re-establishing a greater degree of price stability but at a substantially higher level of relative costs at the going exchange rate.

Such an appreciation will slow down the rate of price increase by holding down the cost of imports of primary products and goods and services competing with domestic output. It will have some effect in moderating the rise in the cost of living and wage increases, conceivably setting off "virtuous circle" effects. But the appreciation also has the immediate effect of raising the level of costs relative to those of foreign producers and of lowering the prices in domestic currency at which producers in the open sector can sell without being undercut by foreign competition. Even if the rate of cost inflation is brought into line with that in other countries, the initial effect of the appreciation in raising the relative level of domestic costs and contracting output in the open sector is liable to persist.[26] With a capital stock and supply of trained labor specific for the established structure of production and with downward rigidity of nominal wages, rents, and other factor costs, this scenario is liable to involve a protracted period of heavy unemployment and low investment if sustained. However, the shift to a more expansionary monetary stance may precipitate a marked depreciation of the exchange rate, setting off renewed inflation.

The Case for a Gradualist Approach Utilizing Incomes Policy

Certain policies were requisite after 1973 in order to promote the process of bringing down cost inflation together with an orderly adjustment of exchange rates. Although such concepts are unavoidably vague, it was desirable that each country should aim at a "feasible" lowering of the rate of inflation with a "desired" level of real output or real growth, that is, at a lowering of the rate of inflation that could be foreseen to be achieved without an excessive level of unemployment or shock to private investment over the next year or two. These desiderata would imply that countries' policies should be such as to ensure some positive, but not excessively high, level of *real* interest rates in the absence of policy-induced capital flows and that

[26]"Firms could be thrown into bankruptcy on a wide swing of the exchange rate both creating damage to the economy and provoking risk-averting actions which increase costs." Cooper (1977, p. 27). See also Crockett and Goldstein (1976) and Artus and Young (1979).

policies should not be such as to promote large changes in *real* exchange rates.[27]

This account implies that it would have been desirable to adopt a "gradualist" approach to the problem of bringing down inflation after 1973 and to avoid policies aiming at "shock" effects, predicated on the assumption that slowing inflation is all a question of correcting inflationary expectations in a world of rapid price and wage responses, without "built-in" institutional lags. In actual practice, the effect of drastic deflationary policies in some countries was to set in motion shock waves and continuing repercussions that produced greatly increased economic uncertainty in the latter part of the 1970s.

A gradualist solution would have indicated some appropriate range of monetary expansion for each country over the next year or two. Above this range, the authorities could be viewed as implementing an inappropriately inflationary policy, or below it an excessively deflationary policy involving an undesirable depressive shock to the real economy. Given the considerations concerning real interest rates and exchange rates, the appropriate range of monetary expansion represented a constraint for budgetary policy: the budgetary position had to be consistent with the appropriate range of monetary expansion and the private demand for credit at the ruling real exchange rate.

Some examples will help to show what this implied, although the questions involved are too complex for a full discussion here. It was not appropriate, if the monetary authority was pursuing a disinflationary rate of monetary expansion in the face of continuing strong private demand for credit, for the government to implement a large exogenous increase in the budget deficit by lowering taxes or raising expenditure, since this would precipitate an excessive rise in real interest rates and/or the real exchange rate. It was however appropriate that the demand for money should if necessary be sustained at the target level by a, probably endogenous, rise in the public sector deficit.

It was not appropriate if the rate of monetary expansion was lower than desired following a decline in activity, that fiscal measures, intended to secure a reduction in the scale of the structural budget deficit under high employment, should serve to prevent the endogenous rise in the budget deficit resulting from the decline in activity. Nor was it appropriate, in these circumstances, for the authorities to seek to expand activity via deliberate monetary measures to promote the outflow of capital, lowering of the real exchange rate, and expansion of the current account surplus. The simultaneous adoption

---

[27] For simplicity, it is assumed that no large changes in real exchange rates were required after the adjustments that took place in the first half of 1973.

of these inappropriate scenarios by two major countries was bound to provoke very large changes in real exchange rates.

To sum up, it was desirable after 1973 that countries should (1) aim to bring down the rate of monetary expansion to a rate compatible with maintaining a desired level of output and employment at a realistically foreseeable minimum rate of cost inflation; (2) adopt a budgetary stance consistent with an appropriate rate of monetary expansion; (3) forgo the option of raising the real exchange rate as a means of slowing wage increases through its effect in moderating the rise in consumer prices. That is to say, the authorities should refrain from policies tending to strengthen the real exchange rate markedly, by contraction of money growth, by incurring public sector deficits requiring to be financed by heavy borrowing abroad, or by measures to limit imports or subsidize exports. In the opposite case, the authorities should forgo "competitive" depreciation and refrain from implementing a policy mix calculated to lower the real exchange rate as a means of securing the desired level of output and activity; and finally, (4) countries subject to severe ongoing cost inflation should, if possible, implement incomes policy measures to slow down the movement of factor costs so as to achieve the minimum feasible rate of inflation. These considerations applied with greatest force to the major economies.

In order to avoid inappropriate real exchange rates and erratic changes in exchange rates, it was desirable that nominal exchange rates should continue to adjust. In actual practice, however, as has been seen, most governments chose to avoid or delay exchange rate adjustments.

For the governments that undertook to maintain a pegged rate under the European narrow margins arrangement (the "snake") and yet wished to implement expansionary budget deficits to support employment and further social objectives, the combination of objectives required the enforcement of tight monetary policy giving rise to public or private borrowing that served to support the exchange rate by offsetting the current account deficit. Rather similar measures would have been needed to maintain the fixed exchange rate under a rigid par value system. However, pegging of the rate on a strong currency, in the context where several major currencies were floating more or less freely, imposed a stiffer constraint on monetary expansion than would have been required if all rates were fixed. More seriously, it exposed producers in the open sector to additional, and largely unforeseeable, pressure as their competitiveness was reduced by the appreciation of the deutsche mark vis-à-vis nonsnake currencies. Thus, it was more difficult to maintain employment by deficit spending than under the par value system. For those countries (such as Canada, the United Kingdom, and later France) which did not undertake to peg the exchange rate but which were concerned to limit the rise in unemployment, the adoption of a floating exchange rate regime intensified the need for coordination of budgetary and monetary policy because the exchange rate was now highly responsive to monetary policy.

Several circumstances made it difficult for policymakers to derive a useful impression of the way in which demand management by the budgetary and monetary authorities would be affected by the abandonment of the fixed exchange rate system. One was that much of the literature comparing the flexible and fixed exchange rate regimes tended to concentrate on the effects of "pure" monetary policy, government expenditure remaining unchanged, and of "pure" fiscal policy, with money growth unchanged, neglecting the more general case of simultaneous changes in both types of policy. The crucial issue of the interrelationship between budgetary deficit, monetary policy, and movement in the exchange rates was not sufficiently emphasized. Theoretical expositions of the working of the two exchange rate systems also tended to ignore the effect of rigidities and the influence of political considerations and uncertainties.

When a marked rise in unemployment conflicts with strong political priorities—or the government's express mandate—to maintain employment, there is a temptation to try for both price stability and high employment, by combining strict monetary policy that tends to strengthen the exchange rate and a large budget deficit that is financed by borrowing abroad. Such a combination however involves inherent contradictions. The results are achieved by "importing unemployment" in the open sector and then subsidizing enterprises in one way or another to maintain employment there, and/or expanding employment in the public sector as employment in the open sector declines. While price increases in the open sector are constrained by means of the exchange rate, expenditure rises in the sheltered sector, where prices and costs are inherently less subject to constraint. The effect of greater price constraint in the open sector in slowing down the movement of domestic factor costs is liable to be weakened if rising public expenditure causes the movement of wages and salaries in the public sector, or of social security transfers and pensions, to be comparatively unconstrained. Furthermore, efforts to mitigate the decline in employment in the open sector may serve to weaken the constraint on cost increases there in various ways: for example, if public spending is channeled to domestic suppliers regardless of uncompetitive prices; or if the authorities in effect underwrite relatively high wage costs by subsidizing employment in the open sector so as to bring wage costs to the employer more into line with those abroad; or if the government finances production for inventory or protects employment by import protection and export subsidizing devices. All such measures interfere with the working of the integrated market economy and tend to create a context in which business energy is applied to exploiting government programs and securing further concessions instead of seeking out and exploiting market opportunities.

The Role of Incomes Policy

The essential role of incomes policy as a supplement to, not a substitute for, measures of fiscal and monetary restraint was most evident after 1973. Incomes policy and labor market measures were generally adopted as constituent elements in complex mixes of demand policies. In many cases, a restrictive monetary policy, tending to strengthen the exchange rate and to curb the rise in nominal income by restraining wages and prices and/or output and employment, was applied together with expansionary fiscal measures. Monetary policy was supplemented by incomes policy and other measures aimed at maintaining employment and investment. In other cases, a restrictive fiscal policy was associated with an expansionary monetary policy used to promote capital outflows in order to finance a surplus in the balance of payments on current account without an appreciation of the exchange rate. Incomes policy measures limiting increases in nominal wages and salaries and price controls were also implemented in this context. Monetary and fiscal policies, exchange rate objectives, and the recourse to incomes policy were in practice closely interrelated. The results achieved were conditioned by the entire set of policies, and the effect of incomes policy measures can therefore only be assessed in the light of the consequences of the entire set of policies pursued.

In the late 1970s, incomes policies were gradually eased or dismantled in several countries. Weak demand conditions and heavy unemployment in most industrial countries and depressed world markets for commodities dampened the rate of price inflation and moderated wage pressures. The need for incomes policy as an emergency brake had passed. At the same time, opposition to the continuation of broad-based intervention and controls was mounting, and their effective implementation was increasingly threatened by resistance of specific groups adversely affected by the measures. Current weak demand conditions minimized the risk of a flare-up of inflation resulting from the ending of controls and, in some cases, represented an opportunity for terminating a program that was threatening to disintegrate or to generate industrial unrest. By the same token, however, the uncertainties associated with the phasing out of controls tended to promote an especially cautious attitude of the authorities to reflationary policies and a heightened concern with maintaining the exchange rate.

Although the immediate threat of rapid inflation seemed to have receded by early 1978, the rates of price and wage increases being experienced in most countries were still stubbornly high by pre-1973 standards. There was no sure indication that cost inflation would not intensify with strengthening demand conditions, particularly if groups and sectors that had fared particularly badly found themselves in a stronger wage bargaining position or a favorable context for increasing prices and if their actions initiated a general speedup of wage and price increases. Moreover, the general rate of inflation was still sufficiently great to pose specific problems of economic management that essentially called for a coordinated solution within the framework of incomes policy considerations. Among such problems were how to finance the steeply rising costs of social security and state pension schemes and the need to avoid "tax push" effects and growing resistance to taxation, occasioned by rising real tax burdens under unindexed progressive income taxes or by rocketing property taxes related to rapidly rising real estate values.

Thus, the need for incomes policy in the sense of a deliberate and concerted effort by the authorities to secure a moderate rise in nominal incomes by directly influencing the attitude and behavior of those responsible for pricing and wage bargaining decisions had by no means disappeared by 1978. The objectives, however, were different from 1975–76 when the overriding aim was to curb the existing high rate of inflation by relatively simple and uniform controls or restraints on wages and prices or profits and dividends. The disincentive effects of controls and the narrowing of skill differentials and other side effects were then of secondary importance in the immediate context of demand restraint. This, of course, ceases to be so when the basic purpose of incomes policy is to reinforce the effectiveness of stimulatory policies in raising real output, employment, and investment.

A principal objective of incomes policy must be to inform public opinion and develop a consensus on the appropriate rate of increase for most wages and salaries, against which large claims, not justified by special factors, can be judged excessive. Another is to foster general agreement on those cases in which larger wage increases are justified, whether by the need to attract more labor or investment in skills or on social grounds, to avoid "poverty wages" or to compensate for a more rapid rise in the cost of living at the lowest consumption levels. (Union support for wage "solidarity" in the sense of larger relative increases for the lower paid was an important element in mitigating wage pressure and promoting recovery in the Scandinavian countries during the 1930s.)

During the late 1970s, many governments sought to achieve somewhat the same purpose as that served by a wage guideline, by adopting a money growth target explicitly predicated on permitting a certain rate of output expansion with moderate, or moderating, price increases. Efforts were also directed to limiting the increase in public sector incomes and sometimes to reinforcing wage constraint in the private sector by suasion or sanctions such as loss of public contracts or withdrawal of financial assistance for training programs.

A basic purpose of the authorities must be to prevent the emergence of strong competing pressures by organized groups aimed at securing large real income gains for their members, whether by pushing up wages and raising prices, by limiting competition and restricting supply, or by opposing or evading taxes. Such a situation will force up the nominal level of incomes and prices but depress the expansion of real output, employment, and investment. To this end, the authorities need to use all the formal and informal weapons at their disposal (including powers to investigate or delay price increases and measures to limit monopolistic practices). But, in the last resort, the problem is an essentially political one of encouraging the formation of consistent and feasible real income aspirations of organized groups (which can then be translated into nominal increases on the basis of reasonably confident and generally held expectations of the general rate of inflation) and of promoting a system of checks and balances to prevent excessive and disruptive gains by particular groups.

The suggestions outlined earlier in the discussion of the problem of stabilization in an open economy do not touch upon the practical problems of devising and implementing measures to meet these suggested ground rules. Many of these problems are illustrated in the country studies in Chapters 9 and 10. But the need for the government and its economic and monetary advisors to hammer out a consistent and feasible set of policy goals and to devise a set of measures to realize that general design cannot be overemphasized. It will not do to adopt the less demanding strategy of implementing an uncoordinated set of policies aiming at specific, and possibly conflicting, goals. Conflicting goals of monetary and budgetary policy or unresolved differences between politicians and economic administrators result in growing tensions within the economy and are apt to produce sudden shifts in policy and changes in exchange rates. The failure to implement a sustainable mix of policies increases uncertainty and business risks, contributing to hold down investment in the open sector and to keep up unemployment. The instability of exchange rates and interest rates that has constituted an important element in increasing uncertainty and business risks in recent years must be ascribed in large measure to the effect of inconsistencies of policies both within countries and between countries.

Part II
The Scope for Incomes Policy in Theory and Practice

4

Incomes Policy Under Fixed Exchange Rates in the 1960s

This chapter provides a view of the role and nature of incomes policy from the standpoint of the mid-1960s.[1] It describes the nature of cost inflation in industrial economies pursuing full employment policies in an international environment characterized by little, if any, inflation in the price of industrial goods traded in the world market and no evident "excess demand"[2] in the industrial world as a whole. It explains why the underlying tendencies to internally generated cost inflation were likely to be stronger in some economies than in others, when a certain moderate rate of unemployment was maintained, and draws some conclusions concerning the scope for incomes policy. It is argued that the strength of upward cost pressure in an economy is broadly determined by the relation between the rates at which money wages and productivity tend to rise at a given level of unemployment and that the rate at which money wages rise is likely to be influenced by (1) the underlying flexibility of the labor market situation and (2) the degree of "organization" that prevails in product and labor markets. Such features of the labor market as the rate of growth of the population of working age, possibilities of increasing

[1]This chapter is based on Romanis (Braun) (1967).

[2]"Excess demand" was defined as a "volume of aggregate monetary demand which cannot be met at existing prices without exerting undue pressure on productive resources [so that] capacity becomes strained, a general labour shortage develops, and prices and wages are bid up by buyers and employers competing for the scarce supplies" in the Organization for European Economic Cooperation (OEEC) report of 1961. See Fellner and others (1961, p. 33).

participation in the active labor force, and the scope for reducing underemployment in technically backward sectors, such as peasant agriculture and small-scale distribution, condition the bargaining power of the unions and determine the likelihood of wages and prices being bid up by scarcities. The degree of "organization," which comprehends such features of the economy as the extent of unionization of labor, the extent to which the pricing policies of employers are deliberately or spontaneously coordinated, and the extent to which firms are subject to competition from foreign concerns whose costs do not move in line with domestic wage increases, strongly influences the likelihood of widespread cost pressure eventuating in an economy. Productivity growth is also likely to vary considerably between countries, depending on the state of technology and the resources becoming available for investment. The economies which, by reason of the circumstances just described, are most likely to experience quite rapid increases in money wages are probably not those in which the underlying conditions are most conducive to rapid increases in productivity.

The Process of Cost Inflation

The Nature of Wage Bargaining by Unions

Entrepreneurs and unions have come to assume that, by and large, rising productivity in the economy should be reflected in rising money wages and stable prices rather than in stable money wages and falling prices.[3] Union members expect to secure increases in money wages over time and will press such claims unless their bargaining position is too weak to permit them to do so. In general, union members expect some percentage increase in money wages each year and expect this percentage to exceed any rise in the cost of living. Even when the cost of living is stable, there is some minimum range of increase that is considered the least worth bargaining for.[4] However, the aggressiveness with which union members are prepared to press for wage increases tends to diminish above a certain customary range.[5] Wage

[3]See Hicks (1956).

[4]This limit may have an important influence on the form of wage claims: additional paid holidays or a reduction in weekly hours may appear a more substantial gain than a 1 or 2 percent increase in wage rates.

[5]In the sense that, if the cost of living were rising by 1 or 2 percent a year, the rank and file would be less inclined to strike and more prepared to compromise and accept a 6 percent increase against a claim for an 8 percent rise when the union was in a strong bargaining position, than to accept a 3 percent increase against a 4 percent claim even when the union was in a weaker position.

cost inflation is, therefore, less likely when productivity growth is very rapid and exceeds that range than when productivity growth is slight and falls short of the percentage increase in money wages that union members have come to expect each year.

It is difficult to organize wage earners in such sectors as peasant agriculture, small-scale manufacturing and handicrafts, distribution, and personal services, where the typical concerns are small family businesses employing few, if any, wage earners and little capital equipment. Even if a union were to be successfully organized, its power to raise wages in these circumstances would be circumscribed by the considerable scope for substituting alternative labor (of the entrepreneur and his dependents) or additional capital for wage labor. Faced with unemployment, many wage earners themselves would be likely to swell the ranks of family helpers or the self-employed.[6]

It is usually easier to organize wage earners in industries where the freedom of entry of new enterprises is restricted by the need for substantial capital or technical know-how. This is so both because such industries are often characterized by the concentration of considerable numbers of wage earners in relatively few concerns and because capital-intensive techniques imply more or less fixed manning requirements in the short to medium term. Thus, it is as a rule easier for labor to restrain wage competition in those sectors where employers are most favorably placed to restrain price competition. Since it is more difficult for entrepreneurs or labor to restrain entry and competition in the sectors characterized by large numbers of small-scale producers, the population dependent on those sectors tends to increase and per capita incomes there tend to decline relative to those in the more technically developed sectors when there is persistent unemployment in the more technically developed sectors or when aggregate demand is tending to rise more slowly than the potential labor force. Owing to this process, weak demand for labor relative to the growth in labor supply in the past tends to be reflected in current weakness of labor organization and union bargaining power and a low level of output per worker over the economy as a whole.

Generally speaking, union members expect their union to secure larger-than-usual increases when bargaining conditions are exceptionally good. However, they also expect the union to ensure that their earnings rise in line with those of other wage earners. Thus, if any

[6]Differences between countries with regard to the underlying labor market situation and structure of employment during the early 1960s are discussed in a later section of this chapter.

important union succeeds in exploiting an exceptionally favorable bargaining position to secure an unusually large increase in wages and benefits, its success tends to raise the scale of wage claims elsewhere, even if bargaining conditions for other unions remain unchanged. Increases in earnings under existing wage agreements, such as those resulting from higher overtime pay when activity increases, or from higher piecework earnings when productivity rises, may have a similar effect in stimulating wage claims from other groups of workers.

Since the object of a trade union is to advance the interests of its members, the coverage of the different unions and the area to which individual wage bargains relate strongly influence the considerations that are taken into account in pressing wage claims. Competitive union behavior is a potent factor in cost inflation. Just as the individual seller in a market comprising many small producers cannot hope to prevent prices from falling by holding back supplies, so a union that is too small to influence the general movement of wages cannot hope by its forbearance to prevent wages from rising. The small union has no reason to sacrifice the specific interests of its members because the wage increase that it secures may give rise to claims elsewhere, the combined result of which may be to force up the cost of living or to create a threat of unemployment. "Even if each unionist believed that the effect of a series of wage increases in different industries would be nullified by the resulting inflation, it would still be good policy for each union to try to get its increases first and make them bigger than the average."[7] On the other hand, where the individual unions are very large or the union movement is strongly coordinated and the central organization exercises considerable control over the wage claims of individual unions, attention is more likely to be paid to the fact that wages generally cannot rise much faster than productivity without causing price inflation, probable repercussions on the balance of payments, and adverse effects on employment in export- and import-competing sectors.

In the 1960s, the pattern of wage negotiations could be characterized as highly coordinated in the Scandinavian countries; coordinated in Austria, the Federal Republic of Germany, and, at least up to 1966, the Netherlands; and competitive in the United Kingdom, Belgium, France, and Italy. In the United States, Canada, and Japan, where wage bargaining takes place predominantly at the plant level, negotiations were more strongly influenced by the "capacity to pay" of particular enterprises, and hence decisions to press particular wage

[7] Hardy (1946, p. 24). See also Chamberlin (1962, p. 226).

claims were reached somewhat more independently than in European countries. These differences stemmed mainly from differences in the context in which unions developed. In general, the unions tend to be organized in a few large units with strong central direction, often with powerful central coordinating federations, in those countries where they developed in a context of large firms or of strongly coordinated resistance to wage claims by the employers.[8] In other words, the character of union structure seems to be determined largely by the character of the employers' organizations. On the whole, owing partly to less widespread unionization, but also partly to geographical and institutional factors tending to create distinct regional labor markets, there is a real contrast between the United States and Canada, on the one hand, and most European countries, on the other, in the extent to which wages differ and move differently in various regions.[9] There is a similar but less marked contrast between the highly unified labor markets of the United Kingdom and the Netherlands and the regional differentiation of Italy and France.

In considering how increases in wage costs come about, it is necessary to distinguish between (1) negotiated wage increases, which essentially represent a compromise, determined by the bargaining strength of the two sides, between a price at which unions would wish to supply their members' labor and a price at which entrepreneurs hope to employ that labor; and (2) other increases in effective rates of pay per unit of labor brought about by arrangements outside the procedures of collective wage bargaining between the union and several employers in an industry, which inter alia give rise to so-called wage drift.

Negotiated Wage Increases in a Particular Industry

For the sake of simplicity, it may be useful initially to assume that all wages and salaries are in practice determined by collective agreement between the union and employers in the industry. It should be noted that though this simplifying assumption implies that wages are not bid up by individual employers competing for labor, the employers in any particular industry faced with highly favorable demand conditions as a group might concede, or even propose, an increase in wages to the union in the course of wage negotiations in order to attract additional manpower into the industry.

---

[8]Differences in the wage bargaining situation in various industrial countries are discussed later in this chapter.

[9]See Organization for Economic Cooperation and Development (1965).

Influence of Degree of Unionization

It is clear that the attitude of both unions and employers toward wage claims will be strongly conditioned by the extent to which they expect the prospective wage increase to apply to all firms in the industry. The unions are likely to be less aggressive in pressing wage claims if they believe that the wage increases may not apply to all the workers actually employed or potentially available for employment in an industry (or craft); and the employers, if they hold similar views, will be less permissive in granting wage increases. Hence, if there is a large pool of unorganized low-wage manpower in the economy and the possibility exists of shifting production to a rural area and paying lower wages there, the bargaining power of unions in the established industrial areas will be somewhat circumscribed. Moreover, even if the unions in the existing industrial areas do succeed in pushing up wages, the influence of this on costs in the economy as a whole will be mitigated insofar as the effect is to encourage the transfer of production to regions where wages are lower. The possibility of substituting lower-paid women workers for men may also have similar effects in restraining wage pressures in the countries where only a small proportion of the potential female labor force has been employed and organized.

The influence of unemployment (or disguised unemployment) is strongly conditioned by the effective degree of unionization. If a union is able to compel all employers in an industry to pay collectively negotiated rates, the existence even of massive long-term unemployment *outside* the industry need not influence the attitude of the union and its members toward putting forward wage claims. Thus, if an industry is fully and effectively unionized, an increase in unemployment outside the industry may have little influence on the attitude of workers in that industry concerning the wage rates at which they are willing to supply their labor. Only when the union has reason to believe that, because of an actual or prospective weakening in sales or profits, employers in their particular industry are more determined not to raise wages and less likely to yield to union pressures (such as strikes, working to rule, and overtime bans) are wage claims likely to be moderated because the general level of unemployment has risen.

On the employers' side, once the effective degree of unionization is such that an increase in negotiated wages will apply throughout an industry, each employer can assume that his competitors' wage costs will rise more or less in line with his own,[10] and the employers may,

[10]Chamberlin (1962, p. 224).

therefore, be less afraid to raise wages. This, in turn, strengthens the bargaining position of the unions.

A priori it would seem that, because of the greater likelihood of coordinated price behavior, the risk of wage increases pushing up prices is greater when wage negotiations take place on an industry-wide basis, as in many European countries, than when they take place at different times in different concerns, as in the United States and Canada. Other factors, however, such as the greater vulnerability of individual enterprises to strike pressure, work in the opposite direction. Wage claims may have more effect in squeezing profits when negotiations take place with individual concerns. The typical sequence may then be for the union first to press a wage claim against a highly profitable concern, using "capacity to pay" arguments; if the concern accedes, it may not be inclined to raise prices before the union has used this wage settlement as a lever to secure wage increases generally throughout the industry. In such a case, there will be a lag between the initial wage increase and the raising of prices, and wage increases will have some temporary effect in squeezing profit margins, particularly in the most profitable concerns.

Influence of Extent of "Organization" Among Employers

The extent to which the price behavior of entrepreneurs is deliberately, or spontaneously, coordinated strongly influences the danger of cost pressure. The importance of the degree of certainty attaching to entrepreneurs' expectations concerning the probable price behavior of their competitors should be stressed. If some firms are actively seeking to expand their shares of the market by their pricing policies, the risk that they may not pass on higher wage costs in higher prices will be clear to other concerns; and firms generally will be less prepared to accede to union pressure than in a more stable market situation. When a more stable situation exists in an imperfectly competitive market comprising many or few firms, individual employers who are faced with a wage claim that, if successful, will apply to all wage earners (or all wage or salary earners of a certain type) within the industry, can foresee the prospective price behavior of their competitors quite clearly, since they can expect the behavior of other entrepreneurs to be conditioned by much the same considerations as their own. Consequently, the risks for the individual employer of allowing wages (or other monopolistically determined costs)[11] to rise

[11]Which may include costs of raw materials, manufactured components, equipment, or services.

are smaller, and resistance to granting wage claims (or to paying higher prices for other items entering into production) is likely to be weaker, than in more fluid market conditions.

While a stable market situation may apply in different circumstances, a priori such a situation would appear more likely to exist in the more highly developed industrial economies where the scope for expansion of the advanced sectors and for advances in technique and changes in the scale of production is relatively small. Unless quite marked fluctuations in demand are commonly experienced, firms in general are unlikely to maintain large reserves of unutilized capacity. The firm which employs price competition in order to expand its share of the market is, therefore, presumably seeking to increase its capacity and probably is increasing that of the industry. Consequently, difficulties in recruiting more labor or pressures on the building sector that interfere with investment schemes are liable to restrict the extent of price competition in an economy. Moreover, the gains from expanding capacity and securing a larger share of the total market will appear more certain to the firm if the industry as a whole is tending to expand. Thus, to risk a generalization, entrepreneurs in an economy undergoing rapid development of the industrial sector in a technologically "backward" setting (such as Japan and Italy in the 1950s and 1960s) may be more independent in their behavior and hence more inclined to resist union wage claims than employers in an economy in which the room for expansion of technically advanced production is smaller (such as the United Kingdom and Sweden in that period).

If a stable market situation exists in an industry, entrepreneurs can expect that prices will continue to be determined on some conventional cost-plus basis because each concern is mindful of the lowering of profits per unit of output that could result from the resumption of price competition. No firm can afford to raise prices alone, and no firm is willing to initiate price reductions alone for fear of unleashing a price war. But, so long as the demand curve for the industry is somewhat inelastic, it is possible for all firms acting in unison to count on raising prices without experiencing a drop of the same proportion in quantities sold. In stable markets, an increase in negotiated wages throughout an industry not only raises costs throughout the industry but, by doing so, increases the possibility of raising prices, since it creates a situation in which all firms are inclined to raise prices more or less simultaneously. It should be noted that price increases for basic products that constitute an important element in the cost of the products of another industry or industries are likely to have an exactly analogous effect in this respect.

In the advanced economy, many circumstances restrict freedom of entry into various sectors or occupations and enable existing producers to keep up prices and realize a certain habitual margin of profit per unit of output except under extraordinary demand conditions. Imperfect knowledge on the part of both producers and consumers, limited mobility of factors, technological progress and limited diffusion of the latest know-how, scarcity of skills, important economies of scale even for very large enterprises, and scope for product differentiation by advertising are all important in this connection.[12] Thus, it cannot be assumed that the output of the industry will be expanded to the point where no additional profit can be made by doing so. Nor will the existing rate of profit represent the *minimum* return required to induce producers to supply the actual (or planned) level of output.[13] Hence, a raising of wage costs by union action need not involve a reduction in present (or planned) output whenever demand for the industry's output is not perfectly inelastic.

The factors that tend to restrict entry of new firms into certain industries, of course, militate against the equalization of rates of return to capital and management in different industries and restrict alternative employment opportunities for management and capital. Consequently, it does not follow that higher wages obtained at the expense of profits and remuneration of management in a particular industry will necessarily reduce the returns to capital and management below those elsewhere and provide inducement for entrepreneurs to contract the industry. Nor does it follow that a reduction in returns below those obtaining elsewhere would quickly lead to reduced employment in the industry in question, since it is difficult for management and capital employed in a particular industry to shift out of that industry into more profitable fields. Eventually, if the rates of return were to remain below those that could be obtained in accessible alternative openings for management and capital over a prolonged period, the lower returns might lead to disinvestment and reduced willingness of entrepreneurs to enter, or to remain in, the industry. However, such an outcome would depend on a number of factors, such as whether returns to capital and management in other industries had also been

---

[12]Sraffa (1926).

[13]For example, in a monopolistic industry, comprising a few firms exploiting a new product or technique (where it may be relatively easy to organize the workers, especially if there are heavy capital requirements or special factors anchoring production in a particular area), the union may be able to push wages above the going wage rate in other industries, somewhat reducing the monopoly profits of firms in the industry.

squeezed by rising wage costs in the meantime or whether higher wage costs throughout the economy had been accommodated by monetary policy, making it possible for firms generally to raise their prices.

In an advanced economy, demand for an industry's output is usually somewhat inelastic. The bounds of an industry are extended by mergers between the producers of goods that constitute alternative objects of expenditure, and the elasticity of demand is also reduced by product differentiation, advertising, and the like. The existence of imperfect competition in other product markets, or in the supply of labor and other factors to industries producing alternative goods, renders demand for each industry's output somewhat inelastic. This is so because the elasticity of demand for the output of any industry is determined not only by the extent to which a rise in the price of the product tends to cause buyers to switch to other goods but also by the response of producers of those other goods to increased demand for their products. (If, for instance, there were to be no increase in the supply of the other goods for which demand had tended to increase, their prices would merely tend to rise until buyers were satisfied with about the same pattern of expenditure as before,[14] and the demand for the original industry's product would be almost or completely inelastic.) Thus, when a union succeeds in pushing up costs to all existing or potential producers in an industry, producers may find that higher wages can be passed on to the consumer with little or no reduction in the total output of the industry, provided that higher prices in this industry induce equivalent increases in prices or costs, rather than expansion of output, in other sectors. When this tends to occur, the widespread existence of monopolistic conditions in product and labor markets in effect renders the general price level unstable in the face of upward cost pressure originating in a single industry.

It follows from this description that price behavior in a single industry cannot be fully understood in isolation, without taking into account the behavior of management and labor in other sectors and the degree of control exercised by the monetary and fiscal authorities in the interest of maintaining price stability. The nature of generalized cost inflation in the industrial economy as a whole is discussed in the section on the effectiveness of aggregate demand policy, below.

Influence of Openness of the Economy

It may be useful to consider how the openness of the economy influences wage bargaining within particular industries. Where the

[14] That is, unless the consequent price increase was so large as to have significant income effects or to influence the choice between spending and saving.

production of certain products is concentrated in the hands of a few very large concerns in several countries, producers may be able to reach market-sharing arrangements without fear of attracting new entrants. In general, however, a stable market situation is much more likely to exist among firms in a single country than among firms in different countries. A principal reason for this is that changes in wages and other costs are more likely to be experienced in common by firms within an industry in one country than by firms in different countries. The relative unit costs of firms in different countries are more liable to change over time, both as a result of differences in the bargaining power of the unions and as a result of changes in national policies affecting the pressure of demand on national resources or the conditions for foreign trade (such as budgetary and monetary policies, tariffs, and exchange rates). Thus, the inducement for firms in different countries to seek to expand their share of an international market by lowering prices is liable to vary considerably over time, and may sometimes be very strong.

Entrepreneurs in export-oriented industries, or in industries selling in a home market where imports are of major importance, are aware that their foreign competitors' costs are not raised by domestic wage increases. Hence, managements are more likely to resist union wage demands, since they have less assurance of being able to raise prices in line with rising costs. There is, consequently, less danger of internally generated cost inflation in small countries, such as the Netherlands and Sweden, where very large concerns are inevitably dependent on exports and even those firms that depend mainly on the home market are generally competing with more or less close substitutes produced abroad, than in larger countries. It is possible, however, that the exceptionally large size of the United States tends to reduce the risk of cost inflation, by allowing regional conditions to have more influence on wage rates[15] and by reducing the tendency toward "organized" price behavior in the home market.

Wage Drift

In practice, wage and salary payments are not determined exclusively by collective agreements between unions and employers, and increases in effective rates of pay per unit of labor also result from arrangements outside the recognized procedures of collective bargain-

[15]Regional considerations apparently have greater influence in wage determination in the United States and Canada than in many European countries, but this is in part the result of the lower degree of unionization.

ing between the union and employers. It is customary to regard such wage drift as reflecting demand pull, but though the extent of wage drift is likely to be related to the scarcity of manpower available to those sectors where collective bargaining applies, wage drift is not occasioned solely by pressure of demand for labor.[16] It is apt to occur whenever systems of payments by results are applied, as a consequence of learning on the job and improvements in the organization of production after piece rates are established. Furthermore, the most progressive enterprises in each industry, which are successful in achieving above-average increases in productivity, frequently are willing to pay higher wages than those stipulated in the collective agreement for the industry (or to grant increases in wages before the agreement is revised), in order to facilitate the introduction of new methods, to reduce labor turnover, or to command the pick of available manpower.

At any given level of aggregate demand, wage drift will usually be greatest in those industries or economies where systems of payment by results are most prevalent[17] and where the actual process of wage determination in the individual plant or enterprise is least closely regulated by the procedures of collective bargaining. Since the majority of union members cannot raise their earnings by increasing effort per unit of time, the timing and scale of a union's wage claims tend to be strongly influenced by changes in average earnings per unit of time in similar occupations. Thus, regardless of whether increases in pieceworkers' average earnings per hour (or per week) are earned by greater labor input or justified by higher output per hour, they are liable to give rise to claims on behalf of timeworkers elsewhere. The classic example of this process is to be found in the postwar history of wage negotiations in the engineering and shipbuilding industries in the United Kingdom. All the authorities on the subject emphasize the vital role of workshop bargaining over piece rates in providing the stimulus for claims elsewhere in the plant or elsewhere in the industry.[18] Recent empirical studies of wage drift have emphasized the difficulties that incentive schemes may cause.[19]

[16]In statistical studies, wage drift is usually defined as the difference between the actual rate of increase in earnings and the rate of increase which would have resulted from the provisions of the collective wage agreements concerning changes in time and piece rates, overtime rates, and so forth. Complications may arise in using this concept, however, when the growth of actual earnings is influenced by marked changes in the degree of utilization of labor. See Hansen and Rehn (1956), Rehn (1959), and Phelps Brown (1962b).

[17]See Lerner (1965).

[18]United Kingdom, National Incomes Commission (1965). See also Knowles and Robertson (1951), Hill and Knowles (1956), and Phelps Brown (1962b).

[19]See, for example, Pym (1964).

The character of union organization at the plant or local level has an important bearing on the likelihood of wage drift. If all the workers in a plant are organized in one union with a single representative, the wage structure will tend to be formalized, and the employer will be conscious that increases in certain workers' earnings will quickly give rise to claims by other workers. The risk of cost pressure originating in wage drift may be reduced by a tradition (such as exists in the Netherlands and the Federal Republic of Germany) of systematic job evaluation recognized by the unions and of written agreements covering many aspects of rate and earnings adjustments,[20] resulting in an accepted concept of an orderly wage structure for the plant (or industry) as a whole.[21] Wage increases for particular workers or groups are likely to be granted less lightly where earning differentials are explicitly fixed than where they are not fixed, but strong pressures for other workers' earnings to be brought into line are subsequently liable to develop.[22] In sum, the risk of wage drift occurring is reduced when it can be foreseen to have unfavorable repercussions for the employer concerned.

Clearly, the extent of pressure on negotiated wage rates arising from wage drift is likely to be related to the tightness of the underlying labor market situation in the economy.[23] Wages actually paid are obviously more likely to rise faster than is provided for in collective agreements if employers are competing for scarce labor. The employers' attitude toward the labor market situation, conditioned by past experience and knowledge of such factors as population trends, is therefore of considerable importance in influencing the likelihood of wage drift. If the labor force is growing rapidly and there are many new entrants, or if there are large numbers of workers in low-productivity sectors

[20]See Oettinger (1964) and Markmann (1964).

[21]In Germany, the trade unions themselves, led by the engineering and metalworking unions, were pressing in the early 1960s for a revision of the traditional occupational classifications to make them more appropriate for modern industrial conditions. See Markmann (1964, pp. 332–33).

[22]It has been suggested that in the United Kingdom, wage drift "has occurred sometimes on the initiative and generally without the active resistance of management" and that wage drift "will be checked only as managers accept responsibility for their domestic wage structures, and move away from extemporisation and its chain reactions towards, for instance, the negotiation and consistent application of works agreements." Phelps Brown (1962a, p. 353).

[23]Under conditions of heavy and persistent unemployment, there may be some converse tendency to "negative wage drift," in that collective agreements may be less effectively enforced; if employees are conscious of competing for jobs, pressure on costs may be reduced by the weaker attitude of workers toward wage fixing practices at the plant level (i.e., less insistence on payment of the rate for the job, "loose" piece rate fixing, and the like).

willing to take up industrial employment at going wage rates, the tendency for employers to offer higher wages to overcome local labor shortages may only appear when reported unemployment has almost disappeared, if then. To the extent that employers are able to hire more workers at going wage rates instead of offering higher wages or having recourse to overtime, one major cause of wage claims by other groups of workers in the same plants or industries, that is, to maintain their relative position in the earnings scale, is avoided.[24] If, on the other hand, large employers are inclined to regard the available labor supply as a more or less fixed pool from which they must secure an increasing share in order to expand production, they are likely to fight for scarce labor with wage incentives of all kinds.

Wage drift is liable to be an important factor in cost inflation because the organization and the behavior of unions are such that increases in wages offered to certain workers serve to trigger claims for increases in negotiated wages by other groups. Though the scale of wage drift depends on employers' attitudes and decisions, it strongly influences the decisions of unions and their members on whether to press for increases in negotiated wage rates. This means that wage increases which employers in one industry are willing to offer, because of rising productivity or increasing demand, are liable to cause cost pressure from unions in other industries.[25]

How the Spread of Wage Increases Influences Business Expectations

Both the danger that a successful wage claim in one sector will set off widespread cost pressure throughout the economy and the risk that general cost pressure may arise from wage drift in particular industries depend on the extent of unionization in the economy and the bargaining strength of the unions in various sectors. Each of these

---

[24]Corina (1962) illustrated the importance of this process in causing the collapse of the 1949–50 pay pause in the United Kingdom.

[25]Increases in negotiated wages that exceed productivity gains are often regarded as evidence of cost-push; but when demand for labor is strong, increases in negotiated wages may merely serve to bring official rates more closely into line with wages already being paid by employers in the industry. This point was not made clear in the main text of the influential 1961 OEEC study. See Fellner and others (1961). However, in the separate note on "Wage Drift" (p. 67), it was conceded that indications of wages actually being paid, including wage drift, were often an important factor in wage negotiations and that "generally speaking the collective agreements have provided a large number of upward moving pegs to which the wages actually paid have remained tethered." That analogy does not, of course, rule out the possibility that the pegs were moved precisely because the correspondence between wages actually being paid and official rates was becoming strained.

processes will, of course, pose a less serious problem in an economy where wage comparisons tend to be confined to a single enterprise, a particular locality or region, or a group of related industries than in an economy where each union is concerned to maintain its position in the national scale of earnings. It is no accident that the problem of wage drift has commanded so much attention in Sweden, where the system of wage negotiations is highly centralized and there is a long tradition of solidarity in the labor movement and coordination of incomes in different sectors, and in the United Kingdom, where wage bargaining usually centers around a set of so-called league tables showing relative wages in different occupations at various dates.

The probable spread of upward wage movements has an important influence on the extent to which managements are prepared to accede to union wage claims and to tolerate, or even initiate, wage drift, since it influences their views concerning the risk they take if they let costs rise.[26] So long as increases in wages and other money incomes are confined to a few sectors of the economy, they will of course not tend to color the views of producers generally concerning the possibility of selling the same quantities of output at higher prices. Increases in the purchasing power of those dependent on certain sectors will be, in part if not entirely, offset by reductions in the real purchasing power of the population dependent on other sectors of the economy. But the wider the spread of an increase in wages and the more nearly the country in question approximates a closed economy, the greater the influence which the increase in wages is liable to have on the prospective level of aggregate demand. In this respect, too, the danger of internally generated cost inflation is likely to be less pronounced in small countries where one third to one half of all goods and services are sold abroad than in larger countries where the bulk of all goods and services produced is sold in the home labor market.[27]

It follows from this account that insofar as a country approximates a closed economy, the aggregate demand and supply curves are not independent of each other. Where virtually all wages are subject to collective bargaining and self-employment has been reduced to relatively small proportions (as in the United Kingdom), a situation may arise where

> the coverage of the collective bargain has been tacitly extended from the industry to the whole economy in the sense that an "annual round" of wage settlements

---

[26]Phelps Brown (1962b, p. 354). The individual employer "may even suspect that the general round of wage increases will generate sufficient demand to absorb an undiminished supply at higher prices" (Streeten, 1962, p. 725).

[27]See section on factors influencing cost inflation in particular countries and especially Tables 4–6, below.

> has become an accepted institution—settlements coming at much the same time are made for much the same amount. This spontaneous coordination extends beyond the bounds of each separate industry the assurance that other firms' costs are being raised equally.[28]

This context influences employers' attitudes, making them more ready to accede to wage claims unless they are primarily selling abroad. As Downie noted,

> If any particular set of employers know that the rate of wage increase they grant will be generalized throughout the economy, they will not be restrained from granting it by the knowledge that it will be necessary to raise prices to compensate for it.[29]

Of course, as Downie went on to say, if the authorities were able to keep the money supply constant, the rise in prices would eventually be halted through lower pressure of demand on resources and through unemployment of labor and capacity caused by rising interest rates and scarcity of credit. But in order to make it impossible for entrepreneurs to count on being able to raise their prices in those economies where the institutional factors are strongly conducive to the rapid spread of wage increases, the authorities would have to pursue an active monetary (or fiscal) policy, deliberately restricting aggregate purchasing power at the first sign of any large wage increase. Such a policy may well not be politically feasible in the context of strong and widespread union organization that is considered here.

It is true that the likelihood of generalized cost pressure developing is strongly influenced by employers' expectations, which are conditioned by the extent to which upward movements of costs and prices have in the past been accommodated by the monetary authorities. However, if the government is committed to preventing more than minimal unemployment, employers may reasonably suppose that the authorities will permit and, if need be, promote the expansion of the monetary circulation necessary to allow production to be maintained at higher prices.[30]

The analysis in this section has indicated that where there are a number of firms in an imperfectly competitive market, the danger of cost pressure eventuating is essentially the combined result of the degree of organization, both of labor and of entrepreneurs—that is to say, the effective unionization of workers and the extent to which employers are able to maintain, or push up, prices by reason of individual monopoly power or by open or tacit coordination of their

[28] Phelps Brown (1962a, p. 174).
[29] Downie (1964, p. 163).
[30] Phelps Brown (1962a, p. 174).

pricing policies. In practice, wage costs tend to rise while there are still unemployed resources in the economy, not solely because of pressure by the unions but also because an increase in wages throughout an industry provides a favorable situation for entrepreneurs to raise their prices more or less simultaneously. Employers may be prepared to *let* wage costs rise if their effective joint monopoly power enables them to maintain profits.[31] Consequently, the role of monopolistic pricing in inducing cost inflation is not confined to the efforts of producers to raise profit margins;[32] its importance derives from the power of groups of entrepreneurs (matching that of the unions to maintain wages) to maintain existing profit margins, if need be by raising prices, when there are still unemployed resources in the economy.[33]

When organization extends to many industries and sectors of the economy, an increase in wages or prices in one industry may set in motion the process of cost-push in other industries, either by encouraging entrepreneurs in competing industries to seek higher returns for management and capital by charging the higher prices which the market will now bear, or by stimulating union pressure for wage increases in other sectors. The power of entrepreneurs in each industry jointly to raise prices without fear of the consequences is substantially increased, since they can foresee increases in prices for other products and in aggregate monetary demand.

Effectiveness of Aggregate Demand Policy in Countering Cost Inflation

Problem of Generalized Cost Inflation

In a world of imperfect competition, it is unreasonable to suppose that whenever prices rise there is "excess demand" and that unless "excess demand" exists, entrepreneurs are prevented from raising their prices by the authorities' control over the monetary situation. Obviously, in each economy there is some level of aggregate monetary demand so high that market prices would rise solely because of scarcities, even if there were no cost-push by entrepreneurs or unions;

[31] Profits per unit of output will rise by the same proportion as unit wage costs where oligopoly pricing is based on a percentage markup on costs.

[32] As, for example, the OEEC experts implied. Fellner and others (1961, p. 69).

[33] It is therefore misleading to suggest that, if "collective bargaining results in wage increases greater than supply and demand forces alone would have yielded" and in excess of the growth in productivity, this is the result of wage-push and not, in part, a consequence of the fact that the monopolistic power of certain producers enables them to pass on increased costs to the buyer. See Fellner and others (1961, pp. 45–46).

conversely, there is some level of aggregate demand so low that entrepreneurs and union members would be unable, or unwilling, to push up or even maintain prices and wages by concerted action, since they would be competing for such restricted markets and employment openings. However, owing to the scope for monopolistic behavior, prices and wages are apt to rise before there is a situation of excess demand as entrepreneurs and unions take advantage of a strengthening sellers' market to raise their respective prices; and some upward pressures on wages and/or prices persist even at a low level of output and employment.

Policy is therefore usually concerned with a range of demand within which increases in the general price level are not solely due to pressure of demand or to cost-push.[34] At any given level of activity within this range, there will be some greater or lesser tendency for prices and wages to move upward, depending on (1) the pressure of demand upon existing capacity and labor resources, and hence the extent to which scarcity of particular outputs or factors of production causes bidding up of certain prices or wages, and (2) the degree of organization prevailing in product and labor markets, and hence the extent to which entrepreneurs and union members are able and inclined to push up prices and/or wages autonomously in particular sectors or to ensure that their earnings rise in line with increases occurring elsewhere in the economy.

Whenever a comparatively high level of activity prevails, the authorities will probably be able to reduce the rate of inflation, at least temporarily, by lowering the level of aggregate demand and so creating a greater margin of spare capacity and unemployed manpower. Although a moderate reduction in the level of demand that is not expected to be permanent is unlikely to produce a permanent change in the pricing policy of firms, employers will be less prepared for the time being to raise prices in the context of rising inventories and declining utilization of capacity. Wage increases may be postponed both because of greater resistance on the part of employers and because the bargaining position of the unions is weaker as the weapons of strike and working to rule lose much of their effectiveness in this context. If any union succeeds in pressing a substantial wage claim, there will be less likelihood than usual of this giving rise to wage claims in other sectors; and if any industry raises its prices, causing demand

[34]See Kahn's evidence before the Radcliffe Committee. Kahn (1960, Vol. 3, p. 142, especially paragraphs 35–37). Kahn was a member of the OEEC expert group but disassociated himself from their analysis in terms of excess demand. Fellner and others (1961, p. 33).

to be diverted to other goods and services, the price increase will be less likely to induce other increases owing to the underutilization of capacity created by the change in aggregate demand policy.

INTERPRETATION OF THE PHILLIPS CURVE

It is, therefore, to be expected that the rate of increase of money wages will vary with the level of activity and of unemployment in the course of cyclical fluctuations, since wage increases can be postponed or accelerated and so are likely to be bunched in the most favorable periods. Such a relation was shown to exist in the Phillips curve[35] and corroborated in other empirical studies.[36] There is, however, a difficulty in interpreting these results. It is commonly suggested that the relation observed between the rate of unemployment and the rate at which money wages actually increased over periods, when the level of unemployment was subject to marked short-term fluctuations, can be taken to indicate the rate at which money wages would be likely to increase if a certain level of unemployment were to be maintained continuously. Paish (1966) provides a very clear statement of this thesis. However, to take his example, it is questionable whether the rate of increase in wages observed to be associated in the United Kingdom with an unemployment rate of 2¼ percent, occurring for short periods when unemployment was usually much lower, provides a valid indication of the rate at which wages would tend to rise if unemployment were maintained at 2¼ percent of the labor force for a longer period. The rate of increase might well prove substantially higher in these circumstances, and perhaps not lower than the average rate of increase over the period 1945–66 when unemployment averaged about 1.6 percent.

An accurate assessment of the "trade-off" between maintaining a higher level of unemployment than was customary in some European countries under "full employment" policies and achieving a greater degree of price stability would clearly be very useful to policymakers. As Massé remarked about the experience of France, if a 5 percent annual growth rate could have been achieved with price stability, it would probably have been preferable to a growth rate of 5½ percent followed by a check to expansion. However, he doubted whether

[35]Phillips (1958) and (1962).

[36]Such as Dicks-Mireaux and Dow (1959); Klein and Ball (1959); and Lipsey (1960). However, Bhatia (1961) did not find a significant relationship between unemployment and the rate of change of money earnings in the United States. Griffin (1962) concluded that, with regard to the postwar U.S. data, "the notion of the Phillips curve can be subjected to any interpretation one desires!"

lasting price stability could be achieved by such a small safety margin. The attempt to secure stability by restraining aggregate demand was, he believed, more likely to result in a relatively low rate of growth and quite significant unemployment.[37]

Unfortunately the Phillips curve does not provide a measure of the relation between unemployment and cost pressure. As has been noted, such statistical studies are likely to overstate the sensitivity of the rate of increase in money wages to the level of unemployment over the medium to long term.[38] Moreover, such studies fail to take into account the influence of the level of aggregate demand on the rate of growth of productivity. Even if the rate of increase in money wages were to be reduced by maintaining a somewhat higher level of unemployment, upward pressure on costs would not be similarly reduced if productivity growth also was sensitive to the level of activity and to demand in the economy both in the short and longer run.

Feasibility of Countering Cost Inflation by Demand Policy

In practice, even in the short run, the feasibility of countering cost inflation by monetary and fiscal policies depends on the importance attached by the electorate (or those who ultimately decide government policy) to the maintenance of high employment in the economy. If the cost of attaining greater price stability by restraining domestic demand is held to be too high by those with a voice in political decisions, restraint will be regarded as a temporary measure and the policies applied will have only a limited effect on the attitudes of management and unions.[39] Employers accustomed to difficulties of recruitment will be disinclined to lay off workers because of a temporary reduction in demand. Employment and the wage bill will then be rather insensitive to reductions in aggregate demand, whereas productivity and profits will be highly vulnerable.[40] If it appears easier to make up the investment later rather than to restore a depleted labor force (particularly should the firm acquire the reputation of a "bad employer"), employers may prefer to postpone investment rather than to cut down the wage bill by layoffs; employers in a squeeze because of tighter credit conditions and declining profits may choose to cut back

[37]Massé (1964, p. 7).

[38]The changing theoretical interpretation of the Phillips curve is described in Chapter 6.

[39]In such a case, the position of the authorities necessarily "contains an important element of bluff. [If] any government [tries] to give absolute priority to price stability [and] this involves heavy unemployment, it may not remain in office." MacDougall (1959, p. 387).

[40]See Marchal (1964). See also Dow (1964) and United Kingdom, Treasury (1965).

investment rather than reject wage claims.[41] Reducing the level of aggregate demand will then bear more heavily upon investment than upon consumption.

The authorities can prevent very rapid cost inflation by avoiding a situation of severe pressure on the labor market. However, below that degree of excessive pressure on labor resources, in the long run the tendency for costs to rise in the organized sectors of the economy would probably not be much reduced by continuously maintaining a somewhat lower level of demand relative to labor resources. Many of the forces restricting the entry of new firms or the employment of nonunion labor in unionized industries would not be much less powerful merely because the rate of unemployment was maintained at, say, 3–4 percent instead of 1–2 percent in an economy with little self-employment; or because the self-employed population in agriculture was declining more slowly in an economy with a large peasant agriculture. In many industries a stable market situation might not be much less likely to exist just on this account; the size of the industry would be adapted to the habitual level of demand; the demand curve for the industry as a whole would still be somewhat inelastic; and the inducement for producers to raise prices in line with wages in order not to risk erosion of profit margins would still apply. In those cases where the greater availability of labor did encourage increased competition, the result might well be the appearance (or survival) of a greater number of small concerns using labor-intensive rather than advanced techniques.[42]

Should aggregate demand policies result in the maintenance of a considerable margin of unutilized capacity intermittently over a period of years, this situation would seem likely to reduce the incentives for investment in the economy, especially in those sectors subject to fluctuations in demand, and hence to slow down the growth in capacity and the speed with which improvements in technique resulting in higher productivity are taken up. Thus, although the bargaining power of the unions and the tendencies to wage drift would probably be somewhat weaker than if the industrial sector were expanding more rapidly, the growth of productivity would probably also be lower. Even if prices were to rise less rapidly in these

---

[41] Such behavior is not irrational if rejecting a wage claim exposes the concern to the risk of a prolonged strike and a substantial loss of profits which cannot be made up in the future, or to the possibility of a permanent reduction in its share of the market. Marchal (1964, p. 855); and Massé (1964, p. 7).

[42] In the Netherlands, the effect of restrictive fiscal and monetary policy in making a rising supply of labor available to the import-competing sector at a favorable level of wages was reflected in just such a development during the 1960s. See Chapter 10.

circumstances, the gain achieved would not be easy to assess. Greater observed price stability associated with less advanced technology is not necessarily preferable to an apparently faster rise in prices associated with more improvement of existing products and greater development of new goods and services (both of which are notoriously difficult to measure statistically).[43]

The observations made above suggest that it may be misleading to assume that a country can, in some meaningful sense, always count on achieving a lower rate of cost inflation and a strengthening of its international competitive position merely by maintaining a lower level of demand pressure and somewhat higher unemployment.

Factors Influencing Cost Inflation in Particular Countries

Earlier sections have described the nature of cost inflation in an industrial country. This section examines why some countries may be less likely than others to encounter internally generated cost inflation.

Duesenberry (1966) suggested that in the contemporary international environment, the strength of upward pressure on costs in an industrial country could be regarded as roughly determined by (1) the rate at which money wages tend to rise when a certain level of unemployment is maintained in the economy (that is to say, the relationship which the Phillips curve unfortunately fails to measure), (2) the rate of growth of productivity, and (3) the level of unemployment that the authorities choose to maintain. This section considers intercountry differences in these three respects.

Differing Exposure to Cost Pressure

The rate at which wages will tend to rise when a certain proportion of the labor force is unemployed is likely to differ considerably in different countries. As has been seen, the tendency for wages to move upward will be influenced by (1) the pressure of demand on supply in the labor market, which conditions the bargaining power of the labor unions and determines the likelihood of prices and wages being bid up as a result of scarcities, and (2) the degree of organization which prevails in product and labor markets.

---

[43] See Turner and Zoeteweij (1966, pp. 30–31).

Elements of Flexibility in the Labor Market

A certain unemployment rate may be associated in different economies with widely differing degrees of tightness in the labor market. Unemployment does not constitute the principal element of flexibility in an economy where large numbers of young persons are joining the labor force each year; nor in one where there are large numbers of persons willing to transfer from technically backward, low-income sectors to better-paid employment or where there are large numbers willing to enter or rejoin the labor force if more jobs become available.

The important differences between various industrial countries with regard to such elements of flexibility in the labor market during the first half of the 1960s are illustrated in Table 4. The annual growth of the population of working age amounted to about 2 percent of the labor force in Canada, the Netherlands, the Federal Republic of Germany, and Japan. It reached about that rate in France and the United States later in the 1960s, but declined in Germany, owing to the low birthrate in the immediate postwar years. The growth rate was only about half as great in Denmark, Italy, Norway, Sweden, and the United Kingdom and was negligible in Austria and Belgium.

The proportion of the population of working age outside agriculture[44] who were outside the active labor force in 1964 ranged for men from as high as 12–15 percent in Belgium, Canada, France, Italy, and Japan, to no more than 3–6 percent in Austria, Denmark, the Federal Republic of Germany, and the United Kingdom; and for women from more than 70 percent in Italy and the Netherlands to less than 50 percent in Sweden and the United Kingdom. These differences were in part related to differences in the age structure of the population. (They were associated, for example, with differing proportions of retired persons, of students undergoing full-time education, or of women occupied in bringing up children, in the adult population.) Nevertheless, they were also indicative of substantial differences in the degree of flexibility in the labor market.

The data in Table 4 suggest that in the mid-1960s, even when a low rate of unemployment was maintained, there was likely to be a considerable degree of flexibility in the labor market in some countries, notably Japan, France, Italy, Canada, the Netherlands, and the United States in approximately that order. On the other hand, severe

[44]As explained in Table 4, footnote 2, it is necessary to exclude agriculture in order to have a roughly comparable measure of activity rates in different countries.

Table 4. Factors Influencing Degree of Tightness in Labor Market, 1960–64

Average Annual Growth of Potential Labor Force, 1960–64[1]		Employment in Agriculture as Percent of Potential Labor Force, 1964		Activity Rates Outside Agriculture, 1964[2]				Average Unemployment Rate, Adjusted, 1960–64[3]	
				Men		Women			
Austria	0.0	United Kingdom	2.7	United Kingdom	97	Sweden	52	Germany, Fed. Rep. of	0.8
Belgium	0.1	Belgium	3.9	Denmark	96	United Kingdom	51	Netherlands	0.8
		United States	4.1	Germany, Fed. Rep. of	95				
		Netherlands	5.6	Austria	94				
		Canada	5.6						
Italy	0.8	Germany, Fed. Rep. of[4]	8.5	Sweden	92	Denmark	48	Austria	1.2
United Kingdom	0.8	Sweden	9.2	Netherlands	91	Austria	47	Japan	1.2
Norway[5]	0.9	Sweden	9.2	Norway	91	Japan	45	France	1.3
Sweden	0.9	Norway	10.4	United States	90	Germany, Fed. Rep. of	44	Norway	1.3
Denmark	1.1					United States	43	United Kingdom	1.5
								Sweden	2.0
								Denmark	2.0
								Belgium	2.4
United States	1.6	France	12.1	Canada	88	France	37	Italy	3.6
France	1.7	Denmark	12.9	France	88	Belgium	37	United States	5.8
Canada	1.9	Italy	14.5	Japan	87	Canada	34	Canada	6.4
Netherlands	1.9	Austria	15.2	Belgium	87	Norway	34		
Germany, Fed. Rep. of	2.0	Japan	18.4	Italy	85	Netherlands	27		
Japan	2.4					Italy	24		

Source: Based on data from Organization for Economic Cooperation and Development, *Manpower Statistics, 1954–1964*, 1965.

NOTE: In each column countries are ranked in descending order of the likelihood of cost pressure. The three groupings distinguish countries in which the degree of pressure in the labor market resulting from each feature was apparently great, moderate, or slight.

1. Growth of population aged 15–64.
2. Activity rates appear higher in agriculture than in other sectors because the concept of employment in agriculture differs from that in other sectors. Consequently, it is necessary to exclude agriculture in order to have a more or less comparable measure of the activity rates in the different countries. Figures show the percentage of all men or women, outside agriculture, who were members of the active labor force.
3. Adjusted to exclude self-employed persons and unpaid family help in agriculture, that is, the figures show the average number of unemployed in 1960–64 as a percent of the labor force outside agriculture plus wage earners in agriculture.
4. 1963.
5. 1960–63.

tensions in the labor market were likely to be encountered at a low level of unemployment in the United Kingdom and Sweden, and, to a lesser extent, in Germany. Austria, Belgium, Denmark, and Norway were in an intermediate position.

It should be noted that the reduction of employment in technically backward sectors need not raise production costs. Unless there should happen to be a great increase in demand for the output of those sectors resulting in upward pressure on prices, the largely unorganized workers will not be in a better position to secure increases in wages that raise unit labor costs until there are shortages of labor. As the number of persons dependent on sectors such as agriculture, retail distribution, and personal services is reduced, those remaining may be prepared to work more intensively, or for longer hours, in return for higher per capita incomes that do not raise unit labor costs. If unit labor costs do rise, there is likely to be scope for reducing labor inputs by rationalizing the scale of production, so as to permit more efficient use of labor and greater mechanization. Indeed, a rise in hourly labor costs to a level more nearly commensurate with that in the advanced sectors is actually needed in order to stimulate the employment of more capital and so to bring the productivity of labor more into line with that in the advanced industrial areas of the economy.

Marked increases in prices and wages in the less advanced sectors frequently stem from sharply increased demands upon those sectors following rapid development of the industrial sectors or from deliberate intervention by the authorities to ensure that incomes of politically powerful groups, such as farmers, increase in line with those in the advanced sectors. Often the inability of the less advanced sectors to meet greatly increased demands from other sectors would not be alleviated even if the existing small-scale enterprises were to retain more labor. In these circumstances, the appropriate remedy must be to encourage rationalization and possibly greater dependence on imports. When the authorities intervene to support agricultural incomes, a continuing reduction of the agricultural labor force may actually be necessary if inflationary increases in the cost of food are to be avoided.[45]

[45]Since expenditure on food does not rise in line with income as the standard of living rises, it is virtually impossible for agricultural incomes to rise as fast as those in manufacturing and services, at the same time as the relative prices of food and other consumer goods remain unchanged, unless the proportion of the population engaged in agriculture is declining.

Organization of Product and Labor Markets

Important differences also exist with respect to the degree of organization of product and labor markets in the various industrial countries, but these are much more difficult to measure. Some rough indicators can be found concerning the coverage and strength of labor unions and the effect of certain structural factors conditioning their bargaining power; but there is little basis on which to judge how far employers in each country are in a position to determine the prices at which they sell their output, or are subject to price competition. One element of some importance in this connection, namely, the openness of the economy, can, however, be roughly measured.

The proportion of incomes in each economy potentially the subject of union pressure for wage increases would seem to be related to the proportion of wage and salary earners in the labor force. However, it may be best to consider the relative scale of self-employment in agriculture as a special factor since government fixing of agricultural prices in most industrial countries renders the position of farmers' organizations vis-à-vis the authorities in some ways analogous to that of a union vis-à-vis the employers. Then, because it is difficult for the unions to organize workers or to press successful wage claims in sectors comprising numerous small family enterprises, the ratio of wage and salary earners to workers on own account (employers, self-employed, and unpaid family help) may provide one rough indicator of the scope for union pressure for wage increases in the nonagricultural sectors of various economies. (The ratio may indeed constitute something of an index of the degree of organization likely to exist both on the side of employers and of labor in different economies.) The figures given in Table 5 suggest that on this account, the scope for union action was greater in the United Kingdom and Sweden, and lower in Italy and Japan, than in other industrial countries during the 1960s.

The coverage and effective bargaining power of labor unions differ greatly between industrial economies, both for historical reasons (such as the time period over which labor organization has been carried out and the legal impediments or encouragements to such organization) and because the bargaining power of unions is conditioned by the extent of coordinated resistance to wage claims on the part of employers. Some of the resulting differences in the wage bargaining situation of industrial economies in the mid-1960s are summarized in Table 6.

The effective coverage of the unions is not very satisfactorily indicated by the number of paid-up union members, owing to marked

Table 5. Relative Importance of Dependent Employment and Self-Employment, 1964

	Percentage of Civilian Labor Force					Ratio of Wage Earners to Workers on Own Account Outside Agriculture[4]	
		Workers on Own Account[2]					
				Other sectors			
	Wage and salary earners[1]	All sectors	Agriculture	Total	Unpaid family help[3]		
United Kingdom[5]	91.3	8.7	2.0	6.7	1.7	United Kingdom	13
United States	86.4	13.6	4.3	9.3	0.8	Sweden	12
Sweden	85.0	15.0	8.1	6.9	0.6		
Canada	83.5	16.5	7.6	8.9	0.9		
						Canada	9
Germany, Fed. Rep. of	79.7	20.3	10.1	10.2	2.4	United States	8
Netherlands[6]	79.0	21.0	9.0	12.0	. . .	Netherlands	8
Denmark	76.2	23.8	15.3	8.5	. . .	Denmark	8
Norway	74.0	26.0	14.8	11.2	0.8	Germany, Fed. Rep. of	7
France	73.8	26.2	11.5	14.6	3.7	Austria	7
Belgium	73.3	26.7	5.3	21.4	6.9	Norway	6
Austria[7]	73.0	27.0	17.0	10.0	2.4	France	6
						Belgium	6
Italy	65.1	34.9	14.7	20.2	4.4	Italy	3
Japan	57.3	42.7	24.7	17.9	3.0	Japan	3

Source: Based on data from Organization for Economic Cooperation and Development, *Manpower Statistics, 1954–1964*, 1965.

NOTE: Countries are ranked in descending order of the likelihood of cost pressure. The three groupings in the first and last columns roughly distinguish those countries in which the degree of pressure in the labor market resulting from each feature was apparently great, moderate, or slight.

[1]Including all unemployed persons.

[2]Employers, self-employed, and unpaid family help.

[3]The figures for the United Kingdom, France, Belgium, and Austria are author's estimates.

[4]Figures show the ratio of wage and salary earners to self-employed persons outside agriculture. Figures for the United Kingdom, Denmark, Norway, France, and Belgium are partly based on author's estimates as indicated in footnotes 3, 5, and 6.

[5]The figures have been adjusted to include estimates of unpaid family help, which is not covered in the national sources.

[6]All figures are author's estimates.

[7]1963 data.

Table 6. Structural and Institutional Factors Influencing Likelihood of Cost Inflation in Mid-1960s

	Openness of Economy[1]		Character of Wage Bargaining by: Employers' federations[2]	Character of Wage Bargaining by: Unions[3]	Degree of Unionization[4]	Scope for Union Pressure on Account of: Flexibility of labor market[5]	Scope for Union Pressure on Account of: Structure of employment[6]
Uncoordinated wage bargaining							
United Kingdom	Slight	20	Uncoordinated	Competitive	High	Great	Great
France	Slight	14	Uncoordinated	Competitive	Slight	Slight	Medium
United States	Slight	5	Uncoordinated	Independent	Slight	Slight	Medium
Canada	Medium	25	Uncoordinated	Independent	Slight	Slight	Medium
Belgium	Great	37	Uncoordinated	Competitive	High	Medium	Medium
Coordinated wage bargaining							
Germany, Fed. Rep. of	Slight	19	Coordinated	Coordinated	Medium	Great	Medium
Sweden	Medium	26	Coordinated	Coordinated	High	Great	Great
Austria	Medium	26	Coordinated	Coordinated	High	Medium	Medium
Denmark	Great	31	Coordinated	Coordinated	High	Medium	Medium
Norway	Great	42	Coordinated	Coordinated	High	Medium	Medium
Netherlands	Great	47	Coordinated[7]	Coordinated[7]	Medium	Medium	Medium
Scope for union action limited by labor market situation							
Italy	Slight	17	Uncoordinated	Competitive	High	Very slight	Slight
Japan	Slight	12	Uncoordinated	Independent	Medium	Very slight	Slight

Sources: Based on data from U.S. Department of Labor, *Directory of Labor Organizations: Europe (1965), Western Hemisphere (1964), and Asia and Australia (1963)*; U.S. Bureau of the Census, *Statistical Abstract of the United States, 1965*; Organization for Economic Cooperation and Development, *Manpower Statistics, 1954–1964*, and *General Statistics: National Accounts*, January 1965.

[1]The figures show the average of exports and imports of goods and services expressed as a percentage of GNP in 1964.

[2]The characterization is based on the description given in the text.

[3]The characterization is based on the description given in the section on the nature of wage bargaining by unions.

[4]The characterization is based on the percentage ratio of paid-up union members to wage earners in each country shown below, modified to allow for the fact that the proportion of wage earners who actively support the unions but fail to pay their dues was higher in Italy, the United Kingdom, and France than in the other countries.

High				*Medium*		*Slight*	
Sweden	67	Belgium	59	Netherlands	41	Canada	27
Austria	62	Italy	49	Germany, Fed. Rep. of	37	United States	25
Norway	62	United Kingdom	37	Japan	33	France	21
Denmark	61						

[5]The characterization is based on the summarization of Table 4 given in the text.

[6]The characterization is based on the three groupings shown in the last column of Table 5.

[7]The coordination of wage bargaining in the Netherlands was secured within the incomes policy institutions, and weakened greatly after the mid-1960s. See Chapter 10.

differences in the proportion of wage earners who actively support unions but fail to pay their dues. The paid-up union membership tends to be higher in a strongly coordinated labor movement or where the unions administer benefits such as pensions or insurance. Allowing for this factor, it is probably safe to conclude that in the mid-1960s the coverage of the unions was not much lower in the United Kingdom or Italy than in the Scandinavian countries, Belgium, and Austria, but that it was somewhat lower in Germany, the Netherlands, and Japan, and lower again in Canada, France, and the United States (see Table 6, footnote 4).

The pressure for wage increases actually exerted by the unions is conditioned both by the extent of coordination between employers in wage bargaining and the relative openness of the economy. These factors are not unrelated. Broadly speaking, strongly coordinated employers' federations came into being in those economies where the leading enterprises were exposed to foreign competition when they first encountered widespread pressure for wage increases from the developing unions. Thus, in four of the six smallest and most open industrial economies—and in only one large economy, the Federal Republic of Germany—coordinated employers' federations have faced coordinated labor unions, whose structure was dictated by the need to bargain with highly centralized employers' organizations;[46] on the other hand, in six of the seven larger industrial economies, uncoordinated labor unions have faced uncoordinated employers' organizations.

Despite their dependence on foreign markets, industrialists in Belgium and the United Kingdom did not have the same inducement to coordinate their wage bargaining at the time when unions were developing because they possessed a commanding technical leadership and because union pressure for wage increases developed gradually in a highly localized and uncoordinated manner. In France and the Netherlands, the threat of union pressure was tempered by the fragmentation of the unions and their weak legal status vis-à-vis the individual employer. In North America and Japan, the employers had little stimulus to coordinate their opposition to the unions, since for historical and legal reasons, the unions were organized to bargain with individual enterprises.

[46]The former group includes the three Scandinavian countries and Austria, but excludes Belgium and the Netherlands. (See Chapters 9 and 10.) In the Netherlands, coordinated wage bargaining was a consequence, not of a strongly coordinated employers' organization, but of the establishment of centralized institutions for wage determination in connection with the postwar incomes policy.

Japan and Italy are probably best regarded as countries where, for various reasons, concerted union pressure for wage increases only became possible during the 1960s. Unions had been prohibited before and during World War II, and even after they were fully established, their bargaining power was restricted by the large number of new entrants to the industrial labor force from sectors of low-income self-employment. A similar situation had existed in the Federal Republic of Germany during the 1950s when there was a large influx of refugees and when the unions were only gradually rebuilding their organization and finances after having been legally prohibited for 12 years before 1945.

One may summarize these findings as follows. Five of the seven large industrial economies were characterized by considerable flexibility of the underlying labor market situation even at a low level of unemployment in the mid-1960s. This was especially true of Japan, Italy, and France; it was also true to a lesser extent of Canada and the United States. The effective degree of unionization among wage earners was comparatively low in France, Canada, and the United States. In Japan and Italy, the unions covered a higher proportion of wage earners, but their bargaining power was circumscribed by the exceptionally large proportion of self-employed workers in the labor force.

In the two other large economies, Germany and the United Kingdom—as also in Sweden—a greater degree of tension in the labor market was likely to exist at a low level of unemployment. In Germany and Sweden, but not in the United Kingdom, coordinated wage bargaining by the employers and unions limited competitive wage claims.

In the smaller industrial economies, the degree of tension in the labor market at a low level of unemployment was probably less than in Germany and the United Kingdom or Sweden. The openness of the smaller economies lessened the scope for upward movements of costs in excess of those experienced in other countries. Except in Belgium, this fact was reflected in coordinated wage bargaining. In Belgium, as in the Netherlands, unions and employers' organizations remained fragmented and uncoordinated, as they had historically always been. However, the bargaining power of Belgian unions was limited by relatively heavy unemployment until the early 1960s.

It is difficult to assign weights to the various factors covered in Table 6, but the information given there suggests that the underlying tendencies to cost inflation were stronger in Belgium, France, Germany, Sweden, and the United Kingdom than in Austria, Canada, Denmark, Italy, the Netherlands, Norway, or the United States. The tendencies to cost inflation were probably least powerful in Italy and Japan.

PRODUCTIVITY GROWTH

Further study is needed of the factors determining the growth of productivity in the different industrial countries and of the relation between the demand for labor and the growth of productivity within an economy. It seems reasonable to assume that at any period there is some potential range of productivity growth in each industrial country and that the actual growth of productivity is related to the strength of internal and external demands upon the economy's resources. The potential range of productivity growth is likely to vary between countries, depending on the existing state of technology. In economies where industrial techniques have lagged, it may be possible to achieve rapid increases in per capita output by the application of advanced techniques already in use elsewhere, provided that adequate resources can be secured for investment. As against this, the most advanced economies may be better placed to apply the latest and most complex techniques (such as automation in the 1960s or computerization in the 1980s). In general, the most highly advanced economies with the highest per capita income may be expected to dispose of greater resources for investment and hence to be in a better position to achieve gains in productivity. However, this need not be the case in a world of unfettered international trade and foreign investment. If there is great scope for the adoption of modern techniques in the less organized economies, and if the level of hourly wages is relatively low at the ruling exchange rates and remains so owing to the less effective organization and weaker bargaining power of the unions in those economies, enterprises may be able to realize very high rates of profit on exports with which to finance a rapid expansion of modern industrial capacity, and high rates of profit may encourage substantial investment of foreign capital.

The relative importance of domestic and export markets to producers in the economy is very likely to influence the relation between the level of demand maintained within the economy and the growth of productivity in that economy. For enterprises predominantly selling abroad, a lowering of domestic demand will have comparatively slight effect on total sales while possibly moderating the rise in costs relative to that occurring in other countries; thus profits and so resources available for investment will probably tend to increase. For enterprises predominantly selling in the home market, however, the lowering of domestic demand, besides reducing costs, is likely to result in smaller total sales and lower total profits. The increase in profits from expanded exports or import substitution is unlikely to counterbalance the reduction in profits in the home market. Investment and the growth of productivity are therefore liable to be reduced when a lower level of demand is maintained.

Level of Unemployment Maintained

In practice, the rate of unemployment maintained in an economy tends to reflect such factors as the occupational distribution of the population, the extent of unionization, and the nature of political representation in the country, rather than to be "chosen" by the authorities. The problem of cost inflation is thus compounded by the fact that the criteria of full employment are most stringent in those economies where the labor force is most fully organized and the danger of generalized cost pressure at a given level of unemployment is greatest. In those economies, the authorities are likely to be under considerable pressure to maintain a lower margin of unutilized labor resources and to give the full employment objective more weight in relation to other policy objectives, such as price stability, than is the practice in economies where the labor unions are less powerful.

Tendencies to Cost Inflation in Different Countries

The foregoing description suggests that the level of unemployment that is likely to be maintained, and the rates at which money wages and productivity tend to rise when a certain level of unemployment is maintained, are not independent and that their influence is likely to be mutually reinforcing. Thus, in one economy there may be a willingness on the part of the electorate to tolerate a relatively high degree of unemployment and underemployment associated with a relatively slight tendency for wages to increase at a given level of unemployment and a potentially high rate of productivity growth. In another economy, the electorate may be strongly disinclined to tolerate the maintenance of more than minimal unemployment; wages may tend to increase more rapidly at a given level of unemployment; and the potential rate of productivity growth may be relatively low.

The description given above prompts certain tentative conclusions concerning the relation that is likely to exist in different economies between the rate of increase in wages and the level of unemployment maintained over a period of years. In a relatively closed and highly organized economy—that is to say, one in which there are powerful, widely based labor unions and rather stable conditions of imperfect competition in many product markets—there will probably be some level of activity at which favorable demand conditions in particular sectors, reflected in increasing profits and, probably, in wage drift, will tend to induce quite large wage increases over a broad area of the economy. This will cause unavoidable pressure on prices in the sectors where productivity growth is lower than average and induce further wage claims stemming from increases in the cost of living. Thus, above some critical level of demand pressure, there will be a sharply increasing tendency to price and wage inflation. Below this critical level, however, there may be a range of levels of activity within which the rate of wage increase is not very sensitive to differences in the levels of activity and unemployment and is mainly determined by the strength of autonomous cost-push in particular sectors of the economy. A curve of this nature is indicated by A-A in Chart 2.

Chart 2. Relation Between Rate of Increase in Money Wages and Rate of Unemployment Maintained over a Number of Years in a Highly "Organized" Economy (A) and in a Less "Organized" Economy (B)

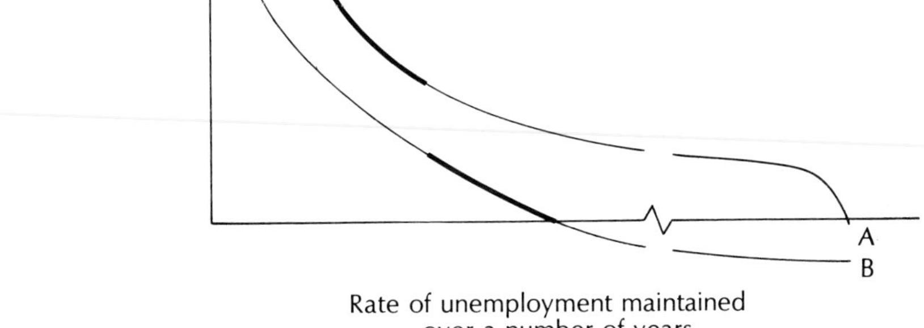

NOTE: The darker portion of each curve represents the range of unemployment rates which is "politically tolerable" to the electorate.

In a less industrialized and less highly organized economy (i.e., one in which greater competition prevails in product markets and the unions are confined to a narrow area of the economy), increasing profits and wage drift in particular sectors will have less influence on the rate at which wages and prices rise in the economy as a whole. Owing to a lower degree of organization of wage earners, the rate at which wages tend to rise will be more sensitive to the level of unemployment and underemployment maintained in the economy. A curve of this nature is indicated by the curve B-B in Chart 2.

If, as has been suggested, the former economy also has the lower political tolerance for unemployment, the authorities there may be virtually precluded from consistently maintaining a level of unemployment at which money wages do not rise faster than those in the less highly organized economy. The competitive position of the more organized economy need not be weakened as a result of this situation, if the rate of growth of productivity was also higher than in the less organized economy at each level of unemployment. However, there seems to be no reason to believe that this would necessarily be the case. If not, the more highly organized economies would be liable to face increasing balance of payments problems. Nevertheless, the strengthening of the competitive position of the less fully industrialized countries vis-à-vis the more highly organized economies would seem desirable from an international standpoint, since it would tend to promote fuller employment in the industrial world as a whole and to narrow disparities between average per capita income in industrial countries, whereas the strengthening or maintenance of the competitive position of the countries with the highest per capita income would almost certainly tend to widen such disparities.

The modifications to Duesenberry's framework of ideas suggested here serve to reinforce his contention that tendencies to payments disequilibria of a long-term character are more or less inherent under a system of fixed exchange rates, given the objectives of national economic policies and certain dynamic aspects of the international economy. It would, however, seem more difficult for any country to check the growth in its deficit and improve its competitive position in the longer run by increasing the level of unemployment, than Duesenberry's analysis might suggest. It might perhaps be more realistic to regard some maximum level of unemployment in the medium term as a politically determined constraint upon economic policymakers, which in practice has priority over other policy objectives.

A country that encounters severe cost inflation when it maintains a politically tolerable level of unemployment may seek to slow down the rate of inflation in a number of ways. The authorities may try to make it more difficult for producers to raise prices in line with wages by eliminating legal or other restraints to competition and barriers to new entrants to certain industries; they may seek to reduce obstacles to the attainment of higher productivity, such as restrictive union policies and obsolete systems of wage payments; they may seek to strengthen labor market mechanisms in order to secure greater mobility and lessen the likelihood of the bidding-up of wages; and they may try to reduce the strength of cost-push by means of incomes policy. The description of the process of cost inflation in this chapter prompts certain tentative conclusions concerning the scope for incomes policy.

The Scope for Incomes Policy in the Mid-1960s

The achievement and maintenance of full employment (comprehending in the term the absorption of underemployment hitherto apparent in very low labor productivity in certain sectors) constituted a new situation in many industrial countries and one that appeared likely to require specific measures to restrain cost inflation. The analysis here has suggested that tendencies to cost inflation were likely to intensify in future because (1) the proportion of incomes and prices determined in noncompetitive markets was likely to increase with increasing industrial employment, growing unionization, and the increasing scale of enterprises; (2) longer experience of a consistently high level of aggregate demand, and of low unemployment with reduced possibilities of shifting labor out of low-productivity occupations, would tend to encourage a more aggressive attitude on the part of labor and a more permissive attitude on the part of employers toward wage increases, leading to a strengthening in the bargaining position of the unions; and (3) with growing international integration, the area of organized price behavior would extend increasingly over national boundaries to firms in different countries if full employment was generally maintained, so that the discipline of international competition would become less effective.

The practicability of incomes policy—that is to say, of deliberate intervention by the authorities in the process of price formation for labor and products aimed at preventing gross (untaxed) money incomes from rising excessively in relation to the growth of national output in real terms—was likely to differ widely between industrial countries. It might well be easier to establish an effective system for influencing the determination of incomes from employment in those countries where the underlying labor market situation and institutions were less conducive to cost inflation and vice versa. The unions were more likely to cooperate when their position was, for various reasons, comparatively weak. The existence of strongly centralized and coordinated institutions on the part of employers and unions, which was usually necessary for the effective implementation of a systematic incomes policy, was itself a factor tending to lessen the severity of wage cost pressure in the economy. Thus, it would seem that if all countries were to adopt incomes policy measures in order to maintain price stability, the effect might be to increase rather than to moderate disparities in the movement of costs as between countries.

In practice, however, under fixed exchange rates the inducement to adopt an incomes policy was stronger in some economies than in others. The inducement was greatest where relative price stability was needed to facilitate expansion of employment,[47] either before or when the employment objective was met or to improve a critical balance of payments position.

In an economy where there was little possibility of expanding employment or of increasing the degree of utilization of manpower resources, incomes policy could not be expected to prevent costs and prices from rising at more or less the same rate as in other countries—that is, unless the external sector was of minor importance, as in the United States. Otherwise, if labor costs were kept stable when prices in other countries were rising fairly rapidly, increasing demand and profits in the export- and import-competing sectors were bound to create pressure on the labor market and probably to give rise to an increasing surplus on current account. The bidding-up of wages by employers in the expanding sectors was bound to occur—as it did, for example, in the Netherlands in the 1960s. Even if the unions exercised some restraint in putting forward wage claims, as in Sweden, wages in the export- and import-competing sectors would tend to drift upward more or less in line with those in competitor countries. At a certain point, prices in protected sectors, such as services and construction, would tend to be adjusted steeply upward to take advantage of the growth in money demand from other sectors and to cover increased costs resulting from heavy wage drift brought about by employers' efforts to attract, or retain, labor.

If the authorities intend to maintain balance of payments equilibrium and a fixed exchange rate, they cannot hope to secure much greater price stability than is being achieved in other countries, unless

[47]Including the need to provide more jobs in other sectors to permit the absorption of manpower out of low-productivity employment in agriculture and services.

there is scope for expanding employment,[48] and need to improve an adverse external balance. In general, the goal of incomes policy can only be to prevent costs from rising faster than in other industrial countries.[49] This is a fact that increases the practical problems of implementing systematic measures of incomes policy by making it difficult to state in advance any general and invariable criteria for permissible increases in money incomes. A policy aimed at securing internal price stability by preventing money incomes from rising faster than productivity is far easier to grasp than a policy that allows incomes to rise considerably faster than productivity in one period, but not in another. However, except possibly in the United States, if wages and prices are rising rapidly in other industrial countries an attempt to prevent money incomes from rising faster than productivity under full employment is doomed to failure. The apparent failure of incomes policy in these circumstances may later render its implementation ineffective when the international situation calls for a greater degree of restraint. It would therefore seem that active intervention by the authorities, designed to ensure that money incomes generally do not rise faster than productivity, might best be limited to those economies where for balance of payments reasons there is a definite need to prevent costs and prices from rising *as fast* as in other countries.

Under a fixed exchange rate regime, the inducement to adopt an incomes policy would then arise in two very different situations: (1) where the tendencies to cost inflation were relatively moderate but the incentive to maintain the advantage was strong, owing to the need to provide for continued expansion of employment opportunities; or (2) where the tendencies to cost inflation were particularly strong and had led to severe deterioration of the competitive position and of the external balance and there was a pressing need to improve the situation if the full employment objective was to continue to be realized. In such circumstances, the need would be to ensure that costs and prices rose less rapidly than those elsewhere.

Obviously, situation (1) would represent an easier task for incomes policy, and past experience suggested that it was more likely to be possible to secure the implementation of incomes policy in these

---

[48] Even if unemployment is very low, there may be scope for expanding employment, as a result of an increasing population of working age, substantial immigration, or the possibility of reducing underemployment in backward sectors. It may be remarked that substantial immigration is more likely to be permitted in countries where the extent of unionization is not great.

[49] If the level of wages is considerably below that in closely integrated economies even this objective may be incompatible with a fixed exchange rate, as the experience of the Netherlands in the late 1960s illustrates (see Chapter 10).

circumstances. To the extent that certain countries successfully achieved their objectives in situation (1), the problem of countries in situation (2) of course became more intractable.

If it appears necessary to strengthen considerably the incentive to export and to lessen substantially the propensity to import in order to right the current account balance at a level of activity corresponding to the full employment objective, internal costs and prices will have to be lowered substantially in relation to those abroad. This may be possible at unchanged exchange rates, if prices elsewhere are rising fairly rapidly and internal prices and unit wage costs can be held virtually stable (or even reduced). However, it may in practice be difficult, if not impossible, to achieve internal price stability without reducing the level of internal activity well below the desired full employment objective, at least temporarily.

To conclude, it would seem desirable to distinguish two different contexts for incomes policy: first, where there is a general need to counter tendencies to creeping inflation when full employment policies are actively pursued; second, where there is a more specific need to ensure that internal costs and prices in a particular economy rise less than those in other industrial countries. One may usefully conceive of two different types of policy as suited for these two different situations. The first, which has been characterized as institutional engineering, would be generally applicable and would cover a wide range of efforts to remedy particular features of the economy that tend to create or reinforce tendencies to cost pressure. The second would comprise more systematic attempts to implement an incomes policy with the cooperation of the parties concerned in wage negotiations and price determination, in order to keep wage and prices increases within limits, more or less clearly stated in advance.

5

The Changed Context for Incomes Policy in the 1970s

Economic history since World War II has to be seen as a long swing from a fragmented international system of isolated and distorted national economies, through a gradual reintegration to the development of increasing strains within the system and growing distortions of national economies, followed by a sudden reversal of the pendulum with the breakup of the fixed exchange rate system, greater independence of national policies, and greater divergence of inflation rates.[1]

It is important to bear in mind that for many years after the war, and again after 1973, developments in the industrial economies were profoundly influenced by the process of readjustment from major disequilibria. This approach will serve as a corrective to neoclassical analysis based on a model in which the economy is presumed to be continuously close to equilibrium. It is also essential to understand the consequences of changes in the industrial world economy during the 1950s and early 1960s, in order to understand why it became increasingly difficult for national authorities to restrain cost pressures and avoid "stagflation" later in the 1960s.

Strengthening Tendencies to Inflation During the 1960s

There were three main reasons for strengthening tendencies to inflation after the mid-1960s.

---

[1] This chapter is based on Braun (1979) and Braun (1981).

(1) During the 1950s and into the 1960s supply conditions were unusually favorable for real output growth with price stability, as the exceptional distortions and inefficiencies of the real economy resulting from the fragmentation of the international system during and after World War II were gradually corrected.

(2) During this era, the paramount economic power and influence of the United States facilitated the operation of the fixed exchange rate system and so long as the United States was implementing conservative policies in pursuit of price stability, fixed exchange rates served to constrain cost pressures in the industrial world.

(3) By the end of the 1960s, the industrial world approximated to a single closed economy with integrated product and capital markets. However, the difficulty of achieving the now closer policy coordination required for the maintenance of fixed exchange rates increased with the emergence of the European Economic Community (EEC) and of Japan as centers of economic and political power. Before national authorities were fully aware of the change that was occurring, the scope for independent demand management had narrowed, at the same time as differences in national policy objectives tended to widen because of the way the fixed exchange rate system was operating. The pursuit of incompatible policy goals led to excessive monetary expansion and the outbreak of very rapid inflation in the early 1970s.

Ending of Exceptional Supply Situation of the 1950s

After the immense disturbance of World War II, the industrial economy of the world was gradually reintegrated under fixed exchange rates during the 1950s through trade liberalization, the lifting of restrictions on current account transactions, and the lowering of tariff barriers. Other circumstances were unusually favorable for the expansion of supply with stable or falling prices:

(1) The supply of primary products in world trade was increasing rapidly as a result of improvements in transportation and technology and the opening up of new sources of supply after the war; primary product prices were stable or falling.

(2) The elasticity of world supply of industrial goods and services, especially of tradable goods, was enhanced by the exceptional opportunities for increasing productivity in the industrial countries outside North America by catching up with advanced techniques.

(3) The elasticity of the supply of tradable goods in the industrial countries was also increased by profitable opportunities for export growth due to wide intercountry differences in money wage levels at existing exchange rates.

(4) Exceptional labor market situations served to prolong the consequent intercountry differences in industrial labor costs.

All four factors were a legacy of the war, though the third was directly related to the level of exchange rates set after the war, particularly for the deutsche mark,[2] the Swedish krona, and the Japanese yen. Other currencies such as the Italian lira and the French franc were subsequently adjusted to bring them more into line with the deutsche mark.

One should note the very great importance of the last three factors in fostering export-led growth. Low-wage countries—at different periods, the Federal Republic of Germany, Italy, the Netherlands, Denmark, and Japan—were able to expand their industrial sectors rapidly by increasing exports. Competition from producers in these countries tended to restrain increases in open sector prices in other countries, especially once the former became important suppliers. Thus, until the mid-1960s favorable exchange rates, combined with scope for increasing utilization of resources in the strong currency countries, served to induce an increasing world supply of industrial products at a virtually stable level of prices, a rising share being provided by Japan, Germany, and neighboring closely associated countries, notably Italy, the Netherlands, and Sweden. These tendencies were reinforced by the ongoing liberalization of trade during the 1950s.

Countries facing profitable opportunities for expansion in supplying the world market for manufactures were able to benefit from a high level of investment and expanding scale of production to secure rapid productivity growth in industry and services generally. Hence nominal and real wages could rise[3] without unit labor costs or prices increasing or profit rates declining. This process continued for lengthy periods because the power of unions to organize labor and the strength of pressures for wage increases at the plant level were circumscribed by the flood of new entrants into the industrial labor force. The inflow of refugees into the Federal Republic of Germany, and the great scope for attracting labor into industry from agriculture in countries such as Italy, Denmark, the Netherlands, and Japan made it possible to

---

[2] While the price level in terms of the GNP deflator in domestic prices rose 5 percent faster in the Federal Republic of Germany than in the United States between 1950 and 1970, the exchange rate appreciated by 14 percent. See Isard (1978, p. 6). It would be hard to argue that the deutsche mark was overvalued in 1970. Hence this comparison would seem to imply that the deutsche mark was substantially undervalued in 1950, even taking into account the exceptionally low productivity and capital stock at that time.

[3] Real wage levels gradually overtook those in countries with initially higher wages such as Belgium and the United Kingdom.

expand industrial employment without wage costs being bid up by employers or forced up by union pressure. So long as real wages were increasing and high profits were associated with high investment, rising productivity, and increasing employment opportunities, the unions were not inclined to treat high profit rates per se as grounds for a rise in the share of labor compensation in total company earnings. This was particularly the case where the leadership of a strongly coordinated labor movement was convinced of the need for high investment to expand employment and raise real incomes, as in Germany and Sweden.

Loosening of Constraint Imposed by U.S. Policies

The problem of restraining inflation in the industrial world was simplified so long as the United States held a paramount position and pursued a strict monetary policy, which imposed a limitation on the rate of expansion of aggregate demand in the industrial countries under the fixed exchange rate regime.[4] The supply factors tending to limit cost pressures at the time made it easier for governments to live with the discipline imposed by the fixed exchange rate system, and the system itself served to reinforce moderation in wage bargaining and pricing behavior. In addition, it had an important effect in promoting tolerance for measures of aggregate demand restraint, since union leaders and wage earners generally feared real wage losses resulting from a devaluation (an outcome that they were not then powerful enough to prevent).[5] (The predominant importance of the current account[6]—since private capital movements were still of relatively minor importance[7]—strengthened the force of the balance of payments constraint because the connection between a very rapid expansion of demand or excessive wage increases and a weakening of the payments position was clear. The converse also applied; a marked slowing down of demand could effect a speedy improvement in the current account and the overall external balance.)

---

[4] McMahon (1978, p. 241) comments that the early success of the Bretton Woods regime was primarily due to the "feature most severely criticised in its later stages: the asymmetry of the system and the unique role played in it by the United States."

[5] Such an outcome was, for example, successfully realized in France in 1958–59.

[6] The balance of payments of most countries effectively consisted of the current account balance plus the balance of official capital transactions and transfers and of leads and lags in financing trade.

[7] It should be noted that Canada and Belgium, the two countries with freedom of capital movements, had already adopted flexible rates (in Belgium's case only for capital transactions).

The rapid industrial growth and integration of the industrial economies and the successful operation of the fixed exchange rate system during this period was not the result of purely economic forces, however, but depended in large measure on politically inspired actions of U.S. Administrations, anxious to restore a strong Europe and Japan and not averse to financing very large current account surpluses that contributed to maintain employment in the United States. This political context in effect created a quite unusual correspondence between the policy objectives of the United States and European governments at this time. Even when the "dollar shortage" ended and the Federal Republic of Germany in particular began to run large surpluses, political reliance on U.S. support in the cold war disposed the German authorities to take steps to finance the surpluses by such measures as restitution payments, early repayments of debt, and funding of the International Bank for Reconstruction and Development. Similar considerations led other national authorities to submit to the constraints of the exchange rate system more readily than they otherwise might have done.

In the final analysis, the existence of a fixed or floating exchange rate system depends upon the constellation of national political goals in the major countries. Coordinated, or at least mutually compatible, national policies are a necessary condition for the maintenance of fixed exchange rates, while widely divergent policies require changes in exchange rates. Consistent policies must, of course, be easier to realize if one power is paramount within the system, as the United States was into the early 1960s. If a fixed exchange rate is a basic policy objective of the dominant power, that country can enforce its preference either by exercising political and economic pressure or by accommodating other countries' deficits.[8]

Diminishing Scope for Independent National Policies

The continued isolation of capital markets by restrictions on capital movements during the 1950s and into the 1960s was another facet of the disintegration of the international system before, during, and after World War II. The establishment of convertibility and a high degree of freedom for capital movements in 1959 was a crucial factor in enforcing closer correspondence of demand conditions among industrial countries, though its effects were not immediately apparent. Up

[8] The United States did not intervene in exchange markets, but it supplied dollars by its reconstruction lending policies or financed surpluses by its acceptance of repayment obligations, restitution payments, and so forth.

to 1959 and for several years afterward—while market participants became aware of opportunities and as new financial instruments and institutions were created—the national authorities possessed considerable control over domestic interest rates and financial conditions in the absence of large capital flows. By the time the United States adopted a highly expansionary policy stance in the mid-1960s, however, effective freedom of international transactions applied in most major financial markets other than Japan. Its implications were not yet fully understood.

Under fixed exchange rates with slight trade barriers and exchange restrictions, the industrial countries now approximated to a single closed economy.[9] The power of any national authority to enforce an exceptionally expansionary (or restrictive) policy was circumscribed by the effects of such a divergent policy stance in precipitating capital outflows (or inflows), in promoting greater (or lessened) reliance on imports, and in causing shifts of production away from (or to) supplying export markets rather than home demands. The effect of an exceptionally expansionary (or restrictive) policy stance in one country tended to be disseminated to other countries, and the strength of demand conditions in all the countries of the group was conditioned by the average of the policies pursued in all the countries, allowing for their relative importance. So long as these conditions prevailed, as they did in the late 1960s, divergence in the realized rates of monetary expansion between the countries of the group was restrained by capital flows and the consequences of changes in balance of payments on current account. Differences in rates of inflation—particularly as measured by price indices for industrial products, less so as measured by GNP deflators—were limited since prices for a wide range of tradable goods and services tended to move in much the same way in each country.

Thus the increasing integration of the industrial countries in the early 1960s was marked by a convergence of inflation rates; and rather similar rates of inflation, as measured by GNP deflators, prevailed in the major industrial countries during the late 1960s.[10] The divergence however widened greatly in the 1970s (Chart 3).

---

[9]One may regard the industrial countries as a closed economy during the 1960s because the rest of the world was not on balance acquiring, or running down, large claims against the industrial countries; and because producers in the industrial countries were not facing competition from the rest of the world whose exports consisted very largely of noncompeting primary products. Both of these conditions ceased with the emergence of the oil countries' surpluses and of large exports of manufactures from developing countries.

[10]The GNP deflator is a measure of the average rise in the price of *national* output due to increases in the cost of domestic factors of production (largely reflecting changes in wages

Chart 3. Seven Major Countries: Inflation Rates, 1962–78

(GNP deflators)

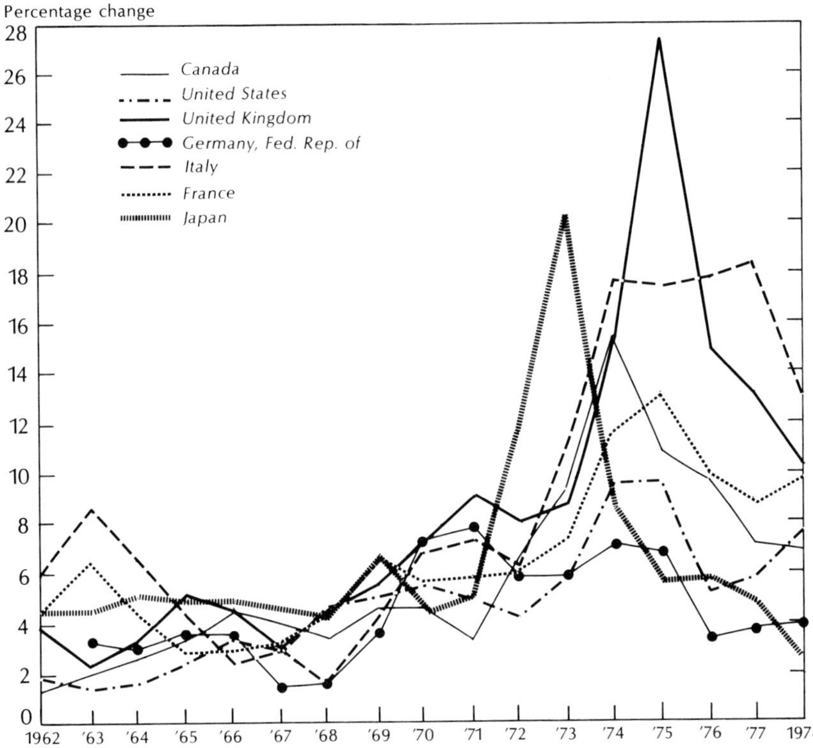

Sources: International Monetary Fund, *International Financial Statistics (IFS)*, 1979 issues.

Growing Divergence of National Policy Goals

National economic policies during the 1950s and 1960s were conditioned by the marked differences between countries in labor market and wage bargaining conditions and in relative wage levels at the exchange rates then existing. Countries faced with structural underemployment of the labor force and with totally inadequate export earnings to pay for imports were naturally disposed to seek export-led growth. The exchange rates established for the deutsche mark and the Japanese yen after the war were expressly set with the

---

and salaries and changes in profit rates). It does not include the direct effect of changes in import prices on the prices of goods and services. The deflator is calculated by dividing the nominal value of GNP in each year by the estimated value of GNP in constant prices of the base year to obtain an estimate of the change in the average nominal value of a unit of real output since the base year.

aim of facilitating export growth and obviating the need for continuing foreign aid.[11] As the expansion of the industrial sector proceeded, the authorities were naturally inclined to buttress their resulting favorable wage cost position by the pursuit of tight financial policies and were disinclined to stimulate domestic demand by deficit spending. The initial high-wage countries, on the other hand, tended to encounter increasing difficulty in maintaining investment and output in the open sector and in sustaining their high postwar levels of employment, as productivity and technology elsewhere improved. This context strengthened the incentive to implement Keynesian "full employment" policies, the effect of which, under the prevailing circumstances, was to expand the size of the sheltered sector and worsen the competitive position of the open sector. Thus some countries, notably the Federal Republic of Germany, Japan, the Netherlands, and Italy during the 1950s, were inclined to follow strict financial policies, while others, notably the United Kingdom, Belgium, France, and the United States after 1960, were predisposed to deficit spending.

This dichotomy posed increasing problems of balance of payments adjustment following the freeing of capital movements. With the reintegration of capital markets heavy inflows of foreign direct investment and portfolio capital were attracted to countries with highly competitive wage levels at going exchange rates. Such flows resulted in very large payments surpluses if they were not associated with a rapid expansion of aggregate demand and an offsetting worsening in the current account of the recipient country. Thus, heavy capital inflows tended to eliminate the relative wage cost advantage *either* by inducing stronger demand pressure and a faster rise in wages in the recipient economy *or*, if reflected in persistent surpluses and reserve accumulation, by creating pressures for exchange rate adjustment. Hence, the relative level of costs tended to be brought more into line with that prevailing elsewhere in the now integrated industrial group. For some years, however, this process was postponed by policies to neutralize the domestic expansionary effects and by deliberate measures to avoid exchange rate changes by official transfers and capital movements and the building up of large foreign exchange reserves. Surplus countries were in effect prepared to finance their surpluses by lending to the United States so long as they could maintain a fair degree of price stability and a strong competitive position and growing stake in the international market by doing so.

By the mid-1960s, the strong currency countries were close to full employment with the absorption of underutilized manpower in

[11] See Romanis (Braun) (1965, p. 20).

agriculture and services, and they began to experience strengthening cost pressures, under the influence of tighter labor markets and high export profits at going exchange rates. The growing tendency for wage increases to exceed productivity growth was essentially part of the equilibrating process within the fixed exchange rate area that has just been described. However, faced with faster wage and price inflation, the surplus countries sought to restore price stability by restrictive demand management. As a result, the shift to highly expansionary policies in the United States at the time of the Viet Nam war coincided with reduced activity in most other industrial countries. This conjuncture greatly increased the spillover of demand from the United States to other industrial countries in 1968–69.

Enforced Coordination of the Realized Policy Stance

Under fixed exchange rates and freedom of international transactions, the realized policy stance in any country is the outcome of domestic policies and of policies in other countries. The wider is the divergence between national policies, the greater will be the tendency for the effects of demand policies to spill over from one country to another. The national authorities can only hope to realize a certain policy stance if they set domestic policies to achieve that result, allowing for the impact of other countries' policies. Clearly this leads to problems if the policy goal of one major country, or a group of countries, is basically incompatible with that of another; for example, if one is determined to accelerate the expansion of demand, the other to slow it, in order to moderate price increases. The former will seek to promote a faster rate of domestic credit expansion, the latter a slower rate to offset the impact of the other's policies—but by doing so each makes it more difficult for the other to realize its desired policy stance and intensifies the balance of payments imbalance between the two areas. This, in essence, was the problem in the early 1970s.

The influence of the fixed exchange rate regime in enforcing coordination of the realized policy stance in the United States and other industrial countries is apparent in Chart 4[12] which shows that the rate of monetary expansion in other industrial countries fluctuates in line with that of the United States during the 1960s,[13] while the

---

[12]See footnote 17 describing the coverage, sources, and methods of calculating series shown in Charts 4–7.

[13]Except in 1966 and 1969 when money growth is sharply reduced in the United States and declines less in the other countries, monetary expansion is about 3 percentage points higher outside than in the United States during the 1960s. The difference mainly reflects the faster secular rise in the demand for money balances associated with rapid development, urbanization, and rising incomes in countries such as Japan and Italy.

correspondence disappears after 1970. In 1971 and 1972, the rate of monetary expansion accelerates in the other countries, far exceeding that in the United States, where it levels off. Subsequently—in striking contrast to the 1960s—the rates of expansion move in opposite directions in the two regions, after decelerating together in 1974 when the authorities in the United States and in Germany and Japan all sharply restricted credit.

Chart 4 illustrates the need, when considering the economic experience of the last two decades, to distinguish between the era of fixed exchange rates under slight trade barriers and exchange restrictions, marked by strong pressures for the coordination of demand conditions throughout the group, and the era of greater exchange rate flexibility inaugurated in 1973, when exchange rates between the U.S. dollar and other currencies were changing frequently.[14] It also highlights 1971–72 as an awkward interregnum, when the fixed exchange rate system was no longer operating in the same way as during the 1960s. The sharp acceleration of monetary expansion concentrated outside the United States calls for attention as one crucial factor in precipitating the rapid inflation of 1973–74.

The Industrial Countries as a Closed Economy

In order to understand the causation of inflation in any single industrial country, it is helpful to start with a simplified picture of developments in the integrated industrial world economy; rather as, if one wished to study the development of real output and inflation in, say, the state of Georgia, one would need to focus first on developments in the United States. Treating the industrial countries as a group[15] is helpful both as a means of securing a broad and simplified picture of what was occurring at different times and in order to understand the mechanics of inflation under fixed exchange rates. It is not possible to explain the process of inflation—in terms of aggregate demand expansion and changes in nominal expenditure, real output, and prices within a single open economy—without considering the impact of changes in other countries' policies and the effect of the combination of all countries' policies. In the closed economy, however, changes in nominal and real income and prices are determined by the policies implemented or the autonomous forces operating *within* the economy.

[14] Continental European currencies, other than the Italian lira, were generally moving more or less together with the deutsche mark against the U.S. dollar.

[15] This approach was pioneered in the 1970s by the "international monetarists," notably Musa (1976) and Swoboda (1977).

Chart 4. Rates of Monetary Expansion in the United States and Group of Eight Other Industrial Countries, 1961–77

(Curves show $\Delta M_{t'}$)

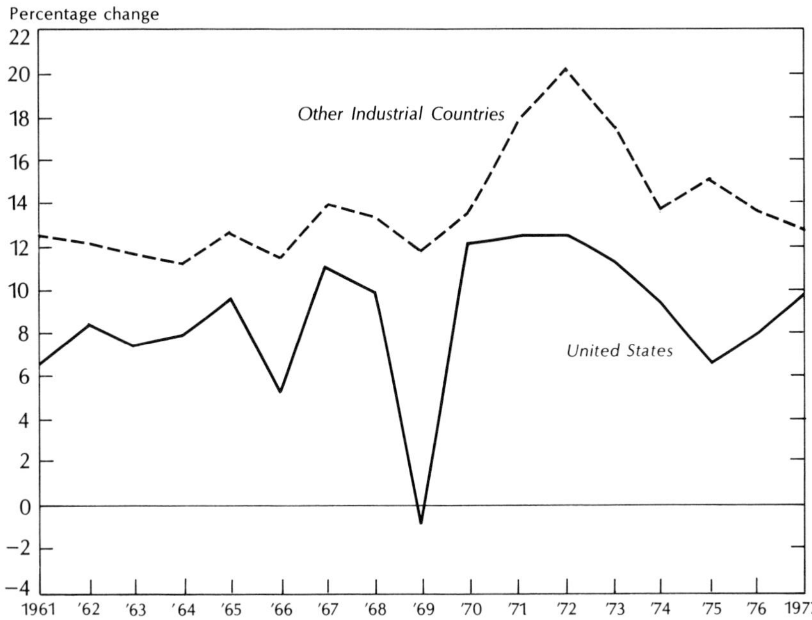

Sources: International Monetary Fund, *International Financial Statistics (IFS)*, 1979 issues. See also footnote 17.

One may treat the group of industrial countries as a closed economy under fixed exchange rates and freedom of trade and payments, so long as overall payments between the group and the rest of the world were kept more or less in balance, the industrial countries normally financing a current account surplus by private capital flows and official aid. Under these conditions, the prior stance of fiscal and monetary policies would determine the rise in nominal GNP generated by home demand and net exports.[16] This was no longer the case when the industrial countries ran very large current account deficits following the oil price increase.

[16] In the closed economy the rise in nominal GNP is equivalent to the rise in nominal expenditure, unlike the case of an open economy.

Within the closed economy, one may expect that the rate of monetary expansion will provide a good indicator of the forces influencing the rise in nominal expenditure in a subsequent period. One may suppose that the rate of monetary expansion reflects the effects both of autonomous changes in fiscal and monetary policy upon the rate of expansion of demand and of the accommodation, or restraint, of any autonomous changes in demand by the policies maintained *within* the economy. In other words, the rate of increase in M provides an indication of the rate of expansion in nominal demand that the economic authorities are prepared to tolerate over time.

By contrast, in a single open economy under fixed exchange rates, the *realized* policy stance, as indicated by monetary growth, may be influenced by domestic or foreign policy measures; and the rise in nominal expenditure within the economy also may exceed (or fall short of) that resulting from the prior realized policy stance *within* the country, due to spillovers of demand from (or to) other countries.

THE AGGREGATE EXPERIENCE OF 1965–74

After experiencing moderate and similar rates of inflation in the mid-1960s—as measured by changes in the average price of national output—the industrial countries individually and as a group experienced a marked worsening of inflation in 1968–70 and a further, much more striking acceleration in 1973–74 (see Charts 3 and 5). These developments followed a shift to more expansionary policies in the mid-1960s, and the occurrence of a highly expansionary aggregate policy stance in 1967–68 and a quite extraordinarily expansive stance during 1971–72, as is indicated by the expansion of broad money (M2) in Chart 5.[17]

---

[17]Charts 4–7 relate to the United States and 8 other industrial countries (Canada, France, the Federal Republic of Germany, Italy, Japan, the Netherlands, Sweden, and the United Kingdom) which together accounted for more than 95 percent of total expenditure and real output in all 14 industrial countries. The charts are based on material prepared for Braun (1981), using *International Financial Statistics* data available in early 1979. The data do not take into account later changes in coverage or revisions in the published series. In particular, the definition of broad money, M2, for the United States differs from the series published later, mainly because large certificates of deposit were formerly included. Observations for nominal GNP, real GNP, and the price deflator show percentage changes, year *t* over year *t*–1. Observations for the rate of monetary expansion prior to year *t*, $\Delta M_{t'-1}$, show the change in broad money M2 *during* year *t*–1 (that is from end-year to end-year). The notation *t'* is used to distinguish changes *during* year *t* from year-to-year changes in the case of variables other than money. In the series for a group of countries, the percentage change in M2 for each country is weighted by the dollar value of M2 at the end of the preceding year, at the exchange rate then prevailing. The change in nominal GNP for the group is the year-to-year change for each country weighted by the dollar value of its GNP in the year *t*–1, at the exchange rate then prevailing. The change in the price deflator is the average year-to-year change for each country weighted by its share in aggregate real GNP (valued at 1970 prices and 1970 exchange rates) in year *t*–1. The change in real GNP is the change in aggregate real GNP of the group valued at 1970 prices and 1970 exchange rates.

Chart 5. Group of Nine Industrial Countries: Prior Monetary Expansion and Changes in Nominal GNP, Price Deflator, and Real GNP, 1962–78[1]

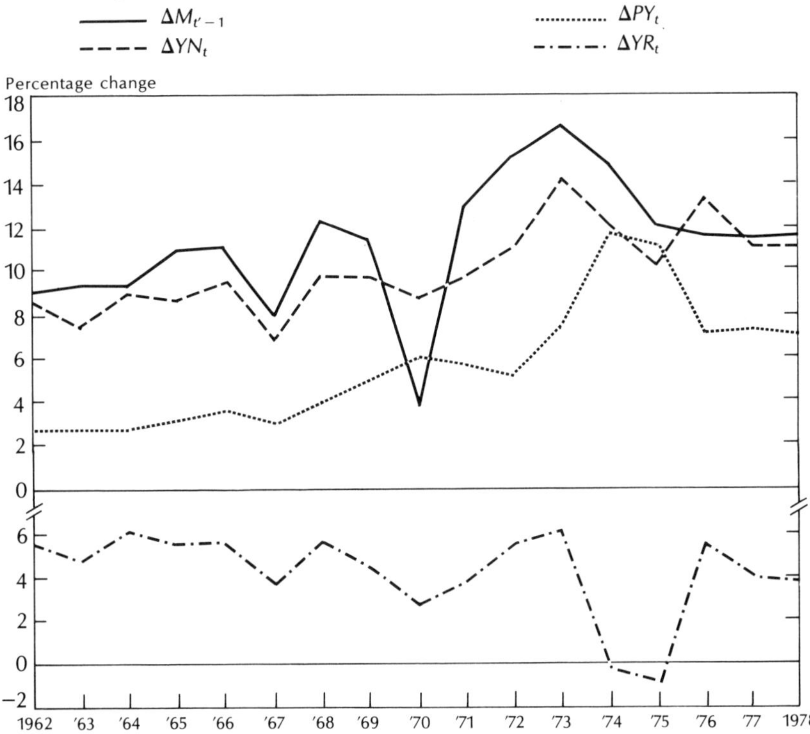

Sources: International Monetary Fund, *International Financial Statistics (IFS)*, 1979 issues. See footnote 17.

[1]Changes in broad money during the preceding year ($\Delta M_{t'-1}$); year-over-year changes in nominal GNP (ΔYN_t); year-over-year changes in price deflator (ΔPY_t); year-over-year changes in real GNP (ΔYR_t).

Chart 5 suggests that the rate of increase in nominal expenditure for the industrial countries as a group reflects the prior aggregate policy stance—taken to be indicated by the rate of increase in the broadly defined money supply during the previous year[18]—while the rate of inflation reflects the rate of increase in nominal GNP with a lag of about a year. Charts 6 and 7 show the same series for the United States and for eight other industrial countries as a group. It should be emphasized that the change in money supply is used as a convenient

[18]Because of the secular tendency for increased holdings of money in the group excluding the United States, ΔYN_t is usually lower than $\Delta M_{t'-1}$ and the expected rise in nominal expenditure, $\Delta YN_t^e = \Delta M_{t'-1} - \mu$.

Chart 6. United States: Prior Monetary Expansion and Changes in Nominal GNP, Price Deflator, and Real GNP, 1962–78[1]

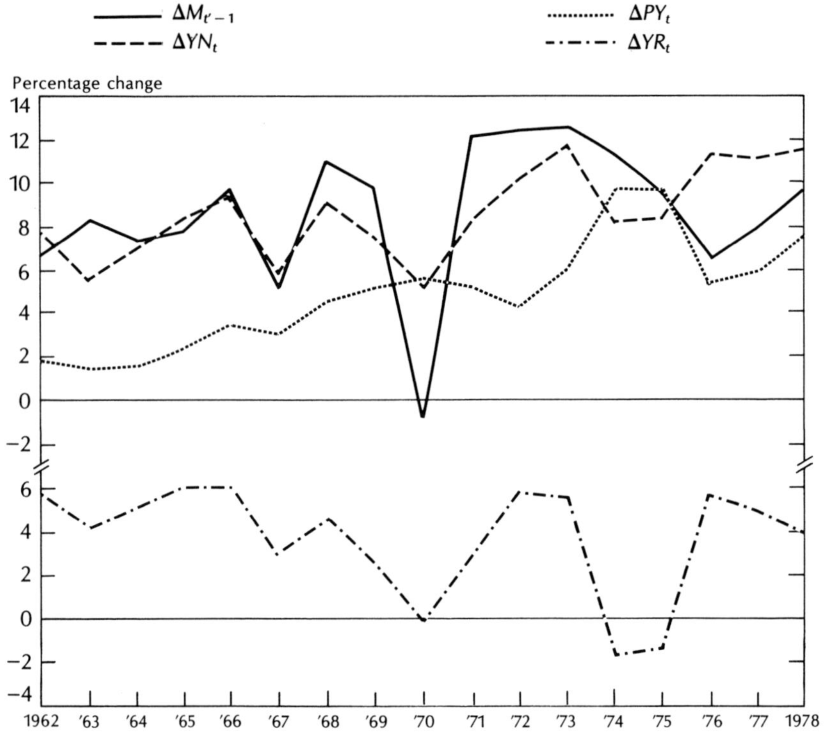

Sources: International Monetary Fund, *International Financial Statistics (IFS),* 1979 issues. See footnote 17.

[1]Changes in broad money during the preceding year ($\Delta M_{t'-1}$); year-over-year changes in nominal GNP (ΔYN_t); year-over-year changes in price deflator (ΔPY_t); year-over-year changes in real GNP (ΔYR_t).

Chart 7. Group of Eight Other Industrial Countries: Prior Monetary Expansion and Changes in Nominal GNP, Price Deflator, and Real GNP, 1962–78[1]

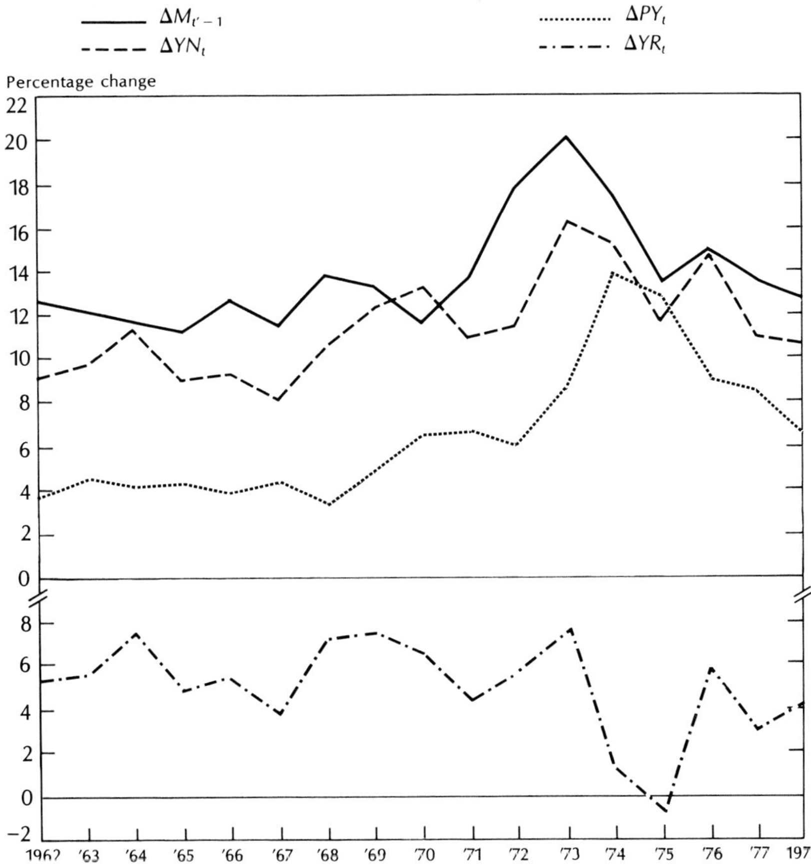

Sources: International Monetary Fund, *International Financial Statistics (IFS)*, 1979 issues. See footnote 17.

[1] Changes in broad money during the preceding year ($\Delta M_{t'-1}$); year-over-year changes in nominal GNP (ΔYN_t); year-over-year changes in price deflator (ΔPY_t); year-over-year changes in real GNP (ΔYR_t).

and reliable measure of the strength of the aggregate demand factors influencing the subsequent growth of nominal expenditures. This presentation should not be taken to imply that the change in the quantity of money per se is the force that determines the changes in nominal expenditure and prices.

It is important to notice that the sharp acceleration of inflation in 1973 and 1974 was not out of line with earlier experience, given the extraordinarily expansive aggregate policy stance of 1971–72 (Chart 5). This contradicts the widespread belief that the sharp acceleration of inflation in 1974 was mainly due to the oil price increase and a change in economic behavior brought about by an explosive change in price expectations. The chart suggests that the acceleration of inflation to double-digit figures in the mid-1970s was primarily due to the combined policy stance of 1971–72, resulting in a very rapid increase of nominal expenditure in 1973–74; and, similarly, that the earlier acceleration of inflation in the late 1960s was due to the expansive aggregate policy stance in 1967–68.

One may formalize the relationships during the fixed exchange rate era up to 1974 broadly as follows. The effective stance of aggregate demand management in the industrial countries during year $t-1$, taken to be indicated by $\Delta M_{t'-1}$, is reflected in ΔYN_t, the rise of nominal expenditure from year $t-1$ to year t. The rate of increase in nominal spending conditions the rise in the price deflator ΔPY with a year's lag. The size of ΔPY_{t+1} reflects the extent to which ΔYN_t exceeds the "secular" potential for real output growth from year to year without an acceleration of inflation.[19] This seems to have been about 3 percent in the United States and 5 percent for the other industrial countries as a group in the late 1960s and early 1970s. Because of the lagged price effects of demand expansion, real output growth reflects the difference between the rate of increase in nominal expenditure and the predetermined rate of inflation.[20]

Thus, real output will usually be below the "secular" potential growth rate following a deflationary shift in policy and above the "secular" rate under an accelerating rate of demand expansion.

[19]The concept of "secular" potential growth rate under imperfect competition is described in Chapter 7, which provides a further account of the relationships outlined here.

[20]That is, the expected growth in real income,
$\Delta YR_t^e = \Delta YN_t^e - \Delta PY_t^e$, where the expected rise in nominal income,
$\Delta YN_t^e = \Delta M_{t'-1} - \mu$ and the expected price rise,
$\Delta PY_t^e = \Delta YN_{t-1}^e - \beta = \Delta M_{t'-2} - \beta - \mu$, provided that
$\Delta M_{t'-2} > \beta + \mu$, otherwise $\Delta PY_t^e > \Delta M_{t'-2} - \mu - \beta$, also
$\Delta YR_t^e < \beta$ when $\Delta M_{t'-2} < \beta$ if $\mu = 0$.

Furthermore, some minimum rate of expansion in nominal demand is necessary for the achievement of the "secular" potential growth rate, because wages and prices are inflexible downwards in the short run. It cannot be assumed that the same rate of real output growth will apply in the long run, whatever the rate of monetary expansion that is consistently maintained.

Anomalous Developments of the Early 1970s

While these relationships generally apply, it will be noticed from Chart 5, that there was almost no slowing of the rise in nominal expenditure, ΔYN, in 1970 despite the sharply restrictive aggregate policy stance in 1969. This came about because the rise in nominal expenditure outside the United States actually accelerated in 1970, under the impact of a steep rise in inflation, that apparently reflected the acceleration of the rise in nominal GNP in 1969 (Chart 7). The rapid rise in nominal GNP in both 1969 and 1970 is quite out of line with the prior realized policy stance for the group. This stands out as one of the two major anomalies in the charts. The other is the much more rapid acceleration of money growth in the other countries than in the United States after 1970 referred to earlier, which is illustrated in Chart 4.

These anomalous developments are important in understanding why such a rapid rate of monetary expansion came to prevail in 1971 and 1972. The two are connected, because the rapid rise in GNP outside the United States in 1970 contributed to bring about an extreme contrast in monetary conditions in the United States and the other countries in 1970–71.[21] That contrast imposed an intolerable strain upon the fixed exchange rate system and had a vitally important effect in predisposing the system to a very rapid acceleration of monetary growth outside the United States thereafter.

Acceleration of Inflation Outside the United States in 1968–70

Charts 6 and 7 help to show how the acceleration of nominal expenditure outside the United States in 1969–70, which is commonly ascribed to a spontaneous increase in "cost-push" forces, arose. A strongly expansionary policy stance in one country is likely to give rise

[21] In the United States, the shift to a highly expansionary monetary policy stance in 1970 in the face of a marked deceleration of the rise in nominal expenditure led to easy monetary conditions, whereas in the other countries a moderately more expansionary realized policy stance, coinciding with the continued acceleration of inflation and expenditure, resulted in little or no easing of financial stringency by 1971.

to a spillover of demand affecting expenditure in other countries with a lag, and causing nominal expenditure to be held down relative to the prior policy stance in the expansionary country. One could expect such spillovers to be important in the context of the expansionary shift in U.S. policies in 1967–68. Such effects seem to be evident in Charts 6 and 7, in the lowering of ΔYN_t relative to $\Delta M_{t'-1}$ in the United States in 1968 and 1969, and the raising of ΔYN_t relative to $\Delta M_{t'-1}$ for the other countries in 1969 and 1970. As another consequence of spillovers, $\Delta M_{t'}$, the realized rate of monetary expansion during year t, will tend to be lowered in the expansionary country, while in the other countries it is increased by capital flows and the monetary consequences of changes in the balance of payments. When the rise in nominal GNP has been held down by a spillover of demand, the rate of expansion of nominal GNP to be expected in the next period will be greater than is indicated by the prior rate of monetary expansion, $\Delta M_{t'}$, and vice versa.

Table 7 provides an account of forces influencing the rise in expenditure and the rate of inflation in the United States and the other industrial countries during 1967–74 within the conceptual framework sketched here. The main elements of the story are as follows. Strongly inflationary U.S. policies in 1967–68 reflected in ΔYN^e for 1968 and 1969 provoke a marked acceleration of inflation and heavy spillovers of expenditure to other countries in those years. These additions to spending augment the rate of increase in nominal GNP outside the United States by about 1.1 and 3.2 percentage points in 1969 and 1970 and raise the "predetermined" rate of inflation correspondingly in 1970 and 1971. The U.S. shift to a drastically restrictive policy stance during 1969, however, induces capital inflows contributing to reduce the expansiveness of the effective policy stance outside the United States in 1969 and tending to sustain the rise in nominal GNP and accommodate inflation in the United States in 1970.[22] For the other countries as a group, the capital outflows of 1969 coupled with the faster rise in nominal GNP due to spillovers have the effect of sharply

[22] Apart from the large discrepancies between the actual and the "predetermined" rise in nominal GNP in the United States in 1970 and in the other countries in 1971, which are associated with the sudden, sharp reversal of restraint in the United States in 1970, a discrepancy in one area is associated with an opposite discrepancy in the other. Apparent spillovers to or from the United States in 1967–69 are reflected in lower or higher-than-expected GNP increases outside the United States in the following years (presumably because of lagged multiplier effects of current account changes and changes in reserves. It should be recalled that at this time the two regions were of similar size in terms of nominal GNP). After 1971, the opposite effects are simultaneous, reflecting the effect of very large capital flows from the United States in accommodating increases in nominal expenditure outside the United States and lessening the rise in nominal expenditure in the United States.

Table 7. United States and Other Industrial Countries: "Predetermined" and Actual Increases in Nominal GNP and GNP Deflators, 1967–74

	Changes in Nominal Expenditure				Changes in Prices			
	Expected changes[1] ΔYN^e (1)	Expected changes[1] ΔYN^{e*} (2)	Actual change ΔYN (3)	Difference (3)–(2) (4)	Expected change[2] ΔPY^{e*} (5)	Price effects of spillovers[3] (6)	"Predetermined" ΔPY (5) + (6) (7)	Actual ΔPY (8)
United States								
1967	5.1	. . .	5.8	0.7[4]	6.4[4]	. . .	. . .	2.9
1968	10.8	10.1	9.1	−1.0	2.1[4]	0.7	2.8	4.4
1969	9.9	10.9	7.7	−3.2	7.1	−1.0	6.1	5.0
1970	−0.9	2.0	5.0	3.0	7.9	−3.2	4.7	5.4
1971	12.1	8.9	8.2	−0.7	. . .	3.0	. . .[5]	5.1
1972	12.3	13.1	10.1	−3.0	5.9	−0.7	5.2	4.2
1973	12.3	15.3	11.6	−3.7	10.1	−3.0	7.1	5.8
1974	11.2	11.9	8.1	−3.8	12.3	−3.7	8.6	9.7
Other countries								
1967	8.4	. . .	8.0	−0.4[4]	4.6[4]	. . .	4.6	4.2
1968	10.8	11.2	10.4	−0.8	3.4[4]	−0.4[4]	3.0	3.3
1969	10.3	11.1	12.2	1.1	6.2	−0.8	5.4	4.7
1970[6]	8.6	7.5 (10.5)	13.1	5.6	6.1	1.1	7.2	6.4
1971[6]	10.7	5.1 (8.1)	10.8	5.7	2.5	5.6	8.1	6.5
1972	14.9	9.2	11.5	2.3	0.1	5.7	5.8	6.0
1973	17.1	14.8	16.2	1.4	4.2	2.3	6.5	8.5
1974	14.6	13.0	15.2	2.2	9.8	1.4	11.2	13.8

Source: See text and footnotes 17–19.

[1] $\Delta YN^e = \Delta M_{t'-1} - \mu$. For the United States $\mu = 0$, for the group of other countries, $\mu = 3$. ΔYN^{e*} represents expected rate of increase in nominal GNP adjusted for spillovers or other disturbances in period t–1.

[2] ΔPY^{e*}, the rate of inflation, as measured by the increase in GNP deflators, expected to be associated with ΔYN^{e*}_{t-1} is equal to ΔYN^{e*}_{t-1} minus β, the "secular" tendency for real output growth, assumed to be 3 percent per annum in the United States and 5 percent for the group of other countries in the period shown. When $\Delta YN^{e*}_{t-1} < \beta$, as for the United States in 1971, it is assumed that the secular real growth rate will not be realized and ΔPY^{e*}_t must be positive. See Chapter 7.

[3] Lagged effect of apparent spillover shown in Column 4.

[4] Assuming that there was no spillover or disturbance in 1966 so that in 1967 $\Delta YN^{e*} = \Delta YN^e$.

[5] Probably substantially exceeding 3.0.

[6] The figures in parentheses allow for the effect of severe financial constraint in 1970 and 1971 in preventing the usual net acquisition of money holdings.

reducing the expected rise in nominal GNP for 1970. The actual rise in nominal expenditure, however, accelerates in 1970 under the impact of lagged multiplier effects of the spillover of demand from the United States in 1969 and of a sharp rise in the "predetermined" inflation rate, owing to the positive spillover effect on nominal expenditure in 1969 following a negative effect in 1968. (The faster rise in expenditure is made possible in part by reduced net acquisition of money holdings,[23] in part by the easing of monetary restraint in the United States, which has some effect in accommodating the rise in nominal spending in both areas during 1970.)[24] The rapid rise in nominal spending and income outside the United States in 1970 results in intense financial constraint in 1971 when, even assuming no net acquisition of money holdings, the "predetermined" rise in nominal GNP, ΔYN^{e*}, barely equals the "predetermined" inflation rate.

The contrasting monetary situation in the United States and in the rest of the industrial world, and growing speculation against the dollar, induces heavy capital outflows from the United States. (These precipitate the floating of the deutsche mark and the Netherlands guilder in May 1971 and the effective devaluation of the U.S. dollar in August.) The capital flows contribute to promote the marked acceleration of monetary expansion outside the United States during 1971, helping to accommodate the high "predetermined" rate of inflation and support the rise in expenditure outside the United States in that year. Together with other factors, notably the price-wage freeze imposed by President Nixon in the fall, the capital outflows tend to limit the rise in expenditure in the United States. In 1972, the "predetermined" rate of inflation is higher for the group of other countries than for the United States, whereas the accommodated increase in nominal GNP ΔYN^{e*} remains markedly lower than for the United States. Hence the contrast between monetary conditions in the two areas persists. Once again, the rise in nominal expenditure outside the United States is sustained by very large capital flows and a further acceleration of monetary expansion.

This interpretation suggests that the acceleration of inflation in the late 1960s was primarily due to a shift to highly expansionary policies

---

[23] That is, ΔYN^{e*} approximates to $\Delta M_{t'-1}$.

[24] The drastically restrictive U.S. policy stance of 1969 in the face of a high "predetermined" inflation rate provoked a sharp decline in activity and rise in unemployment in 1970 and induced the swift reversal of restraint. One might be inclined to view the rapid money growth during 1970 simply as a case of overly expansionary demand management. It would be more realistic, however, to recognize that the *realized* policy stance was the result of greatly easing monetary constraint at a time of strong predetermined upward pressures on costs and prices, both in the United States and abroad.

in the United States, together with a less marked shift for the other countries as a group, in 1967.[25] The lagged impact of the inflationary U.S. policy stance in 1967–68 is the major factor in explaining the disproportionately rapid rise in nominal GNP outside the United States in 1969–70, relative to the previous realized policy stance. This in turn largely explains the subsequent coincidence of a higher rate of inflation with aggregate demand constraint and increased unemployment in 1970–71. The lagged effect of U.S. policies at the time of the Viet Nam war on the rate of inflation outside the United States also is a factor in explaining the acceleration of money growth outside the United States in 1971–72. In effect, the conjuncture of a highly accommodative monetary policy in the United States with a high "predetermined" rate of inflation and monetary stringency outside the United States resulted in U.S. monetary expansion accommodating ongoing cost pressures in other industrial countries. The acceleration of money growth concentrated outside the United States, and the simultaneous effect of spillovers in keeping down nominal GNP growth in the United States and raising it in the other countries during 1972–74 are both facets of this situation.

National Experience of Increasing Inflationary Pressure, 1968–70

While inflation was an international phenomenon in the closely integrated industrial world under fixed exchange rates, it had its roots in national conditions and policies and could only be tackled by national authorities. The sudden, unpredictable shifts in the U.S. policy stance, during and after the Viet Nam war, greatly increased the difficulty of achieving a compatible set of national demand policies in the industrial countries at a time when, as has been seen, the need for coordinated policies had recently become much more compelling. The initial external shock of inflationary U.S. policies followed several years of demand restraint in major EEC countries, aimed at resisting strengthening pressures for upward adjustment of the exchange rate or of the domestic level of costs, and at maintaining price stability at the going exchange rate. As will be seen, the economic and political

[25] The acceleration of inflation in the United States between 1967 and 1970 can be seen as mainly reflecting the acceleration of the predetermined rate of increase of nominal expenditure from 1966 to 1969. The apparently continuous year-by-year acceleration of ΔPY from below 3 percent in 1967 to 5.4 percent in 1970—a phenomenon important for adaptive expectations theorizing about inflation—seems to be the result of the sharp 1967 downturn in holding back price increases in that year, and of the excessive stimulus in 1968 in adding to U.S. inflation in 1969.

consequences of those restrictive policies were important in shaping the experience of the late 1960s and early 1970s.

In 1966–67, the impact of a strongly deflationary policy in the Federal Republic of Germany, coinciding with a brief downturn in the United States, caused a sharp drop in activity in Germany and a marked slowdown in neighboring countries. The first postwar experience of severe recession led to the election of a Social Democrat Government, pledged to promote higher activity and to raise social expenditure. Thus, a very marked policy shift in Germany, as well as the United States, underlay the initial episode of an unduly expansive aggregate policy stance in industrial countries.

In the United States, unemployment had already been reduced to a historically low level by 1966, and the strong demand for labor resulted in a bidding-up of the wages of unorganized workers not covered by collective bargaining and a more rapid rise of wages in the nonunionized sector. This had the consequence of strengthening union wage demands when long-term contracts subsequently came up for renewal. By 1968 the acceleration of inflation had resulted in a marked loss of competitiveness vis-à-vis European countries. The competitive advantage of European producers was strengthened by the ready availability of capacity and labor and by moderate recent wage increases. It was also enhanced by marked improvements in productivity in key industries, such as chemicals, automobiles, and electronics, and closer integration with the U.S. market, brought about by large-scale investment by U.S. companies in Europe (investments that had been influenced by the wish to acquire production facilities behind the EEC external tariff barrier).

Thus, the stage was set for an intense export boom and surging industrial profits outside the United States in 1968–69. Within Europe, the effects of U.S. policies[26] were reinforced by the extraordinarily expansive realized policy stance in the Federal Republic of Germany, occasioned by a rising balance of payments surplus coinciding with the first recourse to deficit financing since the war.[27]

The industrial boom in Europe occurred against the background of increasing social tensions. Rising industrial activity, often involving heavy immigration or large internal population movements, exacer-

---

[26] The external impact of U.S. policies was aggravated by their unpredictability. In several countries (notably Canada, the Netherlands, Norway, and Sweden), the acceleration of credit expansion was influenced by increases in budget deficits and in public sector borrowing intended to protect the economy from the deflationary impact of a slowdown in the United States and Germany.

[27] The broadly defined money supply increased by an unprecedented 17½ percent between March 1968 and March 1969.

bated the consequences of earlier restrictive demand policies in limiting the supply of low-cost housing, public utilities, educational facilities, and social services. In many countries housing shortages and deteriorating urban living conditions were reflected in larger wage claims and more aggressive bargaining attitudes of union members. Student unrest became epidemic, influenced by increasingly inadequate grants and the overcrowding of university facilities, and by growing unemployment among the young, which was intensified by the rise in their numbers due to the postwar bulge in birth rates. Protests mounted when consumer prices started to accelerate with steeply rising world commodity prices in 1967. A wave of political and industrial unrest, that began with the student-led uprising of May 1968 and subsequent very large wage increases in France, was an important factor in predisposing the industrial world to rapid inflation during the early 1970s.

The French crisis served to reinforce inflationary pressures throughout Europe in several ways. Most obviously, it made employers and governments less inclined to resist wage claims, or demands for higher government spending, for fear of provoking similar political unrest and violence. It also disposed union leaders to be more aggressive for fear of being supplanted by unofficial action. The crisis drew public attention to widening disparities in real per capita income and to inadequacies in the social services and rallied the forces supporting reforms, making electorates more demanding and politicians more inclined to propose major increases in social expenditure. Thus it contributed a powerful stimulus toward more expansionary budgets and increases in public expenditure as a share of GNP. In France and Italy particularly, the events of May 1968 predisposed the authorities to highly accommodative demand management for the next several years. In France, this took the form of permissive monetary policy,[28] in Italy, of large and mounting public sector deficits.

The German wage explosion of 1969 stemmed more directly from the extraordinarily rapid expansion of demand in 1968. Real output could not keep up with the rise in nominal demand, and industrial prices rose sharply, in contrast to earlier years, when industry had raised prices only after costs increased.[29] This change in pricing behavior created a very different context for wage restraint, the need for which had been accepted by the union leaders, first in support of the Adenauer Government's efforts to restore price stability, and then

[28]See Salin and Lane (1977, pp. 550–51).
[29]See Fels (1977, p. 629).

in solidarity with the new government. Rising prices and sharply increasing profits, together with the unions' policy of restraint in wage bargaining, provoked a wave of wildcat strikes, leading to large wage settlements in the fall of 1969 that substantially raised the level of German production costs.[30] The threat posed by the unofficial strikes to the unions' control over collective bargaining caused a shift to more aggressive attitudes among union officials, interrupting their cooperation in the concerted action program until the onset of the oil price crisis. This change in attitudes caused wages to become more responsive to strong demand conditions than before, and in 1970 and 1971 German wages rose by 15 and 12 percent over the preceding year.

The extraordinarily strong demand conditions in the Federal Republic of Germany and marked rise in German prices in 1969 contributed to the sharp increase in industrial profits in other closely integrated economies, notably Denmark, Italy, the Netherlands, and Sweden—creating conditions strongly conducive to large wage settlements or to heavy wage drift under existing settlements. In Italy the unions were able to exploit the favorable demand conditions for large industrial enterprises and the political climate inspired by the unrest in France, to secure very large increases in real wages and benefits. Thus, it would appear that the episode of excessive demand pressures in Germany in 1968–69 was an important factor in strengthening cost inflation in the neighboring countries.

Even in the United Kingdom—where the acceleration of wage increases in 1970 has usually been treated as a case of "pure wage push," or as an example of the tendency for wages to rebound after a period of incomes policy controls[31]—there are indications that external factors influenced the outcome of more aggressive wage bargaining. It is true that the hardening of union attitudes represented a reaction to the change in government, to proposals for legislation limiting union

[30] See the discussion of the case for wages indexation in the Federal Republic of Germany in Chapter 8 and the description of the wage bargaining system in Chapter 9.

[31] Gordon (1977b), for example, included a special dummy in his wage equation for the United Kingdom, "for the 1970 episode that has made wage push a byword among British economists." He concluded that the episode did not "represent any profound sociological phenomenon, but simply an attempt to catch up for losses in real income during the preceding period of restraint" (pp. 444–45).

Godley (1977) attributed the spurt in wage increases to "a kind of backlash" due to "the holding down of pay increases of the main groups of public-sector workers, by means of the incomes policy started in 1966. When this policy finally disintegrated, very large increases of almost unprecedented size were awarded to public sector groups that had fallen behind" (p. 456). However, the three very large wage awards he cites occurred late in 1970, in 1971, and in 1972 (p. 470).

prerogatives, and to the raising of direct taxes and charges for social services at the same time as direct taxes on higher incomes were reduced; and that the larger wage increases occurred without a previous acceleration of consumer prices, when the pressure of demand was low and falling. However, in the industrial sector, more intense pressure for wage increases at the local and central level met with reduced resistance due in part to the marked rise in prices of competing foreign products. During 1970, earnings in the private sector were going up faster than in the public sector as wages were rising rapidly in industry and in associated services such as commerce and road haulage. Over the 12 months to October 1970, average weekly earnings in manufacturing rose by 14½ percent, and hourly earnings rose even faster.[32]

External and Domestic Causes of the 1968–70 Wage Explosions

In 1977 a group of experts appointed by the OECD could find no "compelling explanation" for the series of "wage explosions" in the 1968–69 period "other than the prior lag in growth of real disposable incomes—the 'conflicting shares' thesis—in combination with accommodating demand management."[33] The account given here, however, points to the very rapid expansion of nominal demand in the industrial world in 1967 *before* the wage explosions occurred, and to the development of highly inflationary demand conditions in Germany in 1968 *before* strong wage pressures were encountered there, as the missing explanation for the widespread, almost synchronized, upward adjustment of wage levels in Western Europe. Had it not been for the extraordinary surge in demand upon the open sectors of those countries in 1968–69, it is difficult to see why the explanations advanced by the McCracken group, such as "the arrival of the postwar generation to maturity, high employment expectations based on presumed government 'full employment' guarantees, growing inflationary expectations based on extrapolation of recent experience . . . receding memories of unemployment," and "growing imperfections and rigidities in labour markets" should have had a sudden impact on wage developments over a short period of time.

Wage explosions, which were commonly attributed to underlying sociological forces causing an autonomous hardening of attitudes in

[32] See Braun (1971, pp. 160–61).

[33] McCracken and others (1977, pp. 49–51). Kaldor (1976) expressed a similar view. He rejected the notion that the explanation was to be found in the international transmission of the demand inflation in the United States associated with the Viet Nam war for reasons which are not very convincing.

one country after another, actually would seem to have been primarily due to the impact of the extraordinary shift in U.S. and German policies, in creating conditions conducive to very large wage increases in the industrial sector in response to more aggressive wage bargaining. This effect was compounded by the influence of structural imbalances in intensifying wage demands. Such structural imbalances were themselves connected with the response of national authorities to the growing pressures making for a realignment of domestic cost levels during the 1960s. In economies where restrictive policies had been applied for lengthy periods in the effort to maintain price stability and a strongly competitive level of wage costs at the going exchange rates, the result had been to promote the growth of the open sector (producing tradable goods and services) at the expense of the "sheltered" sector supplying goods and services to the home market (in particular public services).

It is worth considering how the external shock provoked the wage explosions in somewhat more detail, since this was the setting for efforts at incomes policy. Briefly, an unforeseen sharp rise in world demand for industrial goods promotes increased activity, a faster rise in the cost of living through rising commodity prices, and sharply higher profits in export- and import-competing sectors. Exceptionally favorable wage bargaining conditions in particular industries cause a marked rise in relative earnings (through increasing overtime, easier setting of piece rates, accelerated wage drift, greater responsiveness to wage pressures on the shop floor, and higher negotiated settlements). The resulting disturbance to established wage contours[34] then creates stronger pressures for wage increases in other industries, and in sheltered sectors producing goods and services sold (or utilized) almost exclusively in the country where they are produced (such as construction and public services).

The general movement of wages is influenced not only by the level of demand versus supply within each sector but also by the tendency for a high rate of increase in one sector, due to exceptionally strong demand conditions there, to spread to other sectors. That tendency will of course be intensified if, because of a low level of investment in the past, rising activity and higher earnings in particular industries are quickly reflected in housing shortages, sharp increases in rents and urban living costs, and inadequate public transportation. The sharper

[34] Fixed relationships between wage rates for different jobs or in different occupations are known as "wage contours" in institutional labor economics. For a statement of the view that wage inflation stems mainly from disruptive shocks to established wage contours, not only from a scarcity of labor, see Piore (1978).

the relative rise in earnings in some major industries or occupations, the greater the tendency for the dissemination of higher wage increases to other sectors. Hence, the occurrence of exceptionally strong demand conditions in certain industries, when the general level of demand and activity is quite restrained, will tend to push up the average rate of wage increase above what might otherwise have been expected from overall level of demand and supply in the economy. This view of wage behavior is not consistent with the monetarist assertion that the general level of prices is independent of changes in relative prices—at least over a period of some years.

Consequences of Delayed Adjustment of Exchange Rates

We have seen how rapid cost inflation originated in the late 1960s. Why was inflation not brought under control at the beginning of the 1970s and why did the aggregate policy stance of the industrial countries become so extraordinarily expansive in 1971–72, foreshadowing explosive inflation in 1973–74? The answers to these questions are closely related to developments in the international payments system.

In hindsight it appears a mistake that the strong currencies—particularly the deutsche mark and the yen—were not revalued or allowed to float freely by early 1969 at the latest. In that case, the very large increases in industrial wages during 1969, the subsequent very rapid rise in primary product prices, the onset of rapid price inflation, and the huge increases in oil prices could most probably have been avoided. At the time, however, there was tremendous psychological resistance to action that might endanger or destroy the Bretton Woods system, which had worked so well for more than two decades. Furthermore, it seemed that the prospective ending of the Viet Nam war and the strongly restrictive U.S. policy stance in 1969 would soon induce a slowdown, as in fact occurred in 1970. In the aftermath of the French crisis, politically harassed European governments were disinclined to risk aggravating the expected rise in unemployment by allowing the exchange rate to appreciate. Even if they had been willing to do so, there was the difficult problem of swiftly agreeing a concerted set of exchange rate changes for EEC countries, without wrecking the Common Agricultural Policy, whose prices were fixed at the existing parities.

In the prevailing political climate, European governments were also unwilling to curb inflation by raising taxes or cutting public expenditure, preferring to rely on the less "political" alternative of monetary restraint by the central bank. However, this tool became ineffective when the United States adopted a strongly expansionary monetary policy in 1970.

By early 1971, the disparity between the financial policies of the United States and those of other industrial countries had created irresistible pressures for exchange rate changes and the deutsche mark and the Netherlands guilder were permitted to float. There followed the dramatic change of U.S. economic policies, with the sudden abandonment of gold convertibility and the effective depreciation of the dollar in August 1971, coupled with the imposition of price and wage controls. The U.S. action signaled the demise of the Bretton Woods system, but an awkward interregnum ensued before flexible exchange rates between the U.S. dollar and most other industrial countries' currencies were finally adopted in early 1973.[35]

Breakdown of the Fixed Exchange Rate System

The initial episode of an unduly expansive policy stance in the industrial world at the end of the 1960s intensified the pre-existing pressures for adjustment of relative cost levels at going exchange rates, first setting off cost increases in the United States, and then in combination with other factors, precipitating much larger cost increases in the other countries. This first worsening of the "Phillips curve" relation between the level of employment and the rate of inflation in the industrial world in 1970[36] took the form of a marked rise in unemployment with little change in inflation in North America, while there was a marked acceleration of inflation and a slight rise in aggregate unemployment in the other industrial countries. Consequently there was bound to be a sharp divergence of policy goals thereafter, with the reduction of unemployment commanding first priority in North America and the restraint of inflation attracting most attention in the majority of the other countries, especially where the rate of inflation was increasing dramatically, as in Germany, Japan, the Netherlands, and Sweden.

After 1970, high and rising unemployment motivated the governments of the United States, Canada, and the United Kingdom to seek

[35] Almost all the currencies were floating between August 15 and December 1971 when fixed rates were reinstituted for most currencies under the Smithsonian agreement. However, the pound was again permitted to float in June 1972, followed by the Swiss franc in January 1973, the Italian lira and the Japanese yen in February, and all other major currencies in March. Eight of the continental European countries then instituted arrangements for joint floating.

[36] The worsening is illustrated in McCracken and others (1977, Chart 15, p. 105), which relates the rate of inflation to the size of the "gap" between actual and potential GDP.

faster growth by expansionary policies, permitting the exchange rate to depreciate if necessary, while attempting to stave off the inflationary consequences by means of price and wage policies.

Following the abrupt reversal of restraint in the United States, restrictive monetary policies in other industrial countries had perverse effects in inducing very large capital inflows that served to accommodate rapid wage increases. Huge capital inflows were encouraged by higher nominal interest rates than in the United States and by expectations of depreciation of the U.S. dollar, despite the higher inflation rates prevailing outside the United States. This situation still persisted after the Smithsonian adjustments of exchange rates in December 1971, and only ended when Japan and Germany enforced strong monetary restraint by allowing their exchange rates to appreciate in 1973.

Once again, it is difficult with hindsight to justify the decisions of the Smithsonian agreement. One should recall, however, that the changes in U.S. policy aroused fears of greatly increased U.S. competition in world markets and raised the specter of a round of competitive devaluations if no international agreement was reached. Those countries that had prospered under export-led growth were not inclined to favor a substantial upward adjustment of their exchange rates that would impose a need for structural change within their economies, and the rapid wage inflation of the last few years reinforced the authorities' reluctance to accept a marked appreciation. Consequently, the exchange rate changes agreed to under the Smithsonian agreement were not large enough to convince the market that they would hold. As the Governor of the Central Bank of Canada pointed out, "in the highly uncertain environment [of the early 1970s] many countries were reluctant to see their exchange rates move as far as was appropriate at that time, although in the end vast changes became necessary. I doubt whether it is generally appreciated how important a factor this was in laying the foundations for the worst outbreak of inflation of the postwar period."[37]

Legacy of the Early 1970s

The adverse combination of reduced real output growth, increased unemployment, and continuing rapid inflation in the industrial

[37] Bouey (1975, p. 15). Erik Hoffmeyer also commented that "it was quite clear that the authorities were not willing to adjust exchange rates sufficiently—with the advantage of hindsight, the size of adjustments in the Smithsonian Agreement could have been doubled." Hauge and Hoffmeyer (1978, p. 25).

countries in the years after 1973 stemmed from efforts to curb, or adjust to, the consequences of the policies pursued in 1972–73. Almost all of the industrial countries bear some responsibility for the emergence of rampant inflation in 1973–74, either because—as in the United States, the United Kingdom, Italy, and, to a lesser extent, Canada—the authorities implemented highly expansionary policies in pursuit of a rapid rise in real output and reduction in unemployment, or because—as in Japan and the Federal Republic of Germany—the authorities sought to maintain their traditional reliance on export-led growth under a favorable exchange rate, in a highly inflationary world environment. Thus, we can identify two closely interrelated causes out of which the stagflationary experience of the mid-to-late 1970s originated, namely the failure to allow exchange rates vis-à-vis the dollar to adjust freely sooner, and the associated failure to contain the aggregate expansion of nominal demand in the industrial countries.

Had the Japanese yen and the deutsche mark been allowed to float freely vis-à-vis the dollar throughout 1971 and 1972, the United States would have experienced a stronger impetus to real growth, investment, and employment, especially in the open industrial sector; but it would also have been more fully exposed to the inflationary consequences of its policies in inducing exchange rate depreciation and domestic price and cost increases. The U.S. authorities would probably have come under stronger pressure to tighten monetary policy, while Japan and Germany would not have experienced the intense export boom and the accelerating cost pressures that caused the adoption of sharply restrictive policies in 1973.

The earlier implementation, or continuation, of freely floating exchange rates for the major strong currencies (with the probable pegging of other strong currencies such as the Netherlands guilder and the Swedish krona on the deutsche mark) would have obviated the huge capital outflows from the United States to other capital markets and the unusually favorable current account balances experienced by many countries. The United Kingdom and Italy—which pursued flagrantly inflationary policies in 1972–73—would not have been presented with the opportunity for expansion offered by an exceptionally easy external position. Tighter policies in the United States would have mitigated the external inflationary pressures upon the Canadian economy occasioned by intense foreign demand and much higher prices for its exports of food and primary products; thus the development of boom conditions in 1973, which gave rise to persisting pressures on costs in 1974–75, could probably have been avoided. France and Italy would have had to accept an earlier adjustment of their exchange rates vis-à-vis the deutsche mark and the U.S. dollar.

The authorities would then have come under greater pressure to curb domestic credit expansion in order to realize the objective of re-establishing the exchange rate vis-à-vis the deutsche mark. Smaller countries, such as Austria, Belgium, the Netherlands, Norway, and Sweden, which wished to maintain the value of their currencies vis-à-vis the deutsche mark, would have been obliged to follow a broadly similar monetary policy to that of Germany—in respect of domestic credit and interest rates—but would have been able to do so without finding their policies frustrated by the monetary consequences of balance of payments surpluses.

As it was, the sharpening conflict of national priorities culminated in the implementation of extraordinarily discordant policies in 1973. Germany and Japan slammed on the brakes while the United States, Canada, the United Kingdom, and Italy continued on their expansionary course. The extreme divergence of national policies enhanced the movement of exchange rates leading to very sharp changes, and this had the effect of intensifying the resulting upward pressure on costs and prices in the expansionary countries and the downward impact on output and employment in the deflating countries. The sudden, sharp depreciation of the dollar was a not unimportant factor in precipitating the large increase in oil prices at the end of 1973, which greatly increased the difficulty of achieving a slower rate of inflation and compounded the tendencies to stagflation in the industrial countries resulting from the deceleration of the expansion of nominal demand after 1973.

6

Incomes Policy and Economic Theory

Between the 1940s and the late 1970s there was a tremendous shift in the prevailing attitude of economists to incomes policy. From being considered an essential adjunct of Keynesian full employment policy in many countries incomes policy had come to be regarded as an unnecessary appendage to a deflationary money growth target. A shift in the primary emphasis of policy from maintaining employment to controlling inflation had occurred in response to, and under the political impact of, rapid inflation after 1973.[1]

The Monetarist Counterrevolution and Theory of Unemployment

Within the economics profession, the displacement of Keynesian economics as the dominant orthodoxy by the monetarist "counter-revolution" had involved the substitution of a very different theoretical model of the underlying economy. While Keynesian economics postulated a continuing need for aggregate demand management to maintain full employment, in an economy inherently subject to fluctuations in investment and the level of activity, the new orthodoxy returned to, and sought to justify, the model of a real economy characterized by powerful tendencies to general equilibrium, resulting from optimizing behavior of individual economic agents in competitive markets. Under resurgent neoclassical economics, there was *by assumption* no need for employment policies or fine tuning of the economy, or for incomes policy interventions. The forces of competition and rational optimizing behavior would promote steady real growth at the "natural rate" of employment without inflation,

[1]This chapter is based in part on Braun (1976a) and Braun (1981).

provided there was stable monetary expansion in line with the long-run trend of real output growth, taken to be determined by autonomous technological and real factors.

The rise to ascendancy of monetarist economics in the "contest for the minds of economists, policy-makers, and the general public" was facilitated by the "recent history of unsatisfactory economic performance and a general impression—right or not—that policies and prediction based on opposing doctrines [had] gone wrong."[2] The monetarist view had been justified by events, in the sense that the primary cause of the inflation of the mid-1970s was the destabilizing impact of an excessive expansion of nominal demand in the industrial world associated with the financing of the Viet Nam war and with efforts to maintain full employment and retain fixed exchange rates. However, events did not justify the wholesale discredit of Keynesian demand management that followed.[3] Inflation was not the inexorable result of sensible employment policies involving deficit financing and accommodative monetary policy: it was the outcome of excessive deficits and monetary ease in some countries, and of incompatible national policies under fixed exchange rates. In short, inflation was brought about by failure to observe the quantitative constraints on policy in the short run. The trouble was not Keynesian policies but bad policymaking.[4]

The gradual acceleration of inflation in the United States would seem to support the monetarist interpretation that creeping inflation was gaining force as expectations adapted, causing the Phillips curve to pivot toward the "natural" rate of unemployment. One should however recall that what actually occurred was a sharp initial inflationary shock, which had direct consequences such as devaluation of the dollar, the effects of which took time to work their way through the system.[5]

Role of Incomes Policy Under Keynesian Demand Management

An important role for incomes policy was foreseen when full employment policies were initiated in the United Kingdom and other

[2]Tobin (1980, pp. 20–21).

[3]See, for example, Lucas (1981).

[4]It is ironic that the term "fine tuning" was applied to the policies of the Johnson and Nixon Administrations and of the Heath Government in the United Kingdom, and to those of some other governments in the late 1960s and early 1970s. See McCracken and others (1977, pp. 190–92).

[5]See Charts 4–7 and discussion in Chapter 5.

European countries after World War II. Expansionary fiscal and accommodative monetary policies were to be used to maintain full employment: a wages policy would be required to control inflation since full employment would eliminate the effect of unemployment in restraining wage claims.[6] Since the need to prevent a recurrence of the heavy unemployment experienced in the prewar decade commanded almost universal support, there was a tendency "to assume that, if only the unemployment consequences of anti-inflationary policies were properly understood, society would cheerfully agree to adopt and implement an incomes policy instead";[7] indeed that was the case in the immediate postwar period, as Chapter 2 has shown.

When moderate rates of wage and price increase were encountered at low levels of unemployment during the 1950s and early 1960s, under the impact of special circumstances which have been described, and of the moderate rate of expansion of nominal demand in the industrial world, it seemed that incomes policy was not needed after all. The publication of Phillips's noted article in 1958 and Lipsey's 1960 interpretation[8] suggested that it was feasible for demand management to achieve an acceptable "trade-off" of inflation and unemployment without recourse to incomes policy. Phillips himself, like Paish, interpreted his results as showing that price stability could be maintained in the United Kingdom provided the unemployment rate was kept at 2¼ percent.[9] However (as the present writer pointed out in 1966), it was questionable whether the rate of increase in wages associated with 2¼ percent unemployment occurring at the low point in regular cyclical fluctuations could be taken to indicate what the rate of wage increase would be if 2¼ percent unemployment was to be maintained indefinitely.[10]

Metamorphosis of the Phillips Curve

The Phillips-Lipsey Version

Phillips's original estimates were the subject of telling criticism by Routh and others,[11] and Lipsey's explanation in terms of excess demand in micro-labor markets was implausible as a description of wage bargaining in the United Kingdom. However, the numerous empirical studies with statistically significant results appeared to

[6]See Artis (1981); see also Kalecki (1944) and Worswick (1944).
[7]Johnson (1971b, p. 6).
[8]Phillips (1958) and Lipsey (1960).
[9]Phillips (1962) and Paish (1964).
[10]See Chapter 4, p. 77.
[11]For example, Routh (1959), Knowles and Winsten (1959), and Griffin (1962).

support a key proposition of the neo-Keynesian synthesis. As interpreted by Lipsey, the Phillips curve quickly became accepted doctrine because it fitted perfectly into the neoclassical model of a real economy made up of efficient markets adjusting to balance supply and demand.[12] The proposition that the change in money wage rates will reflect demand and supply conditions *within the labor market* appeared to be an elementary principle of economics. For the neo-Keynesian theorist, the Phillips relation "seemed to fill in a missing box in the Keynesian system: it endogenised the money wage to the economy" as modeled in his system.[13] However, the concept that the rate of change in wages was a function of the level of unemployment was totally at variance with Keynes's thinking in the General Theory. The acceptance of the Phillips curve relation marked the beginning of the eclipse of Keynesian economics.

Nevertheless, the Phillips curve equation became a highly valued tool for the authorities in the formulation of Keynesian macroeconomic policies. As long as the relationship seemed to be stable, the Phillips curve served the policymaker as a handy slide rule cum alibi.[14] With an accepted wage or price equation that performed well in terms of mathematical tests, the economic advisor could quickly work out the various policy options, in simple form and scientific guise, for politicians and the electorate. Furthermore, if unemployment was to be reduced, the policymaker was absolved from responsibility for increasing inflation, and vice versa.[15] The "choice the Phillips curve presented was simple, and, moreover, one that could be implemented by using the demand management tools of monetary and fiscal policy. . . . Indeed, one could go further . . . [because some of the other factors included as variables influencing the trade-off, such as the dispersion of excess demand across micromarkets, were also variables susceptible to policy influence] it seemed possible to improve the terms on which the unemployment inflation trade-off had to be made rather than simply take them as given."[16]

Starting with the Klein-Goldberger model of 1955,[17] virtually all the econometric models of the 1950s and 1960s made the rate of change of the nominal wage a variable determined by the volume of unemploy-

[12]For an account of early use of a Phillips equation by Tinbergen and others see Wilton (1980, pp. 9–19).

[13]Artis (1981, p. 8).

[14]See reference to Duesenberry (1966) in Chapter 4, pp. 80 and 92, for a typical use of the relation in the late 1960s. See also Rees (1979).

[15]Wilton (1980, pp. 16–17).

[16]Laidler (1976, pp. 56–57).

[17]Klein and Goldberger (1955).

ment and past changes in the price level. "When combined with an equation that determined the price level as a 'normal full-cost markup' over the wage rate and prices of raw materials, the Phillips curve wage equation provided a consensus description of inflation dynamics that formed the basis for the economic policy prescriptions of the 1960s."[18] Thus, in most large econometric models, the Phillips curve provided the vital link between changes in aggregate demand and changes in the rate of inflation, in conformity with the neo-Keynesian view that expenditure determines output, inflation resulting "if aggregate demand rises persistently relative to supply, and the degree of capacity utilization gets too high."[19] When much greater rates of wage and price increase were encountered in the late 1960s and early 1970s than would have been predicted at the going rates of unemployment from earlier experience, repeated efforts were made to recover a stable relation between unemployment and inflation.[20]

The "Expectations-Augmented" Phillips Curve

For many economists, the notion of a stable relation between a nominal variable and a real variable was however suspect. One way of resolving this difficulty, which was suggested by the writer in 1970,[21] would have been to investigate whether the short-run Phillips curve was not in fact a relation between two nominal variables—that is, between the cyclically changing rate of expansion of aggregate nominal demand, *proxied* by the changing level of unemployment, and the rate of wage or price increase. This view is implicit in the account of the inflationary experience of the industrial world during the late 1960s and 1970s given in the previous chapter. For the neoclassical economist, however, the natural reaction was to accept the short-run Phillips curve as a real phenomenon, reflecting a causal relation between the real variables of the level of unemployment and the rate of increase in real wages, and to treat the change in nominal wages as comprising the change in real wages *plus* the expected change in the general level of prices.

This interpretation implied that the observed short-term relation between unemployment and the rate of increase in nominal wages could not be stable. If the occurrence of low (or high) unemployment was associated with a positive (or negative) rate of change in unit labor costs and prices, maintenance of the same rate of unemployment

---

[18] Gordon (1981, p. 503).
[19] Peston (1981, p. 3).
[20] See account of efforts to justify the general equilibrium approach, below.
[21] In a study subsequently published as Braun (1971b).

would cause an accelerating rate of increase (or decrease) in nominal wages as wage bargainers came to foresee the implied rate of price inflation. In other words, the short-term Phillips curve would tend to pivot into a more steeply sloping, or vertical position in the long run. Thus only a slightly, if at all, higher level of employment would be secured by maintaining a faster rate of expansion in nominal demand.

To the Phillips relation, in the notation of Artis (1981),

$$\dot{p} = -\alpha(u - u^*) \tag{1}$$

where u and u^* are the actual and the steady-state equilibrium rates of unemployment and $\dot{p}$ is the rate of inflation, there should be added an inflation expectations term $\dot{p}^e$,

$$\text{so that } \dot{p} = -\alpha(u - u^*) + \beta\dot{p}^e. \tag{2}$$

In the monetarist view of the early 1970s, with given price expectations, inflation would be low in a depressed economy ($u > u^*$) and high in an overexpanded economy ($u < u^*$); β, the coefficient on expected inflation would be equal to unity in the absence of money illusion; and, on the basis of some error learning adaptive expectations, any constant rate of inflation would come to be fully anticipated. The American neo-Keynesian view was essentially similar as regards the first term, but held that β was less than unity, implying that, though the inflation cost of expanding output was higher in the long run than in the short run, there was still some scope for Keynesian policies even in the long run.[22]

The Natural Rate of Unemployment

Assuming that certain conditions were satisfied,[23] the monetarist view implied that there was an equilibrium rate of unemployment (u^*) compatible with any constant rate of inflation and that it would be impossible permanently to reduce unemployment below this "natural rate" by expansionary policies.[24] For neoclassical theorists, such a "natural" rate of unemployment was an inherent attribute of the stable real economy which they postulated. The vertical long-run Phillips curve represented real equilibrium in the labor market at which the marginal physical product of labor was equal to labor's

[22]Laidler (1981, pp. 8–9).

[23]The necessary properties of the wage and price equations are set out very clearly in Auld and others (1979, pp. 32–33).

[24]Friedman introduced the concept by analogy with the natural rate of interest, in an effort to separate real forces from monetary forces. Friedman (1968, pp. 8–9).

supply price.[25] If the actual rate of inflation corresponded to the expected rate, there was only one level of unemployment that could be maintained (that at which the real wage, equaling the real product of additional work, was just sufficient to compensate for the disutility of the extra effort or sacrifice of leisure on the part of the labor force). Consequently, the rate of unemployment over the longer run could not be changed by altering the rate of monetary expansion. The natural rate of unemployment was inevitable in the long run. Hence in its expectations-augmented form, the Phillips curve provided "the missing equation in the monetarist model of inflation" permitting Friedman to demonstrate that ultimately movements in the general price level were an essentially monetary phenomenon.[26]

The Phillips Curve as an Aggregate Supply Curve Under "Rational Expectations"

Whereas Phelps (1967) and Friedman (1968), like Lipsey (1960), still treated unemployment as a signal that conveyed to economic agents the desirability of changing prices, later theorizing interpreted the expectations-augmented Phillips curve as an aggregate supply curve.[27] In this view, it is the divergence of the actual from the expected level of prices that causes the deviations of the level of employment and output from the long-run equilibrium level. The augmented Phillips curve can then be written as:

$$\dot{p} = \gamma y + \beta \dot{p}^e + v \tag{3}$$

where y is equilibrium output and v is a vector of all other systematic as well as random influences.[28] Equation (3) is derived on the assumption that $\gamma = 0$ when $p = p^e$, so that

$$y = \frac{1}{\gamma}(p - p^e) \tag{4}$$

and when $\beta = 1$ in the absence of money illusion, the expected rate of inflation is defined

$$\dot{p}^e \equiv p^e - p_{-1}. \tag{5}$$

Clearly, however, such a purely backward-looking process of forming price expectations would give rise to systematic errors

[25] Friedman, however, had emphasized that the term was not intended to suggest that the "natural rate" was "immutable and unchangeable. On the contrary, many of the market characteristics that determine its level are man-made and policy-made" (and include market imperfections). Friedman (1968, p. 9). See Chapter 7, footnote 21.

[26] Laidler (1981, p. 10) and Friedman (1970, pp. 221–34).

[27] Laidler (1981) cites papers by Alchian, Lucas and Rapping, Gordon and Hynes, and Mortensen in Phelps and others (1970).

[28] Laidler (1981, pp. 8–10; the notation has been changed).

whenever there was a marked change in macroeconomic policies; and one must suppose that rational market participants would become aware of this. Hence, a natural outgrowth of the aggregate supply curve view of the Phillips relation was the hypothesis that economic agents make future-oriented decisions on the basis of "rational expectations" of the influence of *all* known relevant variables, including government policies. While this reasoning drew attention to the problem of modeling expectations, it has actually served as the basis for many empirical studies using highly simplistic and mechanical assumptions about how expectations are formed.[29]

The Empirical Phillips Curve as a Cyclical Phenomenon

Both the "natural rate" and the "aggregate supply curve" equations require, first, that there should be some *consistent* manner in which *confident* price expectations are derived by market participants and, second, that there should be a *consistent* short-term relation between unemployment and the rate of price increase relative to the expected rate of inflation. That is, each hypothesis requires the existence of a sloping short-term Phillips curve, if steady-state equilibrium at the natural rate of unemployment u^* is to be established or maintained, though the direction of implied causation differs in the two cases.[30]

The monetarist model of the real economy implies that the Phillips curve should not be flat—and monetarist theorists therefore were predisposed to accept the empirically observed sloping curve. However, there was reason to suppose that the true relation between unemployment per se and the rate of wage (or price) increase might be neither steep nor stable.

> Although widely interpreted as such, the [Phillips] relation does not indicate a trade-off between the level of unemployment maintained and the increase in wage rates. The observed tendency for slight differences in the level of unemployment to be associated with marked differences in increases in wage

[29] These studies often predicate that the expected value of a variable is derived simply by regression of its current value on its own lagged values. Tobin (1980) comments: "Since this calculation does not utilize the inter-variable structure of the model, it is an *ad hoc* procedure whose superiority to other one-variable *ad hoc* procedures is far from obvious" (p. 28; see pp. 25–29 for a critique of rational expectations theorizing).

[30] In the "natural rate" approach, the term $-\alpha(u - u^*)$ in equation (2) must be well established and the coefficient α must be quite large, otherwise the economy will be prone to persistent unemployment. In the aggregate supply approach, the term γy in equation (3) must be well established and the coefficient must be quite large, or any disequilibrium will tend to persist.

> rates arises in large part from the postponement, or advancement, of wage claims in the course of short-term cyclical fluctuations.[31]
>
> Short-term demand conditions that induce employers to offer a relatively high (or low) level of jobs also predispose them to be more (or less) willing to accede to wage claims; and the size and timing of the unions' wage claims are strongly influenced by cyclical fluctuations because the strike weapon is less effective against enterprises that are working below capacity or accumulating inventories. Thus, the relative level of unemployment in the course of short-term business fluctuations constitutes a good index of the change in wage bargaining conditions from one year to another.[32]
>
> This does not mean that the level of unemployment per se is the causal factor that influences the bargaining power of the unions. The cause of the strengthening (or weakening) in the bargaining position of the unions is not the changing pressure of demand for labor relative to the available manpower supplies but the strength of aggregate demand in the economy [compared to the average customarily experienced]. Thus, the inverse relation between unemployment and the rise in wage rates should be seen to arise from two distinct effects of the same underlying cause, namely, the variation in aggregate demand. . . . E.H. Phelps Brown has emphasized that the Phillips curve association between changes in wage rates and the current level of unemployment arises because the latter is an indicator of the current stage of a more or less regular cyclical fluctuation in activity.[33]
>
> It is difficult to see how a meaningful "steady-state" relation can be derived from the short-run observations, if the association between the rate of increase in wages and each level of unemployment reflects not only the level of unemployment but also the expectation of continued cyclical fluctuations, in the manner described.[34]

This reasoning suggests that, were it not for more or less regular cyclical fluctuations in demand, a much weaker relationship between unemployment and the rate of inflation would be observed. In the absence of marked year-to-year changes in aggregate demand, the relation between the level of unemployment and the rate of wage increase would probably be an S-shaped curve, almost flat over a considerable range of unemployment levels[35] but rising steeply at a

---

[31]Braun (1971b, p. 170).

[32]Braun (1971b, p. 138).

[33]Braun (1971b, p. 168 and footnote 27; words in brackets added here). The references are to Phelps Brown (1968, p. 13) and Phelps Brown and Browne (1968, pp. 72–85).

[34]Braun (1971a, p. 63).

[35]See Braun (1971b, p. 170, footnote 31). The long-run curve (LL) might then compare with the empirically observed short-run curve observed under short-term fluctuations in demand as in the diagram reproduced below.

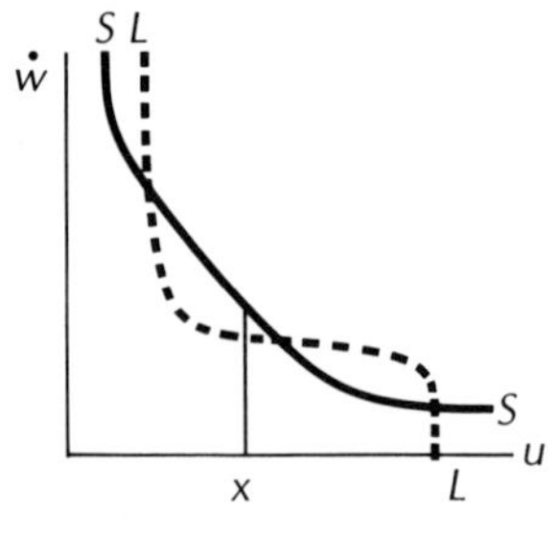

low level of unemployment at which wages would be bid up by employers competing for labor, and falling steeply at a very high unemployment level at which wage earners would be unable to maintain agreed wage levels. The textbook concept of the Phillips curve as a sloping line tending to pivot at the point representing the "nonaccelerating inflation rate of unemployment" (NAIRU) would then be without empirical support, and the foundations of the "natural rate" and the "aggregate supply curve" theories would be undermined. In effect one is left with a range of unemployment levels, over which the existence of any particular unemployment rate of itself exerts little, if any, influence on the rate at which nominal wages and prices will rise for a given expansion of nominal demand. An acceleration of inflation may occur at widely different levels of unemployment, or a certain rate of inflation may persist with rising or falling unemployment. "Correct" (ex post validated) price expectations may be established at different, or changing, levels of unemployment.

This skeptical view of the Phillips relation is described more fully in the final section of this chapter. The reasons for accepting this rather than the neoclassical view will be seen from an examination of the underlying assumptions of that approach which follows.

The Monetarist View of the Economy

The monetarist tradition derives from a model of the real economy and the demand for money, whose mechanisms ensure that the economy will be in equilibrium at the natural rate of unemployment,[36] unless there is a change in the rate of expansion of nominal demand due to a change in monetary policy or possibly to a major exogenous shock.[37] In its purest form—in the aggregate supply curve approach—this view implies that "fluctuations in output and employment [occur] in response to price level variations [and] represent the voluntary choices of individuals operating in markets *which are continually clearing*. . . . It is to locate the cause of unemployment, not. . . in *ex ante* mutually satisfactory trades, but rather in a failure of markets. . . to convey sufficient information to enable the expectations upon which those trades are based to be formed accurately in an economy subject to stochastic shocks."[38]

---

[36]See Mayer (1978) and comment by Johnson (1978).

[37]The notion of a pervasive autonomous shock other than a monetary disturbance is, however, alien to the assumption of an economy composed of many independent markets subject to random shocks. (See pp. 141–43 and 167 below and Reder (1982, pp. 11–12).)

[38]Laidler (1981, pp. 10–11; italics added).

Hence, when there is an autonomous change to a new rate of monetary expansion, it is simply necessary to establish "correct expectations" that the new rate will be maintained. The overall rate of inflation will change accordingly and equilibrium in the real economy will be restored. Unemployment will return to the "natural" rate, and steady real output growth will be re-established, at a rate determined by underlying real supply factors (of technical progress, demography, etc.). During the transition, incorrect expectations are liable to produce price and wage increases inconsistent with the maintenance of unemployment at the "natural rate"; higher (or lower) unemployment at lower (or higher) than equilibrium real output will temporarily prevail. Given the model, the problem is to explain why persistent fluctuations in real output and employment occur instead of rapidly responsive changes in the rate of inflation.

The skeptic may feel intuitively that if competitive behavior in markets can ensure that Pareto-optimum equilibrium[39] normally applies when there is no change in monetary expansion, then the workings of the system must be such as to ensure that the equilibrium level of output and unemployment would be quickly re-established after a monetary shock. The fact that incorrect price expectations can persist suggests that markets do not work as postulated.[40] But in that case, the mechanism by which equilibrium is re-established at the "natural rate" of unemployment, with no involuntary unemployment, is defective or lacking.

Even leading proponents of the market clearing paradigm now recognize that the "problem of reconciling the natural rate hypothesis with *some* adequate treatment of output and employment fluctuations is genuine. . . . If one accepts some idea of monetary neutrality as being central, how does one simultaneously accept the idea that instability in the quantity of money has been a principal source of real instability? If a particular policy variable has the power to account for historical employment movements up and down the business cycle, why can this power not be put to good use by the deliberate manipulation?"[41]

The message of the general equilibrium model and the aggregate supply curve approach is clear. The policymaker should be concerned

---

[39]See definition given below.

[40]Such skepticism will be justified by a glance at the kind of assumptions that rational expectations theorists are driven to make in order to demonstrate the paramount importance of incorrect expectations about the general movement of prices as *the* cause of markets failing to clear.

[41]Lucas (1981, p. 561).

with monetary stability not with full employment, since the economy, as modeled, will generate economic full employment (involving no "involuntary" unemployment) if left free from destabilizing policy interventions. Its workings rule out influencing the level of unemployment by demand management except in the very short run. "The central question of macroeconomic policy [then is] that of determining a workable set of limits on the scope of governmental influence over economic activity and of devising institutional arrangements which can make these limits stick."[42] To accept this conclusion, however, one must be convinced of the realism of the general equilibrium model as a description of the actual or potential workings of the economy over the short to medium term.

Basic Postulates of the General Equilibrium Model

Reder has described the highly specific assumptions on which the widely accepted version of general equilibrium model, as developed at Chicago, rests.[43] The model predicates that Pareto-optimum equilibrium normally applies: that is to say "that decision makers so allocate the resources under their control that there is no alternative allocation such that any one decision maker could have his expected utility increased without a reduction occurring in the expected utility of at least one other decision maker" (p. 11). Economists in the Chicago tradition supplement this hypothesis with other assumptions to derive a model that provides testable hypotheses. In the version which Reder terms "Tight Prior Equilibrium" theory (TP for short), it is typically also assumed that:

> (1) *most* individual transactors treat the prices of all goods and services that they buy or sell, as independent of the quantities that they transact; (2) the prices at which individuals *currently agree* to transact are market clearing prices. . .consistent with optimization by all decision makers; (3) information bearing on prices and qualities of all things bought and sold, present and future [like any other commodity] is acquired in the quantity that makes its marginal cost equal to its price;. . . (4) neither monopoly nor government action. . .affects relative prices or quantities sufficiently to prevent either marginal products or compensation of identical resources from being approximately equal in all uses (p. 11).

Although none of these assumptions is believed to hold exactly, each is commonly treated as a valid first approximation. Tastes, techniques, and resources, as well as information, are affected by *random* disturbances, and the quantity offered by any one transactor is subject

[42]Lucas (1981, p. 566).

[43]Reder (1982, especially pp. 10–22).

to *random* variations. "*Random* disturbances are such that it is possible to devise a stochastic analogue of the exact (non-stochastic) competitive general equilibrium model" in which "expected price and expected quantity are treated as proxies for the corresponding price and quantity in the exact model."[44] There are no stable empirical relationships among prices, quantities, and disturbances other than those with analogues in the exact general equilibrium model.

The mutual independence (randomness) of disturbances can however be assumed to apply only under steady-state conditions. It is recognized that at any given moment, the effect of long-term contracts or the existence of durable assets acquired earlier implies that current demand and supply schedules are affected by past errors and imperfect forecasts. Nevertheless, in their applied work, economists of the Chicago school tend to assume that, unless there is definite evidence to the contrary, observed prices and quantities may be taken as "good approximations" to their long-run competitive equilibrium values.[45]

It is of course difficult to maintain the "good approximation" assumption when pre-existing contracts or existing stocks of assets (such as capital equipment) are not optimal.

> If prices were completely flexible (i.e., differing from long-run equilibrium values only to the extent implied by *transitory* [random] disturbances) then, subject to the *quantity* constraints created by past outlays and contractual commitments, all transactors would optimize at current prices and all markets would clear. However, as Chicago economists have always recognized, prices (especially wage rates) are sticky in the short-run. Thus, there is a long-standing problem of reconciling the fact of price stickiness with the maintained hypothesis of continuous optimization.[46]

There is no agreement on how to apply TP when explaining price-quantity adjustments over time in markets where long-term contracts are important, but "there is continuing resistance to institutional explanations that are incompatible with the assumption of optimization as of the moment of decision making."[47]

The existence of imperfect competition constitutes a major threat to the general equilibrium model, as Joan Robinson, Hicks, and others

---

[44]Reder (1982, pp. 11–12; italics added).

[45]Reder (1982, p. 12). For an example of the difficulty this causes in analyzing actual situations, see the account of Friedman's case for indexation in the United States in Chapter 8.

[46]Reder (1982, p. 13).

[47]Reder (1982, p. 15). TP theory "says very little about the day-to-day movements of prices and quantities during the life of the contract, beyond insisting that, *at every moment*, parties either observe or violate contracts as present expected value maximization. . .dictates. . . . A wide variety of behavior. . . can be rationalized as expected value maximization" (p. 14).

pointed out in the 1930s.[48] Hence TP requires that monopoly should be "of infrequent occurrence and limited impact." According to Reder, "the TP view is that most of what appears to be monopoly [or market imperfection] is ephemeral, being eliminated by free entry." The economy is taken to comprise a large number of distinct products each of which is associated with a market that could be competitive or not, and a relatively small number of productive agents (factors) each with its own market. While "prices in some subset of the product markets may be set monopolistically, ... this does not appreciably affect equilibrium prices in the factor markets which are (approximately) competitive.... Put differently, long-run monopoly is not important enough to invalidate the contention that prices of factors are good approximations to the opportunity cost of using them" (p. 15).

Reder comments that the assumption that equilibrium prices in factor markets are approximately competitive might need to be modified to take into account the effect of strong unionism on wages, but this has not been done so far. He also notes that "the secondary importance ascribed to long-run monopoly" implicitly "reflects an (alleged) absence of interaction between deviations of equilibrium prices and quantities from competitive levels in any single product market, or combination of product markets, and equilibrium prices in the factor markets" (p. 15). In practice, there is of course a potent interplay between the existence of noncompetitive market conditions for products and for factors, as is discussed below and illustrated in the country studies of Norway and the Netherlands in Chapter 10.

Efforts to Justify the General Equilibrium Approach

Since the mid-1970s, many academic studies have sought to demonstrate that persistent fluctuations in output and unemployment can be reconciled with the basic postulates of general equilibrium theory, involving continuous optimizing behavior by individual decision makers in atomistic competitive markets, market clearing in the absence of monopoly, and the concomitant property of monetary neutrality.

Largely ignoring key issues concerning price determination in factor markets—particularly those concerning wage determination—monetarist and neo-Keynesian economists have set out to show, first, that fluctuations in employment need not be inconsistent with market

---

[48] "It is, I believe, only possible to save anything from this wreck...of the greater part of general equilibrium theory—if we can assume that the markets confronting most of the firms...do not differ very greatly from perfectly competitive markets." Hicks (1946, p. 84), cited by Reder (1982, p. 17).

clearing; or next, that incorrect expectations concerning the warranted overall rate of inflation may prevent market clearing by inducing inappropriate pricing decisions in micro-markets when the rate of monetary expansion changes; and more recently, while still stressing the dichotomy between the overall rate of inflation and specific pricing decisions, that price "stickiness" and nonmarket clearing prices for specific products or factor services may in fact be characteristic of profit maximization over the longer run.

The first strand in the literature attempted to show "that unemployment can be treated as a form of choice and can be derived from an optimizing behavior [so] that a situation of unemployment is not necessarily a situation of 'disequilibrium.'"[49] This approach treats unemployment as a consequence of (1) choice of time spent in job search; or (2) the intertemporal substitution of leisure for work in lifetime employment; or (3) as arising from innate differences in ability and hiring and training costs. Reasoning along the lines of (1) and (2) has fallen into the background as heavy unemployment has persisted.

The second strand—the rational expectations literature—focused on inadequate information as the reason preventing *price taking* agents from realizing market clearing aggregate output and employment.[50] Again the purpose is to demonstrate, without relaxing the basic postulates of optimizing behavior, that changes in the level of unemployment can occur within the neoclassical model of a system normally tending to equilibrium. As such, rational expectations is a proposition concerning the workings of the general equilibrium model not the real world. Unless the basic postulates of the model adequately capture the features that govern the actual workings of the economic system and aggregate economic behavior, there are no grounds for believing that competitive equilibrium will prevail after a disturbance, if only "correct" expectations of the general rate of inflation can be re-established. Nevertheless, belief in the overriding importance of correcting inflationary expectations as the paramount—if not the sole—requirement for ensuring recovery after a deflationary policy shift became widespread during the 1970s, notwithstanding the fact that few politicians, bankers, or economic advisors would have been prepared to accept the assumptions of the rational expectations theorists as a plausible picture of the actual behavior of markets over the medium term.

---

[49]Brenner (1979, p. 837). The literature is enormous. See, for example, Phelps (1967); Lucas and Rapping (1970); Azariadis (1975); Lippman and McCall (1976a and 1976b); Wachter (1976); Hall (1980); and Okun (1981).

[50]For a critical review of this literature, see Gordon (1981, pp. 504–12).

More recently, efforts have been made to introduce a greater degree of realism into the neoclassical model, by substituting for market clearing prices the very different paradigm of nonmarket clearing prices with price setting agents (which is in the Keynesian tradition). This involves demonstrating that "price stickiness" under *price setting* is not inconsistent with efficient markets and optimizing behavior,[51] because it serves the purpose either of providing customers with information about prices[52] or, when combined with changes in inventories and order books, of stabilizing production relative to sales.[53]

Gordon has suggested that, given pervasive heterogeneity of final products and inputs, gradual adjustment of prices is a necessary feature of profit-maximizing behavior, as a means of economizing transactions costs and as a consequence of decentralized decision making.[54] While he notes that heterogeneity of products makes each firm a monopolist in the short to medium run (p. 520), he does not question how far the heterogeneity of products may stem from efforts to secure the power to fix prices rather than being the reason for price setting. In general, the literature stressing that price setting may be a feature of profit maximization over the longer run ignores the question whether the power to set prices of specific products or factor services for considerable periods—and to maximize over the longer run—is not directly associated with fundamental, and persisting, restrictions on entry. Intuitively, one may doubt whether a system in which some suppliers are able to set and maintain prices or wages in the face of marked changes in aggregate demand can be one which is characterized by competitive markets such as to ensure the maintenance of "Pareto-optimum" equilibrium under stable demand conditions.

[51]See Gordon (1981, p. 494 and p. 517).

[52]Okun (1981).

[53]Blinder (1982); see also Carlton (1978) and (1979).

[54]Gordon (1981) examines whether each contribution provides an explanation of price stickiness that is derived from maximizing behavior rather than from "extraneous assumptions," that is, whether "it assumes its answers in advance rather than deducing them from the behavior of individual agents" (p. 495). He sets himself the task of constructing "a simple model of price adjustment that explains as many as possible of the. . .outstanding questions. . .with the smallest possible set of assumptions. If the resulting framework is to have any appeal to proponents of the new classical equilibrium macroeconomics, two of these assumptions must be rationality and profit-maximizing behavior on the part of economic agents." A third essential assumption, he suggests, is "the pervasive heterogeneity in types and quality of products, and in the location and timing of transactions" (p. 517). Most revealingly, he suggests that "the general-equilibrium analysis of a quantity-constrained economy is already in place, *once the reasons for partial price adjustment have been explained*" (p. 495, italics added). However, that apparently implies that the reasons for partial price adjustment are not "extraneous" and damaging to the assumptions of the general equilibrium model.

An Alternative View: Discontinuous Adjustment Under Imperfect Competition

For the monetarist economist, marked variations in the price-output response of the economy to changes in nominal demand over time constitute an anomaly. The operation of competitive markets is *assumed* to ensure that there can only be a transient change in the level of activity as the result of an inflationary or deflationary monetary shock, or a temporary change in the overall price level as a result of a real shock not accompanied by a change in the money supply. Therefore, money is neutral and, except in the short run, changes in the overall price level are a purely monetary phenomenon: changes in the rate of monetary expansion do not give rise to lasting changes in the structure of real output, distribution of income and expenditure, or other variables. The system will not possess these properties if some, or all, nominal product or factor prices are inflexible or respond only slowly or erratically.

"Rational" Decisions Under Uncertainty

It is not surprising that the price-output response should vary over time in a system which is actually marked by wide differences in the degree of competition applying in various markets, and by a changing incidence of monopoly over time.[55] Under these circumstances, the market participant's problem in reaching "rational" decisions concerning quantities and prices in specific markets is fraught with great uncertainty. Risk cannot then be adequately represented by mathematical probability theory[56] since expectations are liable to be unstable and contagious, so that business confidence becomes an important factor. The market participant's problem then is one of guessing how the market may judge the situation and react on this particular occasion and of securing insurance against the adverse consequences of being mistaken. The prevalence of even "ephemeral" monopoly is highly important in this connection, as a factor increasing uncertainty at the microlevel and inducing "defensive" rather than "continuously optimizing" behavior on the part of other agents.

Influence of "Ephemeral" Monopoly in a Dynamic World

The monetarist contends that monopoly is a temporary phenomenon tending to wither away with free entry.[57] But, in a dynamic

---

[55]Some aspects of the working of such a system are sketched in Chapter 7.

[56]Townshend (1937) and Shackle (1973).

[57]Reder (1982, p. 12, footnote 28) refers to Harberger (1954) as an important exception, accepted because it showed the output loss from resource misallocation due to monopolistic behavior to be small.

setting, the power to maintain prices for a time at a substantially higher level than would prevail if entry were unrestricted also confers the power to maintain that advantage in various ways. The enterprise earning high profits can devote the proceeds to developing new products or investing in new technology, and is favored in raising financing in the market. The advantage which innovative techniques or large-scale, capital-intensive, production confers in limiting the threat of new entrants is a powerful inducement in promoting technical progress and the realization of economies of scale, and so in encouraging rapid capital replacement. Heavy expenditure on advertising to develop a large-scale market and to "differentiate" the product in the mind of consumers[58] constitutes another barrier for new entrants.

The restrictions on entry which give the enterprise, or the oligopolistic industry collectively, the power to set and maintain prices for a time, though not indefinitely, also make it possible for wage earners to maintain wages in the face of unemployment, as was discussed in Chapter 4.[59] The specific characteristics of wage bargaining in industrial economies reflect the factors making for imperfect competition in industrial product markets. Labor organization depends upon, exploits, and itself contributes to buttress the market power of large-scale enterprises. Thus the characteristics of product and labor markets are closely linked, and their conjoint nature has a crucial role in determining how an advanced economy responds to an inflationary or deflationary shock. The actual characteristics of wage and price determination processes could not exist under the atomistic competition between suppliers modeled in general equilibrium theory. That is the reason why monetarist theorists are unable to provide a satisfactory account of wage and price behavior in the short to medium term.

The Nature of Wage Determination in the Large Enterprise Sector

One may summarize the main features of the wage determination process over a wide area of the industrial economy characterized by restricted entry of new producers, as follows:

(1) Wages are set in nominal terms, usually for periods of a year or longer. For reasons that are discussed below, it is only when rapid inflation has prevailed for some time that automatic adjustment for

[58]Heterogeneity of products is promoted since producers have an incentive to establish a monopoly position in supplying a specific type of demand, thereby maintaining a relatively high markup on costs in that submarket.

[59]See also Chapter 10 on Norway.

price increases becomes widespread.[60] When it exists, indexation of wages is implemented with a lag, and almost always provides less than complete protection against price increases.[61]

(2) Ignoring indexation clauses for the moment, there is some inertia in nominal wages over and above the fact that wages are often set for a definite period or are negotiated at fairly lengthy intervals. This arises because changes in wages have to be secured by agreement. Employees have to get the agreement of the employer(s) to a rise in their wages and vice versa; and changes may be resisted.

(3) Except in very small undertakings, wage bargaining typically takes place between the enterprise (or industry) and employees as a group (or groups), not with individuals.

(4) The conditions under which large and technologically advanced enterprises operate, endow the existing labor force (or segments of the labor force), with considerable leverage vis-à-vis the employer,[62] and, in particular, with considerable power to discourage the enterprise from hiring new employees at less than the going wage rates.

(5) It follows that, contrary to monetarist accounts of the working of the labor market, in many fields of production the unemployed person does not have the choice of accepting less than the going wage in order to secure a job.[63] This fact, together with the difficulty of new firms entering the industry, tends to insulate the level of wages over an important part of the economy, from downward pressure due to rising

---

[60]"Ordinary experience tells us, beyond doubt, that a situation where labour stipulates (within limits) for a money-wage rather than a real wage, so far from being a mere possibility, is the normal case. Whilst workers will usually resist a reduction of money-wages, it is not their practice to withdraw their labour whenever there is a rise in the price of wage-goods." "It would be impracticable to resist every reduction of real wages, due to a change in the purchasing-power of money which affects all workers alike; and in fact reductions of real wages arising in this way are not, as a rule, resisted unless they proceed to an extreme degree." Keynes (1936, p. 9 and p. 14), cited by Brenner (1979, p. 839 and p. 840).

[61]See Chapter 8.

[62]Among the factors that contribute to strengthen the wage bargaining position of the labor force are the heavy cost of idled capacity in capital-intensive industries, the need for a cooperative work force to ensure good quality control or avoid damage to capital equipment, the comparative ease of organizing labor when large numbers of employees work in a plant, and the difficulty of replacing all, or much of a numerous and specialized labor force in the near term. (Although in the longer term, the enterprise may keep down costs by arranging subcontracting, or may be able to locate new plants in low-wage areas.) Furthermore, the high profits to be made from leadership in innovation gives the enterprise a strong incentive to get changes adopted quickly. In this context, enterprises are inclined to accede to employees' wage claims in order to secure changes in the organization of work. The enhanced power of the labor force vis-à-vis the employer under monopolistic competition serves to promote a distribution of income which creates a mass market for advanced consumer goods within the advanced production sectors.

[63]This however is not what is meant by involuntary unemployment in the General Theory. See below.

unemployment. Given this situation, it is quite misleading to imply that "heterogeneity of labor" and "investments in training" are the main reason why "unemployed workers [cannot] substitute for employed workers at a lower wage rate without cost," or that these are the principal factors which confer "a degree of monopoly power on each employed worker."[64]

The Keynesian Concept of "Involuntary Unemployment"

Keynes defines "involuntary unemployment" as existing if labor in general would be prepared to work for a lower real wage due to a small rise in prices.[65] He does not consider the case of a reduction in the real wage attained by the lowering of money wages, since he contends that in a closed economic system labor in general cannot ensure a reduction in average real wages by the alternative route of accepting wage cuts. If labor were to respond to "diminishing employment by offering its services at a gradually diminishing money-wage, this would not, as a rule, have the effect of reducing real wages and might even have the effect of increasing them, through its adverse influence on the volume of output."[66] Expectations of wage and price reductions "would lower the marginal efficiency of investment and increase the marginal efficiency of holding money."[67]

Nominal Versus Real Wage Bargaining

For orthodox economists (of the 1930s or the 1970s–80s) accustomed to thinking in terms of *real* wage bargaining by *individuals* concerned to equate the utility of a real wage with the disutility of work, the idea that there could be a different response to a change in real wages due to a rise in prices or to a reduction in the nominal wage seems paradoxical, requiring to be explained in terms of money illusion.[68] But once it is assumed that wage contracts are set in money

[64]Gordon (1981, p. 526). See also Okun (1981, Chapters 2 and 3).

[65]"Men are involuntarily unemployed if, in the event of a small rise in the price of wage-goods relatively to the money-wage, both the aggregate supply of labour willing to work for the current money-wage and the aggregate demand for it at that wage would be greater than the existing volume of employment." Keynes (1936, p. 15).

[66]Keynes (1936, p. 269). See further discussion of this point on pp. 152–53, below.

[67]Lerner (1952), cited by Brenner (1979, p. 847).

[68]Keynes's account of the resistance to cuts in nominal wages, like that given here, focuses on the resistance of *employed* workers to a reduction in money wages (see Keynes (1936, pp. 8–9)) and is consistent with the idea that work is offered to the unemployed worker at the going rate bargained with *employed* workers. Because this conflicts with the atomistic competition in the labor market postulated by monetarists, it is difficult for them to present a satisfactory account of Keynes's argument. See, for example, Brenner's extraordinary definition of involuntary unemployment in his stimulating article: "Those

terms, and changes in nominal remuneration rates normally have to be negotiated, the explanation is obvious. A fall in real wages due to a change in the price level comes about automatically, whereas the employer has to secure the wage earners' agreement to a cut in money wages. They have to secure the employer's agreement to a rise in nominal wages or to indexation, in order to prevent a decline in real wages when prices rise. The fact that wage bargaining normally relates to money wages represents a decision made by enterprises as well as wage earners. The question is not why do wage earners respond differently in the two cases, but why does a system providing for relatively inflexible unindexed money wage contracts so often apply?

For the large enterprise, a system of set money wages, not adjusted very frequently and not involving bargaining with individuals, clearly has advantages in keeping down personnel management costs and lessening occasions for disputes. Even apart from the opposition of existing employees to the hiring of new workers at less than the going wage, managements might not be keen to hire individuals at less than the going wage, as predicated in monetarist accounts of the labor market. Cost accounting in a large enterprise in which individual workers had been hired at widely different rates for the job would be a nightmare.

Automatic compensation for price increases involves the sacrifice of some bargaining freedom by the enterprise, and increases the risk that wages may go up faster than the price of its output if market conditions for its product are relatively unfavorable. Indexation may make it possible for wage earners to secure a faster rise in nominal wages than if indexation did not apply, as workers may well be able to secure increases over and above indexation when demand for the company's product is strong. Indexation will impose incidental costs on the enterprise if it involves frequent changes in nominal pay. Thus, employers are unlikely to agree to indexation unless it is strongly pressed for by employees. For their part, wage earners—and more particularly union leaders—may feel that they can do better without indexation unless prices are rising quite rapidly, because indexation lessens the incentive to organize and press for wage increases. Faced with militant unions and a strong market outlook for its products, the large enterprise may nevertheless see an advantage in granting,

---

actually employed do not expect somebody looking for a job to accept a real wage lower than the one they are currently earning. Therefore, when somebody is offered a wage lower than the actual real wage and does not accept it, he is considered in Keynes's model as involuntarily unemployed." Brenner (1979, p. 841).

generally less than full, indexation for price increases as a means of securing long-term wage contracts, so avoiding negotiations with the risk of possible work stoppages, for several years.[69] An offer of indexation as an alternative to a large immediate wage increase may also be favored by the enterprise when rapid inflation is expected to slow down.

Two implications of the situation described here need to be emphasized. First, the extent to which wage bargaining refers to "real" increases *automatically* adjusted for price changes is liable to vary over time and between countries, largely depending on whether the economy has been subject to rapid inflation within recent experience. Second, the price/output response of the economy to autonomous shocks is likely to be influenced by the prevalence or absence of provision for automatic indexation of wages. Contrary to the assumptions of general equilibrium theory, wages are not consistently bargained in real terms, and the economic system can be expected to show a differing price/output response to autonomous shocks at different times. Moreover, even when pervasive indexation does exist, the fact that indexation provisions typically provide incomplete protection against price increases and are implemented with a considerable lag, means that real wage bargaining as assumed in the theory does not apply. These and other issues relating to indexation are treated in Chapter 8.

"Rational" Resistance to Wage Reductions

It has been suggested that in many sectors of the advanced economy, employees are able to resist the hiring of additional workers at less than the going wage, and that this, together with the various obstacles preventing new concerns from entering the industry, enables wage earners to resist reductions in wages accorded under existing contracts except in dire economic conditions.

---

[69]Garbarino (1960, pp. 1–2) describes the costs of wage negotiations which predispose U.S. managements to seek multiyear settlements as follows:

"...each contract negotiation has the potential of upsetting the external balance of power in the relationships with union leaders, political leaders, government agencies, customers and competitors. This consideration is reinforced by the intraorganizational turmoil that may result from the negotiations. For a period of months before the expiration of the current contract the union and the company may be engaged in a public debate over the anticipated issues in bargaining. Actual negotiations typically occupy the two months before the contract deadline and may run beyond that date in an atmosphere of increasing tension, sporadic stoppages, and decreasing work efficiency. Even if a strike is avoided, the changes in the new contract have to be integrated into the operating practices of several levels of supervision and adjudication of differences of interpretation through the grievance procedure may have to be undertaken."

Resistance to wage reductions of course lessens firms' willingness to lower prices when there is a reduction in nominal demand. However, if the restriction on entry has hitherto been associated with favorable markups, a high rate of investment in new techniques, and rapid replacement of capital, the enterprise has the option—when faced with a fall in demand—of maintaining the same markup and prices and realizing lower aggregate returns on smaller sales *or* of lowering markups and prices in the hope of realizing higher, or about the same, aggregate returns as in the first case through larger sales. Hence, given the importance which the firm attaches to expanding or maintaining its share of the market, it does not follow that refusal to accept a wage cut will necessarily lead to lower output and employment *within the enterprise* than acceptance of a cut. Wage earners in the enterprise therefore need not fear that resisting a wage cut will inevitably pose an increased risk of the loss of their jobs in the first instance: that is, unless aggregate demand conditions become highly unfavorable. The more probable immediate consequence is a cutback of the firm's investment, and/or a deterioration in its asset position, due to increased borrowing to support continued investment and smaller net expansion of, or even a failure to maintain, its real assets. If so, the reduction in employment occurs outside the enterprise, and by preventing a decline in wages, the typical wage earner secures an increased share in the gross receipts of the enterprise, at the cost of the shareholders.

Employment within the industry may contract because hiring practices become tighter, or because weak firms go out of business. But in large enterprises that experience a gradual reduction of output, natural wastage and possibly encouragement of early retirements may suffice to protect the existing work force from redundancy. It is not clear, therefore, how much weight the existing regular employees of large enterprises should, or do, give to the risk of a prospective reduction of employment opportunities within the enterprise if they insist on maintaining their actual or relative nominal wages. Against this, there is a clear risk of reducing real wages if they accept a cut in nominal wages or a markedly lower rate of wage increase than wage earners generally are securing. In these circumstances, should employees consider that the probable reduction in real wages will yield a counterbalancing benefit, in improved employment prospects? Proponents of this argument often seem to assume that, despite the assumption of maximizing behavior on the part of the individuals, wage earners or individual unions are altruists who care about the general level of employment.[70] In actual fact, the overall level of employment may only be taken into account directly in wage negotiations under centralized bargaining, as in the Scandinavian countries, or where industry-by-industry settlements are negotiated by individual unions within a strongly coordinated union movement, as in the Federal Republic of Germany.

Response of the Economy to Deflation

The price setting/wage bargaining context of the large enterprise sector has a vital bearing on how the advanced economy responds to a deflationary monetary shock. Output and employment within large enterprises is likely to be better maintained than their previous (high) rate of capital replacement and net investment. The principal casualty in a downturn therefore is business investment, along with housing investment; the reduction in investment, of course, involves a further weakening of demand for other sectors' output. In a closed economy an attempt to raise output and restore profits in this situation by lowering money wages will be ineffective because its immediate effect will be to lower aggregate demand, further weakening the incentives for investment. The same will be true if all the industrial countries, or all those in a group trading very largely among themselves such as the EEC, attempt such a policy.

Lowering wages could only be counted upon to prevent the reduction in nominal demand affecting the level of real output and employment in the unreal case of perfect competition, where all prices were absolutely flexible and responded instantaneously to any change in demand. In the real world, a general lowering of the level of nominal wages and salaries (if it can be realized) will reduce the level of aggregate demand and real output unless any resulting decline in wage and salary earners' real expenditure is *simultaneously* offset by increased real purchases, and higher investment spending, by businesses, shareholders, and holders of financial assets. This is a most unlikely contingency on practical grounds, even if these groups did not tend to hold back purchases in the expectation of price declines.[71] Of course, once the reduction of wages and salaries has an impact in

[70]See, for example, Gordon (1981, p. 526): "Each worker may believe that a uniform wage reduction would help boost output in a recession [which may not be true], yet no single worker has the power to convince all employed workers to accept an immediate wage cut" [Why should he, if his own job looks safe?].

[71]Kalecki (1966, Chapter 5) and (1971).

lowering sales and increasing layoffs, its effect in bringing down aggregate demand will be reinforced by precautionary reductions in expenditure by those fearing unemployment or reduced business earnings.

The goal of restoring investment and output may be realized, however, if an expansion of nominal demand can be achieved without an offsetting rise in nominal wages; and if contagious business expectations of a recovery prompt a higher rate of investment, inducing a further rise in nominal demand, higher utilization of output, and higher aggregate profits, associated with a decline in *unit* labor costs. However, there need be no automatic tendency for output and employment to recover to its previous (or a "natural") level because "correct" price expectations must be re-established if a stable monetary policy is pursued. The monetarist scenario relies upon a steady stream of technical progress to provide the incentive for an increase in investment to ensure this outcome, but it has been suggested here that the opening up of new technical possibilities is itself not independent of the ruling rate of profit.

Need for a More Realistic Theoretical Framework

The workings of an advanced economy described here do not constitute a system to which the underlying postulates of general equilibrium theory—basic to most current economic thinking—can be applied as a useful simplification, in the analysis of developments over the short to medium run.

Far from being a generally applicable theory, the general equilibrium model is a rigorous and illuminating analysis of an abstract special case. Conclusions deriving from the model are apt to be misleading when dealing with a system in which relative prices and quantities traded are not tightly determined in competitive markets in response to a largely invariant structure of real demands and supplies.

In neoclassical theory, the observed stability of the relative price structure results from the consistent maximizing behavior of great numbers of individual suppliers and users of products and factor services, in markets over which they individually have no control. Relative prices are assumed to be flexible, the price of each product or wage for the job being freely determined by changes in demand and supply. Under the conditions assumed, slight changes in relative prices rapidly elicit equilibrating changes in the composition of real supply and demand, so that changes in the relative price structure do not persist unless there is a fundamental change in real supply conditions or the composition of demand.[72]

The industrial economy, as we know it, exhibits rather stable relative price (or wage) relationships and shares of profits and wages in national income. But contrary to the neoclassical assumptions, such economies are characterized by considerable rigidity of prices and wages, especially in large enterprise production and in organized labor markets, and by sticky and erratic responses of prices and wages to changes in aggregate demand. The observed stability of the relative price and wage structure seems to arise in large part from causes "extraneous" to the postulates of the general equilibrium model, and from behavior which it is difficult to represent in terms of optimizing individuals. The stability of relative wages over considerable areas of some economies in particular seems to derive in large part from a preference for "equitable" wage relationships. In practice, this generally involves the maintenance of customary differentials because a sharp rise in another group's income is seen either as a threat, or of itself as a reduction in others' "welfare." These characteristics of pricing behavior are closely associated with the fact that in many markets, suppliers and/or purchasers possess some degree of market power to influence prices and quantities traded. This often originates in the scope for individual buyers and sellers to improve their gains by acting in concert, particularly given the characteristics of production and distribution in advanced economies, under economies of scale and technical innovation. While the power to influence prices or quantities traded also often derives from regulation and controls, it is not solely occasioned by such interventions, as is often contended.

If disequilibrium prices and heavy unemployment can persist for considerable periods, it would seem that this cannot be explained solely by incorrect expectations of a determinate general level of prices, but arises because the basic assumptions of the model do not apply.[73] The view of the economy as readily tending to attain a general equilibrium therefore is misleading. The more realistic paradigm is that of an economy prone to fluctuations, in which there is reason to

---

[72]When it is *assumed* that relative prices are flexible, it is also assumed *ex hypothesi* that the general level of prices, or the rate of inflation depends solely on the quantity, or changes in the quantity, of money.

[73]Suppose, for example, that despite the existence of competitive markets, because of incorrect price expectations, prices were not adjusted after a sizable reduction in the nominal quantity of money. Any enterprise that did reduce its prices when it observed that quantities sold in the market were declining would increase its sales, and any unemployed wage earner who accepted less than the going wage would get a job. Incorrect price or wage expectations could not persist once anyone adjusted his expectations.

expect that the price/real output response to changes in nominal demand will *not* be consistently the same over time, or symmetrical as between accelerations and decelerations of nominal demand. Chapter 11 contains an account of the industrial world as an economy with these characteristics. Once the assumptions concerning the nature of markets and prevalence of optimizing behavior are relaxed, we are no longer dealing with a system whose inherent properties can be counted upon to generate the "optimum" allocation of existing resources and development of resources over time, provided that monetary stability is ensured. Instead we have a system in which relative prices, incomes, and demands are determined very largely by countervailing monopoly forces, which are subject to change, and which are influenced inter alia by changes in the rate of expansion of aggregate nominal demand. This is not a world in which it is possible to assume that the underlying trend rate of real output growth and capital formation, or the realized rate of technical progress is independent of the aggregate demand conditions maintained in the system over a period of years.

Relation Between Unemployment and Inflation in a Closed Economy

To conclude this chapter, let us take another look at the relation between unemployment and inflation in a closed economy. If a consistent, steady expansion of nominal demand were maintained, one could expect that there would be some low level of unemployment at which the rate of inflation must tend to accelerate as difficulty in hiring labor induced the bidding-up or pushing up of wages. This, or lower levels, of unemployment could not be sustained if the same rate of nominal demand expansion was maintained and was confidently expected to be maintained. Similarly, there would be an opposite limit, at some very high level of unemployment, at which point labor would be unable to prevent downward pressure on wages, and at which the growth of nominal demand and the rate of inflation would tend to decelerate. This or a higher level of unemployment could not be sustained, if the same rate of nominal demand expansion was maintained.[74]

[74]It should be emphasized that the stabilizing properties of the system under extreme labor market conditions require the maintenance of steady demand expansion in the face of accelerating or decelerating wage inflation. As there are likely to be tendencies for the expansion of credit and rise in nominal demand to speed up, or slow down in these circumstances, the system would be prone to periods of sustained low unemployment with accelerating inflation and periods of very high unemployment with decelerating inflation, unless deliberate policies were implemented to maintain the steady demand expansion by restricting credit expansion or promoting demand for credit.

The stationary state long-run unemployment position, if it existed, would lie somewhere between the two limits. If there had ever been a change in the rate of nominal demand expansion, the stationary state unemployment/inflation locus would probably be influenced by the course of demand before the steady expansion of nominal demand was established. More realistically, however, even after steady demand expansion had been maintained for a period of years, the economy would still be subject to a continuing shifting of the aggregate level and structure of output and employment, reflecting the consequences of earlier changes in demand, the extent to which those consequences were accommodated or constrained by the now stable demand policy, and the effects of past and recent autonomous shocks such as political events.

Suppose, for example, that the rate of nominal demand expansion had been fluctuating within moderate limits for a number of years, and had been such as to promote a moderate average rate of price inflation and a similar moderate *expected* rate of inflation. Now suppose that there is a marked acceleration of nominal demand expansion. One may expect that the extent to which the acceleration is reflected in higher inflation or higher real growth will depend on the scale of the acceleration relative to the average rate of expansion recently maintained. For various reasons set out in Chapter 7, a marked acceleration is likely to produce *proportionately* more price effect and relatively less effect in raising real output than a slight increase, which may be wholly reflected in higher real output and employment, with no change in the inflation rate. The opposite case of a sharp deceleration would be likely to produce *proportionately* more effect upon real output and unemployment and relatively less effect on prices than a slight change mainly associated with a squeezing of profit margins and lowering of auction market commodity prices.

One must therefore distinguish between a slight acceleration of nominal demand, which may be associated with a reduction of unemployment without an acceleration of inflation, and sharp acceleration, which may give rise to a somewhat larger reduction of unemployment accompanied by an acceleration of inflation. Reinforcing this distinction is the fact that there is some threshold for increases in consumer prices, which, if exceeded for more than a limited time, will promote explicit or de facto indexation of wages,[75] producing a closer link between the recent rate of price inflation and the rate of wage increase. The lags in the process imply that even if a marked

[75]See Chapter 8, p. 181.

acceleration of nominal demand is soon reversed, deflation will be initially associated with higher nominal wage increases, limiting the deceleration of price inflation, despite declining profits and commodity prices.

By strengthening the response of $\dot{w}$ to $\dot{p}$, the occurrence of rapid price inflation causes the flat range of the Phillips curve to shift upward. In subsequent periods, $\dot{p}$ will tend to decelerate gradually because of the squeeze on profit margins, and the lowering of commodity (auction market) prices and of real asset prices, influenced by declining real output and higher nominal interest rates, and because of moderating wage increases; but $\dot{w}$ will still be relatively well maintained because of lagged price effects. In effect, the flat short-term curve will shift slowly downward under the slower expansion of nominal demand: but that response will be weakened if there has been a prior experience of rapid price inflation. The effort to check a rapid price inflation that has taken hold, by a very sharp deceleration of nominal demand, is therefore liable to be very costly in terms of unemployment, real output losses, and reduced investment. If there is a continued effort to bring down inflation by decelerating monetary expansion, the effect will continue to be felt in increasing unemployment and reduced real output growth, up to the point where very heavy unemployment, underutilization of capacity, and mounting business failures induce a dramatic change in the rate of inflation by provoking a crisis of confidence, intensifying price competition and lowering wage claims, and/or strengthening employers' resistance to granting wage increases. At that point inflation may come down very rapidly, but there may be no tendency for a speedy recovery of investment, activity, and employment. The economy remains prone to steady-state growth, under price stability or inflation, at close to the lower-limit employment position.

7

Demand Expansion, Inflation, and Real Output Growth Under Imperfect Competition

This chapter discusses certain aspects of the workings of an industrial economy which cause changes in the rate of expansion of nominal demand to be reflected to a varying degree in price changes or in changes in real output growth.[1]

Unsymmetrical Response to Acceleration or Deceleration of Demand

It was suggested in Chapter 5 that treating the industrial economies as a single closed economy under fixed exchange rates, one could regard aggregate broad money growth $\Delta M_{t'-1}$, as an indicator of the demand forces promoting a foreseeable expansion of nominal spending ΔYN^e in period t.[2] As a first approximation, the rate of increase in the GDP deflator ΔPY^e_{t+1} could be expected to depend on the extent to which ΔYN^e_t exceeds β the "secular" tendency for real output to grow from year to year under a steady expansion of nominal demand. That is

$$\Delta PY^e_{t+1} = \Delta YN^e_t - \beta$$

[1]This chapter is based in part on Braun (1981).

[2]See Chapter 5, pp. 108–15. For simplicity it is assumed here that there is no secular tendency for real money holdings to increase faster than GNP, i.e., $\mu = 0$.

and foreseeable real output growth

$$\begin{aligned}\Delta YR^e_{t+1} &= \Delta YN^e_{t+1} - \Delta PY^e_{t+1} \\ &= \beta + (\Delta YN^e_{t+1} - \Delta YN^e_t) \\ &= \beta + (\Delta M_{t'} - \Delta M_{t'-1}).\end{aligned}$$

That is to say because of the lagged response of prices and costs to the rate of expansion of nominal demand, real output tends to be higher under an accelerating rate of demand expansion than under a stable or decelerating one, and real output is likely to be lower than the "secular" rate under a deflationary policy slowing the expansion of nominal expenditure. However, the maintenance of higher than "secular" real growth involves accelerating inflation. The factors determining the size of β are considered later in this chapter.

This preliminary formulation ignores any actual constraints on real output growth or wage and price flexibility. Now consider the constraints on ΔYR and ΔPY.

In practice there is obviously an upper limit to the annual rate of output expansion under peacetime conditions, because of real supply constraints and logistics.[3] Even starting from a low level of capacity utilization, there will be a physical limit to the expansion of real output that can be achieved at short notice from one year to the next. Such a physical limit is likely to be more stringent for the industrial countries as a group, than for any one country, owing to their interdependence and common reliance on international transportation, sources of primary commodities, and suppliers of specialized equipment. In practice, however, owing to the prevalence of imperfect competition, and restrictions on entry, it is the exercise of market power to push up prices and wages in the face of rising demand and tightening supplies, or to maintain wages and prices in the face of declining nominal expenditure, that often sets the upper limit on aggregate real output growth or enforces downward flexibility of real output. The effect of physical constraints on the expansion of real output is felt largely through their impact in enhancing or inducing the exploitation of market power.

Thus one may postulate, first, that under normal business conditions actual (and hence expected) real output growth cannot exceed the "secular" growth rate by more than a certain margin z, which is not large for reasons that are explained below. Hence,

$$\Delta YR,\ \Delta YR^e \leq \beta + z$$

[3]Under wartime emergency conditions, some constraints can be overcome by exceptional measures and incentives.

Therefore, if

$$\Delta YN_t^e > \Delta PY_t^e + \beta + z,$$

that is if $\Delta M_{t'-1} - \Delta M_{t'-2} > z$ when $\Delta YN_{t-1} = \Delta YN_{t-1}^e$,

$$\Delta PY_t > \Delta PY_t^e.$$

That is to say, an acceleration of the expansion of nominal demand that exceeds the maximum feasible rate of real output expansion in the short run will result in a more than proportionate acceleration of the rate of inflation in the subsequent period.[4]

Second, one may postulate that there is usually some downward limit to the year-to-year change in the GDP deflator, because most nominal wages and salaries are fixed by contract, and are rarely adjusted downward. Thus, there is in effect a floor to the rate of inflation if the "secular" rate of real output growth is to be maintained. This limit is inversely related to ξ, the rate at which productivity is tending to rise with technical progress,[5] so ΔPY^e, ΔPY cannot decline by more than minus ξ if real output growth β is to be secured. There is some minimum rate of nominal demand expansion necessary for the achievement of the secular rate of growth of real output and productivity.

These equations represent a system under which, in the short run, changes in prices or in real output reflect the interplay between two changeable flows: the flow of nominal spending, which is responding to changes in the stance of monetary and fiscal policies, and the potential aggregate flow of real output, which under given underlying conditions and abstracting from the influence of financial policies, is responding to natural forces and technical progress, occurring gradually over time or as sudden shocks.[6] At any point in time, there is a

---

[4]Conceivably, there may also be a slight tendency for a delayed expansion of nominal demand with ΔYN_t falling below ΔYN_t^e as order books lengthen, keeping down ΔYN_t and resulting in delayed increases in nominal and real expenditure (higher ΔYN_{t+1} and ΔYR_{t+1}). In the opposite circumstances, one may suppose that in a dynamic environment, when new capacity is coming into production and productivity is rising rapidly, real output growth may not respond immediately to a sharp restriction of nominal demand leading to involuntary investment in unsold inventories in the hands of producers and distributors.

[5]Note that ξ could be negative due to declining productivity resulting for example from exhaustion or increasing scarcity of natural resources.

[6] Since the real output response to underlying conditions such as population growth and scope for improvements in technique is not independent of financial conditions in a monetary economy, it is misleading to view the trend growth of real output over the long term solely as the outcome of real factors, as the neoclassical and the monetarist approach supposes. To do so is to treat the stream of real output as a river, which no matter what interventions are made in its course always reaches the same rate of flow later downstream. In fact it is more reasonable to suppose that, no matter how long a stretch is considered, the average rate of flow will be affected in some measure by any interventions decreasing or increasing the flow before or during the stretch under study. The present flow of real output has to be seen as a stream determined by both natural factors and macroeconomic policies, upstream and here and now.

certain tendency for real supply to rise (or fall) as a consequence of the opening up or exhaustion of natural resources, climatic factors, the growth of the labor force, and growth of the capital stock (including the stock of human skills, which reflects the recent rate of investment in physical capital and education and training) and the recent rate of improvement in techniques. However, the tendency for real output to increase (or decline) is also influenced by the extent to which competitive forces (including those stemming from efforts of enterprises to acquire a larger share of an oligopoly market or to profit from economies of scale) tend to restrain the exercise of market power; that is, to prevent enterprises, professional groups, or unions from responding to higher nominal demand by raising prices by more than the going rate of inflation, or wages by more than the inflation rate plus the rise in productivity.

Differing Response to Marked or Gradual Changes in Demand

One may suppose that the lagged relation—between the rate of increase of nominal expenditure and the rate of inflation in industrial countries—comes about because a change in nominal expenditure tends to be accommodated by a change in real output *while* the change in nominal expenditure sets in motion wage and price adjustments that take time to be realized.[7] This is so both because many prices and most wages are governed by contracts that are renegotiated at fairly lengthy intervals and time is required for renegotiation, and because the dissemination of price and wage increases across the national, or international, economy takes time.[8]

Price Behavior in "Auction" and "Administered" Markets

The effect of a change in the rate of expansion in nominal demand is first reflected in the rate of price increase in auction markets, where prices of goods or services are freely determined by demand and supply under competitive conditions (such as markets for many

[7]Blinder (1982).

[8]Wage and salary increases are commonly negotiated at annual intervals—on the basis of less than up-to-date information on prices and profits. If indexation applies it is usually implemented with some delay, also on the basis of less than up-to-date price data. Consequently, unit labor costs and ΔPY are liable to reflect changes in nominal demand with a considerable lag. In the aggregate relation between changes in nominal expenditure and changes in GNP deflators for the industrial countries as a group, the lag will be extended by the time which it takes for changes in expenditure in one country to influence wage and price developments in other countries.

primary commodities, for simple manufactures not requiring substantial capital investment or the use of advanced techniques, and for casual labor). The speed of the expansion in nominal demand, relative to the rate at which real output is tending to rise for structural reasons, influences the market power of businesses and labor to push up prices and wages within the administered (fix-price) markets.[9]

Prices of primary products and lightly processed goods entering into world trade[10] respond more swiftly and sharply to changes in the rate of expansion of nominal demand in the industrial countries than does the price of their own output, as measured by the GDP deflator. Furthermore, since the value of GDP is net of the cost of imports, the deflator does not reflect the immediate direct effect of changes in the cost of imports upon the level of consumer or wholesale prices. For this reason, and also by reason of their coverage, the cost of living and wholesale price indices are more sensitive to changes in the rate of expansion of nominal demand, and are likely to respond more quickly, than the level of unit wage costs or the GDP deflator.[11]

Changes in the nominal price of national output of industrial countries—that is, in their GDP deflators—are predominantly determined in administered markets, since prices for only a relatively small fraction of their GDP are determined in auction markets. In Western Europe and to a lesser extent in Japan, the movement of wages and salaries is dominated by developments in organized labor markets, domestic agricultural prices are not freely determined, and the great bulk of auction market primary products is imported. In the United States and Canada, which are large producers and exporters of auction market primary commodities, some, but not all, agricultural prices are influenced by supply and demand in world markets; and, as also in Japan and Italy, the movement of production costs in general is influenced by wage developments in unorganized labor markets. Even in these countries, however, prices for only a minor fraction of total GDP are freely determined by supply and demand.[12]

In industrial countries, the movement of the GDP deflator largely reflects changes in the level of "normal" average labor cost per unit of

---

[9]For a discussion of pricing behavior in administered markets and of the role of auction markets and administered markets in the international economy, see Hicks (1974). See also Nordhaus (1976, pp. 59–64) and Braun (1976b, pp. 30–31).

[10]That is excluding agricultural commodities traded at fixed prices within the EEC.

[11]Primary products and other "auction market" goods having a larger weight in the indices than in the total value of GDP.

[12]This description suggests that in North America and Japan the movement of the GDP deflators may be more directly and swiftly affected by changes in the rate of expansion of nominal demand than in Western Europe.

output: that is, changes in average nominal wages per unit of real output after abstracting from the effect of cyclical variations in the level of real output upon labor cost, which are largely offset by opposite fluctuations in profits per unit of output. Nevertheless, highly responsive auction market prices play a vital role in causing the general level of administered labor costs and prices to respond to changes in the rate of expansion of nominal demand.[13]

Prices of freely traded primary commodities vary strongly with changes in the rate of expansion of demand in the industrial countries because the short-run price elasticities of supply and demand typically are low and because fluctuations in the demand for industrial output are associated with sharper fluctuations in demand for primary products owing to changes in the incentive to hold commodity stocks. A rise or fall in demand for commodities typically produces a large change in prices both because supply is more or less fixed in the short to medium term by such factors as annual harvests, long tree crop cycles, difficulty of changing, and real costs of reducing, mining output,[14] and because of the high cost of holding stocks of perishable and bulky commodities and the inability of a myriad small agricultural suppliers to influence prices. In an industrial country, a restrictive shift in demand policy leads to inventory accumulation of manufactures and a drawing down of commodity stocks, followed by cutbacks of industrial output. At the downturn, declining profits, high

[13]Kaldor (1976) provides an account of the processes involved: "the rise in commodity prices has a very powerful inflationary effect operating on the *cost* side. The rise in the price of basic materials and fuels is passed through the various stages of production into the final price with an exaggerated effect—it gets 'blown up' on the way by a succession of percentage additions to prime costs which mean, in effect, an increase in cash margins at each stage. This causes (initially) a rise in the share of profits in the value added by manufacturing which in itself is a powerful factor (in countries where trade union power is strong) in causing pressure for wage increases. Added to this is the price-induced rise in wages caused by what Sir John Hicks called 'Real Wage Resistance'—the reluctance of workers to accept a cut in their standard of living (which is not paralleled by similar reluctance to accept a rise). . . . The industrial sector with its superior market power, resists any compression of its real income by countering the rise in commodity prices through a cost-induced inflation of industrial prices" (pp. 706–707). Kaldor considers the basic problem to be the difficulty of "securing continuing adjustment between the growth of availabilities and the growth in requirements for primary products in a manner conducive to the harmonious development of the world economy" (p. 707). He does not suggest, as is done here, that any rapid expansion in nominal demand in the industrial world is likely to set off cost pressures in the administered sectors through its disproportionate and swift effect on auction market prices. In his opinion, "the inflation in industrial countries was not the result of excess demand, either for labour or for the products of labour: if anything, it was the result of excess demand for primary products (food and raw materials) which is quite a different thing" (p. 706, footnote 1).

[14]Because mines have to be kept open to avoid flooding or labor is hired by the year or longer.

interest rates, and falling commodity prices increase the inducement to run down stocks and cut back purchases of materials. Strengthening demand necessitates rebuilding commodity stocks quickly and prospective increases in interest rates and commodity prices also promote speedy rebuilding of stocks.[15] In effect, therefore, commodity prices tend to fluctuate sharply with changes in the rate of expansion of demand in the industrial countries, and changes in commodity prices lead changes in industrial output, costs, and prices.

Role of the Consumer and Wholesale Price Indices

The fact that the consumer and wholesale price indices are sensitive to changes in the price of primary commodities and foodstuffs and tend to "lead" and condition the changes in administered wages and salaries and industrial prices causes the indices to play a major role in disseminating the effect of an acceleration in demand from auction markets to administered markets.[16] Because of this effect, a marked rise in commodity prices—such as that due to the oil price increases of 1973 and 1979—is likely to be associated with a larger, and swifter than usual, rise in the level of nominal unit labor costs and in the deflator, together with a smaller than usual rise in real output. In the opposite case, rapidly growing world supplies of primary products and the declining trend of their prices in the 1950s and early 1960s served to facilitate increases in real output rather than prices, by moderating the rise in the consumer and wholesale price indices, thereby lessening the impact of increases in nominal demand in raising the general level of wages and prices of domestic output.[17]

---

[15]See Hicks (1950).

[16]An acceleration of the rise in the consumer price index induces larger wage increases under indexation schemes and tends to increase the size of wage claims and strengthen union militancy when negotiations become due, and vice versa. The rate of increase in the wholesale price index or its constituent series also serves as a yardstick in generating common expectations of an acceleration, or deceleration, of the rate of price increase among industrialists generally or in particular sectors. Furthermore, if markups are maintained or increased, as is likely if the expansion of nominal demand is sustained, an acceleration of the wholesale price index will be associated with rising nominal profits in those industries in which auction market commodities constitute a major part of costs (such as food processing, basic metal manufacturing, and food distribution). Thus rising auction market prices are likely to go with favorable wage bargaining conditions in a range of basic industries. Even if the initial level of capacity utilization is low over the economy as a whole, and if firms do not raise their markups on normal costs, the acceleration of demand will be reflected in rising total profits as higher capacity utilization lowers overheads per unit of output. Hence, wage bargaining conditions become more favorable for unions.

[17]This description suggests that the scope for expanding the supply of auction market primary products may set an upper limit on the range of moderate steady-state rates of expansion of nominal demand, over which there is some positive association between the rate and the expansion of real output and above which higher rates of demand expansion are merely reflected in higher inflation. See concluding section of Chapter 6.

Influence of the Rate of Acceleration of Demand

Largely irrespective of the existing level of unemployment and capacity utilization, a sharp acceleration of the expansion of nominal demand is liable to provoke a faster rise in the cost of living, to create conditions favoring large wage increases in some industries that may set the pattern for wage claims in other sectors, and to improve wage bargaining conditions for employees generally. The force of cost of living effects arising from auction market price increases, and of relative wage effects, as well as the extent of the strengthening in the wage bargaining position of labor in many sectors, depends on the speed of the acceleration in nominal expenditure. The vitally important consequence of this is that the rate of change in the overall price of domestic output becomes in part a lagged function of the acceleration in the rate of expansion of nominal expenditure, rather than a function of the level of capacity utilization or unemployment, as postulated in neo-Keynesian theory. The implications of this for the working of the system have been sketched in the last section of Chapter 6.

"Secular" Versus "Structural" Potential Real Output Growth

It was suggested earlier that, as a first approximation, the rate of inflation in the price of industrial countries' output could be taken to reflect with a lag the excess of the rate of expansion in nominal demand over the "secular" potential growth rate β at which real output tends to rise from year to year under a steady expansion of demand. Let us now consider what determines β.

At any period, one may suppose that there exists some *structural* potential for real output to grow annually (or conceivably to decline) which depends on supply factors such as (1) the availability of additional agricultural land and the discovery or exhaustion of natural resources; (2) the natural growth of the labor force, including the effects of changes in the age/sex composition of the population, and the effects of long-term social trends influencing the participation rates of various age/sex groups; (3) scientific progress making possible advances in technique increasing labor productivity or efficiency in the use of resources and fixed capital; and (4) the past level of investment in capital and training which determines the age structure and level of the capital stock and the skills of the labor force. (Prior investment determines the level of investment that is needed to prevent declining efficiency of the capital stock or shortages of skilled manpower, etc., and also influences the rate at which technical advances can be realized in practice.)

In a perfectly competitive economy, one could assume that, in the absence of political shocks and government intervention, real output would tend to grow at a rate determined by such structural factors, with employment at the level corresponding to the full or natural rate of unemployment, and the general price level responding to changes in the money supply.[18] Thus, in the general equilibrium theory, which is essentially concerned with the allocation of existing resources, not with the dynamics of economic growth, the actual trend rate of real output is taken to correspond to the structurally determined, potential real output growth rate. It is postulated that the actual level of real output can diverge only briefly from the structural potential level under the influence of changes in the rate of expansion of nominal expenditure or autonomous real shocks.[19]

Dropping the assumption of perfect competition, one may suppose that, given the structural *potential* for real output growth at any period, there will exist a "secular" rate of real output growth under stable demand management, representing the growth rate that can be realized without an acceleration of inflation. The actual trend growth of real output will correspond to the "secular" growth rate *provided* a more or less steady expansion of nominal demand is maintained, *and* there is no marked change in competitive conditions.

In order to understand the difference between the "structural" and the "secular" rates of real output growth, it will be helpful to see what each implies, assuming for simplicity an unchanging labor force and supply of natural resources, so that in either case the trend of real output only reflects productivity developments.

In the competitive steady-state, the rise in productivity, π^c, would be the outcome of the *unvarying* competitive market response to structurally determined changes in relative prices and factor costs.[20]

[18]See footnote 20.

[19]"Monetarists are [now] willing to agree that factors such as the activities of OPEC, unexpected real shocks, or sudden changes in the level of indirect taxes, can affect the behaviour of the price level 'temporarily' against the background of long-run trends determined by monetary factors" (Laidler, 1981, p. 9). However, factors such as "the activities of OPEC" are inconsistent with the underlying postulates of their model of the economic system.

[20]With given consumer preferences, including preferences for employment yielding purchasing power versus leisure restricting purchasing power, the stability of the competitive model requires that unimpeded competition in all markets should ensure that maximizing behavior results in optimizing "utility" for all individuals. With given real resources, real income and the distribution of income and employment are determined by profit maximization and preferences for goods or leisure. At that "full employment" level of real income, the level of saving versus consumption demand (reflecting consumer preference) determines the share of investment in total output through its influence upon the real interest rate.

The rate of productivity increase would be solely determined by consumer preferences and technical and scientific advances. One may then conceive of a self-sustaining steady-state growth of real output under an autonomous, and presumably rather stable rate of scientific progress. Under imperfect competition however, even if a steady demand policy were to be maintained, the rate of technical progress—and more specifically the rate at which innovation proceeds in different areas of production—could not be taken to be solely determined by consumer preferences and an autonomous "technological progress." The trend growth of productivity over a period of years would be affected by the prevailing but not immutable, changeable but not "ephemeral," distribution of market power within the system.[21] The extent of market power would be liable to be affected by autonomous events.

Relaxing the assumption of unchanging natural conditions of supply and allowing for political changes, it is not difficult to see that the "secular" rate of real output growth, β, may differ widely at different periods, depending not only on differences in the growth of population and natural resources and autonomous advances in technique but also on the influence of the conditions of imperfect competition prevailing. Any major change in natural conditions, political institutions, national boundaries, and conditions governing international trade or the determination of exchange rates, is liable to influence the working of the economic system and hence the take-up of scientific advances. The influence of some of these factors upon productivity growth since World War II was referred to in Chapter 5.

Assuming that atomistic competition could exist in all markets, the existence of impediments to competition and the concomitant possession of market power by some groups and individuals would represent interference with the optimal allocation of *existing* resources for

[21]Friedman (1968, p. 8) defined a "normal" secular rate of real output growth as "a rate that can be *indefinitely maintained* so long as capital formation, technological improvements, etc."—*and*, as is made clear later "the actual structural characteristics of the labor and commodity markets, including market imperfections"—"remain on their long-run trends" (italics added). The "normal" secular rate of real growth and the "natural rate of unemployment" "would be ground out by the Walrasian system of general equilibrium equations," capital formation and technological improvements proceeding at a steady rate under the *consistent* effect of competitive forces limited by market imperfections. In practice, however, the influence of noncompetitive forces in the system is essentially unstable, and may change markedly in the conditions created by major autonomous events such as wars and revolutions, or by prolonged destabilizing policies. In the absence of powerful shocks of this kind, one may suppose that though the influence of noncompetitive conditions typically may be tending to strengthen or weaken gradually over time, the secular rate of real output growth will remain approximately unchanged for some years at a time.

maximizing present individual "utility." However, these very circumstances may serve to promote a high rate of real investment and innovation.[22] It cannot be assumed that the development and application of new techniques would proceed as fast or faster under a more competitive system. In other words, the rate of productivity growth, π^{t}, which is associated with "secular" real output growth of β under imperfect competition, *may* be higher than π^{c} (the "structural" growth of productivity under perfect competition). Hence imperfect competition *may* create the possibility of a faster rise in aggregate real income and consumption over time. On the other hand, the imperfectly competitive system lacks the equilibrating properties which serve to ensure equality of supply and demand in the abstract competitive model and which justify the view of the economy as tending to maintain steady-state growth with full employment, provided there are no exogenous disturbances, such as government policy interventions. A more rapid average rate of technological advance over the longer term under imperfect competition may occur in bursts of investment activity followed by slowdowns of overcapacity and reduced rates of investment. Furthermore, prevalence of imperfect competition implies that, as was emphasized earlier in this chapter, the actual trend of real output and productivity growth over a period of years or decades will not be independent of the demand policies pursued over the period, as is commonly assumed in monetarist writings.

Productivity Growth and the Level of Employment

Let us now try to see how productivity growth is likely to be affected by changes in the rate of expansion of nominal demand, given imperfectly competitive markets and downward wage inflexibility. Let us first consider what is the minimum rate at which nominal demand must rise in an economy with a growing labor force, if the unemployment rate is not to increase and the technical potential for an increase in productivity is to be fully realized. and then consider what will happen if nominal demand rises at less than this rate.

A Crucial Problem

One major conceptual and practical difficulty must be mentioned at the outset. This concerns the fact that under imperfect competition, the measure of productivity growth is problematic since the weighting

[22]See Chapter 6, "Influence of 'Ephemeral' Monopoly in a Dynamic World."

of different outputs as shares in total "real" output reflects the degree of market power exercised by the producers. If the relative remuneration of factors in different employments is systematically influenced by noncompetitive conditions in some markets, the assumption that observed relative prices may be taken as "good approximations" to their "utility maximizing" long-run competitive values is unjustified. It is then not possible to postulate that value added in different activities represents a measure of "real" output in the sense of relative "utility" created.[23] In calculating real output and overall productivity growth, relative "real" output in different employments is taken to be the relative *nominal* value added in the base year. Thus for instance, if the pharmaceutical industry is able to keep the value of per capita output high by means of exclusive patents, real output per capita in pharmaceuticals is taken to be high. Though this difficulty is fundamental, we shall ignore it here.

Minimum Nominal Demand Expansion to Avoid Rising Unemployment and/or Losses in Productivity

Let λ be the natural growth rate of the labor force with constant participation rates. Then, if rates of pay are inflexible downward in the short run, the wage bill must rise by at least λ percent, from one year to the next, if the same unemployment rate is to be maintained with unchanged participation rates and an unchanged distribution of employment at going wage rates. We may start by assuming there is no current improvement in technique. If we suppose that a reduction in profit margins will not occur without an increase in unemployment or a reduction of productivity due to underutilization of employed workers, the rate of monetary expansion and the increase in nominal expenditure must be at least λ if unemployment/underemployment is not to increase. In this case, the general level of prices cannot fall ($\Delta PY \geqslant 0$), and real output will rise by λ or less. Now suppose that real output would rise by $\lambda + \pi^f$, where π^f is the scope for annual improvement in technique and efficiency with a fixed distribution of employment.[24] When π^f is positive, if profit margins are on average maintained, this implies that the rise in productivity is on average passed on in lower prices, and that in the notation used earlier $\xi = \pi^f$ and ΔPY equals $-\pi^f$ and is negative. But, if not every increase in productivity is passed on in lower prices, this may not be offset by

[23]See Chapter 6, "The Monetarist View of the Economy."

[24]For this condition to be fulfilled, if π^f is not the same in all sectors, the relative rates of productivity growth would have to be exactly matched by changes in the relative growth of product demands and outputs, induced by the requisite relative price changes.

more than proportionate reductions in other cases so that ΔPY would exceed $-\pi^f$ and could be positive. In this case, if the rate of monetary expansion was kept at λ or less, real output would rise by less than $\lambda + \pi^f$, implying some increase in unemployment or underemployment and reduced capacity utilization.

In practice, however, if technical progress is uneven in different sectors, the distribution of employment will probably be tending to change. So even if all rates of pay remain unchanged, the outcome of technical progress, noncompetitive product and factor markets in some sectors, and of consumers' and real investors' preferences will probably be to cause the maintenance of the same rate of unemployment to be associated with changes in the distribution of employment and composition of output that involve some change in average wages per capita and in average profit markups. Even if wage rates remain unchanged as assumed, the maintenance of the same unemployment with average productivity growth π^t and real output growth of $\lambda + \pi^t$ will be associated with a change in average wages per capita of w^t. The minimum rise in the wage bill consistent with the maintenance of the unemployment rate and the achievement of productivity growth π^t will be $\lambda + w^t$. The minimum rate of increase in nominal expenditure to avoid an increase in unemployment, if all profit markups were to remain unchanged, would be $\lambda + (w^t + g)$, where g is the effect of the change in the composition of output in changing the average markup.

Under imperfect competition, markups vary from sector to sector, so that a change in the composition of output may be associated with a change in the average markup, even if all individual markups remain unchanged. But, the assumption that all margins remain fixed is much less realistic than the assumption that money wages are inflexible downward in the short run. One may suppose however that, although particular profit margins are changing as a result of technical progress, the average markup does not decline unless unemployment is rising. Moreover, since the *average* markup is a fairly small fraction of the wages and salaries bill, a slight change in the average markup will be reflected in a very small value for g.

In this example, $\lambda + (w^t + g)$ represents the minimum rise in expenditure necessary to maintain the same unemployment rate and realize productivity growth π^t over the coming year, and ΔPY probably cannot be less than $(w^t + g) - \pi^t$ if unemployment is not to increase. That is to say, if technical progress and the responsive, changing pattern of demand involves a shift of output and employment toward high wage and salary, high markup sectors—characterized by market power and restricted entry—the rise in output per head will be associated with a rise in average wages and salaries per head and, most probably, with an at least proportionate rise in profits (i.e., $g \geqslant 0$).

Given the technical advantages of large-scale enterprises in exploiting many new techniques, and the usually restricted access to major technical breakthroughs, resulting in market power, $(w^t + g)$ seems more likely to be positive than negative under normal circumstances. Conceivably technical progress could be associated with a reduction in the degree of "market power," that is, a reinforcement of the forces of competition within the economy—for example, if it involved the development of efficient small machines making it easier for small enterprises to enter and compete in specialized fields.[25] But the most likely context for rapidly rising productivity associated with a declining degree of market power is not the situation considered here—of technical progress under normal circumstances. The favorable combination is most likely to occur when the normal take-up of technical progress has been impeded by circumstances such as wars and postwar scarcities or by prolonged recession. In these circumstances, the spread of existing techniques to regions of heavy unemployment and disguised unemployment can constitute a strengthening of competitive forces throughout the open sector of the entire industrial world.

Influence of the Rate of Deceleration of Demand

What happens when the nominal expansion of demand is below the minimum needed to maintain employment and productivity growth? Let us start by abstracting from current technical progress. There are then no technically induced changes in the composition of output and employment. Let us first consider the case under conditions of preexisting price stability, where $\Delta PY^e = 0$.

Now, recall that relative "real" output per capita, as measured by nominal value added divided by numbers employed in the base year, is typically high in capital-intensive occupations (notably large-scale enterprises and the production of investment goods) and in sectors exploiting scarce resources, including specialized human skills; and that these are sectors characterized by difficulty of entry for new producers and unionization, or professional organization, of the labor force.

[25]Changes in technique facilitating production in small enterprises (and subcontracting by large enterprises to small-scale producers) are likely to occur when the spread between wages in the large enterprise (unionized) sector and the small enterprise sector is very wide.

If $\Delta YN^e < \lambda$, after having been equal to λ in previous periods, the immediate consequences will be a smaller rise than before in the nominal value of sales; declines in auction market prices; and, in administered markets, rising inventories of unsold products, increasing underutilization of labor and plant, and/or layoffs and higher unemployment, together with associated reductions in profits. There will also be rising unemployment and declining participation rates among new entrants to the labor force. As a result, as time goes on there will be mounting pressure of new entrants in sectors of unrestricted entry, including casual labor and self-employment. Because of the association between high per capita output as *measured* and restricted entry (either for enterprises or labor), the tendency will be for a restricted expansion in nominal demand, relative to the growth of the potential labor force, to result in an increasing proportion of employment in low, as measured, productivity occupations. In this case, abstracting from technological improvements in productivity, the result will be a declining trend in average output per capita over and above any effect of increased underutilization of labor employed in capital-intensive sectors. If π^t was positive, the demand-related changes in the distribution of employment under imperfect competition would have the effect of offsetting part or all of the technical scope for raising productivity.

Thus, a stiff constraint on the expansion of nominal demand, in the face of an increasing labor supply, will tend to strengthen competition in certain less "organized" areas of the economy, causing a tendency for declining wages, prices, and returns to enterprises there. The decline in wages may come about not through reductions in nominal wage rates of existing employees—but through replacement of existing members of the work force by new entrants employed under different conditions: for example, through enterprises going out of business, retirees not being replaced by similarly paid employees, and substitution of existing workers by others (especially new entrants) working on a temporary or part-time basis or employed by subcontractors. Competitive sectors may then make some inroads on the market of the organized, administered price sectors of restricted entry.

One may postulate therefore that, in a closed economy, or in the industrial countries as a group, constraining the rise in nominal demand in the face of rising labor supply over a period of years is likely to hold down or reduce wages, prices, and returns to enterprises in some sectors relative to those in more strongly organized "administered" markets. Hence, relative prices, the composition of output and employment, relative real output per capita in different occupations as measured, and the average growth in productivity per capita[26] are all liable to be influenced by the rate of expansion in nominal demand that is maintained relative to the natural growth of the labor force. If a more restrictive monetary policy is pursued, the structure of the real economy will be different from what it would have been had the expansion of nominal demand been sufficient to permit nominal GDP to rise in line with the increase in the wages and salaries bill associated with employing the growing labor force at the going wage rate for each particular job.

For simplicity we have considered what may happen in the case of pre-existing price stability (ΔPY_{t-1}, $\Delta PY^e = 0$). But the processes described will be intensified under inflationary conditions (when ΔPY^e_t substantially exceeds zero), if ΔYN^e_t falls short of $\lambda + \Delta PY^e_t$ by a substantial margin.[27]

Consider the case where inflationary policies have applied and $\Delta\overline{M}$, the rate of monetary expansion maintained over a period of years, has been equal to $\lambda + \Delta\overline{PY^e}$. Again abstracting from current technical progress, suppose that ΔM_t is reduced to λ, the rate consistent with noninflationary growth under pre-existing price stability. Then

$\Delta YN^e_{t+1} = \lambda$, but

$\Delta PY_{t+1} = \Delta\overline{PY^e}$

$\Delta YR_{t+1} = \lambda - \Delta\overline{PY^e}$, that is to say, real output growth ΔYR declines by $\Delta\overline{M} - \Delta M_t$,

$\Delta YN^e_{t+2} = \lambda$, but

$\Delta YR_{t+2} < \lambda$ because

ΔPY_{t+2} still exceeds 0.

This comes about because the market power of strong enterprises in administered sectors ensures that their organized employees can secure nominal wage increases that compensate in some considerable degree for earlier inflation. So we may suppose that the rate of nominal wage increase and the change in the GNP deflator for administered

---

[26]If wages and profit margins are lowered in the "competitive" markets relative to "administered" markets, the relative level of real output per capita in the former, as compared to the latter, will decline when the real output index is rebased with new nominal value weights.

[27]Profits in administered market sectors will decline with underutilization of capital and labor (especially if redundancy provisions limit cost reductions through layoffs). Efforts by the strongest firms to improve profits by securing a larger share of the market, possibly by accepting somewhat lower profit margins per unit of output (and increasing nonprice competition or moderating price increases, discounting prices) may typically result in the restricted output of the "organized" sector being concentrated in fewer large producers with strengthened market power, who are subsequently able to restore profit margins.

sectors of the economy, ΔW_{t+2}^{ad} and ΔPY_{t+2}^{ad} are related in period $t+2$, to the size of ΔPY_{t+1}, as well as to the more marked deceleration of ΔPP, the rate of increase in auction market prices (notably for imported primary products) in period $t+1$. The latter, as we saw, is usually sensitive to the concurrent change in nominal expenditure. So very crudely,

$$\Delta PY_{t+2}^{ad} = x[b\Delta PP_{t+1} + (1-b)\Delta PY_{t+1}]^{28}$$

$$0 < x > 1$$

$$\Delta PP_{t+1} = h(\Delta YN_{t+1}^{e} - \Delta YN_{t}^{e}).$$

In this example, the rate of price and wage increase in the administered sectors will still be influenced by the initial rate of inflation under the policy prevailing three years earlier, though moderated by the subsequent change in policy.[29]

The value of the coefficient x, which is likely to be related to the rate of inflation (ΔPY^{e}) and the time for which it has persisted, will probably rise steeply if inflation approaching, or exceeding, a double-digit rate obtains for more than a year or two—and once established a high coefficient may persist for a long time. The higher is ΔPY_{t}^{ad} relative to ΔYN_{t}^{e}, the greater will be the tendencies for rising unemployment or declining participation rates, and/or reductions in average output per capita due to changes in the distribution of output and employment.

In effect, the downward inflexibility of nominal wages in the short run under conditions of price stability has its counterpart in a limit on the rate of deceleration of nominal wage and price increases under conditions of pre-existing inflation. Attempts to secure a steeper deceleration than this are likely to be very costly in terms of losses in real output and lower investment, unemployment, and reduced productivity growth, and these losses will not guarantee the maintenance of a low rate of inflation over the medium term. Only if a low level of demand is sustained for a very considerable period, may the existence of large pools of manpower in low-productivity employment, not subject to union organization, serve to create a favorable opportunity for the expansion of high-productivity, large-scale enterprises, with slight wage cost pressure.

---

[28]Where b is the effective weight which auction market prices have in determining the movement of administered market prices, including their effects on wage claims described earlier in this chapter.

[29]It should be noticed, incidentally, that in the period $t+3$ the effect of the now stabilized slower expansion of nominal demand upon auction market prices will be much smaller or negligible, consequently the rate of increase in nominal wages and prices in the administered sectors may be closer to the rate of inflation in the preceding year than was the case in period $t+2$. This is likely to be seen by commentators and politicians as a case of hardening cost pressures and failure of restraint.

8

Indexation of Wages: A Monetarist Prescription

The monetarists' view of inflation as a phenomenon of the general movement of prices level induced by monetary expansion led them to advocate indexation as a means of ensuring a rapid adjustment of nominal wages (and prices) to changes in the quantity of money, thereby preventing monetary disturbances from provoking fluctuations in the level of real output and distortions of the structure of production due to mistaken expectations concerning the general movement of prices.[1] They particularly emphasized that if the authorities were seeking to bring down the rate of inflation by reducing monetary expansion, indexation could be helpful as a means of avoiding the dislocation of production and unemployment that would occur if wage settlements were based upon continued expectations of the previous rate of inflation.[2]

The issues raised by indexation illustrate the difficulty of applying principles derived from general equilibrium theorizing to a concrete wage bargaining situation. As has been seen in Chapter 6,[3] the idea that the real economy itself is continually subject to powerful "autonomous shocks" is alien to the monetarist approach. In a real environment in which competitive markets and freedom of entry for new enterprises and wage earners are by no means general, even when a certain rate of inflation has been maintained for some time, the movement of particular prices and/or wage rates will still be liable to accelerate (or decelerate) as a result of "real" factors. (Since the

[1]This chapter is an abridged version of Braun (1976a).
[2]See Friedman (1974) and Giersch (1974).
[3]Pp. 139 and 141–43.

economy is continually liable to largely unpredictable changes in the degree of monopolistic organization of business and labor in different sectors, and in political forces, both within the economy and within the world at large.)

Hence it will in fact be difficult for firmly held price expectations and general agreement concerning the probable rate of inflation to become established. Changes in the strength of price and cost pressures in particular sectors, together with the degree of constraint implied by constant growth of the money stock, will always be liable to produce an acceleration (or deceleration) in the average rate of price increase and a tendency for the level of employment and real output to fall (or rise) at the going rate of monetary expansion. Furthermore, the possibility of the changing situation provoking a change in monetary policy will always exist.[4] Nevertheless, there are constraints and frictions that mitigate and slow down the impact of autonomous shocks and contribute to the apparent stability of the real economy (including the usually cautious reactions of economic agents under imperfect information, resistance to change, and lack of mobility). One of the stabilizing checks and balances is the existence of a monetary system.

This view of the economy poses a question that does not arise in the monetarist view of things, namely, whether wages indexation would render the movement of prices in general more sensitive to price and cost pressures developing in particular sectors of the economy. If so, it could make the task of the monetary authorities more difficult by increasing the risk that changes in the real economy could set off a faster rate of inflation and rising unemployment when the same rate of monetary expansion was maintained.

To understand the effect of indexation on the macroeconomic behavior of the economy one must consider the influence of wage bargaining on the flexibility of relative prices in the economy, and how this is likely to be affected by the rate of inflation.

Wage Bargaining and Indexation

The average rate of wage increase in an enterprise, an industry, or the economy as a whole is influenced by several factors, one of which is the actual or expected rate of increase in prices. Wage increases are also sought or conceded on the grounds of rising productivity, high

---

[4]The monetarist approach begs the question of whether it is legitimate to treat the economy as tending to steady-state equilibrium, under a constant rate of monetary expansion, if some paths to the steady state are politically impassable.

profits, or scarcities of particular, or all, types of labor; and the level of wages in a particular sector may be raised as a result of strengthened organization of wage and salary earners there. These grounds for increases are not mutually exclusive but may be in part alternatives.

Price Expectations in Wage Bargaining

When wage bargaining relates to particular enterprises or industries, the rate of wage increase granted is likely to be influenced both by the actual or expected movement of the cost of living, which influences the size of wage claims, and by the actual or expected movement of prices for the specific output of the enterprise or industry, as this affects its profitability and the size of wage increases likely to be granted. These two influences do not necessarily correspond for the economy as a whole. Not all domestic output enters directly into consumption, and consumption is not met exclusively out of domestic output. There are imports and exports, and outputs of capital goods (whose prices often fluctuate more widely than those of consumer goods).

The fact that in a "partitioned" labor market the influence of price expectations operates in part from specific price expectations to particular wage settlements has important consequences. With shifting patterns of demand and supply, it means that, at any moment of time, wage and salary earners will be in a position to secure above average gains in real income in those sectors where demand is strongest, or where productivity is increasing exceptionally rapidly.[5] Over any short period, certain industries and professions will be able to increase their share in total value of output relative to their share in employment. Other sectors then have to accept a relative decline in the price of their outputs, if the average rate of price increase is not to accelerate, and the overall level of output and employment, associated with the given rate of monetary expansion, is not to decline. Thus, even when the authorities pursue a consistent monetary policy, demand conditions and price movements in particular sectors are liable to be influenced by the uncertain outcome of labor-management and supplier-buyer confrontations in other sectors; and possibly also by unintended changes in the monetary and fiscal situation brought about by changes in the rate of inflation and the level of output. Since

[5]This process is illustrated in the account of wage developments in the Netherlands and in Norway in Chapter 10. Charles L. Schultze is the leading exponent of the concept of inflation originating neither in an overall excess of money demand nor in autonomous upward wage push but in shifting excess demands on particular sectors in an economy characterized by price and wage rigidities. See Schultze (1959).

in most economies there are marked differences in the degree of organization and bargaining power of wage earners as between sectors, the average rate of wage increase is likely to be higher or lower, depending on which sectors are experiencing relatively strong demand.[6]

The Rate of Monetary Expansion and Relative Price Flexibility

There are grounds for thinking that it may be easier to maintain a high level of employment with a moderate rate of monetary expansion that permits a gradually rising average price level than with either a lower rate of expansion, requiring a stable or falling price level if employment is to be maintained, or a faster rate of expansion that permits rapid price inflation. In other words, contrary to the monetarist view, there is likely to be a lasting trade-off between the rate of monetary expansion and the level of unemployment experienced over time, at least over a certain range of expansion rates.

The reason for thinking so is that a moderate positive rate of price increase is likely to be associated with greater flexibility of relative wage rates at the going level of employment, rendering the average movement of prices, and hence the level of employment, less vulnerable to above average price and/or wage increases in particular sectors than under conditions of strict price stability or rapid inflation.

Consider an economy with a fixed labor force and a trend growth of productivity of π percent per annum. The money stock is permitted to expand by $\Delta\overline{M}$ percent per annum, and the existing level of employment is maintained when prices rise on average by $\Delta\overline{M} - \pi$ per annum. Suppose that the desired level of employment has been sustained with this rate of inflation for some time, but one sector then is able to secure a much larger increase in the price of its output than previously, as a result of some autonomous change in the structure of demand or supply, or as a result of more monopolistic organization. This will tend to cause some weakening of demand in other sectors at the going rate of monetary expansion. If the desired level of employment is to be maintained with the same rate of monetary expansion, prices in other sectors must rise less rapidly than before.

As long as moderate rates of inflation are experienced, wages and salaries are commonly fixed, by contract or convention, in money

[6]The importance of differences between economies in the scale of the competitive sector and the pervasiveness of labor organization in determining the overall response of the economy to monetary and exogenous shocks was illustrated in Chapter 4 and is considered further in Chapter 11.

terms and are adjusted for price changes by wage bargaining at relatively infrequent intervals (of a year or longer). Money wages are inflexible downward; rates of pay are not likely to be cut unless the level of employment is substantially reduced for some considerable period of time. Upward adjustments of wages can however be postponed if an enterprise or industry faces a weakening of demand. Hence, the effective floor to the distribution of rates of wage increase *without a marked rise in unemployment* is the maintenance of agreed money wages. The fact that prices are known to be rising by, say, 3 or 4 percent per annum has little if any effect in preventing the postponement of wage increases in sectors faced with a weakening of demand. So, if certain industries succeed in pushing up their prices at a higher rate and increasing their share in total expenditure, there is some scope for reducing the rate of wage increase in sectors facing weakening demand, in spite of the downward inflexibility of money wages.

If, however, the monetary authority were to limit the growth of the money supply strictly to that consistent with overall price stability at the expected rate of productivity growth, price increases in some sectors would require price reductions in other sectors, which (as has been seen in Chapter 7) most probably could not be achieved without unemployment, given the downward inflexibility of money wages under wage contracts.

Thus, over some range, a higher rate of monetary expansion associated with a higher (but still moderate) rate of inflation may increase the possibility that an acceleration of price or wage increases in one sector can be offset by postponement of wage and price increases in other sectors. The average rate of price increase and level of employment may therefore be less apt to change as a result of increased price or cost pressures in particular sectors of the economy. In other words, the authorities will be less likely to face the need to choose between validating a faster rate of price increase or tolerating a higher level of unemployment. If demands and supplies are price elastic, one may suppose that when there is greater short-term flexibility in relative wages and prices between industries, shifts in the structure of output and employment can be achieved with less unemployment and the maintenance of a higher level of real output over time.[7]

---

[7]Note that widespread rapid growth in productivity would have a similar effect to a moderately rising price level in permitting greater flexibility of relative wage and price movements to be achieved. This was a moderating factor under the exceptional conditions of the 1950s and early 1960s as is described in Chapter 5.

Friedman and the monetarists assume that whenever a certain rate of inflation has persisted for some time, a situation resembling that under price stability will apply, because all prices and wages will be swiftly adjusted for the correctly anticipated rate of price increase. There is, however, an important difference in this respect, between a rapid and a moderate rate of inflation, because a moderate rate of price increase does not cause wages to be fixed in real terms by explicit or implicit indexation. Experience suggests that a continued moderate rate of inflation does not lead to widespread adoption of indexation clauses, or to frequent renegotiation of wage rates in order to maintain the real value of wages. Neither the extra effort of frequent negotiations, nor the real cost involved in frequent changes in pay scales (or in any prices), is justified when prices in general are rising on average by no more than 1–1½ percent a quarter. There is also likely to be resistance to the idea of indexation, both on the part of employers, who fear that it may expose them to difficulties should the prices of their products tend to rise less than consumer prices in general or that it may raise the size of wage increases that they are forced to concede, and on the part of union leaders, who see it as detracting from their power and influence.

By contrast, the onset of rapid inflation quickly leads to greater insistence on the maintenance of real, as opposed to nominal, wages. That is to say, wage fixing in real terms seems to depend more on the rate of price inflation experienced than on the length of time that inflation has persisted. Contrary to the view of some monetarists, notably Friedman, the weakening of money illusion in wage bargaining seems not to be a gradual process of adjusting expectations for rising prices but rather a swift response to the more obvious effects of large price and wage increases. Under rapid inflation, both the loss of purchasing power associated with fixed money wages under annual, or less frequent, wage settlements and the conspicuous relative gains of those wage earners who have just secured new wage contracts become sufficiently great to justify the extra effort and cost of wage bargaining at more frequent intervals or of adjusting wages automatically by indexation.

Under widespread indexation (providing close to, or full compensation, for changes in prices at short intervals) a sharp acceleration of price increases in one sector would provoke a faster rise in wage costs in other sectors, even while increasing monetary constraint due to the faster rise in money incomes and prices was tending to cause a weakening of demand. Thus, indexation would appear to make it more difficult to maintain the existing level of employment with the existing rate of monetary expansion.

The situation need not be very different without explicit indexation, however, if the realization that real wages had declined significantly led to greater militancy and the refusal to permit postponement of wage settlements, even in the face of a weaker demand situation for the enterprise or industry, and if some groups were insisting on swifter compensation than usual for price increases outside, or under, customary bargaining procedures.

In sum, rapid price inflation soon leads to greater insistence on maintaining the real value of wages in the short run, by indexation or other means, and thereby lessens the relative flexibility of labor costs in different industries. The average rate of price increase becomes more likely to accelerate with any acceleration of the rate of price and wage increase in specific sectors of the economy, and it becomes increasingly difficult to maintain an existing, desired level of employment without validating an accelerating rate of price increase by faster monetary growth. Thus, it is probably easier to maintain a moderate rate of inflation for some considerable period of time than to maintain either a stable price level or a double-digit rate of inflation. Rapid inflation would not seem likely to come about through a gradual acceleration of creeping inflation. It would usually be the result either of some quite unduly rapid expansion of monetary demand relative to real output potential or of some unforeseen catastrophic decline in real output potential owing to natural or political causes.

Effect of Indexation

Indexation is merely one of the ways in which greater insistence on maintaining the real value of wages in the face of rapid inflation makes itself felt. There are, however, certain differences compared with the achievement of a similar degree of compensation for price increases by more insistent wage bargaining and more frequent wage negotiations: (1) indexation is more automatic, (2) it continues until abrogated, and (3) it can be foreseen with greater certainty. Because of (1) and (2), indexation will most probably cause nominal wage increases to be less responsive to the existence of substantial unemployment and real wages to be better maintained when unemployment is heavy but prices are still increasing. Contrary to the view of its advocates, indexation is therefore likely to prolong the impact of rapid price inflation and to delay the response of wage settlements to an easing of demand conditions. Because of (3), indexation may increase the certainty with which producers in any particular sector count on money wage rates, prices, and probably, money income in other sectors rising in the immediate short run, in response to current price increases, even though the rise in money incomes may require to be validated by a faster rate of monetary expansion.

It is often suggested that if a macroeconomic wage equation shows that an average level of wages responds to changes in the price level with a coefficient of unity, money illusion is absent, and indexation is unlikely to have an important effect in enhancing inflation. This need not be true, however.

The fact that wages on average keep up with prices does not, of course, imply that all wages do so continuously. It may result from a continuing combination of rising real wages in sectors of rapidly increasing productivity, or of high profitability associated with increasing demand, or in sectors where union power is increasing, combined with wages falling behind the average rise in prices in sectors of low growth, declining demand, or weak labor organization. The introduction, or extension, of indexation to these latter groups (for example, as a consequence of the adoption of an indexed minimum wage) may then cause their wages to rise more rapidly than they otherwise would. It is not possible to say, a priori, what effect this will have on the average rate of wage increase. But it seems probable that the initial effect will be to promote a more equal rise of money wages throughout the economy around a higher average rate of increase[8] (since the power of less favored groups to ensure that their wages rise more closely in line with other wages will probably not be offset by a reduction in the power of the most favored groups to secure above average wage increases).[9]

The rate of price and wage increase that is actually experienced must of course be influenced by the degree of financial constraint imposed by the authorities' control over the budgetary situation and the supply of money and credit. But it is not obvious that it will be an easy, or politically acceptable, task for the authorities to prevent wages in general rising faster if indexation has the effect of increasing the rate at which wages rise in the weaker or less strongly organized sectors of the economy.

In an economy such as the United States, characterized by wide differences in the degree of competition prevailing in various sectors and a large nonunionized segment of the labor market, it would

[8]See the account later in this chapter of a detailed study of U.S. experience with escalator clauses in Soffer (1959a).

[9]A possible exception to this situation may occur in an open economy, which maintains a fixed exchange rate in relation to its principal trading partners, as foreign competition may set a ceiling on the rate of price and wage increase in the more highly organized sectors of rapid growth in productivity.

appear that if all wages and salaries[10] were automatically indexed on the previous rate of inflation, the effect of generalized and "full" indexation of wages would be to make inflation less painful and socially disruptive, but faster and more difficult to brake.[11] Consequently, a reduction in the rate of monetary expansion aimed at halting inflation could well produce a larger immediate rise in unemployment, loss of output, and economic dislocation (bankruptcies, companies going out of business, depressed areas, etc.) than if indexation did not apply. A shift to tighter financial conditions would tend to be associated with more unemployment precisely because there would be less effect in holding down wages and prices in the sectors most affected by weakening demand.

The argument that the introduction of indexation may serve to lessen the strength of cost-push is most persuasive when labor is strongly organized both for wage bargaining at the industry or plant level throughout the economy and in exercising political influence—with the result that the maintenance of full employment commands a high priority among policy objectives.[12] In such a case, any well-publicized wage settlement, much in excess of the current rate of price increase plus the expected average rate of growth in productivity, will be likely to unsettle price expectations, even when it is believed that the authorities intend to maintain the existing degree of financial restraint and rate of monetary expansion. If wage earners in other sectors can secure similar wage increases, the rate of price increase will be apt to accelerate, and the level of employment to decline when the rate of monetary expansion is maintained. It is not clear that the monetary authority will be able to avoid validating the higher rate of inflation, given the strength of political pressures for maintaining full employment. To be sure of protecting themselves against a decline in their relative real wages and a possible fall in their absolute real income in these circumstances, wage earners have to seek wage

---

[10]Friedman's advocacy of wages indexation in the United States, and his commendation of the Brazilian system, actually applied only to wage settlements in the unionized sector.

[11]"Because of its uneven impacts, then, our existing system throws sand into the gears of inflation. Indexing would oil the gears and speed the process of inflation," Heller (1974). "The 'escalator' features of the GM-type formulas make the general level of wages highly sensitive to even small fluctuations in the Consumers' Price Index," thereby limiting the effectiveness of mild monetary or fiscal policies to check inflation. "Reducing the lags, frictions, delays and uncertainties which slow the average rise in wages probably lubricates the inflationary process." Soffer (1959a, pp. 54–55).

[12]The United Kingdom was the most obvious case but these conditions also applied, in the early 1970s, in the Federal Republic of Germany, Sweden, and Austria (as well as in Belgium, Denmark, and the Netherlands, where indexation was already widespread).

increases that match the highest rate of increase recently granted. That is to say, they are bound to bargain for matching increases in nominal wages, given the uncertainty over the rate of price increase that may eventuate.[13]

The fact that wage earners will try, as far as possible, to protect themselves in this manner against the unforeseeable outcome of particular groups' efforts to push up their real wages then causes the average rate of wage increase to exceed the growth in real output. In this "scenario" generalized cost-push is, in part at least, due to uncertainty; it does not necessarily reflect the situation that wage and salary earners have "nonnegotiable demands" for increases in real income much in excess of the growth in real output. Protection, via indexation, against the eventual rate of price increase, whatever it may turn out to be, may therefore offer a means of preventing an exceptionally large settlement from setting off a round of similar increases.[14] Indexation on the movement of prices in general should be less inflationary than wage increases matching the highest rate of wage increase recently accorded when that settlement may reflect exceptional factors such as favorable shifts in demand, major changes in technique, or strengthened labor organization. Thus, while it is usually correct to regard indexation as tending to reduce the flexibility of relative wages, in circumstances where great rigidity already exists, indexation may sometimes provide a means of securing increased flexibility. Where wage bargaining over much of the economy is centralized, as in the Scandinavian countries and in Ireland and Israel, indexation is likely to prevail, but this particular benefit will not apply.

Incidence of Indexation

Policy options with respect to indexation of pay are usually limited. In a context of rapid price inflation, the authorities are not likely to be willing or able to resist the spread of some form of cost of living clauses. One may expect that a period of rapid price inflation will result in widespread indexation unless either wage and salary earners

---

[13]As a study by the Australian Department of Labor (1974) observed (p. 12), indexation "avoids a situation where workers base wage claims on the highest expected rate of inflation. If a union is successful in achieving such a claim, this tends to become the norm for which other unions strive and the expected rate of inflation becomes a self-fulfilling prophecy."

[14]A good example of the usefulness of indexation in such a context is to be found in Australia's experience under the Price and Incomes Accord between the Government and the trade unions in 1983–85 described later in this chapter.

are sufficiently strongly organized for wage bargaining purposes to secure compensation for price increases by means of frequent renegotiation of contracts, wildcat strikes, etc., or labor is politically too weak to insist on some form of indexation. Once indexation is widespread, it is only under conditions of severe and rising unemployment induced by strongly restrictive aggregate demand policies of a firmly established government or in exceptional circumstances (such as a balance of payments crisis under fixed exchange rates imposing a clearly apparent need to secure a lowering of relative costs by a large devaluation) that the authorities will be able to secure the abandonment of the system, as occurred in France and Finland. However, indexation may wither away naturally during a prolonged period of price stability.

The apparently haphazard incidence of indexation among industrial countries in the early 1970s can be explained in these terms (see Table 8); in many Western European countries, rapid price inflation during the late 1940s had led to widespread indexation. The countries that had slight recourse to indexation fall into three groups: (1) the Netherlands, Sweden, and the United Kingdom, which experienced less than average open inflation in the immediate postwar period, and in which a politically powerful labor movement was able to protect real wages by other means than indexation, such as rationing, food subsidies, and price controls; (2) the United States and Canada, where the postwar inflation was least severe and where wage earners were a less strongly organized force in national politics than in many European countries; and (3) Austria, the Federal Republic of Germany, and Japan, where the labor movement was exceptionally disorganized and politically weak in the immediate postwar period.

Case for Indexation in the Early 1970s

The case for indexation naturally arose in those countries where it was relatively unimportant, notably the United States, the United Kingdom, the Federal Republic of Germany, and Australia.[15] Interest in indexation was fanned by the determined advocacy of Friedman, Giersch, and some other monetarist economists. It was not always sufficiently emphasized that, while presenting a general case for indexation, these authorities were actually prescribing indexation as a remedy to the highly specific problems of a particular economy at a particular time.

---

[15]In the Netherlands, the adoption of indexation was recommended in a 1969 Report of the Social and Economic Council. See Chapter 10.

Table 8. Extent of Indexation of Pay in 1975

Countries with widespread indexation of wages and salaries, pensions, and social security benefits	
Adopted during the late 1940s	
Belgium	
Luxembourg	
Italy	
Denmark	in the context of centralized wage bargaining
Norway	in the context of centralized wage bargaining
Iceland	in the context of centralized wage bargaining
Israel	in the context of centralized wage bargaining
Adopted during the 1970s	
Netherlands	
Switzerland	
United Kingdom	
Ireland	in the context of centralized wage bargaining
Countries in which indexation remained relatively unimportant	
United States	
Canada	
Sweden	
Austria	
Japan	
Countries in which indexation had been expressly prohibited or abolished	
France	previously widespread indexation, prohibited at time of devaluations in 1958 and 1967, respectively
Finland	previously widespread indexation, prohibited at time of devaluations in 1958 and 1967, respectively
Australia	automatic adjustment of the basic wage, in force since 1921, abolished after the Korean war boom; indexation reintroduced in April 1975
Germany, Fed. Rep. of	all forms of indexation prohibited without express consent

NOTE: For notes on the extent and form of wages indexation in most of these countries, see the Appendix to Braun (1976a).

UNITED STATES

Friedman's 1974 discussion of the case for indexation of wages in the United States illustrates some of the pitfalls in the monetarist approach to the problem of inflation.[16]

When Friedman propounded his ideas on indexation, a round of large wage increases appeared to be in prospect in the United States following the lifting of price/wage controls, which had the effect of sharply reducing real wages. His immediate goal in advocating the wider use of escalator clauses[17] was to enable enterprises to retain the benefits of long-term wage contracts, in obviating the considerable costs involved in frequent wage bargaining, but to avoid the risk of being stuck with excessively large wage increases should the rate of inflation moderate. His case for indexation essentially concerned the introduction of escalator clauses into long-term wage contracts coming up for settlement when more restrictive financial policies were about to take effect and a decline in the rate of inflation was in prospect. He advocated widespread use of escalator clauses merely as a temporary expedient, expecting the use of clauses to disappear once inflation was brought under control.[18]

Friedman's discussion of the advantages of indexation in the specific case of the General Motors settlements of 1967 and 1970 is typical of monetarist writing in its neglect of the fact that changes in the growth in total spending are in practice associated with changes in the pattern of real demand. It is odd that, although he ascribes the inflationary expansion of the money supply to "the sovereign's attempt to acquire real resources," he then seems to forget the effect that the government's use of real resources has in enhancing demand for specific resources, with its consequent impact on the structure of relative prices and wages.[19]

---

[16]For a comment on Friedman's earlier views on indexation, see Soffer (1959a, p. 54, footnote 3).

[17]Less than 10 percent of all nonagricultural employees in the United States were covered by escalator clauses at the beginning of 1975. Automatic adjustments under such clauses did not fully compensate for price increases but, on average, covered no more than half the increase in the consumer price index. Douty (1975). See also Braun (1976a, pp. 253–54 and 267–68).

[18]"Private use of escalator clauses is an expedient that has no permanent role, if government manages money responsibly." Friedman (1974, p. 38).

[19]Friedman considers that the fact that General Motors paid lower real wages than expected, when the consumer price index and aggregate expenditure rose at a faster rate than anticipated after 1967, "was a stimulus to General Motors and no doubt led it to produce at a higher rate than otherwise" (1974, p. 34). This does not necessarily follow, however. It is possible that sharply higher prices for items such as housing, services, and medical care, which contributed to the acceleration of the rise in consumer prices, were

In practice, of course, not only unanticipated inflation but also unanticipated changes in government expenditure, financed out of taxation, may pose problems under long-term wage contracts. Suppose the U.S. Government had financed the rise in expenditure after 1967 out of progressive taxation, or a sales tax on consumer durable goods, or a gasoline tax. The price expectations of General Motors and the United Automobile Workers might have been fulfilled, but General Motors would probably not have been able to maintain the relative price of automobiles and its planned scale of output.

Friedman's support for indexation rests on the implicit assumption that the economy is in steady-state equilibrium with relative wages and prices at their equilibrium levels when an unanticipated inflation or deflation occurs.[20] This explains his tendency to regard changes in relative prices as distortions requiring to be corrected.[21] If, however, one supposes that deflation follows after a period of rising inflation, associated with changes in the structure of real demand, it is at least conceivable that the changes in relative wages and prices produced by the response to inflation in existing wage settlements for some sectors, and the adjustment to deflationary conditions in new wage settlements for other sectors, may tend to reverse the changes in relative wages and prices associated with the changes in structure of demand during the preceding period.[22] More important, as shifts in relative prices are

---

associated with shifts in the composition of aggregate expenditure tending to limit the rise in demand for automobiles. The steep rise in prices of steel and nonferrous metals under the impact of the Viet Nam war should also have had an influence in lessening the company's incentive to produce more cars.

In the context of, possibly sharp, short-term changes in the real economy, it cannot simply be assumed that a fall in the real wages paid would necessarily cause General Motors to expand output more than it would otherwise, or vice versa. Suppose, for instance, that real wages had risen because of a fall in the price of food. Would this be likely to cause GM to produce at a lower rate? As wage earners buy more cars than do farmers, and as the demand for food is inelastic, this situation would seem more likely to induce an increase than a decrease in its output.

[20]See the account of the Chicago version of the general equilibrium model in Chapter 6.

[21]"Different activities have different time-speeds of adjustment. Some prices, wages and production schedules are fixed for a long time in advance; others can be adjusted promptly. As a result, a slowdown of total spending produces substantial shifts in *relative* prices, which will sooner or later have to be corrected; the correction in turn will cause economic disturbances." Friedman (1974, pp. 31–32).

[22]Suppose, for instance, that sectors subject to smaller increases in demand during the inflationary period are the last to conclude wage settlements allowing for the inflationary average rate of price increase, and that sectors that experienced larger increases in demand associated with the inflation are the first to bargain settlements in the expectation of deflationary conditions. The resulting changes in relative wages and prices would then seem to be conducive to securing the relative wages and prices appropriate to the structure of demand in the absence of inflation.

required, it is not clearly desirable to ensure, by widespread indexation, that wages in all sectors move more closely in line.

FEDERAL REPUBLIC OF GERMANY

In the Federal Republic of Germany, where the leaders of the union movement were concerned to avoid provoking a marked inflation of costs, indexation was seen as an answer to the threat of wildcat strikes. It presented a possible solution to the problem of satisfying the interests of their membership and of avoiding a loss of influence to radical groups, while at the same time maintaining the solidarity of the union movement with the ruling Social Democratic Party.[23] As Giersch pointed out, the inclusion of cost of living clauses in wage contracts could provide the unions with a means of avoiding the opprobrium of being responsible for large wage increases, while protecting them against an outbreak of wildcat strikes following upon an unanticipated decline in consumer purchasing power.[24] The unions had reacted to the wave of wildcat strikes in 1969 with inflationary wage demands in 1970, and the same phenomenon occurred again in 1973.[25]

Thus, the advocates of indexation in the Federal Republic of Germany saw it as a means of restoring the controlling role and moderating influence of the union leadership in wage bargaining, as well as a means of combining the advantages of long-term wage contracts with flexibility of nominal wages.

Giersch argued that

> ever since flexible exchange rates and swift adjustments of parity values have become the general practice, we have seen that the central bank is fully able to apply the monetary brakes.... If escalator provisions are forbidden and not in use, there is a strong tendency to build the inflation rate of the past into the new

---

[23]See Chapter 9. One commentator described the "political imperatives" of the situation as follows: "...the party cannot allow inflationary wage increases for blue-collar industrial workers and at the same time retain the allegiance of the new-middle-class voters so critical to its electoral victories; union leaders cannot supply too much flank protection for the government in the face of revolt from the rank and file; and both sides find the unemployment associated with economic slowdown (as in the 1966–67 recession) an intolerable way of fighting inflation—the party for political reasons...and the unions because unemployment is the most dreaded of all their specters." Willey (1974, p. 59).

[24]Giersch (1974, p. 10).

[25]In 1970, collective bargaining settlements raised wages by 13.6 percent, excluding improvements in fringe benefits. "In January 1973, two thirds of those steel workers voting in North Rhine-Westphalia turned down a union-negotiated package of 8.5 percent.... By July, the metal workers' union estimated that over one hundred concerns had been affected by wildcat strikes, and most managements were giving in to the strikers with 'inflation bonuses' of one kind or another." Willey (1974, p. 58).

> collective agreements, especially in those cases where no loss in employment has occurred as yet.[26]

To avoid major repercussions on physical output and the level of employment, it is

> necessary that people keep their price and income demands flexible. These demands should be based not on inflation rates of the past, but rather on those lower future inflation rates which monetary policy will tolerate. This is exactly what will be achieved by concluding agreements containing cost-of-living escalator clauses.[27]

United Kingdom

Essentially similar arguments were advanced by the Trades Union Congress when advocating the introduction of threshold agreements in the United Kingdom at a time of accelerating expectations of price inflation in 1971. The agreements were to stipulate that if, during the period covered by a wage settlement, the increase in retail prices exceeded a certain "threshold" figure, wages would be increased by a set amount related to the additional price increase. The threshold agreement would provide a guarantee of protection against a high rate of price increase, enabling the wage settlement to be negotiated on the basis of a lower rate of increase.[28]

When the agreements were adopted in November 1973, it was reckoned that "there was a reasonable chance that retail prices would rise by only about 7 per cent during the coming year; import prices, it was thought, would level off, and national output would be rising at about 3 per cent a year."[29] However, the National Institute had pointed out earlier that, given the uncertainty about import prices, threshold agreements would be something of a gamble. It had been suggested that the price index used for the threshold should exclude import prices, as had been tried in Denmark, but it was doubtful whether such an index would be accepted.[30]

> If, by giving some insurance against the consequences of a rapid price rise, the basic wage increase figure can be brought down; and if, as a consequence of that low basic figure, the threshold price rise is not reached; then obviously there is a gain. On the other hand, if the reduction in the basic figure is only marginal, and the rise in import prices exceeds the forecast, anti-inflationary

---

[26]Giersch (1974, p. 6).

[27]Giersch (1974, p. 4).

[28]Blackaby (1971, p. 49).

[29]National Institute of Economic and Social Research (February 1974, p. 5).

[30]With the wisdom of hindsight it seems that, given the general expectation that the sharp rise in import prices would not continue, the Government might have been able to secure agreement to hedge its bet by providing that the threshold would be raised should a steep rise in import prices occur.

> policy would probably lose. . . any attempt to compensate for real income losses arising from adverse terms of trade only results in higher prices still.[31]

AUSTRALIA

Indexation was seen as a means of strengthening the influence of the Australian Conciliation and Arbitration Commission over the general movement of wages and salaries and as a means of countering the growing tendency for collective bargaining and strikes concerning "over-award" wages.[32]

The Arbitration Commission rejected indexation proposals put forward by the unions and the Government in the 1974 National Wage cases, but in April 1975 it decided that adjustment of award wages for price increases should begin in the June quarter.[33] In explaining the ruling, the Commission pointed out that the case for indexation rested on three grounds: it would help to moderate inflation; it would provide an equitable basis for wage adjustment; and it would help to lessen the heat generated in industrial relations. The first proposition was based on the notion that the expectation of further large price increases led to large wage claims, which in turn produced the expected rate of price increase. The self-fulfilling element in the inflationary process could be eliminated by indexation. The opponents of indexation—the private employers and the four Conservative State Governments—had contended that an attempt to maintain the real value of wages, which had risen greatly in excess of prices and productivity in 1974,[34] would add to inflation or increase unemployment or both. In their evidence to the Commission, Professors Whitehead and Gates had argued that elimination of price expectations would probably not greatly reduce wage demands, but would impart an additional automatic element to the rise in wages and would cause inflation to accelerate.

The Commission noted that for many years it had rejected claims for automatic adjustment on the ground that it preferred to keep wage movements under its direct control. However, with rapid price increases and large wage increases outside the National Wage cases, it

---

[31]National Institute of Economic and Social Research (August 1973, p. 5).

[32]For a description of these problems and an explanation of Australian wages terminology, see Braun (1974, especially pp. 172–76 and 186–92).

In 1974, the Department of Labour suggested that the over-award element of earnings drift had increased "partly because of the inadequate compensation for the impact of inflation on award wages in the 1950s, and the less frequent cost of living adjustment of award wages in the sixties." If wage indexation were to be introduced, "that element of over-award payments catching up with, and anticipating, inflation could be reduced." Australia, Department of Labour (1974, pp. 25–26).

[33]Australian Conciliation and Arbitration Commission (1975).

[34]Average weekly earnings rose by 7.2 percent in real terms in 1974.

had recently been difficult to avoid erosion of the real value of National Award rates. The unions and the Government did not rely on indexation as a means of reducing the current rate of inflation but regarded it as "an integral part of an equitable counter-inflationary policy."[35] Indexation could be applied in National Wage cases only if pay increases apart from National Wage awards and indexation provisions were kept within strict limits. "Otherwise it is difficult to escape the conclusion that, even if it removed inflationary expectations from wage claims, indexation carries a high risk of accelerating inflationary tendencies if it adjusts excessive wage increases automatically for price increases every quarter."[36]

Characteristics of Wages Indexation in Practice

In practice, indexation of pay diverges in significant ways from the concept implied in theoretical discussions of the case for generalized indexing, or "monetary correction."[37]

Indexation is rarely, if ever, complete in the sense that it ensures that all wages and salaries are automatically fully adjusted for changes in the overall price level at short intervals and that wage negotiations concern changes in real wages. Indexation provisions seldom apply to all workers or cover the whole pay packet; they often provide for adjustment only with substantial delay, usually on the basis of some less than comprehensive index of the movement of prices in general. Furthermore, there is usually provision for price declines to be treated asymmetrically from price increases—or ignored. Indexation usually applies to negotiated rates of pay but not to additional earnings resulting from wage drift at the plant level, overtime pay, bonuses, or special allowances for working conditions. Sometimes, as for example in Italy up to 1975,[38] indexation is applied to specific basic rates of pay, which have come to account for a progressively smaller share of total wages as time goes on.

---

[35]Australian Conciliation and Arbitration Commission (1975, p. 14).

[36]Australian Conciliation and Arbitration Commission (1975, p. 16). In the event indexation proved to be helpful in the context of the heavy unemployment prevailing in 1975. The increase in award wages and average earnings was less than half the phenomenal rise in 1974, and was almost confined to indexation awards. Industrial unrest subsided. See Braun (1976a, pp. 246–49). National wage cases, providing for full or partial indexation, were held quarterly up to May 1978 and half yearly until mid-1981. After 1978 they were supplemented by separate "work value" cases and over-award payments became increasingly important. Organization for Economic Cooperation and Development (June 1984, p. 12).

[37]For further details of indexation provisions see Douty (1975) and Appendix to Braun (1976a).

[38]See Braun (1976a, p. 265).

The price index on which adjustment is based frequently excludes important items of expenditure, notably housing (as was the case in Belgium).[39] Rental costs are sometimes based solely on rent-controlled housing. Highly processed items of increasing importance in household budgets (such as pharmaceuticals, consumer durable goods, and newly introduced products) and personal services are generally underrepresented in the basic cost of living indices.

Both the partial adjustment of wages and the incomplete coverage of price changes for which compensation is provided are symptomatic of a different underlying objective from that of monetary correction. In many systems of indexation, the basic aim is not to protect the real value of wages in general but to protect the consumption levels of the lowest-paid workers, by ensuring that increases in the cost of basic essentials are reflected in wage rates.

Partial adjustment with a considerable lag means that indexation generally has less powerful effects than might be expected in theory, so that in practice indexation does not tend to cause whatever rate of price increase may result from rising wage costs in the economy to be perpetuated.[40] Incomplete and biased coverage of price changes in the index may have the effect of predisposing the economy to a faster or a slower rate of wage increase in certain circumstances.

Thus the heavy weighting, in consumer price indices, of foodstuffs, and staple items with a high commodity component in their total value enhanced the effect that increasing supplies and falling prices for agricultural products had in moderating wage pressures during the 1950s and the early 1960s. But it also meant that tight commodity supplies and sharply rising prices, such as occurred in 1973–74, would have a disproportionate effect in inducing wage increases irrespective of the employment situation, the automatic adjustment of wages in turn compounding the rise in food prices and leading to further pressure on wage rates. In practice, therefore, contrary to the view of the advocates of "monetary correction," the effect of indexation was to make the general level of prices particularly susceptible to the influence of strong fluctuations in particular prices.[41]

The most striking way in which indexation in practice diverges from the system propounded by its advocates, however, is in respect to the

---

[39]Where home mortgage costs are included in the cost of living index with a substantial weight, as was the case in the United States for many years, the effect is to make the level of wages unduly sensitive to the effect of restrictive monetary policy upon interest rates, and hence to weaken the effectiveness of such a policy in curbing inflation. See White (1967).

[40]See Goldstein (1975).

[41]The special role of commodity price movements in the inflationary process is outlined in Chapter 7, pp. 162–65.

time dimension. Since indexation provisions usually call for semiannual or annual adjustments, indexation is likely to increase the "inertia" of inflation and to retard rather than hasten the effect of deflationary policies, as is claimed by its proponents. In an expansion, lagged correction may cause the adjustment to be superimposed on wage increases that have already been granted rather than to be substituted for negotiated increases. Similar considerations apply if adjustment is called for after a large "threshold" price increase is exceeded. A balancing of considerations of the cost of frequent changes in pay packets versus the disadvantages of delayed adjustment suggests that quarterly changes may be the most favorable interval if the timing of adjustments is to be fixed.

Generally speaking, if indexation is not to be a disturbing factor, it is desirable that adjustments should be made frequently and smoothly, and preferably not on the same basis and simultaneously in all sectors, since lumpy and easily foreseeable changes in the total wage bill provide a favorable opportunity for price increases and tend to promote a relaxation of price discipline, producing greater subsequent wage adjustments than smoother changes.[42]

Experience with Indexation in Selected Countries

Opinions concerning the advantages and disadvantages of wages indexation have differed enormously between countries, and at different times. In practice, views tend to be colored by the success or failure of economic policies pursued in the country concerned. In the United Kingdom, Denmark, Finland, the Netherlands,[43] Iceland, and Israel, indexation has been associated with severe economic problems and has been held to have had damaging results; but in Norway, Belgium, and Luxembourg up to the mid-1970s, and most recently in Australia, wages indexation has generally been regarded as a necessary and useful device.

Threshold Agreements in the United Kingdom, 1973–74

The danger of wages indexation in the context of a sharp autonomous deterioration in the terms of trade is illustrated by the experience of the United Kingdom, where indexation was introduced at an inopportune moment and in an unfavorable form.

---

[42]Differing provisions for adjustment under wage settlements for particular industries may therefore be preferable to widespread adjustments triggered by a single indicator, such as a change in the minimum wage.

[43]The Netherlands experience with indexation is described in Chapter 10.

Threshold agreements were initially introduced for one year in November 1973 with the immediate purpose of gaining union support for Stage III of the Government's statutory price/wage policy, following a 90-day standstill on price and pay increases, and a period of strict control lasting about six months.[44]

In the outcome, the effect of Stage III was to delay the impact of steeply rising import prices and the acceleration of retail price increases (which was actually enhanced by the raising of indirect taxes early in 1974), and to hold down the increase in average earnings for about six months. Thereafter, the increase in average earnings accelerated very steeply, exceeding the rise in retail prices and causing the rate of price increase to continue to accelerate despite the slowing down of import prices.

The form that indexation took in Stage III was liable to increase the severity of subsequent wage pressures. The combination of a pay-rise ceiling with provision for a liberal flat rate adjustment for each 1 percent rise in prices above the 7 percent threshold was unfortunate. The fact that the ceiling was announced *before* the acceleration of price increases occurred led to a widespread feeling that the conditions upon which it had been based had been breached; and the sharp decline in real earnings during the first half of 1974, together with the provision for automatic adjustment, contributed to strengthen wage claims later in the year.

The flat rate adjustment was dictated by the wish to afford the strongest protection against inflation to the lowest-paid workers. The increase of 40 pence a week was equivalent to about 1 percent of the average weekly wage and salary bill, but each 1 percent increase in retail prices caused a rise of considerably more than 1 percent in below-average wages.[45] The operation of threshold clauses was therefore apt to provoke a faster rise in wages than in prices by inducing wage claims for the maintenance of traditional relativities. In sum, in the British context of fragmented wage bargaining and jealous attention to wage relativities, the specific form of indexation that was adopted introduced a very dangerous element of instability into the system by making wages both more swiftly responsive to price increases and apt to rise more rapidly than prices. With a fluctuating

---

[44]See Chapter 9 for an account of the political setting for threshold agreements and their consequences.

[45]In November 1974, the average increase in wage rates due to threshold payments in settlements coming up for renewal was 12.8 percent, but the increases ranged from more than 20 percent for women shop assistants to less than 10 percent for dockworkers. See Wilkinson (1975, pp. 26–27).

exchange rate, this situation was likely to put pressure on the exchange rate, enhancing the rate of price increase and provoking a still faster rise in wages.

Indexation Under Centralized Agreements in Scandinavian Countries

Explicit compensation for increases in the cost of living has almost invariably constituted an element of central wage settlements in the Scandinavian countries, other than Sweden. In Sweden, price movements have influenced the national "frame" agreements more indirectly, the expected increase in foreign prices entering into the calculation of the "room" for wage increases in the open sector. Of the other four countries, Norway's experience shows how the degree of compensation for price movements can provide a useful element of flexibility in nationwide bargaining over increases in nominal income in a favorable political and economic setting. The experience of Denmark and Finland illustrates the difficulty of controlling the rate of inflation, when indexation is pervasive, if there are strong unresolved conflicts over the distribution of income and a divisive political situation preventing the election of a government with a clear majority and mandate for action. Developments in Finland and Iceland also illustrate the problems posed by widespread indexation of wages in an economy subject to marked fluctuations of export prices and the terms of trade.

Broadly uniform provisions for indexation have generally applied throughout the private sector in both Norway and Denmark, under the influence of the wage agreements negotiated, usually for a two-year period, between the central organizations of the trade unions and the employers' associations. The system of wages indexation has been in many ways similar in the two countries, but in Norway the Government has had a much stronger influence on indexation decisions, and has been more closely involved in the process of income determination.

Indexation of wages is calculated to have provided about 70 percent compensation for the rise in the cost of living in Norway during the early 1970s.[46] Up to 1966, indexation clauses generally provided for the so-called semiautomatic adjustment, that is to say, for reopening of negotiations if the cost of living rose by more than a stated number of

[46]Agricultural incomes were also indexed on the consumer price index. Increases in old-age pensions were decided by the Storting (Parliament), usually on the principle that they should go up in line with the general level of incomes. Social security contributions and benefits, including sick pay, were increased automatically in line with the general level of incomes.

points. Later, fully automatic adjustment was provided, with increases of a certain absolute amount being granted for each point rise in the index over an agreed period, frequently one year.[47]

In Denmark, government attempts to curb the inflationary impact of indexation in the face of balance of payments difficulties and declining export competitiveness precipitated repeated political crises during the 1970s. A crucial factor predisposing the economy to inflation has been the unresolved conflict between the general union movement, which is strongly committed to a policy of wages "solidarity," aiming at a more egalitarian wage structure, and the organizations of higher-paid wage and salary earners who are concerned to maintain their existing differentials. In practice, workers in the engineering and machinery industries were prepared to participate in the central wage settlements, which provide fuller protection against price increases and proportionately larger contractual increases on lower wages, because they were confident of being able to restore their relative differentials via wage drift.

The two-year (or sometimes three-year) wage agreements negotiated between the Federation of Trade Unions (LO) and the central organization of employers (DA) covered less than half of all employees during the mid-1970s, but they set the pattern for agreements covering other workers. In the negotiation of the central wage agreement and other wage agreements, three components of wage increases were considered: the contractual increase in the basic wage rate; the cost of living adjustment; and the expected amount of wage drift, which includes wage increases resulting from the raising of piece rates and other increases in wages negotiated at the industry or plant level. The guarantee of automatic cost of living adjustment generally aimed at a flat rate of compensation, providing for hourly wage rates to rise on average by about 0.7 percent for each 1 percent rise in the price index,[48] but provided almost full compensation for the lowest-paid workers. However, since relative wage levels were maintained by wage drift, the Danish system in practice provided virtually full compensation against price increases for all wage and salary earners, as well as state pensioners and recipients of unemployment and social security benefits. Civil servants generally received full price compensation on the ground that they did not benefit from wage drift.

---

[47]See Chapter 10 for an account of later changes in indexation in Norway.

[48]The wage-regulating price index differed from the regular consumer price index as indirect taxes were excluded, and in the weighting of items covered. Indexation was suspended in 1982.

Developments over the period of the first oil price shock provide an example of how the system functioned. The "frame" agreement signed in March 1973 called for "standard" or "minimum" wage rates to be raised by 0.40 kroner per hour for each 3-point increase in the wage-regulating index. This sum represented about 2 percent of the average hourly wage rates but about 2.5 percent of the lowest rates of pay. When it appeared that the automatic indexation formula would trigger a "three-step" increase in March/April 1974 and an even larger increase in September/October, the Government undertook to subsidize employers for 50 percent of the adjustment becoming due in March, the cost being met out of a compulsory savings scheme levied on higher incomes. Price control was to be used to ensure that wage costs covered by the Government were reflected in lower price increases.

Faced with the prospect of further massive adjustments to wages in early 1975, the Government proposed the adoption of a general price-wage freeze. The unions refused on the grounds that the freeze was likely to be more effective in preventing wage increases than price increases, and the Government was defeated on the issue.

Collective bargaining talks failed to produce a new frame agreement, and the state mediator's draft proposal was rejected by both the unions and the employers. In order to avoid a major industrial conflict in an already difficult economic situation, the Government decided to impose the mediation proposal by law. The March 1975 legislation provided for continuance of automatic adjustment for about two thirds of price increases in the private sector, triggered by a larger price increase than previously, and for adjustments in the public sector and for salaried employees fixed in absolute amounts rather than in percentage terms.

Danish experience illustrates how difficult it is to determine whether the existence of indexation per se has had an influence tending to enhance or to lessen cost pressure. Economists advising the Economic Council concluded in 1973 that wage increases under the two-year agreement would have been larger without indexation, because the union leadership had informed them that they would then have insisted on larger contractual increases. It is conceivable, however, that the employers might have resisted the larger wage claims in that case. In fact, indexation does not seem to have played the crucial role in the inflationary process. The essential problem appears to have been lack of an effective constraint, to force the wage bargaining parties to reach agreement on a noninflationary average movement of wages, under a series of minority governments, which were unable to enforce financial control or to resolve the competing claims of the general union movement and of other interest groups.

Indexation-Based Wages Policy in Australia, 1983–85

Recent Australian experience provides an example of the successful use of indexation in favorable circumstances, as a key element of an incomes policy used to bring down the rate of increase in nominal incomes. Since mid-1983 the Government has pursued macroeconomic policies aimed at simultaneously reducing both unemployment and inflation, framed in the context of extensive consultations and the development of consensus solutions. This approach contrasted strongly with that adopted in Australia during the late 1970s and early 1980s, or in other industrial countries over this period. In mid-1985 Australia was entering the third year of economic recovery, after experiencing a more rapid rise in output than most other industrial countries, a marked deceleration of inflation, and a fall in unemployment.[49]

Centralized wage determination was abandoned in 1981 when the Conciliation and Arbitration Commission decided that, with the spread of independent collective bargaining, there was no longer adequate commitment of participants to the system for it to continue making general indexation-based awards in biannual national wage cases.[50] From mid-1981 to the end of 1982, industry-by-industry negotiations resulted in many consent agreements being ratified by industrial tribunals. The general rate of increase accelerated as unions in the strategic minerals and investment sectors won increases in pay and reduced hours and the concept of "comparative wage justice" was invoked to support similar claims elsewhere. (Average award rates rose at an annual rate of almost 17 percent from the second half of 1981 to the first half of 1982, and both award rates and average earnings rose by more than 17 percent from 1981 to 1983.)[51] At the end of 1982 the Arbitration Commission and the State Tribunals implemented a wages pause for six months at the Government's request.

The wages policy applied since mid-1983 is based upon the Accord reached between the Australian Labor Party and the Australian Council of Trade Unions (ACTU) shortly before the party came to power in March 1983. This "social contract" type agreement sup-

[49]Organization for Economic Cooperation and Development (June 1985, p. 7).

[50]See footnote 36.

[51]Organization for Economic Cooperation and Development (June 1985, p. 32, Table 6, and Table E in the Statistical Annex).

ported a return to centralized wage determination and stated as a prime objective of policy that real wages and real incomes of the non-income-earning segments of the population should be maintained and increased through time with movements in national productivity.[52] However, it was recognized that this objective might need to be temporarily forgone at a time of economic crisis. The Accord also set forth principles concerning the development of nonwage incomes, taxation, and the "social wage" (that is to say, expenditures by governments that affect living standards by income transfers or services). After the election, the Government called a National Economic Summit Conference. This issued an agreed communiqué supporting a policy of reducing unemployment and inflation simultaneously by "the maximum fiscal stimulus consistent with the need to reduce inflation and to avoid upward pressure on interest rates" and recognizing the need for an effective incomes and price policy.[53] A Price Surveillance Authority was set up to monitor, but not to control, prices in key sectors of limited competition. It was agreed that the policy on pay should be developed under the auspices of the Arbitration Commission. A set of principles governing national wage cases was established by the Commission in September 1983, after the existing pay pause had been extended for three months at the Government's request.

The principles provided for full indexation every six months for changes in prices over the two preceding quarters, unless the Commission was persuaded otherwise. Unlike 1975, on this occasion the unions individually were required to undertake to make no wage claims outside the system, in order to qualify for indexation. Indexation was to be applied uniformly to all award wages unless the Commission decided otherwise in exceptional circumstances. An application for a productivity-based wage increase would be heard not before 1985. The principles were to be reviewed after two years.[54]

Wage inflation was dramatically reduced in 1983 and 1984 as a consequence of the nine-months pay pause and the subsequent application of the wage fixing principles.[55] The enforcement of the

---

[52]Dawkins and Blandy (1985, p. 39).

[53]Cited by Dawkins and Blandy (1985, p. 40). While there was agreement on the return to centralized wage determination, there was no agreement by the employers to indexation at the conference.

[54]The principles for wage determination in 1983–85 are reproduced in Organization for Economic Cooperation and Development (June 1984, Annex I, pp. 54–57).

[55]Award wage rates rose from half year to half year at annual rates of 3.4, 4.2, 9.1, and 4.3 percent during 1983–84. Increases in average non-farm earnings were similar until the second half of 1984. Over the same periods, consumer prices exclusive of hospital and medical services rose by 9.3, 8.1, 6.1, and 5.5 percent. See Organization for Economic Cooperation and Development (1985, Table 6, p. 33).

wage fixing principles was aided both by the unions' support for the Government's employment and social policies and by the context of exceptionally heavy unemployment.[56] The Organization for Economic Cooperation and Development (June 1985, p. 32) concluded that there was little evidence that over-award wage increases were being negotiated outside the system during the first half of 1985, though some wage drift seemed to be occurring as a result of the job reclassifications within enterprises.

Three factors caused indexation to be exceptionally helpful in bringing down the rate of wage increase. One was the timing of its introduction after the pay pause and the fact that recession had slowed the rise in consumer prices. The second was the special factor of the switch from private to partly public-financed health care and the exclusion of Medicare expenditures from the consumer price index. As a result, the index actually fell during the first two quarters of 1984 and there was no indexation increase in October 1984. The third was the marked appreciation of the Australian dollar between December 1983 and November 1984, which also served to moderate the rise in consumer prices.

During its first two and a half years in office, the Hawke Government pursued an expansionary fiscal policy and a monetary policy set to promote a lowering of inflation while allowing the expansion of demand to proceed. Monetary control was enhanced by the floating of the Australian dollar after large inflows of short-term capital occurred late in 1983; it was associated with a considerable deregulation of the financial sector. The incomes policy implemented under the Accord with the Council of Trade Unions was a major instrument in restraining wage increases and inflation and helped in restoring profits during 1983–85.[57]

While wage and price inflation moderated in 1983 and 1984, rising domestic demand and the strengthening of the exchange rate led to a sharp worsening of the current account deficit and increased import penetration in 1984, and this precipitated a steep decline in the exchange rate during the first half of 1985. The depreciation contributed to raise the consumer price index by about 2 percentage points in each half of 1985. In this context, full indexation of wages posed problems since a real depreciation was required to improve the current account balance and support output and employment.

---

[56]After averaging less than 6 percent during 1975–82, unemployment rose to almost 10 percent in 1983, and remained above 9 percent in 1984.

[57]Organization for Economic Cooperation and Development (June 1985, pp. 7–9).

In September 1985 the Government and the ACTU announced their agreement to extend the Prices and Incomes Accord for two years, with a provision to exclude the effect of the depreciation in wage indexation.[58] The Government and the ACTU agreed to propose to the Conciliation and Arbitration Commission that in the national wage increase of April–May 1986 the percentage increase called for by the rise in consumer prices should be "discounted" by 2 percentage points. (This adjustment is held roughly to offset the effect of the depreciation in raising consumer prices from 1984 to 1985.) To compensate for the effects of the proposed "discounting" on living standards, the Government agreed to reduce marginal tax rates on personal incomes in September 1986. Provision of the tax cut is conditional upon compliance by all concerned, with the principles agreed between the ACTU and the Government, and in particular with the requirement that trade unions not press any claims outside the centralized wage fixing system.

The new Accord also provided for a reduction in the size of the ACTU's claim for a productivity-based wage increase then before the Commission, and a delay in making the award. The original claim for a 4 percent increase in wages was replaced by a 3 percent increase to be given in the form of new or improved occupational superannuation provisions. The award would be implemented gradually (industry by industry or occupation by occupation) over the two years beginning in July 1986. It is estimated that since an increase in superannuation payments does not raise holiday pay, payroll tax, and similar expenditures, the provision would raise employers' nominal labor costs by slightly less than 2½ percent. Since the rise in costs is expected to be smaller than the expected cumulative productivity gains over the three years mid-1985 to mid-1988, the agreed productivity adjustment would contribute to mitigating the direct and indirect effects of the depreciation of the Australian dollar on consumer prices.

Escalator Clauses in the United States in the 1950s

A detailed empirical study of the effect of U.S. long-term wage agreements incorporating escalator clauses at the time of the Korean war[59] concluded that during periods of rapid price increase, automatic wage increases "led" but did not exceed changes in closely related

---

[58]There was a noted precedent for a deliberate cut in real wages in the 10 percent reduction imposed by the Arbitration Court in January 1931, in order to counter the drastic worsening in the terms of trade. Braun (1974, p. 178) and Reddaway (1938).

[59]Soffer (1959a).

wages; that automatic adjustment tended to lessen the effects of short-term restraining influences in industries where wages tended to lag; and that they increased the sensitivity of the general wage level to price changes.

Soffer found that when agreements both with and without provision for automatic adjustment for price increases existed in bargaining units subject to similar demand conditions, escalator clauses tended to have a positive influence on the average rate of wage increase. This came about because during a period of rising prices, it was almost impossible to negotiate wage increases as frequently and for similar amounts as those occurring under escalator clauses. Thus, "time inequities" or temporary divergence in rates of wage increase became widespread. "The more rapid the inflation, the greater are the immediate and expected lags of the relatively infrequently negotiated wages behind the automatically adjusted wages. These lags are rather quickly eliminated by supplementing the smaller increases,"[60] because smaller wage increases than those already granted are likely to be unacceptable to the union and its members. However, if the catching-up with automatically adjusted wages entails relatively larger current increases in other wages, this will be perceived by wage earners who are covered by escalator contracts as an adverse shift in their relative wages, requiring escalator increases to be supplemented by additional negotiated increases. Given this kind of interrelation between automatic and negotiated wage increases, the influence of automatic adjustment on the movement of wages in general could not of course be assessed by comparing the movement of escalated and nonescalated wages, or the share of automatic increases in the average overall increases in wages.

Automatic Adjustment of the Basic Wage in Australia, 1922–1953

Seen in a long-term perspective, the adoption of an effective system of indexation may in some circumstances help to make the economy less subject to cost pressure by retarding, or preventing, the development of a militant union movement, of wage bargaining organizations at the factory level, or of strong unions in the public sector. This seems to have been true in Australia, where from 1922 to 1953 the pay of the majority of wage earners was adjusted upward (or downward) for changes in the purchasing power of the basic wage component.[61]

[60] Soffer (1959a, p. 53).

[61] For a description of the system of indexation over this period, and its effects see Braun (1974).

Under this system, each worker in effect received a fixed minimum real wage plus additional purchasing power, not adjusted for price changes, if, for example, he qualified for a margin for skill or adverse working conditions. Automatic adjustment served to keep the general level of wages and prices moving in line with those of other countries, but problems arose when import prices moved very differently from export prices, or when both were subject to extremely sharp short-term fluctuations, as in the early 1950s. The automatic adjustment of wages meant that an autonomous inflationary (or deflationary) stimulus produced a swift chain reaction on domestic costs and prices. The goal of the system was not price stability but near-stability of real wages and flexibility of money wages and prices.[62]

Movements of the price level in both directions were tolerable because almost all incomes were adjusted for changes in the price level. As Keynes remarked in 1923, "a change in the value of money, that is to say in the level of prices, is important to Society only insofar as its incidence is unequal."[63]

Australian experience may thus be seen as an illustration of Friedman's thesis that while

> widespread escalator clauses would make it easier for the public to recognize changes in the rate of inflation, would thereby reduce the time-lag in adapting to such changes, and thus make the nominal price level more sensitive and variable. . . . But, if so, the *real variables* would be *less* sensitive and *more* stable—a highly beneficial trade off.[64]

It is, however, a revealing special case, since pressures by highly organized groups of workers, in a favorable bargaining position to secure increases over and above the increases in the basic wage component of pay, were restrained by the operation of the compulsory arbitration system. (One evidence of this is the fact that the wage structure that emerged was narrower than that in most other countries.) Thanks to this restraint, indexation did not generally tend to produce a faster rate of inflation than that experienced in other industrial countries, and was not associated with chronic balance of payments difficulties as in some less successful cases.

The Case For and Against Indexation

Discussion of the economic case for indexation has tended to obscure the fact that indexation is primarily a means of mitigating the

---

[62]Braun (1974, p. 176).
[63]Keynes (1923, p. 1).
[64]Friedman (1974, p. 44–45).

political consequences of rapid inflation, and of lessening intergroup conflicts occasioned by changes in the distribution of income. The principal economic benefits stemming from indexation are likely to be the avoidance of industrial unrest and frictions, loss of morale, and time-consuming wage bargaining processes that would otherwise occur, and the effects in promoting conditions more conducive to long-range planning by enterprises and a political climate more favorable to business than might otherwise exist.

Even when there is evidence that wages indexation may have contributed to aggravate the rate of price inflation, indexation may also have been an important element in ensuring the survival of a democratic, free enterprise system. In Finland, France, and Italy, a divisive political situation in the 1950s was rendered less explosive by indexation of wages, and this was still more true in countries such as the Netherlands and the United Kingdom in the mid-1970s. It is rightly emphasized that "it will not be possible to successively apply and abolish indexation in the light of economic policy. . . . It is too closely tied up with tradition and the system of industrial relations."[65] However, the decision to introduce indexation will often be dictated by overriding "short-term imperatives" of the immediate political situation.

---

[65]Geluck (1974, pp. 189–90).

Part III

Wage Bargaining Institutions, Incomes Policy, and Demand Management Since the 1960s

9

Case Studies of Four Large Economies

Chapters 9 and 10 consist of case studies and some general conclusions on labor market organization and incomes policies since the 1960s in the United Kingdom, Japan, the Federal Republic of Germany, and Canada; and in Austria, the Netherlands, and Norway. These studies illustrate the influence of the salient features of the wage bargaining system in facilitating demand management in Japan and Germany, and the characteristics of the incomes policies, results achieved, and problems encountered in the other five countries.

United Kingdom: Incomes Policies of the 1970s

Relatively high unit labor costs at the ruling exchange rate hampered industrial progress and the expansion of job openings in the open sector of the British economy over much of the postwar period. Two major factors contributing to the difficulty of maintaining a competitive level of production costs at high levels of employment were the fragmented wage bargaining system—which tended to produce a relatively rapid rise in nominal wages and salaries as the result of numerous settlements at different bargaining levels—and the slow growth of productivity.[1] The latter stemmed partly from the lower profitability and the lower rate of investment in productive capacity in the open sector of the economy than in most other industrial countries. Strong political demands for full employment and the tendency to cost pressure fostered reliance on actively expansion-

[1] Blackaby (1978a, p. 653).

ary demand policies coupled with various forms of incomes policy.[2] The economic strategy was sharply reversed in 1979 with the coming to power of the Conservative Government.

Institutional Setting

It is not clear why employers in the United Kingdom, unlike those in other strongly unionized countries, did not organize to resist wage claims and to enforce greater coordination of the wage bargaining system and more orderly industrial relations procedures. One reason seems to be that as long as easy labor market conditions prevailed in the industrial sector,[3] separate collective bargaining with numerous groups of workers and "informal" wage settlements without legally binding contracts were not disadvantageous for employers. They became so under conditions of labor scarcity—by permitting the reopening of negotiations at will, and consequent leap-frogging wage settlements for different groups, and by facilitating supplementary wage claims arising out of interpretation disputes. The employers' incentive to press for a reform of the wage bargaining system was limited under conditions of heavy unemployment prevailing in the late nineteenth and early twentieth centuries and during the interwar years.

Another important influence working in the same direction was the considerable degree of protection enjoyed by British producers in the home market and the large overseas markets of the Commonwealth. Though the bargaining power of labor generally was weakened by heavy unemployment, wages in the more capital-intensive industries were kept up by the stronger organization and bargaining power of unions there. Beginning in the nineteenth century, such industries became increasingly dependent on the protected markets. Commonwealth protection was reinforced during the 1930s, and for some years after World War II, British firms benefited from exceptional opportunities in export markets, a booming home market, and import controls.

The lack of coordinated bargaining and formalized industrial relations procedures was strongly felt during both World Wars, when

---

[2] For a comparison of the purpose of incomes policies and the results achieved in the United Kingdom and the Netherlands—both economies marked by pervasive unionization and uncoordinated wage bargaining organizations—see Braun (1985, pp. 144–46). Government policies and the problems encountered before the 1970s are described in Worswick and Ady (1962), Dow (1964), Kaldor (1966), Caves and Associates (1968), Fels (1972), Blackaby (1978a), and Cairncross (1985). The Appendix in Fallick and Elliott (1981) provides a chronology of developments from 1947 to 1979.

[3] As a result of large shifts out of rural employment or of heavy unemployment.

war production rendered it essential to avoid stoppages at the plant level. Wartime expedients had important peacetime repercussions. The need to settle disputes within the plant resulted in the emergence of the shop stewards movement, comprising employees' representatives who were largely independent of the unions. Particularly in the metals and engineering industries, during and after World War II the wage structure came to be a chaotic mix of national basic rates, of local adjustments negotiated with the unions, and of special supplements negotiated with the shop stewards at the plant.[4]

The problem of restraining wage increases became of increasing concern to enterprises in the open sector as trade was liberalized and foreign competition intensified during the 1950s. But, since claims pressed by shop stewards within the plant or enterprise now constituted a major element of wage pressure, coordination with other employers did not appear to be the solution.[5] Instead the focus turned to incomes policy as a means of bringing public opinion to bear in moderating the scale of wage claims.[6]

Previous Incomes Policies

After the Labour Government came to power in 1964, the unions agreed to cooperate in a voluntary incomes policy (as they had in 1948–49) under the national plan to promote faster growth and full employment by a substantial expansion of the public sector. Following two balance of payments crises and devaluation, a statutory incomes policy was introduced in 1967, at a time when the unions were growing increasingly hostile to the Wilson Government. The final months of the Government in 1969 were marked by an ill-conceived attempt to introduce legislation to limit unofficial strikes.[7] The proposal, which

[4] Knowles and Robertson (1951).

[5] It was not until 1979—after the abandonment of incomes policy by the Thatcher Government—that the Confederation of British Industry proposed the initiation of more unified resistance to wage claims with the establishment of a common strike fund modeled on that in the Federal Republic of Germany and Sweden. Owing to the divergent interests of the stronger enterprises and the smaller concerns, the proposal was not supported by the large enterprises. Instead, they acted individually to secure a coordinated wage structure and improved industrial relations within the enterprise.

[6] In February 1962 the Conservative Government set out its proposals for a productivity-based "guiding light" for increases in wages and salaries, and in November the National Incomes Commission was set up as an independent tribunal to deal with specific cases referred to it by the Government. See the U.K. Treasury, *Incomes Policy: The Next Step* (February 1962) and Fallick and Elliott (1981, Appendix).

[7] The proposals initially published in the 1968 White Paper, *In Place of Strife*, would have provided compensating benefits to the unions but these were dropped in 1969. See Flanagan, Soskice, and Ulman (1983, p. 394).

was strongly opposed by the unions, divided the Labour Party and was followed by an unprecedented wave of unofficial strikes in the public sector,[8] after which the incomes policy effectively ceased to apply.

During the 1960s, the explicit purpose of incomes policy was to secure a downward adjustment of relative labor costs, while avoiding a change in the exchange rate. In practice, however, the main effect was to make it possible to maintain very low unemployment by expansionary fiscal policy. Incomes policy helped to secure this option both by shielding the open sector to some extent from wage pressures and so limiting a worsening of the relative cost position, and by constraining the rise in nominal income and so lessening the adverse impact of fiscal policy upon the external balance. The industrial sector was protected from the painful consequences of its worsening technological competitiveness as long as the home market was expanding and there were growing opportunities of selling to the public sector, where control over pricing was lax. This context was not one to encourage aggressive export efforts and the investment needed to maintain competitiveness in the face of heavy investment in up-to-date capacity then taking place in many other countries.

Policies of the Early 1970s

The Heath Government, which came to power in June 1970, restored free collective bargaining. It was hoped to moderate wage increases by permitting a somewhat higher level of unemployment, by stiffer bargaining in the public sector aiming to gradually bring down wage increases there, and by the passage of the Industrial Relations Act.[9] However, incomes policy was subsequently reintroduced in an attempt to contain the consequences of an excessive monetary expansion, stemming from efforts to promote a rapid recovery from the 1971 recession just after long-standing credit controls were relaxed.[10]

---

[8] See Chapter 5.

[9] Smith (1980, pp. 121–27).

[10] In adopting a program of stimulatory measures, the Government had indicated that faster growth would require a relatively rapid rise in the money supply and expressed its determination not to allow the expansion of output and employment to be frustrated by efforts to maintain an unrealistic exchange rate. Both the broadly defined money stock (M3) and domestic credit rose by about 60 percent between 1971 and the end of 1973. Runaway credit expansion was associated with the introduction of a new regime of monetary management in 1971 under which long-established quantitative restrictions on bank lending were abandoned and emphasis was placed on more indirect techniques, involving a greater use of open market operations in pursuit of more flexible interest rates and the introduction of uniform reserve requirements for the whole banking sector. The changes resulted in the banks attracting funds away from other markets, such as the local authorities

The British experience of the mid-1970s represents a classic example of an inflation induced by overly expansionary policies rather than a case of cost-push inflation per se. The consequences of monetary and fiscal policies were suppressed and delayed by price and wage controls in 1972–73 and by policies adopted to prevent, or limit, the depreciation of the exchange rate.

Led by a boom in private consumption, output expanded rapidly in 1972 and early 1973, and unemployment fell steeply. A marked rise in per capita output served to moderate the rise in labor cost per unit of output. The increase in hourly wage rates decelerated somewhat to about 12 percent per annum in mid-1972, but the balance of trade deteriorated sharply. Mounting concern about the balance of payments, industrial unrest, and the re-emergence of severe cost pressure led to a substantial move out of sterling in June 1972. Following the freeing of the rate, the pound depreciated by about 6 percent, and thereafter wage increases accelerated rapidly. Sterling declined by a further 3 percent after the Trades Union Congress (TUC) rejected the Government's initial proposals on prices and incomes.

Statutory Incomes Policy, 1972–74

To forestall the acceleration of inflation and give time for anti-inflation programs to be drawn up, the Government imposed a 90-day standstill on pay, prices, profits, and dividends in November 1972. This was later extended to March–April 1973. There followed a period of strict statutory controls administered by a Pay Board and a Price Commission established for the purpose, lasting about six months (Stage II), and a continuation of the strict controls on prices, profits, and dividends, with somewhat greater flexibility on pay in Stage III (intended to apply for one year).

In Stage II, pay increases were limited to £1 a week, plus a sum equivalent to 4 percent of the average pay bill per head for the group covered over the preceding 12 months. The flat rate increase resulted

---

and intercompany lending, and made it difficult for the authorities either to influence or to judge the scale of the expansion. The Government's wish not to impede investment delayed and limited measures to secure control over credit expansion until late 1973. Public sector borrowing increased from about 1.7 percent of GDP in 1970/71 and 1971/72 to 3.9 percent in 1972/73 and 6.3 percent in 1973/74 but the increase had a comparatively slight additional impact on the money supply. The monetary expansion was associated with a very sharp rise in real estate prices, speculative purchases of houses and commercial property for improvement, and a marked increase in private housebuilding. The importance of the very steep rise in property values as a factor exacerbating inflationary pressures throughout the economy was recognized in a White Paper of April 1973, outlining measures to assure additional low-cost housing.

in larger-than-average percentage increases for lower-paid employees. An upper limit of £250 a year was set for the increase to any individual.[11] It was also laid down that wage settlements should not be made at intervals of less than 12 months.

Price controls included restrictions on the type of costs that manufacturing and service enterprises could pass on in domestic prices and on net percentage profit margins for domestic sales.[12] In order to promote stiffer resistance to wage claims, enterprises were generally required to absorb one half of increases in unit labor costs in a "productivity deduction." (This provision was later eased for labor-intensive enterprises.) Distributors' prices were controlled by limiting their gross profit margins, increases in dividend payments were restricted, and business rents were frozen.

Large firms, or smaller firms supplying a substantial share of the home market for certain important items, were required to obtain prior consent before raising prices. Such firms, and medium-sized firms, were required to provide the Price Commission with quarterly reports on costs, prices, and profit margins. Nationalized industries and other public enterprises were subject to the same price controls as comparable private enterprises.[13] A nationalized industry in deficit was not to increase its prices by more than allowable cost increases, except to avoid an increase in its deficit.

Threshold Agreements

In the fall of 1973, agreement was reached with the TUC for the continuation of controls for one year, with provision for "threshold" indexation arrangements. When Stage III came into effect in November 1973, the scope of price surveillance was widened but certain provisions were added to ease the financial position of enterprises.[14]

---

[11] Pay increases were monitored under a four-tier system: (1) settlements affecting more than 1,000 employees were to be notified eight weeks in advance and were not to be implemented until the Pay Board had given its approval or the eight weeks had lapsed; (2) settlements affecting 100–1,000 employees were to be notified to the Board and periodic returns were to be provided of increases in earnings under schemes of payment by results; (3) firms with more than 10 employees were required to keep records of pay increases and their effect on the wage bill; and (4) smaller firms were exempt.

[12] Net profit margins were not to exceed the average level of the best two years of account prior to April 30, 1973. If that limit was exceeded, price reductions were to be required, unless the return on capital or net profit margin was exceptionally low.

[13] Some prices, specifically for coal and most iron and steel prices, were excluded by reason of U.K. membership in the European Coal and Steel Community.

[14] Specifically (1) enterprises making losses or earning very low profits were permitted to raise their prices to yield a minimum return of 8 percent on capital, compared with 5 percent in Stage II; (2) price controls were eased for capital-intensive industries operating

Pay increases of up to £2.25 a week or 7 percent were permitted, subject to a ceiling of £350 a year. The 7 percent included a 1 percent allowance for correcting anomalies and obstacles to the better use of manpower. Protection against price increases could be provided via "threshold agreements" should the retail price index rise by more than 6 percent. Under the agreements, additional payments of 40 pence a week were permissible for each 1 point rise in the index after it reached 106 (October 1973 = 100). This represented full compensation for price increases at the average level of wages, and more (or less) than full compensation at lower (or higher) than average wages. Consequently, the operation of the threshold clauses tended to induce wage claims for the maintenance of traditional relativities and so to provoke a faster rise in wages than in prices.[15]

The Government was anxious to reach an agreement with the unions, but with the prospect of further depreciation, the provision for indexation, particularly in a form likely to set off wage/wage competition, was a dangerous step. After the defeat of the Government in an election called over the miners' insistence on a large wage increase,[16] Labour came to power in February 1974, pledged not to rescind "threshold" agreements or to reintroduce stricter wage controls.

The effect of Stage III was to delay the impact of steeply rising import prices until the first quarter of 1974; thereafter the increase in average earnings accelerated very steeply as the further surge in import prices triggered threshold payments sooner and more frequently than had been anticipated. In the event, the "threshold" agreements served to ensure that in the United Kingdom, unlike many other industrial countries, the impact of sharply rising commodity prices and of the oil price increase was fully compensated in nominal wage increases.

"Voluntary" Incomes Policies After Mid-1974

The "Social Contract" of 1974–75

The Labour Government abolished statutory wage controls in July 1974 and instituted a system of voluntary wage restraint under the

---

well below capacity at the beginning of the controls program; and (3) it was provided that precontrol profit margins should not be reduced by more than 10 percent by the operation of price controls. To encourage investment, increased depreciation could be taken into account in justifying proposed price increases. Dividend increases were still limited to 5 percent a year, but some latitude was permitted where new capital had to be raised for investment.

[15] See the account of the experience with threshold agreements in Chapter 8.

[16] The miners' case for a larger-than-average wage increase had some justification on grounds of the urgent need to expand production and the greatly increased value of coal output following the oil price rise. Relative wages in coal mining had fallen greatly over the postwar period.

Social Contract negotiated with the TUC. In return for a commitment by the Government to improve welfare benefits and pensions and to implement legislation favorable to the union movement, the TUC issued guidelines on pay, providing for a minimum interval of 12 months between settlements and calling for increases in general not to exceed the rise in the cost of living during the 12 months to August 1975. However, larger increases were specifically provided for the lower paid, and the Government also authorized special increases for some groups, mainly public sector employees, whose remuneration had fallen relative to other groups during the period of statutory controls. In practice, many settlements exceeded the rise in consumer prices as special increases for particular groups tended to spread to others to maintain or restore differentials. Escalating expectations of price inflation caused the unions to press for wage increases covering not only past but also anticipated price increases. Very severe fiscal drag occasioned by rapidly rising nominal incomes was a further source of wage pressures.[17] Over the 12 months average weekly earnings rose by nearly 28 percent.

The Government was precluded from reintroducing controls on nominal incomes by the mandate on which it won the election. Its subsequent acceptance of the principle of full compensation for price increases under the Social Contract compounded the danger that depreciation would induce an explosive acceleration of inflation. Depreciation could be avoided, or at least postponed, because large autonomous inflows of funds to the London market from oil producing countries supported the rate. The United Kingdom had a comparative advantage second only to that of the United States in attracting such funds. Thereafter, the very large volume of outstanding short-term foreign exchange liabilities posed the risk that a moderate depreciation could set off a heavy outflow of capital, precipitating a sharp decline in the rate, and inducing spiraling wage inflation and depreciation. Hence, later policies were aimed at avoiding depreciation of the exchange rate, while endeavoring to bring down the rate of inflation by securing the unions' agreement to more moderate wage settlements. The Government in effect relied on a very large public sector deficit,[18]

---

[17] See Chapter 3.

[18] The budget for 1974/75 initially provided for a marked reduction in public sector borrowing, achieved mainly by raising the corporation tax rate and employers' national insurance contributions. Food subsidies and indirect taxes on less essentials were increased, with the combined effect of raising the retail price index by 2 percentage points. In July 1974, faced with stagnating output and accelerating inflation, the Government took steps to slow domestic price increases and restore the cuts in purchasing power made in the budget—by lowering the value-added tax from 10 percent to 8 percent and further increasing food subsidies, thereby holding down threshold payments. Relief was provided

financed largely by continued foreign borrowing, both to provide a stimulus to the economy and to support the exchange rate, thereby moderating price increases. Such policies, however, served to reinforce the impact of above-average wage inflation on the exposed industrial base of the economy.

The chain of developments affecting the movement of nominal wages between November 1973 and August 1975, combined with the maintenance of the pound by public sector borrowing abroad, caused British unit labor costs to go up by 10 percent compared to its competitors. Worsening cost competitiveness and the increasing penetration by foreign suppliers of U.K. producers' home and export markets intensified the effects of the external recession upon industrial output and employment.[19] These effects were aggravated by fiscal drag, which caused higher nominal wage and salary bills to be associated with *reduced* after-tax purchasing power of wage and salary earners. The consequent weakening of household demand led to increased public expenditure on unemployment benefits and public assistance and to demands for higher public spending to maintain employment. While it served to promote increased employment in the public sector,[20] expansionary public spending failed to sustain industrial employment because of the leakages due to increasing imports and the unfavorable climate for industrial investment. It was illogical to expand real public expenditure in order to provide a stimulus to the economy, without at least offsetting the impact of fiscal drag in limiting real private demand and aggravating cost pressures.[21] It

---

from local taxes and the regional employment premium was doubled. In November, the value-added tax on gasoline was increased to 25 percent, and the tax on stock appreciation was deferred and price controls were eased to lessen the acute financial strain on enterprises. The Government also announced a fund of £1 billion to be made available over two years for medium-term financing of productive investment. In the event, the lowering of value-added tax and of corporation tax merely offset the higher tax yields resulting from the rise in personal incomes. The very large increase in the public sector borrowing requirement in 1974/75 was almost entirely due to increased expenditure.

[19] Between 1973 and 1976 industrial employment fell by 6.8 percent, while other employment rose by 3.4 percent.

[20] Greatly increased tax collections and social security transfers themselves required a large expansion in public service employment. For example, the number of tax inspectors concerned with P.A.Y.E. (direct taxes on wages and salaries) rose by 30 percent from 1974 to 1977.

[21] The effect that the unprecedented rise in nominal wages was having in increasing rates of direct taxation in 1974–75 only attracted attention some time later. In February 1977, a National Institute study pointed out that "real disposable earnings per employee remained virtually unchanged in 1974 and 1975. This flattening off was not, as one might have suspected, attributable to the recession and the poor productivity performance of labour. In fact, real gross earnings rose by an average of 3¾ per cent in the two years 1974 and 1975, a faster rate of growth than occurred between 1970 and 1973, but this rise was almost completely offset by tax increases." National Institute of Economic and Social Research (1977, p. 14).

might have been preferable to provide the stimulus in part by cutting real direct tax rates instead of expanding public expenditures.

This solution was ruled out by the terms of the Social Contract with the TUC. It is interesting to compare the attitude of the TUC and its Norwegian counterpart toward tax reductions in compensation foı wage restraint (see Chapter 10). In the United Kingdom, it was not until the unions ceased to cooperate in the policy of wage restraint in mid-1977 that the Government sought to use reductions in taxes to moderate wage pressures (see p. 221). It is not excluded that the earlier granting of tax concessions as an accompaniment to the stiff wage restraint of 1976–77 might have helped to secure continued rank and file support for incomes policy in 1977–78. The measure might have been timed to coincide with the introduction of cash limits on government expenditure (see below).

Voluntary Wage Restraint, 1975–77

Over the next two 12-month periods, limits for wage increases were agreed between the Government and the TUC. Phase I set a limit of £6 a week for increases in pay over the year August 1975–July 1976, subject to an upper cutoff point of £8,500, above which no increase was permissible. The £6 limit represented a 10½ percent increase in average earnings. With exceptions, such as those permitting further progress toward equal pay for women and commitments entered into before the beginning of the policy, the limit implied an increase in average earnings of about 12 percent. The actual increase for the year ended July 1976 was 13.9 percent, about half that of the preceding 12 months. There were no reported breaches of the £6 limit. Higher-than-estimated earnings drift appears to have been due to changes in the composition of the work force and an increase in average hours worked. The growth of average earnings in the public sector was kept about 2–3 percentage points below that of earnings in the private sector.

The Price Code was gradually relaxed late in 1975 and during 1976, with the aim of improving profits and cash flow and encouraging investment. Tax relief—permitting 70 percent of stock appreciation to be excluded from profits—was granted for two years. The "productivity deduction," whereby only 80 percent of any increase in wage costs could be passed on in prices, was abolished. In order to encourage investment, firms were permitted to pass on 50 percent, instead of 17½ percent, of firmly budgeted expenditure on capital investment in higher prices and profit margins. As in 1975, weak demand conditions seem to have pre-empted any effect that the price controls might have had in keeping down prices. Gross profit margins were halved between 1975 and 1976—a steeper fall than in almost any other country. Many companies' survival depended on the large reductions in corporate taxes provided by the stock appreciation relief and investment allowances.

An important step in the direction of securing control over the rate of inflation was taken shortly before the start of Phase II, with the introduction in April 1976, at the behest of the International Monetary Fund, of cash limits for about three fourths of all voted government expenditures, other than social security benefits, and for central government grants to local authorities.[22] The estimated total financing requirement of the nationalized industries in the form of loans, grants, and dividend capital was also treated as a form of cash limit. Any new spending plans during the financial year had to be within the limits of the contingency reserve incorporated in the budget. The increasingly strict enforcement of cash limits had a marked effect in limiting public sector expenditure[23] during the first half of 1977—partly because the shortfalls of some departments were not offset by overspending by others—and it seems to have been an important factor in restraining the rise of wages in the public sector.

Much stricter wage limits were agreed for Phase II. Pay increases for the 12 months beginning August 1976 were not to exceed £2.50 for those earning less than £50 a week or 5 percent for those earning £50 to £80, with a maximum weekly increase of £4. The overall increase averaged 4½ percent. With earnings drift estimated to add about 2 percentage points, it was foreseen that average labor earnings would rise by about 7 percent. Average earnings actually rose by 9 percent.

Although the observance of the pay limit by employees was voluntary, the policy was backed by the threat of sanctions that could be imposed on employers making settlements outside the limit, and the existing system of price controls was amended so as to prevent pay settlements that exceeded the limit being reflected in higher prices. The Government announced that discretionary assistance under the Industry Act would not be given to companies that contravened the pay limit, and that, in its purchasing policy and in the awarding of

---

[22] The need for nominal limits on the public expenditure, even under expansionary policies, as an essential element of incomes policy is discussed below. Cash limits were first introduced in 1975 but then applied only to public sector building and construction programs. In 1976–77, limits were set for 126 expenditure blocks. At the same time, a new system of monitoring actual expenditure was developed in order to prevent expenditure overrunning the limits.

[23] In the event, the new system was almost too successful, resulting in very substantial underspending below that called for in the budget.

contracts, it would take account of a firm's record of observing the pay limit. It would also refuse to cover excessive wage settlements made by local authorities or the nationalized industries by increasing subsidies and it would use its control over borrowing by other public sector entities in such a way as to ensure their compliance with the pay limit.

At the close of Phase II, a new Act relating to the Price Commission came into force. This empowered the Commission to investigate price increases proposed by companies and gave it authority, modeled on the powers of a similar organization in Belgium, to recommend price freezes or to delay price increases for up to a year. At the same time, a key provision of the original 1973 legislation, that price increases in manufacturing and services were to be permitted only to the extent that they reflected an increase in allowable costs, was abandoned.

Wage Restraint Without TUC Endorsement, 1977–79

There was mounting dissatisfaction with the limits on wage increases as Phase II came to an end. The narrowing of differentials, growing anomalies in wage structures, and a refusal to permit a synchronization of settlements with different unions in the negotiations with British Leyland were adduced to justify a return to free collective bargaining. A more potent cause of the mounting opposition to continued wage restraint was, however, the fall in real wages during Phase II. Whereas average earnings had risen in line with consumer prices during Phase I, during Phase II the rise in earnings had decelerated to 9 percent, while the increase in retail prices had accelerated to an annual rate of 22 percent in the six months to April 1977 under the impact of the steep fall in the exchange rate, a sharp rise in food prices, and increased indirect taxes and lower subsidies.

By July 1977, it became clear that the unions would not agree to any explicit Phase III of the voluntary wages policy. In seeking to achieve an orderly gradual return to normal collective bargaining, the Government reiterated the importance of compliance with the TUC's call for continued observance of the 12-month rule as a means of preventing a free-for-all and resulting wage explosion.[24] Without announcing a guideline for individual settlements, the Government urged that, in general, settlements should be such as to ensure that earnings did not rise by more than 10 percent on average, requiring that most settlements be well within single figures. It also emphasized that it would not be possible to correct anomalies of pay quickly and

[24] Continued observance of the rule meant that the next wage settlement for the majority of employees would not take place before the first half of 1978.

that only very severe distortions could be tackled over the next 12 months. Pension improvements were removed from the pay code restrictions.

In August, the Government reaffirmed its intention to maintain strict control over public expenditure with no change in the cash limits and announced a series of measures intended to ensure that the target for wage increases was realized. Controls over dividends and profit margins were extended for one year—the limit on dividends remaining at 10 percent. Companies that broke the 12-month rule for wage settlements were to have their statutory profit margin ceilings reduced by the amount of the settlement (for capital-intensive industries, the reduction was greater). If profits exceeded the reduced ceiling, the firm would have to reduce its prices. Companies that granted excessively large wage increases would continue to be discriminated against in public purchasing and industrial assistance. (However, the Government abandoned its proposal to use the investigatory powers of the Price Commission in such cases.) Tax reliefs were granted to moderate pressures for wage increases and to create a favorable climate for an orderly restoration of collective bargaining.[25] Schemes were initiated to give training and work experience to young people and to provide temporary employment opportunities for adults.

The sanctions against companies were hotly opposed by the Confederation of British Industry and employers generally. The Government became involved in legal action and lost its case in at least one instance where a contract was blocked. As with many punitive provisions, sanctions were more powerful as a potential threat than when they were actually invoked.[26] In practice, it was difficult to penalize a large supplier without interfering with the efficient operation of the public sector and even action against a small subcontractor could have damaging repercussions on its customers who had not broken the rules. For these reasons the Government used sanctions sparingly, but cannily, for demonstration effects in Phase III, not however without raising serious issues of "equity." When it adopted

[25] The basic tax rate was reduced from 35 percent to 34 percent and marginal tax rates on smaller incomes were lowered by increases in personal allowances. Children's allowances (payable to mothers) were increased, but tax allowances for children were lowered. This had the effect of reducing the father's take-home pay. Family income supplements were granted to bring the income of lower-paid workers up to the level of social security benefits. The rise in consumer prices was alleviated by a large reduction in the duty on gasoline, an increased milk subsidy, and higher income limits for free school meals. The price of electricity was reduced for families receiving supplementary benefits.

[26] See the Australian experience in the attempt to implement penal sanctions against strikes in the late 1960s. Braun (1974, pp. 174–75 and 205–206) and Phelps Brown (1971b).

the tighter wage guideline after July 1978, it appeared to be contemplating more drastic use of sanctions.

Despite the unions' refusal to endorse the Government's Phase III policy, there was no immediate rash of higher settlements in late 1977. Indeed, there was a tendency for major settlements to be delayed until the "going" rate of increase could be established.[27] A certain apprehensiveness about the Government's powers of blacklisting firms worked in the same direction. The first major settlement, for Ford Motors' manual workers, was for a 12 percent increase and no government action was held to be called for. There were relatively few apparent breaches of the 10 percent limit, in part because the scope for self-financing productivity deals permitted under the policy provided a loophole for larger increases as the genuineness of the deals could not easily be assessed. In the public sector, the 10 percent rule was enforced, with some important exceptions that foreshadowed growing unrest. After a long and bitter strike, the firemen obtained an immediate 10 percent increase and larger guaranteed increases in the next two years. The police received a special settlement under a committee of inquiry. The miners who had opposed a national productivity deal eventually agreed to very generous local productivity agreements and a 10 percent settlement.

The annual rate of increase in average earnings fell below 8 percent at its lowest in the late summer of 1977, but by April–May 1978, it was up to 12½ percent. Nevertheless, a wage explosion had been avoided, the 12-month rule was generally upheld, and there were no outrageously high settlements.[28] This outcome was achieved however in a highly favorable context, the annual increase in consumer prices having decelerated from 22 percent in the six months to April 1977 to about 7 percent in the six months to December. Unfortunately, the higher rate of wage increase under Phase III could be foreseen to bring the rate of price increase back into double digits by the end of 1978.

By June 1978, when the next stage of the Government's policy was about to be announced, the rate of increase in earnings was up to almost 15½ percent. In July—in a Canute-like move—the Government announced a 5 percent limit for pay settlements other than self-financing productivity deals in 1978–79 and also ruled out reductions in normal working hours, unless output would be unaffected. Pensions, sick pay, and job security provisions remained exempt from the limit, and larger wage increases were permitted where necessary to bring earnings up to a minimum of £44.50 a week. Settlement dates

[27] National Institute of Economic and Social Research (May 1978, p. 16).
[28] National Institute of Economic and Social Research (May 1978, p. 16).

were to respect the 12-month rule, with possible exceptions to rationalize bargaining units, subject to the 5 percent limit being observed. Statutory control on dividends was extended to July 1978, with some relaxation permitting a company to exceed the 10 percent limit in line with higher earnings.

During the early months of its operation, the policy swung almost weekly from confrontation and imminent collapse to apparent acceptance and success. The effort to enforce the 5 percent limit in the public sector, however, led to severe industrial unrest during the "long hard winter" of 1978–79, generating widespread resentment against the unions and culminating in the overthrow of Labour and election of the Thatcher Government, pledged to end wage and price controls.

Lessons from the Experience with Incomes Policy

Any account of British experience with incomes policy requires some consideration of the connection between public expenditure policies and tendencies to cost inflation. In the concluding chapter of a volume of studies of the British economy during 1960–74, Blackaby emphasized the problem of "generalized inefficiency" in the economy. While he conceded that the lack of continuity and frequent changes and reversals of policy—especially in the areas of incomes policy, industrial relations legislation, and measures to promote industrial investment and reorganization—were damaging, he saw these shortcomings of policies as the outcome of two basic problems confronting policymakers in the United Kingdom. These were (1) a relatively inefficient manufacturing sector that "has not competed successfully in world trade in manufactures" and (2) "the tendency of the particular form of free collective bargaining which exists in Britain to deliver very high figures for the annual increase in money earnings." Since, in his view, this tendency could only be moderated at very high levels of unemployment, "it was not possible simply by demand management to obtain a reasonable combination of the standard objectives of economic policy" involving wage settlements consistent with the maintenance of price competitiveness and a tenable balance of payments position at fairly low levels of unemployment.[29] Worswick put it more strongly: "If demand management is earmarked for keeping down unemployment, it is not available also to control inflation. Whether this matters depends on the kind of inflation which present institutions for free collective bargaining and price fixing deliver at full employment."[30]

---

[29] Blackaby (1978a, p. 653).
[30] Worswick (1977, p. 12).

Incomes Policy and Control of Public Expenditure

Can one however suppose that the rate of inflation "delivered" by the wage bargaining institutions is independent of the terms upon which high employment is maintained by the authorities? Blackaby himself points out that "public expenditure planning throughout most of this period [1960–74] was in constant price terms, with an implicit undertaking to finance inflation."[31] Consider a closed economy in which the government undertook to maintain full employment and set no limit on government expenditure in nominal terms or on monetary expansion, there would be *no trade-off* between inflation and unemployment and no constraint to prevent the wage bargaining institutions "delivering" a high rate of wage increase. Concern on the government's part to inject just the right volume of *real* expenditure so as to avoid excessive or inadequate demand for labor would not suffice to prevent inflation in imperfectly competitive labor and product markets. Alternatively, consider an open economy under a fixed exchange rate where the government refused to intervene to maintain employment. The level of output and unemployment would then be sensitive to the rate of cost inflation relative to that abroad. Employers in the open sector would be conscious that if wage increases outpaced those in competing countries, they would be unable to maintain both their profit margins and their market shares; labor would be conscious of the risk of loss of jobs to foreign competition and the prospect of reduced industrial investment. Wage bargaining would take place in the context of an evident trade-off between high wage increases and reduced employment. In such a case, there could be no question of "the particular form of wage bargaining" consistently "delivering" an excessive rate of wage increase when industrial employment was maintained at a high level, since high employment would not be maintained if the increase in wages was excessive.

Obviously the situation in the United Kingdom, or in any other industrial country in which the authorities seek to maintain employment by public expenditure, lies between these extremes. When public spending accounts for a considerable share of GNP, the wage bargaining climate cannot be independent of the degree of control over costs exercised by the public authorities. The government cannot simply undertake to provide a certain real volume of expenditure in pursuit of its full employment goal, because if the increase in the prices

[31] Blackaby (1978a, p. 638). It should be remarked that the unindexed, highly progressive income tax system was a major reason why the U.K. authorities could afford to adopt a relaxed attitude toward control of nominal public spending, without fear of serious budgetary consequences. See Chapter 3, pp. 37–38.

and wages it pays is excessive, prices and wages in the private sector will be influenced and employment and investment in sectors exposed to foreign competition will suffer.[32] If the authorities are committed to maintaining a fixed exchange rate, the inescapable choice is between avoiding an excessive rate of domestic cost increase or accepting a reduced rate of growth—or even an outright decline—of employment in the open sectors of the economy, together with an increasingly stringent balance of payments constraint due to a weakening current account.

This would suggest that, under a fixed exchange rate, the government's real expenditure target to maintain employment must be made contingent upon a targeted rate of wage and price increase not being exceeded. That is to say, nominal expenditure must be subject to limits, calculated from the desired real volume of stimulus and a tolerable rate of inflation, such as not to jeopardize the competitive position of the open sector. A system of cash limits on expenditure such as was introduced in 1976—though not necessarily so stringent—should be a permanent feature of public expenditure control.[33]

It would not be simple to determine appropriate "target rates" for price and wage increases in setting public expenditure limits. If the nominal expenditure limit was set too low, the full employment objective would be sacrificed; if too high, cost inflation would be unconstrained. Clearly, the allowable increases should not be far out of line with expected changes in prices or wages in competing countries based on their recent experience and current policies.[34] The announcement of the "permissible" rate of inflation might tend to

---

[32] Empirical studies attempting to show whether the rate of wage increase was determined by developments in the public or private sector are hard to interpret because it is difficult to establish the direction of causality. Lax control over price and wage behavior in the public sector, and belief that the volume of public purchases and employment will not be affected by their rising cost, influence the attitudes of employers and labor in the private sector, coloring labor's view of the risk of unemployment and employers' views of the danger of permitting costs to rise. (If, for example, they expect to pass on higher costs in sales to the public sector and expect that the effect of increasing penetration of the home market by foreign goods will be mitigated by buoyant home demand.)

[33] Strict expenditure limits for public construction projects could almost certainly have held down the rate of wage increase in building and civil engineering, which was a leading element in wage inflation in the United Kingdom during the early 1960s. The enforcement of such limits, however, required effective government control over local authority spending. Some other types of expenditure would be more difficult to control if there was an excessive increase in costs. The total for public sector expenditure might therefore need to be fixed, with certain programs being contingent on the cost of more vital, or less flexible, elements not exceeding their proposed limits.

[34] A sustained effort to ensure that public sector wages rise less than wages in the open sector are going up under the influence of international conditions is bound sooner or later to generate labor unrest and pressures for a destablizing large adjustment. See Chapter 2, footnote 45.

make it a floor under actual price or wage increases. But the government could announce limits for the rate of increase in expenditure without explicitly stating the rate of price/wage increase assumed.

The enforcement of such a budgetary limit would bear a distinct resemblance to the monetarist prescription for "fixing the money supply according to some rule and sticking to it as another form of incomes policy"[35]: a firmly held target for money growth, *consistent* with the desired real stimulus and price and wage behavior might serve somewhat the same purpose. But the "budgetary rule," if firmly applied, would have the advantage of making the trade-off between price or wage increases and employment in the public sector more explicit and effective than under a monetary policy. Under such a rule, the government would accept the responsibility for maintaining "full employment," *provided* the rate of increase in prices and wages did not exceed a certain limit. By doing so it would make the trade-off explicit, thereby encouraging "self-policing" tendencies in the system, as other unions and economic groups saw their own jobs or income prospects worsened by "excessive" wage settlements or price increases. Thus, there could be a tendency to promote a more coordinated system of wage bargaining and greater resistance to monopolistic price increases. The acceptance and determined enforcement of the rule would have other beneficial effects such as making it more difficult for the authorities to accede to large wage claims in the public services or in nationalized enterprises (thereby reducing the risk of such damaging developments as the very large increase in civil servants' pay in the United Kingdom in 1974 and the frequent government interventions to secure the settlement of wage disputes in key nationalized industries at the cost of an overgenerous award). It would also provide guidance for arbitrators in the settlement of disputes.

Over the period from mid-1975 to mid-1978, incomes policy contributed to moderate the general rate of wage increase and aided in establishing a consensus, at least concerning what was to be judged an "excessive" rate of increase. In general, the provisions of the different "phases" had satisfied union demands for equity. However, despite its effects in moderating the rate of wage increase, incomes policy had not greatly eased managements' difficulties in maintaining profitability under increasingly severe competition from foreign goods and in the context of the more restricted growth of home demand after 1976. "The more the senior shop stewards had been required to impose wage restraint, the less they were prepared to accept redundancies. (Part of

---

[35] Worswick (1977, p. 13).

the price paid. . . for the reductions in real wages of 1975–77 consisted of a battery of formal and informal devices for preventing redundancies in large plants.)"[36] Consequently, for the individual business, by 1978 the pressing need appeared to be to secure greater authority and discretion for management.[37]

Policies Since 1979

The new Conservative Government held that the lack of managerial authority was a major factor impeding rationalization and even in explaining the weak record of postwar economic growth in the United Kingdom. Higher unemployment was needed to shift the balance of power from the unions. "Whether or not the Labour incomes policy had restrained the growth of real wages, it had restrained the growth of productivity."[38] The task of moderating wage increases and promoting the achievement of higher productivity by reducing overmanning was now assigned to demand management. To support this approach, the Government concentrated on propositions deriving from the microeconomics of a competitive closed economy, assuming away those characteristic features of the advanced economy described in Chapter 6 that are not consistent with the assumptions of the neoclassical model.

Japan and the Federal Republic of Germany: Wage Bargaining Systems

Economists have recently focused their attention upon Japan—as they had earlier studied the Federal Republic of Germany—in an effort to discover the reasons for the outstanding performance of the economy in terms of technological progress, continued growth, and absence of severe cost pressure at low recorded rates of unemployment.

Neither Japan nor Germany has depended upon the weapon of incomes policy. Each pursued a strategy of export-led growth for many years; first exploiting low money wages at the going exchange rate and exceptional labor market conditions that limited cost increases, later maintaining a strong competitive position by consistent and repeated use of domestic demand restraint. Early application of fiscal or monetary brakes as expansion got under way or when wage increases

[36]Flanagan, Soskice, and Ulman (1983, p. 438).
[37]See Dawkins (1980, pp. 80–84) on the effect of incomes policies during the 1970s.
[38]Flanagan, Soskice, and Ulman (1983, pp. 437–38).

accelerated, combined with demand-sensitive wage determination systems, served to protect the competitive position and reinforce the inducement for export promotion.

Since demand management in these two countries has often been taken as exemplary, it should be emphasized, first, that their success cannot be generalized. Over long periods their continuing rapid growth was made possible by the expansionary policies pursued in other industrial countries. Export penetration of those countries' domestic markets did not induce protective measures, both because their levels of employment were sustained by expansionary policies and because of the strong international commitment to free trade. Second, the effectiveness of restrictive demand management in Japan and Germany was itself in large measure due to certain exceptional features of the wage determination system, which are described below.

The distinctive character of union organization and collective bargaining is more obvious in Japan than in Germany. In both economies, wage bargaining behavior was strongly influenced for many years after 1945 by the period of authoritarian rule, extending to labor management, before and during the war; by the disbandment of unions and their reintroduction under the aegis of the Occupation forces;[39] and by an exceptional labor market situation after the war, owing to damage to the capital stock[40] and the heavy inflow of refugees into Germany up to 1961, and the pent-up outflow of manpower from agriculture in Japan. These circumstances limited the risk of generalized cost pressure for many years and served to prevent the emergence of wage pressures at the plant level because wage earners were afraid of losing their jobs.

Wage Bargaining in Japan

The desirability of implementing an incomes policy was widely discussed in Japan during the early 1970s. However, the experts appointed to consider the question after the oil price increase rejected the idea on the grounds that "Japanese enterprise unions do not have a strong enough position in the labor market to raise wages more than is appropriate."[41]

The unique character of the Japanese collective bargaining system makes it especially easy to perceive the influence that the institutional framework exerts on macroeconomic demand management. The

---

[39] Similar circumstances applied in Austria.

[40] In Germany's case, a considerable fraction of the productive capital had been lost through boundary changes.

[41] Shirai and Shimada (1978, p. 280).

following features of the Japanese labor market and trade union organization profoundly affect the working of the economy:

(1) In the private sector, unions and collective bargaining are concentrated in large enterprises and are not as widely disseminated as in other countries. There is a relatively large self-employment sector,[42] a large agricultural sector, and a preponderance of employment in small-scale enterprises serving the home market (Table 9).

(2) The very large unions in the public sector come under a different law than unions in the private sector: they are legally prohibited from striking and their rights to organize employees and bargain collectively are restricted.[43] They negotiate directly with the government; wages and conditions of work are set by legislation in highly political decisions, and the unions themselves are highly politicized. They do resort to strikes, though subject to severe disciplinary action. However, the fact that unions in the public sector operate under different legislation and in a totally different context for wage bargaining has limited the development of solidarity and common interests with wage earners in the private sector.

(3) The labor market in larger enterprises is distinguished by three closely interdependent features: pay systems based on age and length of service; lifetime employment; and enterprise unions, covering both white-collar and blue-collar employees. These characteristics serve to give the work force a strong interest in the fortunes of the enterprise.

Institutional Framework

The Nenko-System

The wage determination system had its origin in historical developments. Rapid industrialization and technical change obliged Japanese industry to hire inexperienced workers and train them within the enterprise. The employer was concerned to hold onto trained workers; wages and other benefits graduated by length of service provided a powerful means of restraining employees from changing jobs. By the 1920s, large corporations had developed a complex set of rules governing the allocation of jobs and rewards for work, known as the *nenko*-system. There was a tendency for workers to organize within the

[42] Self-employment still accounts for about 30 percent of employment in Japan, a larger share than in any other industrial country.

[43] This difference originated with the denial by the Supreme Commander of the Allied Control Forces of the principle of collective bargaining granted under the 1947 Law Governing Trade Unions, following severe unrest in 1948.

Table 9. Selected Industrial Countries: Comparative Statistics, 1981 or Five-Year Averages to 1981 or 1982

	Period	Japan	United States	Canada	United Kingdom	Italy	Fed. Rep. of Germany	Netherlands	Austria	Norway
Population (in millions)	Mid-1981	117.7	229.8	24.4	56.0	56.5	61.7	14.2	7.5	4.1
Employment (in millions)[1]	1981	55.8	100.4	10.9	23.8	20.6	25.6	4.9	3.3	1.9
Of which (as percent)										
Agriculture		*10.0*	*3.5*	*5.5*	*2.6*	*13.4*	*5.5*	*5.0*	*8.8*	*8.5*
Industry[2]		*35.3*	*30.1*	*28.3*	*35.7*	*37.5*	*43.5*	*30.2*	*39.5*	*29.8*
Other		*54.7*	*66.4*	*66.2*	*61.7*	*49.1*	*51.0*	*64.8*	*51.7*	*61.7*
Foreign trade[3]	1977–82	12.7	7.5	21.2	20.9	23.1	25.0	46.9	26.2	29.4
Growth of real GDP (in percent)	1976–81	4.6	2.8	2.8	0.5	2.6	2.5	1.4	2.6	3.6
Capital formation[4] (as percent of GDP)	1981	31.0	17.9	23.7	15.9	20.3	22.0	19.0	24.9	27.2
Of which *Machinery and equipment*	1981	*10.5*	*8.1*	*8.7*	*8.1*	*8.5*	*8.3*	*7.3*	*11.7*	*9.1*
Gross saving ratio (as percent of GDP)[5]	1981	31.9	18.9	21.4	17.3	18.9	20.8	20.0	24.5	29.8
Government expenditure (as percent of GDP)[6]	1981	10.1	18.1	19.5	22.3	18.1	20.7	17.9	18.4	19.0
Increase in hourly earnings (in percent)[7]	1977–82	6.2	8.4	9.9	13.4	19.6	5.4	8.1	6.3	7.5
Unemployment (as percent)	1982	2.4	9.7	11.0	13.1	9.1	7.5	12.6	3.7	2.4

Sources: Organization for Economic Cooperation and Development, *OECD Economic Surveys: Norway*, January 1985, annex table, and United Nations, *Monthly Bulletin of Statistics*, September 1985.

[1]Civilian employment.

[2]Mining, manufacturing, construction, and utilities.

[3]Average of imports and exports as percent of GDP.

[4]Gross fixed capital formation.

[5]Gross saving equals gross national disposable income minus private and government consumption.

[6]General government expenditure on goods and services.

[7]Average annual increase in hourly earnings in manufacturing.

confines of the large enterprise, and outside unions found it increasingly difficult to organize workers in these enterprises.[44]

There was no legal protection of trade unions in prewar Japan, and union activity was halted just before World War II. After the war, the establishment of free trade unions was actively promoted by the U.S. occupation authorities. Frequently, the establishment of an enterprise union was encouraged, or even initiated, by the management of the firm. But, from the wage earner's point of view also, the enterprise union was the most natural and workable form of organization given the conditions of employment in large enterprises.[45] Newly established unions tended to concentrate on issues of interest to the enterprise work force as a whole and to press for "egalitarian" settlements granting a similar pay increase across the board. Under the *nenko*-system, job distinctions were quite weak, and unions were unable, and disinclined, to press for pay structures based on craft skills or on rates for the job performed. It was natural and easy for them to bargain on the basis of the existing, easily identifiable characteristics of age, length of service, and educational qualifications.

The *nenko*-system confers great flexibility when management wishes to change the work performed by employees. Improvements in productivity and changes in technique are facilitated because wage earners are not threatened with a drop in earnings when a particular job or skill is supplanted and because increased mechanization or automation is not seen as a threat to the employment of the union's members, but rather as a means to higher earnings if it enables the enterprise to expand sales and profits. This attitude is strengthened by the fact that most workers receive semiannual bonuses, varying in amount with the financial position of the enterprise.

Enterprise Unions

Collective bargaining takes place between each enterprise union and the management. While many unions affiliate with industry-wide federations, only limited control is exercised by these bodies. They do, however, coordinate the union approach in the "spring wage round," during which the unions and employers separately work out a concerted approach, seeking to achieve a degree of uniformity in general wage increases. The outcome is reflected in key wage bargains that set the pattern for other settlements. How closely the lead is

[44] Shirai and Shimada (1978, p. 255).
[45] Shirai and Shimada (1978, p. 277).

followed depends on conditions in the industry and more especially on the profits of the enterprise.[46]

Considerable variation in wage increases tends to occur in times of weak demand in some industries, unions being inclined to accept moderate increases in order to protect the employment security of their members. The Government does not intervene in the wage round, but it is careful to keep the participants informed about the state of the economy and scope for wage increases.

The specific character of the enterprise unions is well illustrated by their staffing. Few have professional staff. Their functionaries are usually white-collar employees who are assigned to union business; while paid by the union, they retain their employee status. In many cases, their attitude is one of strong identification with the enterprise. In large corporations, union leadership may be assumed by graduates with good prospects of entering the managerial elite. As Shirai and Shimada (1978, p. 259) point out, there have been many cases where, during prolonged strikes, this type of leadership has taken over from a more dissatisfied and leftist leadership by forming a second breakaway union, a telling indication of the "organizational frailty of enterprise unionism."

The relatively limited diffusion of the union movement and the special character of the enterprise unions is held by some experts to be a major factor in explaining the low level of social security provisions in Japan compared with other countries at the same stage of development.[47] Unions cover "those employees who are already the best off and most secure in the labour force;"[48] their members' identification with less-favored wage earners and social groups is not great. Consequently, they are less disposed to press for social security and welfare provisions—and less well placed to do so—than the broader-based unions in other countries. Low social security protection has its obverse in a uniquely high and stable rate of household saving (of the order of 20 percent of disposable income). Households make steady provision for contingencies that elsewhere would be covered largely by social security, subsidized public housing, and state pensions.[49]

---

[46] Dean (1980). See also Organization for Economic Cooperation and Development (1977).

[47] See Galenson and Odaka (1976).

[48] Levine (1980, p. 74).

[49] The high rate of household saving seems to be influenced particularly by the need to make personal provision for income after comparatively early retirement and by the extraordinarily high cost of land and therefore housing.

"Lifetime" Employment

"Lifetime" employment might seem likely to create inflexibility in the economy, but it is actually a rather limited phenomenon. Less than half the total labor force—comprising the regular employees of the unionized sector of large enterprises and public sector organizations—enjoys a high degree of job security up to the compulsory retirement age of 55–60. Other categories—such as employees of smaller concerns, subcontract and temporary workers, and women employees—enjoy no such security. Thus, larger enterprises can ensure flexibility of labor supply by hiring temporary workers and subcontracting work out to smaller firms in times of strong demand and by not doing so when demand weakens; the unionized sector is able to provide stable employment for union members to a considerable extent by transferring the impact of fluctuations in demand to the nonunionized sector.

The primary concern of the union is to ensure security of employment for its members who, under the Japanese system, usually face a severe loss of pay and benefits even if they do find similar work in another enterprise. Lifetime employment is not a contractual obligation on the employer; it has obtained since the late 1950s, largely because of the unions' determined resistance to any sizable number of dismissals.[50]

Lifetime job security was greatly facilitated by the rapid industrial growth of the 1960s and the early 1970s. When it became more difficult to sustain under slower growth, the Government stepped in to hold down open unemployment by the provision of employment subsidies to enterprises with redundant labor in 1975. Firms received "employment adjustment subsidies" equal to one half (two thirds in the case of medium and small-sized enterprises) of the wages paid to workers who were temporarily released from work while retaining employee status. As a result, the unemployment figures considerably understate the proportion of idled workers among regular employees at this period. With the rising proportion of older workers in the unionized sector and the rapid increase in the supply of graduates, the problems of maintaining the employment of elderly workers and satisfying the job aspirations of educationally qualified entrants to the labor force have come into increasing prominence.

[50]"Although Japanese unions are moderate in such industrial actions as slowdowns and strikes, once a dispute concerning mass dismissal occurs, they fight most bitterly, often causing protracted work stoppages that continue for hundreds of days." Shirai and Shimada (1978, p. 261). This was a major reason why large corporations did not discharge large numbers of workers, despite heavy redundancies, during the protracted recession of 1973–76.

Industrial Relations and Macroeconomic Policies

Unionized enterprises in Japan possess unusual flexibility, compared with their counterparts in other industrial countries, both in regard to varying the level of employment by temporary hiring of nonunion labor and subcontracting work to the large ununionized sector, and in changing production methods and introducing new techniques in the absence of linkages between wages and specific jobs performed. Such changes are facilitated by union members' general confidence that their employment is not threatened by improvements in productivity and that their earnings will rise with higher sales and profits of the enterprise. The enterprises are also in a strong position to limit nominal wage increases in times of weak demand and low profits because the unions' paramount concern is with the job security of their members, who have a stake in the enterprise in the form of pay and benefits graduated by length of service.

As a consequence, the favorable performance of the economy is strongly influenced by union members' identification with the enterprise and their confidence that they will remain with the firm until they retire. (Hence, the Government's willingness to subsidize "layoffs" within the enterprise after 1975.)

The importance of the characteristics of the organized labor market in predisposing Japanese Governments to pursue macroeconomic policies conducive to export expansion has not received due emphasis. The large enterprise sector relies on export expansion for the sustained growth which is essential for the continued smooth and favorable functioning of the organized labor market. Maintaining employment in large and medium-sized enterprises under conditions of rapid productivity growth and technical advance requires expanding output. Given Japanese specialization in high-technology industries with capacity far in excess of home demands, expansion necessitates export growth, secured through cost competitiveness, technological leadership, and good quality control.

In recent years each oil price shock has been met by strongly deflationary policies, leading to declining sales and pressure on profits, which were reinforced by weak export markets after the oil price increase. Recession promotes wage restraint and declining real wage income. In each case, the inflationary shock has been followed by a marked strengthening of competitiveness, associated with a sustained real depreciation of the exchange rate. Domestic demand was cut back in 1974–75, and its growth halted in 1980–81; but owing to a very sharp increase in net exports, real GNP rose in 1975 and in 1980–81. In each case, this was associated with a marked reduction in relative normalized unit labor costs (that is, unit costs corrected for the effect of cyclical variations in the level of output). In 1980 particularly, relative costs were greatly reduced. They remained well below the level of 1975–76 in 1981 after rising steeply with the appreciation of the yen during late 1977 and 1978.

It is worth considering how this marked improvement in competitiveness came about. Reductions in real personal income associated with wage restraint were reflected in reduced consumption rather than lower savings. This arose partly because those most affected by reductions in real wages and unemployment were the lower paid and unorganized members of the work force who save little and partly because of the characteristic stability of household savings in Japan. Declines in consumption further reduced activity and investment in the small to medium-scale enterprises, predominantly selling in the home market. These enterprises account for 60 percent of all investment in Japan. So, unless increased government spending made up for lower private investment, real wage restraint was liable to be associated with an excess of savings over investment, declining home demand, and an increased current account surplus reflecting lower imports. Strongly restrictive monetary policy and a higher rate of price increase under the impact of the oil price rise caused a reversal of the interest rate differential vis-à-vis the United States and a sharp exchange appreciation in the first half of 1980, tending to weaken exports and reduce the current account surplus.

The authorities then relaxed monetary policy. This had little effect in strengthening home demand under the prevailing weak incentives for investment over most of the economy, but had a pronounced impact upon the exchange rate in the context of restrictive monetary policy in the United States. At the same time the Government decided to pursue a policy of fiscal consolidation prompted by the legacy of high public debt and interest payments left by an expansionary fiscal policy in the second half of the 1970s. Rather than compensating for excess private savings, the policy called for lowering the budget deficit relative to GNP over the medium term and the avoidance of government borrowing to finance current expenditures. To this end, in the 1980–81 budget the Government implemented the largest tax increase and the smallest increase in expenditure for 20 years. Budgetary policies tending to reduce government borrowing, and speedy reductions of the discount rate, limited the tendency for an appreciation of the yen with the advent of lower interest rates in the United States.

In effect, the Japanese authorities countered the impact of the oil price increase by administering a deflationary shock to the economy, promoting an appreciation of the yen when wage increases might have tended to accelerate. In the Japanese wage bargaining context, the resulting recession was effective in promoting wage restraint. The authorities then relaxed monetary policy and followed a budgetary policy that tended to cause an easing of the exchange rate. Industry, for its part, has taken good advantage of the openings provided by favorable export conditions to invest in high-technology, energy-efficient, high value-added industrial capacity.

Wage Bargaining in the Federal Republic of Germany

Institutional Setting

German trade unions and employers' organizations were dissolved in 1933. It was more than two decades before collective bargaining was resumed on an important scale. In the interim, a National Socialist "Labor Front" was responsible for mobilization of labor and for social welfare administration, while state trustees for labor matters took over wage fixing. The labor movement had previously been divided into Socialist, Liberal, and Christian unions. Their wartime collaboration provided the opportunity for a considerable unification in 1949, on the general principle of "one industry, one union." (The unions affiliated in the German Confederation of Trade Unions (Deutscher Gewerkschaftsbund—DGB) accounted for four fifths of all union members in the early 1980s.)

Wage bargaining in the Federal Republic of Germany has come to consist increasingly of a "dual structure" of collective agreements at the industry level and works agreements at the plant level;[51] but for many years negotiations took place predominantly at the industry level between the union and the employers' federation. Bargaining was marked by the strong coordination of the employers' side—not only within the industry but also between industries. This characteristic was scarcely surprising, because although the employers' federations had also been dissolved, enterprises had been closely integrated during the war. Furthermore, state control of wages had established a concept of national and regional wage levels for each industry.

Collective bargaining rights and procedures in the Federal Republic of Germany are clearly defined, and circumscribed, by law. The unions are excluded from bargaining at the plant level, which is reserved for the works council. Wage earners must be represented by a permanent association; this largely rules out action by unofficial

[51] Günter and Leminsky (1978, p. 175).

groups such as shop stewards in the United Kingdom. Wage agreements are legally binding and contain a no-strike clause, breaches of which by union members render the union subject to severe penalties.

Political strikes and sympathetic industrial action by the unions are limited by the requirement that such action can only be taken in connection with a wage negotiation.[52] In general, the official strike has been used sparingly as the weapon of last resort. Many procedural matters must be satisfied before calling a strike, and it has to be preceded by conciliation efforts.

The Federal Labor Court plays a continuing role in interpreting and establishing the law concerning collective bargaining. It has ruled, against the union position, that collectively agreed rates can relate only to minimum wage levels, not to wages actually paid; that collectively agreed benefits for union members only are illegal; and that strikes and lockouts are equally acceptable forms of industrial action. Restrictions on lockouts are less important than in other major European countries, and in some years, such as 1963 and 1971, the number of days lost through lockouts actually exceeded that through strikes.[53]

The fact that regional collective bargaining by the unions only sets minimum wages, often geared to the capacity to pay of the marginal firm, has deprived the unions of control over actual levels of pay; and their exclusion from negotiations over pay or job evaluation within the enterprise lessens their usefulness in the eyes of the wage earners. Employers have traditionally made discretionary payments above the negotiated rates and reserved the right to withdraw these at will.[54]

Evolution of the Unions

The status of unions within the economy, their objectives, and the distribution of power within the movement have changed perhaps more radically in the Federal Republic of Germany than in any other industrial country over the last three decades.

During the 1950s and much of the 1960s, the strategy of export-led growth under the spur of frequent recourse to domestic demand restraint was facilitated by the wage bargaining context and by the widespread support for these policies, reinforced by the general fear of

[52] Carew (1976, pp. 169–70).
[53] Günter and Leminsky (1978, p. 174 and p. 182).
[54] Carew (1976, p. 172).

inflation. Though the labor movement was strengthened by unification and the establishment of a comparatively small number of large industrial unions, the unions were at first financially weak and remained insecure in their hold on public opinion for a considerable period after the war.[55]

Until the late 1960s, cost pressures were restrained by the employers' firm resistance to union wage claims at the industry level and by the weakness of the wage earners' organization at the plant level. Restrictive demand management served to reinforce the employers' stand and was not politically unacceptable so long as the effect was to induce higher employment in export production. Restrictive policies were effective in bringing this about under fixed exchange rates because of the considerable degree of wage flexibility resulting from discretionary payments and piece rates, over and above collectively bargained rates. A further important element of flexibility, similar to that provided by the unorganized labor market in Japan, was provided by the employment of foreign workers, which first became important when the inflow of refugees ceased in the early 1960s.[56] Foreign workers typically experienced much higher rates of unemployment than union members in downturns.

Initially, the unions adopted a short-term program concentrating on immediate aims, such as raising real wages, reducing hours of work, and increasing social protection (disability benefits, etc.). In 1962, the DGB set out a long-term program, which was strongly influenced by the success of the current economic policies and which stressed goals that could be achieved within the existing environment of unrestricted free enterprise. The program also enunciated the unions' wider

---

[55] "Perhaps more than in countries with a longer democratic tradition, economic efficiency is. . . a prime stabilizing factor for the social and political order that was adopted after World War II. Maintenance of conditions considered essential for an efficient market economy, such as sufficient authority for decision making by managers, private ownership, and a favorable investment climate, have become widely shared values in Germany. . . . Against this background. . . refusals of concessions to unions can be presented as being in the general interest. Thus, employers tend to see themselves as the guarantors of a free, efficient society." Günter and Leminsky (1978, p. 171).

[56] The large-scale hiring of foreign workers tended to prevent the usual phenomenon of wages rising in the lowest-paid jobs as full employment was reached. This served to obviate wage claims elsewhere, induced by consequent increases in the cost of living or narrowing of traditional wage differentials. This effect tended to curb the adjustment of relative costs under the fixed exchange rate system as full employment of the German labor force was reached. Between 1970 and 1973 alone, the intake of foreign workers was equivalent to a 3 percent addition to the dependent labor force; and at the peak in 1973, about 2½ million foreign workers represented 11 percent of all employees. (See Günter and Leminsky, 1978, Table 3.5, p. 160.) A substantial proportion of foreign labor is regarded as a permanent requirement of the German economy, since German workers will not accept jobs previously held by foreign workers at the going level of wages.

political objectives of full employment, steady economic growth, an equitable distribution of income, and the right of employees to "co-determination" of their working conditions. In the same year, the Government established the independent Council of Economic Advisors, charged with making an annual review of the economic situation and particularly of the wage bargaining context. This provided a new forum in which the DGB could exert its influence upon the formulation of economic policy, fulfilling its view of its role as a "central part of the democratic infrastructure."[57]

Concerted Action

In 1965 the Council, fearing that the customary implementation of restrictive measures to check a strengthening expansion and curb the 3 percent inflation rate might provoke a severe recession, took the dramatic step of calling a conference of the trade unions and employers' associations to seek a new solution. The conference led to a proposal for tripartite "concerted action" by the unions, employers, and the Government. This represented a proposal to establish a voluntary incomes policy in the private sector in return for the Government's undertaking to support price stability by letting the deutsche mark float upward and by limiting the impact on prices of the financing of public expenditures in 1966 and 1967.[58] For their part, the employers and unions would undertake to maintain the existing distribution of income between wages and profits in the interest of supporting high employment by adhering to a wage formula devised by the Council that was intended to ensure a reduction of the expected inflation rate in wage bargaining by 1 percentage point in each of the next two years. The Council hoped that the Government would permit a gradual appreciation of the deutsche mark to reduce inflation, that the Deutsche Bundesbank would gradually reduce the rate of monetary expansion, and that all those concerned with decision making would seek to moderate inflationary expectations.[59] However, the Government rejected the scheme, and was later defeated when the effects of a sharply contractionary monetary policy coinciding with a downturn in the United States led to a severe recession.

The election of a Social Democrat Government profoundly altered the position of the unions, giving the central organizations far greater

[57] Heinz O. Vetter, President of the DGB, cited in Günter and Leminsky (1978, p. 171).

[58] Large increases in public utility prices to cover the cost of capital construction had been a major factor in the recent acceleration of price inflation.

[59] Giersch (1977, pp. 6–7).

political power and an increased sense of responsibility. The new Government maintained the practice of "concerted action," that is, continuing consultations, under the chairmanship of the Minister of Economic Affairs, between the unions, employers' federations, the central bank, other interest groups, and various ministries. The Government did not, however, accept the case for allowing the exchange rate to appreciate.

The union leaders, along with the majority of the German public, remained convinced of the need for moderate wage increases as a prerequisite for price stability and continued export-led growth, and they could hardly change their stance under the new Government. However, moderate wage settlements during the upswing in 1968 were followed by sharp increases in profits and prices under the impact of external and domestic inflationary forces in 1969. In Giersch's phrase, "the fruits of wage restraint were not internalized by an appreciation of the currency." Thereupon, "trade union leaders lost the confidence of the rank and file, and a wage explosion following wildcat strikes became a quick substitute for a change in the exchange rate."[60]

It is generally agreed that the failure of the unions to adjust their wage policies in the late 1960s was a major cause of membership discontent. The spontaneous strikes of 1969 compelled the unions to adopt a stronger line in pushing for enterprise-oriented bargaining, stronger organization at the plant level, and wage contracts covering shorter periods. Greater union access to the workplace was secured under the 1972 Works Constitution Act.

Concerted action continued until 1977[61] and proved to be useful in promoting wage moderation in 1973–75 following appreciation of the deutsche mark and the rise in oil prices. Under the system the Government supplied documentation concerning recent and prospective economic developments, which was reviewed and commented on by the representatives of the different organizations at regular meetings. Though no formal guidelines were issued, the published reports on the meetings served to inform and influence public opinion.

Wage Bargaining Developments During the 1970s

The 1970s saw a marked change in the activities of the labor movement in the Federal Republic of Germany. The central union organizations commanded, and used, great political power to secure

[60] Giersch (1977, p. 7).

[61] The DGB withdrew from concerted action in 1977 following the employers' action in contesting the 1976 codetermination law in the Federal Labor Court.

benefits for their members through legislation; but increasingly the impetus for industrial action came from the shop floor rather than the leadership.[62] The unions were obliged to accept the shift of wage bargaining more and more in the direction of plant bargaining between union representatives of the plant work force and the enterprise, and the incidence of spontaneous strikes remained fairly high. The coordination of wage bargaining on the side of the unions weakened.

With the increased importance of plant-level bargaining by the works councils, the German wage bargaining system bears some resemblance to that of Japan. It has become common practice for the works councils to adjust the regional (or national) industry agreement by supplementary plant bargaining, and incentive payments are widely negotiated by the works councils. The representation of workers on the supervisory board of the enterprise under the 1972 law and the 1976 codetermination legislation gave the work force more information concerning the firm's management. In the profitable enterprise, the works council can often secure much better wage rates that those agreed in the industry agreement. Terms and conditions agreed between the works council and the employer do not, however, have the legally binding status of collective agreements.[63] Such elements correspond in this regard to the bonus system in Japan.

Several developments during the 1970s tended to strengthen the identification of the work force with the interests of the enterprise and increased the responsibility of the enterprise to provide permanent employment for its employees. Among the former were employer-financed schemes for capital acquisition, included in collective agreements covering more than half of the labor force, and plant-based pension schemes, to which about 60 percent of employees are entitled.[64] The latter included schemes of protection and compensation for workers made redundant, first introduced in the coal and steel industry and subsequently required by the "social plan" law of 1972.

Canada: The Anti-Inflation Program of 1975–78

Whereas incomes policies were repeatedly applied for lengthy periods in European countries marked by pervasive unionization, in

[62] See Chapter 8, p. 190, and Giersch (1977).

[63] Carew (1976, p. 171).

[64] A 1974 law required maintenance of pension entitlement in case of a change in place of employment, eliminating an important obstacle to mobility. Günter and Leminsky (1978, pp. 188–89).

Canada—a less strongly unionized economy—the recourse to a statutory incomes policy in 1975–78 represented an isolated case induced by exceptional circumstances that threatened to cause a wage explosion.[65]

Setting for Controls

During 1974–75 economic policy in Canada had been aimed at maintaining output and employment in the face of recession in most other industrial countries. Real output and incomes had held up relatively well, although unemployment continued to increase. But costs and prices rose much faster than in the United States, and while inflation abroad was moderating, Canada was facing accelerating wage and price increases against the background of very large public sector deficits.

Despite substantial increases in nominal wages in 1973 and 1974, real wages had declined in many sectors of the private economy, while profits were at record levels in these years. Pressures for wage increases were strengthened by marked differences in the size of wage increases in different industries and by the very large increases won by certain groups of public sector employees. (Employees in semipublic enterprises, for example, had secured an average increase of 19 percent in yearly money wages under new contracts in 1974.) During 1975, claims for almost unprecedented wage increases were put forward to restore real earnings, to match earlier settlements, and to guard against future losses in real earnings being caused by the faster rate of price increase that was expected to result from rising costs of housing, energy, insurance, and municipal taxes.

In September 1975, the federal and provincial governments were faced with major disputes in public service sectors and with indicators showing declining industrial production and GNP growth for the first half year. Unemployment was still increasing; prices were rising at double-digit rates, and wage settlements in the second quarter had on average provided for increases of over 18 percent. Public sector deficits (especially at the provincial and municipal levels) threatened to grow out of control unless immediate action was taken to limit spending or increase taxes. The Federal Government wished to mitigate the impact of more restrictive budgetary and monetary policies upon

[65] The program followed attempts to implement voluntary incomes policy in the 1960s, and prior efforts on this occasion to secure agreement to voluntary measures of wage restraint by the imposition of selective price controls for oil and wheat and by indexation of income taxes, pensions, and social security payments and charges.

This account is an abridged version of Braun (1981, Part IV).

employment and lacked the power to enforce wage restraint by provincial and local governments.[66] In the election campaign of the previous spring, the Conservatives had announced their intention to introduce controls—and the proposal had proved surprisingly popular. So taking a leaf out of the Opposition's book, the Government decided to institute a program of specific controls at the same time as it applied general financial and economic policies aimed at gradually bringing down the rate of inflation.

Shift in Monetary Policy

The Anti-Inflation Program was associated with a major change in monetary policy. During the early 1970s, the Bank of Canada had been severely criticized for permitting an excessive monetary expansion following the appreciation of the Canadian dollar in 1970.[67] Just before the Anti-Inflation Program was initiated, the Bank announced that henceforth its policies would aim to ensure that the money supply (narrowly defined) would grow "along a path capable of accommodating a satisfactory rate of real economic growth accompanied by some slowing in the rate of increase of prices."[68] As an aid in bringing about a gradual moderation of inflation and price expectations, the Bank would set a target range, to be adjusted periodically, for the growth in the narrowly defined money supply M1. The achievement of the desired rate of money growth would require that interest rates and the exchange rate be allowed to move in either direction not only over the business cycle but also over shorter periods. The first money growth target was announced soon after the initiation of the program.

Scope of the Program

The Anti-Inflation Program, as presented in October 1975,[69] consisted of four parts. But there were two essential elements:[70]

[66] Christofides and Wilton (1979) suggest that the unexpectedly large wage settlements in the public sector during the second and third quarters of 1975 "might well have been one of the motivating forces behind the introduction of wage controls" (p. 57). They cite Courchene's view that the provinces themselves "felt that wage demands in their respective domains were also out of control" and "played a major role in forcing Ottawa's hand in the direction of instigating the anti-inflation program." Courchene (1976a, p. 88).

[67] See Courchene (1976b).

[68] Bank of Canada (1976, p. 9).

[69] For a fuller description of measures taken under the program, see "Attack on Inflation: A Program of National Action, Statement tabled in the House of Commons by the Minister of Finance on October 14, 1975"; and Canada, Anti-Inflation Board (1976), (1977), (1978), and (1979). The administrative apparatus is described in Allen (1982). Maslove and Swimmer (1980) contains a bibliography of Anti-Inflation Board publications.

[70] Little was heard afterward of the other elements of the program, which comprised structural policies in the areas of energy, food, and housing and proposals for strengthening competition and improving labor-management relations.

(1) General fiscal and monetary policies were to be such as to permit "a sustained economic recovery" with a declining rate of inflation. In support of this, government expenditure policies were to limit the rise in public spending and the rate of increase in public service employment.

(2) The prices and incomes policy—comprising specific controls on certain prices and incomes—was intended to ensure that the rate of increase in consumer prices was brought down from almost 11 percent in 1974 to 4 percent by 1978.

The Anti-Inflation Program established targets for a gradual deceleration of inflation from a rate of 8 percent in the first year to 6 percent in the second year and 4 percent in the third year.

The Anti-Inflation Board (AIB) was set up to monitor the movement of wages, prices, and profits, to disseminate information about the guidelines, and to identify contraventions. Controls were intended to restrain wage and price increases in key areas, where decisions were liable to have an important influence on the general pattern of wage settlements and pricing behavior in the economy. Legally binding guidelines for increases in wages and salaries and in profits and dividends were applied to firms with more than 500 employees and to all firms involved in industry-wide bargaining, to firms in construction with more than 20 employees, and to federal and participating provincial government departments, agencies, corporations, and municipal institutions.[71] Eight provincial governments decided to participate; the other two, Quebec and Newfoundland, established their own programs. Since the participation of provincial governments was vital, the need to secure their agreement to the proposed controls was an important influence in determining the relatively liberal compensation guideline.

In practice the program was—and was perceived to be—mainly aimed at controlling wages. Originally it was announced that the AIB would regulate prices and profits of enterprises subject to controls, both by day-to-day rules based on increases in allowable costs and by year-end tests involving control over corporate profit margins. However, it proved impracticable to administer regulations based on allowable costs because of the huge number of goods and services on

[71] Because of widespread concern over the rapid increase in medical costs and professional fees, all individuals or firms carrying on professional businesses were subject to the regulations—but the numbers involved ruled out any attempt at strict enforcement. Other groupings could be brought under the controls—as was the food-processing industry—if they were considered strategically important in controlling inflation.

the market, and the detailed regulation of prices was formally abandoned in June 1976. The AIB retained the right to require corporations to justify price increases and could order a rollback of price increases which it considered excessive.[72]

Wage and Salary Guidelines

The guidelines for wage and salary increases permitted increases to cover the target rate of inflation in each year of the program, plus a further 2 percent rise, to allow real incomes to rise in line with the projected trend growth of average productivity in the economy.[73] The rise in real income was guaranteed by a provision that if the consumer price index rose by more than the target rate of price increase, the difference would be added to the rate of wage increase for the next year. There was no corresponding provision for wage increases to be reduced should the consumer price index rise by less than the target, and this proved to be a serious omission.

In the first year of the program, had the wage and salary guideline applied throughout the economy and the level of employment remained unchanged, total money income would have risen by at least 10 percent. Since the aim was to promote some rise in employment, fiscal and monetary policies were set to permit a somewhat larger rise in total nominal income—of about 12 percent. Broadly in line with this objective, in November 1975 the Bank of Canada set its first target for the annual rate of increase in the money supply at "not less than 10 per cent a year but not as high as 15 per cent."[74]

An underlying assumption in setting the wage guideline was that prices in all the sectors covered would tend to rise at about the target inflation rate. This soon posed a problem. When the rate of inflation eased in the United States and Japan under the influence of strongly restrictive policies, Canadian export- and import-competing industries were exposed to sharply increased competition. Under these circumstances, the wage guideline tended to keep nominal wage increases in these industries higher than they might otherwise have been. Prices

---

[72] In order to secure compliance with the prices and profits guidelines, major firms were required to provide advance cost and profit information on proposed price increases. This served as an early warning system of price movements and allowed the AIB and firms to analyze and determine permissible price increases under the regulations. The number of firms required to pre-notify price increases increased from 117 at the beginning of 1976 to 342 by mid-1977.

[73] There was provision for smaller or greater increases in cases where pay had risen faster, or less fast, than the guideline over the last two or three years. An absolute ceiling (of Can$2,400) was set on the average increase in pay under any settlement.

[74] Bank of Canada (1976, p. 9).

and profits fell below those projected in the program, and reduced profit margins held down employment and limited investment, lowering employment in the private sector. These effects were aggravated by the appreciation of the exchange rate between mid-1975 and mid-1976, which profoundly affected the course of developments under the Anti-Inflation Program.

When the program was devised, it was foreseen that controls would initially serve to curb the rate of inflation and that restrictive monetary and fiscal policies would take effect when the rate of inflation had already been somewhat moderated. That sequence was not, however, realized. Indeed, the deceleration of wage increases envisaged in the program could not possibly have been achieved without more complete coverage and more stringent rules concerning previously negotiated increases. In practice, the average rate of wage increase was sustained for several months by the continued spread of large increases to the nonunionized sectors not covered by the controls and by the implementation of awards granted under pre-existing long-term contracts or contracts that were being negotiated when the program commenced.[75] Thus, although there was a marked deceleration of first-year increases in major wage settlements within six months of the start of the program,[76] the average rise in labor income per employed person over the preceding year was little smaller than in 1975 (Table 10). In spite of an exceptional rise in productivity (of 3.2 percent) associated with the recovery of a higher level of output, labor costs per unit of output were on average about 4½ percent higher, and some 9 percent higher in terms of U.S. dollars, during the first year of the program than during the first ten months of 1975.

Effects of Monetary Policy

The impact of the new monetary policy in 1976 was heightened by the unforeseen consequences of a prolonged postal strike in late 1975 and of a sharp fall in U.S. interest rates early in 1976. The strike caused an enormous increase in the demand for cash. The consequent rise in the money supply faced the Bank with a problem in establishing the credibility of its newly instituted target and also made it difficult for the public to interpret monetary developments. Responding to a decline in Canadian interest rates (that was associated with the fall in U.S. rates), as well as to some initial difficulties in implementing the

---

[75] See passage from Christofides and Wilton (1979) cited on page 251.

[76] See Canada, Anti-Inflation Board (1977, p. 6).

Table 10. Canada: Prices and Costs, 1974–78

(Year-to-year percentage changes unless otherwise indicated)

	1974	1975	1976	1977	1978
Prices					
Gross national expenditure deflator	15.3	10.7	9.7	6.9	6.7
Consumer prices	10.9	10.8	7.5	8.0	9.0
Excluding food	*8.8*	*10.1*	*9.4*	*7.9*	*7.0*
Industry selling price index	19.0	11.2	5.1	7.7	8.3
Costs					
Labor income per employed person	14.9	14.6	13.2	8.9	6.1[1]
Productivity	−0.7	−0.6	3.2	0.7	0.3[1]
Unit labor costs	15.8	15.3	9.6	8.1	5.7[1]
Unit profits	25.6	−3.0	−2.5	7.3	9.7[1]
Average weekly earnings	11.0	14.2	12.2	9.6	6.2
Wage settlements: first-year increases	17.0	21.0	12.3	8.0	6.8[1]
Other					
Exchange rate[2]	−2.2	4.0	−3.1	7.8	7.3
Import price	23.3	15.6	0.9	11.7	12.4
Labor income as share of GNP[3]	55.1	57.4	57.3	57.9	56.8
Profits as share of GNP	13.6	11.9	10.6	10.6	10.3

Sources: Based on data from Canada, Anti-Inflation Board, *Third Year Report*, 1978, p. 2, and Department of Finance, *Economic Review*, April 1979.

[1]Second quarter 1978, compared with second quarter 1977.

[2]Change in value of U.S. dollar in terms of Canadian dollar.

[3]Includes military pay.

wage and price controls,[77] the Bank decided that the underlying trend of money growth should be reduced and on March 5 raised the bank rate to 9½ percent. This precipitated an unexpectedly sharp increase in short-term interest rates.[78]

The fall in U.S. long-term interest rates constituted a highly favorable opportunity for new bond issues by provincial governments and public enterprises in respect of large capital investment projects in the pipeline. Private Canadian corporations also borrowed heavily in

[77]The constitutionality of controls had been challenged in the courts, the provision for adjustment for past experience was causing difficulties, and a heavy backlog of cases had built up.

[78]Bank of Canada (1976, p. 9).

foreign bond markets. Capital inflows were further enhanced by the widened differential between Canadian and U.S. short-term interest rates. As a consequence of the heavy capital inflows, the Canadian dollar appreciated by about 6½ percent in terms of the U.S. dollar between August 1975 and July 1976.

Operation of the Program

During the first year of the program, the consumer price index rose less than expected, owing to an exceptional decline in food prices and a slowing down of the increase in prices of other goods, but not of services. The year-over-year increase in prices of goods, excluding food, moderated from 9.4 percent to 6.6 percent in 1976, while that for services accelerated from 10.7 percent to 12.2 percent under the influence of the continuing rapid rise in wages and salaries and professional incomes. These developments were influenced by the effect of the appreciation of the dollar in holding down import and export prices in Canadian dollars. Wages decelerated much less than prices and real wages rose sharply, while profits, investment, and the level of employment in industry were severely constrained.

The appreciation of the exchange rate had contributed to bring down the rate of price inflation—gladdening those who believed that a slower rate of increase would contribute to ease the long-term problem of inflation by lessening inflationary expectations. But the achievement of a moderation of inflation by this means was a fragile success. The maintenance of the exchange rate depended on the continuance of heavy capital inflows. When these were curtailed by political uncertainties late in 1976, the value of the Canadian dollar dropped by more than 6 percent in November, and at the end of the year it remained about 3½ percent lower than in October.

At the beginning of the second program year in the fall of 1976, the controls on wages and prices were largely redundant in most sectors of the private economy, in the sense that they were exercising little if any additional constraint on increases, over and above that resulting from the conditions created by monetary restraint and the appreciation of the Canadian dollar. Under these conditions, the guideline for wages may even have tended to limit the effect of the greater-than-expected slowdown of product prices in moderating wage increases. Moreover, because the reduced level of activity rendered the 2 percent productivity growth assumption unrealistic, the 8 percent guideline implied that unit labor costs would rise by close to 8 percent, exceeding the going rate of price increase for industrial goods.

Thus, despite the moderation of inflation achieved during the first year and a half of the program, developments were not altogether satisfactory. The combination of continuing large increases in nominal wages and salaries, declining prices for food, and severe constraints on price increases for tradable goods and services in 1976—together with the fact that the indexation of personal income tax led to a reduction of real tax rates[79]—had resulted in an unwarranted and unsustainable increase in real disposable income from employment. The initial strong support for the Anti-Inflation Program in an emergency setting was in a sense dissipated during the first year and a half of the program, while the rise in real income over this period made it tactically more difficult to moderate wage increases later when the consensus on the need for restraint had weakened.

By the end of 1976, pressures to end controls were mounting. Despite increasing support for the program among the public at large, the unions' hostility to it had been strengthened by the fact that, with fewer rollbacks of price increases than of wage settlements,[80] less restraint appeared to have been applied to prices than to wages and salaries. Their belief that the controls program was aimed mainly at wages was heightened by the abandonment of detailed profit regulation and easing of the profit limitations in June 1976. Business had been prepared to accept the controls program in 1975 for fear of an explosive acceleration in wage increases, but now felt there would be little risk in lifting wage controls. In addition, for many enterprises the effect of foreign competition in holding down prices and profit margins had been eased by depreciation and, consequently, price controls threatened to become an effective, rather than a potential, restraint.

The authorities in Ottawa were still fearful of losing control over wage movements in the public sector. They were also worried that decontrol might provoke a reacceleration of wage inflation, since recent wage contracts had included provision for renegotiation, or immediate increases and restoration of any rollbacks, as soon as controls ended.[81] They were conscious, however, that the full protection of wages against price increases in the program was inappropriate in the context of the depreciation and would negate the hoped-for effects in strengthening the competitive position of Canadian producers. By mid-1977, the Government was actively seeking to replace the

[79]Since the future rise in the price index allowed for in indexing the tax schedules when they were prepared months earlier substantially overstated the actual change in prices between the tax years 1975 and 1976.

[80]See Canada, Anti-Inflation Board (1976, p. 9).

[81]Such so-called AIB clauses were rendered "null and void" by law when the Anti-Inflation Act was amended during the third program year.

controls by more informal arrangements with business and the unions to ensure moderate wage settlements and price increases. Although no such agreements were secured, in October 1977 the Government decided to begin phasing out controls in mid-April 1978 and to lower the final income guideline to 6 instead of 8 percent.[82] The Centre for the Study of Inflation and Productivity was set up to monitor price and wage developments after the ending of the program. The limit on dividend increases was also reduced from 8 percent to 6 percent. In order to soften the impact of the stricter guideline on real incomes and to help maintain real expenditure, a one-time cut of Can$100 in direct taxes payable on lower and middle incomes was implemented at the beginning of 1978.

The fact that the authorities were seeking to close out the AIB during the second year of operation suggests that in their opinion it must have served its purpose during the first year or so, or that its method of operation and principles had become more of a liability than an asset in the prevailing circumstances.

Results Achieved

By the end of 1977, wage and price behavior had improved markedly compared with 1975. Whereas before the establishment of controls wage settlements in major contracts had provided, on average, for an increase of 18 percent per annum over the life of the contract, they were now providing an increase of about 8 percent. Consumer prices were tending to accelerate once more, however, under the influence of the depreciation of the Canadian dollar, the adjustment of government-regulated energy prices, and unfavorable supply conditions for food.

Statistical Studies

A number of empirical studies[83] sought to estimate the impact of the AIB's controls on union-negotiated wage settlements in Canada. The methods and findings of several of these studies are compared in

[82] That is to say, the figure originally envisaged for the third year would be enforced: without a change in the regulations, the guideline would have remained at 8 percent as in the second year of the program, because the consumer price increase in the second year had exceeded the target 6 percent by some 2 percent, and this would have been added to the original 6 percent guideline.

[83] Auld, Christofides, Swidinsky, and Wilton (1979); Christofides and Wilton (1979); Cousineau and Lacroix (1977); Cousineau and Lacroix (1978); Reid (1979); Wilson and Jump (1979); and Maslove and Swimmer (1980).

Christofides and Wilton (1979, pp. 81–92). In their view, the evidence of these studies suggested three qualitative conclusions:

> (i) The AIB exerted a significant indirect effect on wage inflation, depressing negotiated wage settlements below values which might otherwise have prevailed.
> (ii) This indirect AIB impact effect on wages appears to have been greater in the public sector than in the private sector.
> (iii) The indirect wage impact and/or effectiveness of the AIB appears to have increased during the life of the program [pp. 87–88].

Their own study suggests that in the public sector, the AIB had the effect of reducing negotiated base wage settlements on average by some 4–4½ percent per annum during the life of the AIB while in the private sector the effect was in the 3½–4 percent range. They consider that

> the impact of the AIB on aggregate wage levels accumulated very slowly as many workers were "locked-into" pre-AIB wage contracts for much of the early life of the AIB. It was only as these pre-AIB wage contracts expired that the impact of the AIB program could be brought to bear on wage levels. Based on the existing bargaining cycle, we estimate that the cumulative impact of the AIB on private sector wage rates was only about 0.8 per cent after one year and 3.2 per cent after two years, but rose quite dramatically to 6.1 per cent after three years and 7.2 per cent after four years [pp. 88–89].

Estimates by Reid (1979, p. 223) also show a very considerable reduction in wage settlements due to controls, and he concludes that if the "reduction in settlements had been forced on the economy through restrictive monetary and fiscal policy alone, the result would have been an intolerable rise in the unemployment rate."

It should, however, be noted that all the studies cited are alike in assuming that had there been no program, negotiated wage changes after September 1975 would have responded to various factors in the same way as over the preceding decade or so. That is to say, the structural parameters of the wage equation estimated over the earlier years could be used to estimate what the scale of settlements would have been in the absence of the program. This assumes that price expectations would be formed in the same way and that factors such as the strength of labor demand and declines in real wages due to inflation over the life of the previous contract would have had the same influence in determining wage increases after 1975 as they did during the 1960s and early 1970s. This is a strong assumption to make, given the far greater divergence between demand and labor market conditions in Canada and the United States after 1975, the unprecedented shift to a restrictive monetary policy, and the much greater instability of the exchange rate than in the earlier years. It is by no means clear, therefore, that wage settlements would have been as high as those estimated by the authors of the studies had the AIB not existed.

Major Factors Influencing Results Achieved

The outcome of policies over the first 18 months of the program was conditioned by three factors:

(1) The overoptimistic target for wage increases in the first year of the program, which did not allow sufficiently for the difficulty of securing a marked reduction in the average rate of wage increase when large increases were already provided for under long-term contracts concluded earlier. To achieve the target, the program would have had to incorporate measures to curb wage increases provided for under existing wage contracts.

(2) The enforcement of a rate of money growth consistent with the unrealistic target increase in wages during the first year of the program.

(3) The large and growing deficit of the public sector, reflecting an overoptimistic forecast of federal government revenue and continued heavy borrowing by the provinces.

The public sector deficit was incompatible with the enforcement of the tight monetary growth target *and* the maintenance of the going exchange rate. The mounting public sector deficit had *either* to be accommodated by the central bank *or* to be financed at higher interest rates so as to secure a larger share of investable funds in Canada and induce capital flows, in which case the exchange rate would tend to appreciate. In effect, by enforcing its money growth target, the Bank of Canada achieved the target rate of price increase (despite the faster rise in unit labor costs) through the deflationary impact of the appreciation. Thus, the public sector deficit was financed at the cost of raising interest rates and weakening the incentive for private investment, especially in the "open" sectors of the economy. Real incomes increased but employment declined, owing to the worsening of the current account and the decline in private investment.

The Government emphasized that "the decline in profit margins in 1976 was primarily a reflection of slack markets in Canada and abroad, rather than of the controls program. Most firms were unable to earn the margins which the guidelines permitted."[84] It is true that profits would have been cyclically low in 1976 because of weak demand at home and abroad, even if wage costs had not been rising faster in Canada than in the United States and several other major countries. Nevertheless, lower profit margins were in part the consequence of (l) the failure of the controls program to achieve the moderation of wage increases upon which the financial policies of the

[84] Canada, Department of Finance (1977, p. 12).

Anti-Inflation Program were predicated; and (2) the failure to keep the financing requirement of the public sector for 1976/77 down to the same level as in 1975/76, as called for in the program,[85] mainly owing to the overestimate of revenue from personal income tax. The impact of increasing wage costs on profits was intensified by the appreciation of the exchange rate and in some measure by the imposition of price controls.[86]

The wage guidelines, as formulated, in effect guaranteed increases in real wages (except at high-income levels). The impact of tightening monetary conditions, owing to the enforcement of the money growth target in the face of the nonfulfillment of the income guideline and of the target for the public sector deficit, was bound to impinge more heavily on profits, investment, and employment because its immediate effect in slowing wage increases was limited. While the slower rise in prices brought about by weaker demand and the appreciation of the exchange rate was subsequently reflected in wage claims, this effect was soon overtaken by the effect of the subsequent depreciation, and of supply factors influencing food prices, in causing a renewed acceleration of the cost of living.

Lessons from Canadian Experience

It is worth considering how policies might have been improved. A realistic assessment of the difficulty of quickly reducing the average increase in wages to the target rate might have indicated the advisability of not seeking to implement the money growth target immediately, following the abnormal growth in the public's holdings of money caused by the prolonged postal strike. In giving overriding priority to its efforts to moderate price increases and price expectations by this means, the Bank ignored the widening gap between interest rates in Canada and the United States, and therefore strengthened the appreciation of the exchange rate in the first part of 1976.

When it became clear that government revenue was not rising in line with the budget forecasts, tax increases might have been imposed. As food prices were declining, an increase in sales tax need not have caused the rise in the consumer price index to exceed that foreseen in the program and in setting up the wages targets.

The appreciation clearly was not sustainable given the relative movement of factor costs in Canada and abroad. It could have been avoided by more consistent policies on the part of the federal and

[85] See Canada, Budget Speech (May 1976, p. 33 and Table 1).

[86] One should not neglect the effect that the price control provisions may have had during the opening months of the program in holding off price increases to restore profit margins.

provincial governments and the Bank of Canada. If governments had taken steps to limit the public sector deficit and if the Bank had intervened to prevent the exchange rate from rising, prices would have risen somewhat faster, but employment would have been better maintained and profits would have been squeezed less. While the rate of price inflation would have been higher than was actually the case during the first half of the program, the tendencies for inflation to reaccelerate in 1977 could probably have been avoided. A higher level of profits, private investment, and employment would probably have led to greater business confidence in Canada than actually existed at the end of the 1970s.

Two main lessons may be drawn from the Canadian experience with the Anti-Inflation Program.

The first is the need to achieve flexibility in implementation both by measures aimed at correcting any nonfulfillment of targets as it occurs (e.g., in the revenue forecasts) and by the adjustment of other policy variables to be consistent with the actual outcome. The second lesson is the difficulty of achieving a satisfactory outcome if the monetary and fiscal authorities pursue different priorities. Policies adopted in the spirit of countervailing forces are not likely to yield consistent "in-between" results but are likely to produce sudden shifts in policy and uncertainty. At the very least, if overall policy is to be determined by a process of "checks and balances," the contending policymakers must take account of the effect of each other's policy stance in evaluating the probable outcome of their respective policy options.

10

Case Studies of Three Small Economies

Strongly institutionalized incomes policies have been a persistent feature of economic management in Austria, the Netherlands, and Norway,[1] contributing to the achievement of real output growth and high employment over considerable periods. The experience of the Netherlands and Norway illustrates the crucial need to select a compatible set of medium-term economic objectives, the realization of which is economically feasible. Austrian policies have been marked by greater consistency of aims and aided by strongly integrated institutions for devising and implementing policy. It is particularly interesting to compare the experience of Austria and the Netherlands, two economies that were similarly situated in many respects, but which are distinguished by the contrast between a strongly coordinated wage bargaining system in Austria and uncoordinated wage bargaining institutions in the Netherlands.

Both economies are closely integrated with the German economy and are highly susceptible to the influence of the policies implemented in the Federal Republic of Germany. In both, incomes policies were initiated in exceptional conditions of economic dislocation and shortages after World War II and originated out of proposals formulated by employers and labor leaders in wartime. Support for cooperative action was strengthened by resistance to wartime occupation and common purpose in reconstruction. Business and labor leaders had active memories of hyperinflation and subsequent depression after World War II, and particularly in the Netherlands, price stability was a primary goal of economic management.

[1] Table 9 illustrates the relative size and structure of these economies and those studied in Chapter 9.

Early postwar policies were supported by the relatively weak unions, which had little effective organization within enterprises. The evident need to expand employment opportunities in order to avoid the heavy unemployment of the 1930s and absorb rapid population growth and surplus manpower in agriculture provided a strong rationale for wage restraint. Incomes policy was to be an instrument in promoting higher employment, productivity, and per capita incomes and in overcoming the balance of payments constraint through industrialization. The small scale of each economy and the institutional framework allowed incomes policy to be effectively operated by a few influential individuals in close personal contact—a factor that was immensely helpful in permitting a rapid response to problems as they arose, in avoiding conflicts, and in facilitating the coordination of incomes policy with other measures.

Austria: The "Social Partnership"

Austria possesses a unique institutional structure of representative organizations at the local, sectoral, and national level, and there is a long tradition of close association between these bodies and the government in the coordination and implementation of various aspects of economic policy, especially price and wage policies. The organizations of management and labor and the government have been jointly involved in operating the "social partnership" almost continuously throughout the postwar period.[2] The large size of the nationalized sector, comprising basic industries and major banks, is a factor reinforcing the need for the Government to be directly concerned with incomes policy. To a greater degree than in perhaps any other industrial country, the character of Austrian macroeconomic policy since the war has been inextricably linked with the characteristics of its institutional framework.

As in the Federal Republic of Germany and Japan, wage bargaining was influenced for many years by the consequences of the period of authoritarian rule, by the disbandment of the unions and their re-establishment with a reformed structure under the Allied Occupation,[3] and by the exceptional surplus of labor after the war. The strong

[2] See Spitäller (1973) and Farnleitner and Schmidt (1982).

[3] The Occupation, which lasted until 1955, had a severe economic impact. The eastern provinces under Soviet control were effectively cut off from the rest of the country, and Austria was obliged to make heavy reparations deliveries. Postwar recovery was delayed both by the Occupation and by political uncertainties during the Cold War period. As a result, the typical attitudes and policies of the reconstruction era (described in Chapter 2) were evident in Austria in the late 1950s and found expression in the institution of the social partnership in 1957.

impact of generally conservative German demand management upon economic and financial conditions in Austria[4] was not less important than the social partnership as an influence for wage and price restraint.

Institutional Setting

The existence of legally established, autonomous "chambers" representing the economic interests of businesses and professions, labor, and farmers at the regional and the national level constitutes a distinctive and long-standing feature of the Austrian economy.[5] Three of these bodies, the Federal Chambers of Commerce and Industry, of Agriculture, and of Labor are involved in the operation of the social partnership together with the Federation of Trade Unions. Each chamber was set up by an Act of Parliament, and membership of enterprises, agriculturalists, or wage earners is required by law. The Government has no authority to give orders to the chambers, but possesses the means to bring pressure to bear upon them.[6]

The Chamber of Commerce and Industry, also known as the Federal Economic Chamber, is management's principal instrument in wage negotiation. It represents all independent entrepreneurs and managers of enterprises and comprises sections for industry, commerce, trade, transport, tourism, and finance. The Chamber also has authority for the regulation of foreign trade. The Chamber of Labor presents the views of employees, "primarily in their role as consumers," and has no role in collective bargaining. However, there is a close connection between the Chamber and the Austrian Trade Union Federation. The Chamber provides economic information to the unions prepared by its large staff and the Federation effectively decides the positions taken by the Chamber.[7]

The Trade Union Federation was re-established in 1945 with a reorganized structure, which greatly centralized finances and power

[4] The close integration with the Federal Republic of Germany was in part a legacy of political unification between 1937 and 1945. It was reinforced by Austria's postwar isolation, half surrounded by the Communist economies of Czechoslovakia, Hungary, and Yugoslavia.

[5] Several of the chambers were instituted during the Austro-Hungarian Empire to represent the various interest groups in the formulation of legislation; the Chamber of Labor dates from 1920. Separate chambers also exist for lawyers and for physicians and dentists.

[6] For example, the Chamber of Agriculture dispenses the considerable subsidies which the Government provides for agriculture (Mire, 1977).

[7] Mire (1977, p. 14).

within the movement.[8] The affiliated unions, whose members comprise more than 60 percent of eligible wage earners, ostensibly have considerable autonomy in wage bargaining. However, the centralization of authority in the Federation "probably exceeds that of any other democratic trade union movement and vests the federation with considerable influence over the activities of the affiliated unions. In particular, the [Federation] controls the finances of the sixteen unions and appoints and employs the secretary of each."[9]

The labor movement is primarily oriented toward the achievement of full employment, real growth, and income redistribution goals by political means,[10] and the leadership does not view wage bargaining as its prime concern and justification. This attitude mitigates direct wage pressure, but it has other repercussions, one result being that the gap between wages paid and total labor cost is probably higher in Austria than in any other European country.

Organizational Framework of the Social Partnership

The continued existence of the chambers during the Nazi period was a key factor in facilitating the establishment of a coordinated policy for wages and prices under the coalition government after 1945. A powerful incentive promoting collaboration between the economic interest groups at the time was the need to present a united front to the occupation authorities so as to demonstrate that self-government could be safely restored. In 1947, the Federal Chamber of Commerce and Industry and the Trade Union Federation, together with the

[8] The earlier uncoordinated and fragmented union structure, divided by craft and political or religious affiliations, was superseded by 16 unions organized mainly by industry, though the largest organization is now the union of salaried employees in the private sector.

[9] Flanagan, Soskice, and Ulman (1983, p. 52). They also note that the system for electing union officials contributes to increase the centralization of power within the Federation. Union members vote only in the election of representatives to the work councils in the firm where they are employed. In unionized firms, the union representative is usually the local union representative and shop steward. These representatives elect the higher union representatives who in turn elect the officials of the Federation. "The position of most senior union officials therefore seems on the whole insulated from the pressures of the rank and file, an arrangement that may contribute to their freedom to. . .cooperate through long periods in the incomes policy arrangements" (p. 52).

Works councils are legally distinct from trade unions as in the Federal Republic of Germany and exist in nonunionized as well as unionized enterprises. The works council has authority to negotiate plant-level supplements to negotiated wage settlements, and hence is a source of wage drift.

[10] The concern to secure a coordinated movement of wages consistent with the macroeconomic goals of economic policy is illustrated by the fact that the union representatives in the social partnership commissions have frequently urged employers to resist pressures for wage increases in the works councils. See Flanagan, Soskice, and Ulman (1983, p. 56).

Chambers of Agriculture and Labor, set up the Economic Commission with the active support of the Government and signed a national agreement on wages and prices. Three more annual agreements followed, before price inflation moderated and free collective bargaining was reinstituted in 1952. After renewed inflation in 1956, the Parity Commission on Prices and Wages was established at the initiative of the Trade Union Federation, which indicated its willingness to moderate wage demands, provided that industry would curb price increases and that the Government would reduce tariffs and control monopolies. Since 1957 the Commission—the principal organ of the social partnership—has constituted "an integral part of the Austrian industrial system."[11]

The development of the social partnership was connected with the weakening of the coalition between the Austrian People's Party and the Socialist Party, which governed from 1945 to 1966. The social partnership became steadily more important as coalition governments became increasingly unable to reach decisions after 1956. "Whenever solutions [at] the level of the political parties were not obtainable, the task of finding a compromise was shifted to the social partners."[12] The role of the social partnership remained substantially unchanged under minority or majority socialist governments after 1970. As a result, "the responsibility [for] critical issues of everyday policy, such as the problems of prices and wages, [has] been largely transferred from the government to the organizations . . . under such circumstances, prices and incomes cannot furnish ready slogans for electoral campaigns."[13]

While the original goal of the social partnership was to create a favorable climate for growth by controlling inflation, after a Socialist majority government came to power in 1970 the purpose shifted to maintaining full employment, growth, and external balance and promoting an equitable income distribution. To this end, a countercyclical wage and price policy (tending to restrict increases in boom periods and be more generous in recessions) was adopted, together with union "solidarity" on wage increases, favoring the lower paid (the powerful unions supporting the demands of weaker unions and lower-income groups).

Control over wage and price developments is exercised by the Parity Commission and the two subcommissions for prices and for wages and salaries. These organizations are not statutory bodies and their

[11] Mire (1977, p. 13).
[12] Farnleitner and Schmidt (1982, pp. 88–89).
[13] Farnleitner and Schmidt (1982, p. 89).

decisions are not legally binding. The Parity Commission is composed of four members of the Government (the Chancellor and the Ministers of the Interior, Commerce and Industry, and Social Affairs) and eight representatives of the interest organizations (two each from the Chamber of Commerce and Industry, the Chamber of Labor, the Chamber of Agriculture, and the Trade Union Federation). The Subcommission on Prices has six members, one from each of these organizations and the Ministries of Commerce and Finance; it meets once a week. The Subcommission on Wages and Salaries has six members, two each from the Chamber of Commerce and the Trade Union Federation and one each from the Chambers of Labor and Agriculture. It meets every two weeks to consider union applications for the reopening of wage negotiations.[14]

All decisions of the subcommissions must be unanimous. This requirement forces the parties to modify their positions and search for compromise. The subcommissions must act within six weeks or pass the application to the Parity Commission, which must act within five weeks. "However, consideration is never simply cut off. If no agreement is reached within 5 weeks, the report is returned to the [subcommission] as often as is necessary to achieve a unanimous vote."[15]

Issues that cannot be resolved by the Parity Commission are taken to the Presidents' Conferences—ad hoc meetings of the presidents of the four participating organizations, at which final compromises are reached. These conferences were not envisaged in the original undertaking of 1957, but according to Mire (1977) they are given much of the credit for the long survival of the social partnership.

The Subcommission on Prices examines the appropriateness of proposed increases "in the light of the general economic welfare" and of the proviso that increases should be approved only if unavoidable cost increases could not be absorbed by raising productivity. It has jurisdiction over about 200 standard industrial products, raw materials and staple foodstuffs, and a few services, constituting about one third of all consumer expenditure. Companies submit applications for increases directly or through the Federal Chamber of Commerce. Firms that raise prices without approval risk having the Federal Government set prices for six months.[16] Apart from this rule, the system operates without explicit sanctions. The Federal Government

---

[14] The role of the subcommission has been officially described as "influencing the period of validity of collective agreements and helping to ensure a balanced wage policy." See Austrian Federal Press Service, *The Rational Approach to Labour and Industry* (Vienna, 1973, p. 13), cited in Flanagan, Soskice, and Ulman (1983, p. 59).

[15] Mire (1977, p. 15).

[16] Driscoll (1982, p. 15).

has also imposed price ceilings for certain basic foods, energy, and public services.

Farnleitner suggests that price intervention remained acceptable to the entrepreneurs because it quickly became apparent that price controls could only be applied to mass produced outputs and would not apply to services and new products; and because "in practice the climate of control has been realistic and relatively free of politics."[17] Actual prices have tended to be below those recommended by the Commission, mainly owing to import competition. Nevertheless, from the entrepreneurs' standpoint there are "strong disadvantages in the emphasis of pricing policy on cost factors [because] enterprises are usually not permitted to exploit favorable market situations simply to increase profits.... [This] may be one of the reasons for the insufficient equity capital of Austrian industry."[18]

The Subcommission on Wages and Salaries processes routine wage and salary claims; major settlements and those that are liable to cause price increases are dealt with by the Parity Commission. There is no specified wage guideline or rule that it follows, and its powers appear modest in comparison with those of incomes policy institutions in other countries.[19] Control is exercised over the claims of individual unions, however, by the requirement that all their wage requests must pass before the Federation's central committee on wage policy. There the union's proposal is examined for its possible impact on the economy (in terms of prices, employment, and the trade balance) and for compliance with the coordinated wages policy of the Federation. Thus, the Federation itself screens out claims at variance with its general policy and can recommend delays or adjustment before a claim ever comes to the official incomes policy institutions.

For considerable periods the unions sought to obtain an average 3 percent annual increase in real wages. Employers were prepared to take into account the inflation rate of the previous year and the actual increase in productivity in negotiating wage increases. Both sides agreed to above-average wage increases for lower-paid employees.[20]

Incomes Policy Measures Since 1973

Demand management policies pursued in Austria after 1973 were similar, in many respects, to those in Sweden.[21] Austria's greater

[17] See comment in Arndt (1982, p. 210).
[18] See comment in Arndt (1982, pp. 210–11).
[19] Flanagan, Soskice, and Ulman (1983, p. 52).
[20] Farnleitner and Schmidt (1982, p. 92).
[21] See Chapter 3, pp. 40–45. For a description of Austrian economic policies see Seidel (1982), Koren (1982), and other studies in Arndt (1982).

success in combining measures to protect full employment with the maintenance of a fixed exchange rate was aided by the more cohesive economic climate and greater success in moderating inflationary expectations, promoted by the procedures of the social partnership.

Until 1982, Austria was successful in maintaining very low unemployment by expansionary fiscal policies and measures to prevent or discourage enterprises from laying off workers (Table 11). Price and wage increases were moderated by the effects of the "hard currency" exchange rate policy, but at the cost of a very large deficit on current account, a profits squeeze, and an unfavorable climate for private

Table 11. Austria: Labor Market Statistics, 1978–84

	1978	1979	1980	1981	1982	1983	1984
				Annual averages			
Total labor force							
In thousands	3,317	3,321	3,326	3,345	3,342	3,326	3,332
Changes in percent	0.5	0.1	0.1	0.6	−0.1	−0.5	0.2
Dependent labor force[1]							
In thousands	2,816	2,830	2,842	2,868	2,881	2,862	2,875
Changes in percent	1.0	0.5	0.4	0.9	0.5	−0.3	0.4
Dependent employment[1]							
In thousands	2,758	2,774	2,789	2,799	2,766	2,735	2,745
Changes in percent	0.8	0.6	0.5	0.4	−1.2	−0.8	0.4
Industrial employment (in thousands)	623	623	630	616	591	567	564
Foreign workers (in thousands)	177	171	175	172	156	145	139
Unemployment (in thousands)	59	57	53	69	105	127	130
Vacancies (in thousands)	29	31	36	25	17	15	17
Unemployment rate[2] (in percent)	2.1	2.0	1.9	2.4	3.7	4.5	4.6
Vacancies (in percent of unemployed)	50	55	69	36	16	12	13
Foreign workers (in percent of dependent employment)	6.4	6.2	6.3	6.1	5.6	5.3	5.1

Sources: Austrian Institute for Economic Research, *Statistische Übersichten* and *Monatsberichte*, various issues.

[1]After a statistical correction, the 1982 figures for the dependent labor force and dependent employment were lowered by 9,000. The changes from 1982 to 1983 are shown on the revised basis.

[2]In percent of dependent labor force.

investment. The hard currency policy was accepted, with increasing reservations, by employers. It was backed by the unions apparently with some recognition that it would necessitate a more moderate rate of wage increase in return for its effect in moderating the rise in the cost of living. However, for some years after 1973 unit labor costs and consumer prices continued to rise faster than in Austria's principal trading partners, the Federal Republic of Germany and Switzerland;[22] and after 1978 slower growth in Germany intensified the difficulty of attaining the long-term policy objectives.

Price surveillance was extended and strengthened after 1973. The Parity Commission agreed to place a wide range of prices under the control of the Minister of the Interior; in 1975 the Government undertook to promote a voluntary reduction of certain prices including fuel oil. Partly as a result of these measures, the sharp rise in wholesale prices during 1974 and early 1975 was not reflected in consumer prices. While the imposition of price controls may have helped to dampen inflationary expectations in wage bargaining, their full effects are difficult to assess. It has been suggested that the controls may have hindered the subsequent deceleration of price increases because their implementation by the employers' associations may have served to restrain competition.

In 1974 the Government sought to use the occasion of the regular four-yearly tax adjustment to secure wage restraint in return for tax reliefs and increased family allowances, following the precedent of a successful tax-wage bargain in 1967–68.[23] However, the unions rejected the idea that the reduction in taxes should be taken into account in the wage negotiations, and hourly wages increased by almost 20 percent from 1974 to 1975. In the event, the tax reform served as an anticyclical measure, raising disposable income by some 2½ percent. (Other stimulatory measures included the release of contingency funds, labor market policies, and tax incentives for private investment.) In 1977–78, however, the Trade Union Federation succeeded in restraining negotiated wage increases in pursuance of its countercyclical wages policy and did not press union suggestions for a tax reduction aimed at countering fiscal drag.

The social partnership appears to have been an important factor in limiting industrial disputes. In general, the scope for channeling income redistribution issues into the legislative process served to

[22]After rising steeply earlier in the 1970s, Austrian unit labor costs in manufacturing, adjusted for exchange rate changes, were declining almost continuously in relation to those of 13 other industrial countries from 1977 to 1984. Their relative level in 1984 was little higher than in 1972.

[23]See Flanagan, Soskice, and Ulman (1983, p. 62).

lessen the pressures on the collective bargaining system. Joint intervention by the Presidents of the Federal Economic Chamber and the Trade Union Federation provided a useful means of settling disputes within the enterprise without a stoppage.[24] Austria escaped the wave of unofficial strikes and explosive wage increases experienced by many other countries in the late 1960s and early 1970s. The fact that Austria was not exposed to a major inflationary demand shock of external or domestic origin was of great importance in this connection.[25] However, relatively decentralized wage bargaining and the exceptional integration of shop stewards into the union hierarchy[26] were helpful in lessening the gap between the union leaders and the membership.

The institutions of the social partnership were also instrumental in limiting unemployment. Moral suasion was used to prevent layoffs and short-time working. Until the 1980s, the nationalized industries (accounting for 17 percent of industrial employment) refrained from adjusting employment with reduced output, the resulting deficits being subsidized out of the budget. Anticyclical inventory policies were promoted by the use of the public sector's considerable market power.[27] Unemployment was mitigated by conscious efforts by both sides to restrict overtime and by deliberate measures to reduce the employment of foreign workers.[28] There was also a marked expansion of government-financed training programs for underemployed workers and new entrants and of expenditure aimed at increasing labor mobility by improving labor market information. Employment in the service sector rose substantially in 1974–84.

Economic Performance Under the Social Partnership

The performance of the Austrian economy during the 1970s and early 1980s was generally favorable, with a lower inflation rate than in

[24] See Arndt (1982, p. 210). The record of uninterrupted production has given Austrian exporters a comparative advantage in their reputation as reliable suppliers.

[25] The geographic and industrial distribution of its trade and the comparative isolation of its financial system limited the impact upon Austria of the inflationary developments in the industrial world in the late 1960s and 1970s.

[26] In Austria, unlike many other countries, the union organization offers the shop steward the possibility of "moving successively into positions of local or regional union leadership, the regional parliament, and later a national union or party position;" this serves to strengthen his identification with the union position in conducting wage negotiations at the plant level. Flanagan, Soskice, and Ulman (1983, p. 80).

[27] Organization for Economic Cooperation and Development (July 1976).

[28] The proportion of foreign workers was reduced from a peak of almost 9.5 percent of the dependent labor force in November 1973 to 6.8 percent over the year 1975, and less in 1976. The quota system for foreign workers in force during the 1960s was reactivated at the beginning of 1976.

other industrial countries except the Federal Republic of Germany and Switzerland, unemployment at about 2 percent, and higher-than-average, 4–5 percent real growth in most years up to 1982.[29] Although the faster rise in unit labor costs than in Germany and Switzerland, and the marked appreciation of the schilling vis-à-vis currencies other than the deutsche mark and the Swiss franc caused a decline in Austrian cost competitiveness during the 1970s, Austria succeeded better than many other industrial countries in limiting the inflationary impact of the second oil price increase and was able to regain part of the loss in cost competitiveness after 1979. From 1982 to 1984 earnings in industry rose less than productivity (Table 12).

It is difficult to identify the concrete effects of the social partnership in restraining price and wage inflation. Only an informed historical study, based on confidential sources, could establish exactly what role the commissions and chambers have played in the formulation and execution of economic policies since 1957. It is clear, however, that the system provides the authorities with an invaluable channel for informing the various interest groups concerning the economic situation and the Government's intentions and for obtaining the reactions of the economic "constituencies" (in the process forcing the various groups to reveal, and to some extent adjust, their positions).

Table 12. Austria: Wages and Salaries and Productivity, 1978–84
(Percentage changes over preceding year)

	1978	1979	1980	1981	1982	1983	1984
Overall economy							
Minimum wage and salary rates[1]	7.0	5.1	5.4	7.2	7.2	5.1	4.3
Actual earnings	7.1	5.5	6.2	7.7	5.8	4.5	5.0
Productivity[2]	0.2	4.3	2.4	−0.5	2.2	3.3	1.8
Industry							
Minimum wage and salary rates[1]	5.9	5.4	6.0	7.2	7.4	5.5	4.2
Actual earnings	6.1	6.3	7.2	7.8	7.0	5.3	5.0
Productivity (output per man-hour)	5.9	7.3	2.3	0.7	4.3	6.4	4.9

Sources: Austrian Institute for Economic Research, *Statistische Übersichten* and *Monatsberichte*, various issues.

[1] Negotiated minimum pay rates averaged across job categories.

[2] Real GDP per employee.

[29] Driscoll (1982, p. 16).

The system is useful in providing agreed procedures, which encourage the resolution of intra-union and employer-union issues out of the public eye and which tend to discourage the adoption of extremist positions for their publicity value. The social partnership has, however, also contributed to delay necessary structural adjustments. It should be seen mainly as a means of securing and preserving consensus and thereby ensuring the smooth operation of economic policies rather than simply as an instrument of anti-inflationary policy per se.

While its proponents laud the social partnership as a means of avoiding political conflict, it essentially represents an extension of politics in less open, nonparliamentary forums. Faced with the increasing influence of the labor organizations within the political parties, Austrian entrepreneurs have seen the social partnership as a means of influencing political developments. The Parity Commission is based on the principle of parity with equal rights for each member organization, regardless of the size of its constituency. The representation of the four organizations was intended to ensure parity between employers and employees and also between organizations dominated by the Austrian People's Party (the Federal Economic Council and the Chamber of Agriculture) and the Socialist Party (the Chamber of Labor and the Trade Union Federation).[30] However, the divisions are less clear-cut than this would suggest because the largest of the three organizations that make up the People's Party is the Federation of Employees and Workers, which also has considerable influence within the Trade Union Federation. Katzenstein has drawn attention to the effects of this "organizational interpenetration of the unions by business organizations and of business by union strongholds" in tying "political opponents closely together in the policy process" and of consequently inhibiting unilateral initiatives and the formulation of coherent industrial policy.[31]

Flanagan, Soskice, and Ulman (1983) conclude that the Austrian system represents a special case, unlikely to be duplicated in other countries since it requires for its operation (1) a strictly limited number of participants in the wage and price coordinating institutions; (2) strong centralization of powers within the interest organizations; and (3) political power of the coordinated labor movement to

---

[30] Farnleitner and Schmidt (1982, p. 89). Spitäller (1982, p. 99) comments that "the social partnership consists invariably of the same quartet, the three chambers and the Trade Union Federation.... The impression of seeing in action a state within the state ... is not altogether illusory."

[31] Katzenstein (1982, p. 154).

secure income gains through legislation and to obtain such gains and the protection of employment opportunities as a quid pro quo for restraining negotiated wage increases.

It is clearly difficult to duplicate the first condition (which has been vitally important in the successful pursuit of incomes policy objectives at various periods in other small countries, such as the Netherlands, Norway, Finland, and Sweden) in larger and less homogenous economies. But the limited cast of individuals involved in the operation of the social partnership also results from the second condition and the sharply pyramided structure of power within the labor movement mentioned earlier. The institutional framework of the social partnership not only depends upon but also reinforces the centralization of authority within the interest groups—a fact that may not be irrelevant in explaining its survival.

It is fascinating to see how the historic structure of coordinated interest organizations, whose original purpose was to influence legislation, has acquired a new role in the social partnership. A highly centralized, bureaucratic organization of this kind may be held over from a period of authoritarian rule—if for instance the structure of organization at the local and national level formerly utilized for administration is retained. Alternatively, it may be a legacy from a period when an emerging union movement was forced to coordinate its activities in order to combat organized resistance by the employers' organizations (as in Sweden at the turn of the nineteenth century). It is a far different proposition to establish tight control from the center where free collective bargaining is strongly established at the local or sectoral level and where powerful unions predate the setting up of central organizations, as in the United Kingdom, Belgium, Canada, and the United States.

The social partnership has enabled a trade-off to be achieved: industrial peace and some measure of control over wage settlements in return for high budgetary spending on social programs and the protection of employment opportunities (by measures such as subsidies to nationalized enterprises and to support investment by private enterprises in areas of heavy unemployment). While this trade-off mitigated direct wage pressure, it had other less favorable consequences. No adequate evaluation of the benefits derived from the social partnership can be made without an assessment of these other impacts, in particular the effects on public sector finances and the, almost certainly adverse, effects on the allocation of investment. The system results in pragmatic decisions and is conducive to political stability and the operation of a consistent economic policy over time. But the need for consensus solutions may cause short-run expedients to be emphasized at the expense of necessary long-run structural adjustments. For more than a decade, support for the system was conditioned by rising real disposable incomes and the maintenance of very low unemployment. Since 1982 it has been tested by a marked increase in unemployment, tighter restraint on public expenditures, and higher interest rates.

Netherlands: Incomes Policies of the 1970s and 1980s

The Netherlands experience with incomes policy is a revealing illustration of the theoretical and practical problems of devising a national economic policy in a small economy closely integrated within a larger economic system.

The concept of a statutory incomes policy effectuated with the cooperation of the wage bargaining parties may be said to have originated in the Netherlands after World War II. It therefore seems appropriate that this study should include a brief account of the evolution of the organizational framework and nature of the incomes policies implemented during 1945–70—the more so since the principles applied earlier strongly influenced wage bargaining attitudes in the 1970s.

The coordination of wage decisions by means of the incomes policy institutions established after World War II represented a response to the divided and divisive organization of the wage bargaining system in the Netherlands. From the mid-1940s to the early 1960s it enabled centralized annual wage decisions to be arrived at by negotiation and enforced by wage controls. After the late 1960s the Government frequently intervened to impose a settlement on those occasions when no central agreement could be reached.

For some two decades, the system was effective in limiting industrial unrest and contributed to the achievement of a rapid expansion of employment opportunities and a rising standard of living with an almost stable price level. Centralized wage decisions closely meshed with macroeconomic demand policies aimed at maintaining price stability worked well, as long as that goal was compatible with other major countries' policies under fixed exchange rates.

After the mid-1960s, the wage bargaining partners involved in centralized income decisions were repeatedly unable to achieve pragmatic and workable compromises concerning wage increases. The contrast with Austria's success in this respect stemmed mainly from the organizational fragmentation and stronger conflicts of interest between social groups. It was, however, also due to the far greater exposure of the Dutch economy to external shocks.

Institutional Setting

Unlike Austria and the Federal Republic of Germany, where denominational unions were reorganized along industrial lines in the late 1940s, in the Netherlands three major union federations survived until 1976: the Netherlands Federation of Trade Unions (Nederlands Verbond van Vakverenigingen—NVV), a Socialist group; the Netherlands Catholic Trade Union Federation (Nederlands Katholiek Vakbond—NKV); and the Protestant National Trade Union Federation (Christelijk National Vakverbond—CNV). The Socialist and Catholic federations then merged to form the Dutch Federation of Trade Unions (Federatie von Nederlandse Vakbouden—FNV). The three union groupings mirrored a similar division of the employers' associations. The divided structure of the labor market institutions, the lack of discipline and formal authority of the employers' organizations over member firms, and the fact that there was no clear hierarchic union organization of the kind that developed in Austria and Sweden ruled out a system of self-restraint by the "social partners" on the Austrian or Swedish model.

Dutch incomes policies have involved explicit participation of the Government and frequent recourse to statutory controls.[32] This represented the continuation of a long-standing tradition of government involvement with wage bargaining, including the acquisition shortly before World War II of legal authority to extend collective agreements to nonsignatory firms or declare agreements void in whole or part—a measure which, though it tended to preserve the existing divided union structure, was strongly opposed by the employers.[33]

The conflicting interests of the different union groupings, and the increasingly limited influence of the central federations over their constituent unions, hampered the operation of the postwar incomes policy institutions after the early 1960s. The institutions remained in existence and played an important role in informing the authorities of the attitudes and demands of the economic groups and at times in influencing public opinion, but by the 1970s wage restraint was secured primarily by ad hoc government intervention.

---

[32] The following description of the institutional framework and the course of incomes policies up to the early 1970s is based on Flanagan, Soskice, and Ulman (1983, pp. 99–122).

[33] Windmuller (1969).

Dutch economic policy was aimed at limiting inflation by carefully integrated fiscal and monetary management and policy for income development, generally supported by price and wage controls. Price controls were a useful weapon at times, for example when tightened to secure an immediate effect in slowing inflation. But they were usually applied in a relaxed fashion, with numerous exemptions.

Prior Evolution of Wage Determination

The wage determination system established after World War II combined statutory wage controls with collective bargaining between employers and wage earners. Under the Extraordinary Decree of 1945, collective agreements relating to a particular enterprise or industry were subject to approval by the independent Board of Mediators, which functioned as an independent nongovernmental agency with considerable powers.[34] The Board was required to consult with the Foundation of Labor,[35] a body which originated out of wartime meetings between employers and labor leaders. In 1950, the Social and Economic Council was set up to advise the Government.[36]

Synchronized Wage Increases and Objective Job Evaluation

In the immediate postwar period, wage controls were applied as part of the effort to ensure a subsistence real wage to all employees out of the limited resources available for consumption. During the early 1950s, the essential task was to restrain wages and consumption in order to permit high public and private investment in reconstruction and protect the balance of payments position.

Despite considerable unemployment, there was a danger that decentralized wage bargaining by weakly organized employers and competing unions would lead to "leap frogging" claims resulting in an excessive rise in wages, or that wage increases for skilled labor in short supply would have a similar effect by promoting matching claims by

[34] The Board was established to help set wages in wartime. It consisted of prominent academics and members of the professions and not of full-time experts.

[35] The Foundation of Labor was originally concerned primarily with social policies. It consisted of an equal number of representatives of labor and employers and was financed equally by both groups. In practice, all collective agreements came to be passed to the Permanent Joint Committee on Wages set up by the Foundation and it was in its weekly meetings that centralized bargaining between the employer and union federations was carried out. Bhatia and Bouter (1961, p. 358).

[36] The apparent purpose was to create a more conservative advisory body than the Foundation of Labor. The Council comprised 15 members appointed by the Government from various fields of social research, 15 members appointed by the unions, and 15 by the employers' organizations.

other groups. To meet the first problem, the Board of Mediators and the Foundation of Labor in effect sought to transform a decentralized system of wage determination into a centralized and synchronized system of annual wage rounds. The remedy for the second was sought in a nationwide, and supposedly scientific, system of objective job evaluation. This could not, however, overcome the essential problem that the value of the work and the willingness of the employer to pay a certain wage depend not on the measured characteristics of one job versus another but on changing economic factors of demand and supply. Not even the imposition of fines and jail sentences could prevent employers from paying "black market" wages in order to secure or retain scarce skilled workers.

Differentiated Productivity Guidelines

In 1959, following the election of a new government without any Labor Party participation (or ties with the socialist unions) there was a shift toward the greater differentiation of wage increases and decentralization of bargaining, advocated by large employers and the denominational unions. Increases were in part to reflect the rise in productivity in each sector, but wages were to rise more rapidly than productivity in sectors of low productivity growth, and vice versa. Prices were to be reduced in sectors of high productivity growth to counterbalance increases in costs and prices in sectors of low productivity growth. (The system was the precursor of the U.S. guidelines of 1961.) Unfortunately, since objective figures on sectoral productivity were lacking, the policy led to some ludicrous complications and caused even more interference with bargaining than before.[37]

This second "failure to resolve distributional issues by reference to what had been advanced as objectively neutral or scientific formulas" deprived the wages policy of its claim to have an objective basis and cast doubt on whether effective wage and price restraint could be achieved under decentralized bargaining with less government intervention.[38]

Negotiated wage increases accelerated sharply under the new system, and as labor markets tightened with a marked cyclical upswing in Europe in 1960–61, wage drift far exceeded that of the 1950s. When the deutsche mark was revalued in 1961, the Dutch authorities reluctantly decided to follow suit in order to limit the rise in

[37] Pen (1963).

[38] Flanagan, Soskice, and Ulman (1983, p. 112).

consumer prices and reduce excess demand in the labor market. The resulting rise in labor costs in terms of other foreign currencies and the smaller balance of payments surplus heightened anxiety over wage inflation and impelled the Government to intervene. Its action in bypassing the Board of Mediators and prohibiting the negotiation of further wage increases until existing contracts expired set off unrest, and many of the relevant directives were ignored. Toward the end of 1961, the Government asked the Social and Economic Council to suggest criteria for wage increases other than the differentiated productivity guidelines.

Return to a Uniform Wage Norm

The shift toward decentralization and unrestricted bargaining had been opposed by the nondenominational employers' associations, whose smaller, less efficient, and less profitable, member firms feared the effects of decontrol during a period of labor shortage. With the active support of the Governor of the Netherlands Bank, a general norm based on the expected annual growth in overall average productivity was reinstituted in 1963. The figure was to be negotiated between the Foundation of Labor and the Government, guided by recommendations of the Social and Economic Council based on the economic forecasts of the independent Central Planning Bureau. Following discussions with the Government, the central union and employer federations were to meet with their constituent organizations in various industries to ensure that individual settlements would not contravene achievement of the overall target. Thus, the central wage bargaining organizations took over the task of supervising and reviewing settlements from the independent Board of Mediators. However, the Board retained the power to set aside a proposed settlement if the Foundation could not agree on its appropriateness or if the Board believed the settlement exceeded the target. The Government also had power to impose a temporary wage freeze should the Foundation and the Government fail to agree on the central norm.

Conflicting Policy Goals

Throughout the 1960s, Dutch policies were predicated on the belief that price stability would be achieved provided that the rate of increase in nominal spending was not permitted to exceed the potential for real income growth. Carefully integrated monetary and fiscal policy could ensure stability of the domestic price level, with price controls and wages policy together serving to prevent money wages from rising faster than productivity.[39] This approach ignored the extent to which, in a highly open small economy under a fixed or pegged exchange rate, the movement of prices and wages must be influenced by those abroad. Therefore, if "there is inflation in the world as a whole, the reasonable goal for a wage policy in a country like the Netherlands is not absolute price stability but a rate of price increase which will enable the country to maintain its competitive position in international markets."[40]

Despite the faster rise in wages experienced under the differentiated guidelines, Dutch unit labor costs in manufacturing remained well below the average for the major industrial countries in 1963 (Chart 8), and they had actually declined relative to those in the Federal Republic of Germany between 1958 and 1963. In an increasingly integrated world economy, the maintenance of this differential, let alone the widening probably implied by wage increases geared to domestic price stability, was likely to generate large balance of payments surpluses. Hence, the guiding principle of wages policy was in conflict with the fixed exchange rate objective. Unless they were prepared to revalue, the authorities would, sooner or later, have to acquiesce in a faster average rise in wages than in productivity.

Collapse of Centralized Wage Determination

In practice, the noninflationary guideline was not likely to be met, given the forces making for larger wage increases in the export industries. Large enterprises, using capital-intensive techniques and selling much of their output abroad, were able and willing to grant

---

[39] In the formulation of policy, the increase in spending was taken to be governed by monetary expansion originating from the short-term borrowing of the public sector, from credit to the private sector determined by the Netherlands Bank, from limited changes in velocity, and from the balance of payments position. The rate of monetary expansion (defined as including the increase in holdings of short-term government debt) that would be consistent with the maintenance of price stability was derived from the five-year projections of real GNP growth estimated by the Central Planning Bureau. The target growth of public expenditure and revenue was then decided with reference to the projected medium-term trends in the economy, the norms for the acceptable "structural budget deficit" being established after taking into account the expected pattern of financing surpluses and deficits in the economy. The structural budget deficit was to equal the projected financial surplus of the rest of the economy in a cyclically neutral situation, defined as one of moderate current account surplus and private investment and savings ratios at their trend levels. A large balance of payments surplus tending to produce an excessive liquidity expansion relative to the projected rate of real output growth was to be compensated by the Government withdrawing liquidity through a financing surplus, achieved by reducing expenditure, increasing taxes, or by long-term borrowing beyond current needs. See Holtrop (1962, p. 216).

[40] Bhatia and Bouter (1961, p. 372).

Chart 8. Netherlands: Relative Labor Cost per Unit of Output Compared with Trading Partners

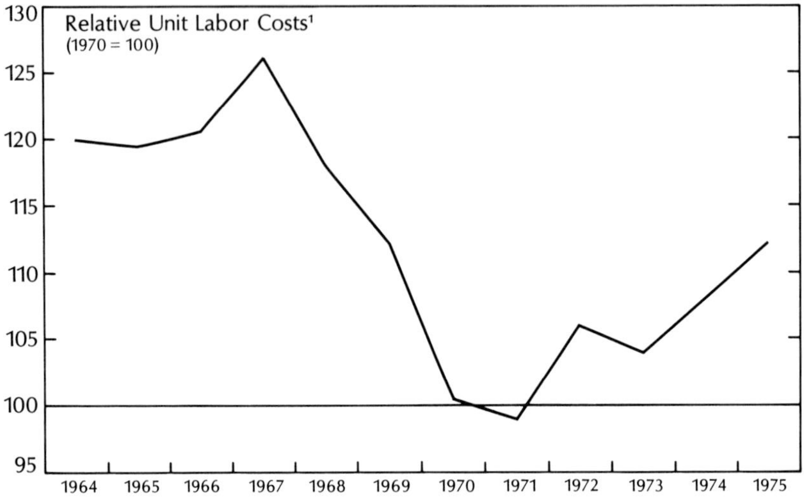

Sources: Swedish Employers' Confederation; OECD.

[1] Unit labor costs in industry in the Netherlands expressed as a percentage of ULCs in a trade-weighted average of important partner countries (Federal Republic of Germany, Belgium, France, United Kingdom, Italy, Switzerland, United States), both in U.S. dollars.

Reproduced from Organization for Economic Cooperation and Development, *OECD Economic Surveys: Netherlands* (Paris, February 1977), p. 24.

substantial wage increases in order to attract additional labor and avoid losses of skilled workmen, or to promote good industrial relations and achieve multiyear settlements, so that they could forecast cost developments in planning output and investment. Such settlements in contravention of the norm posed an insoluble dilemma for their opponents in the Foundation of Labor (in the main, the associations of smaller firms and the NVV), who were unwilling either to confirm the agreements, or, in the case of the NVV, to support the Government in overruling a negotiated settlement. Consequently, the new system virtually ceased to function after 1965. The norm for 1963 of only 2.7 percent having been substantially exceeded, the norm for 1964 was set at the 10 percent proposed by the unions, a figure far in excess of the 4 percent estimated productivity growth. In the event, negotiated wages rose by 14 percent, but productivity increased by 9 percent. This unexpected outcome raised fundamental questions concerning incomes policy. Had the unions been too cautious? Would a more aggressive wages policy have led to higher productivity growth by promoting greater efficiency and increased mechanization and investment?[41]

In 1965 the Foundation of Labor reached a deadlock over a settlement that provided for indexation on the model of U.S. wage contracts, in violation of the wage norm. No norms were agreed for 1966 and 1967, but the Government issued its own. Price control legislation expired at the end of 1966.

The late 1960s were marked by abortive efforts by the Government to acquire greater control over wage movements by means of new legislation authorizing it to intervene in specific negotiations and to impose a general wage freeze in an economic emergency.[42] These efforts had the effect of reinforcing union militancy and rendering it more difficult for the central union federations to collaborate in efforts at restraint.

Spread of Indexation

When price inflation accelerated in 1969, demands for indexation became general and the Social and Economic Council recommended the insertion of indexation clauses even in one-year agreements. By 1971, practically all collective agreements provided for some form of automatic adjustment. The minimum wage and public sector pay were later indexed on the movement of negotiated wage rates. In the early 1970s, the procedure of equal percentage adjustment produced an evident widening of *nominal* wage differentials, which was unacceptable to the unions. Hence, wage contracts came to provide for graduated compensation, with full compensation for the lowest paid and declining percentage compensation in higher wage brackets. This had the effect of narrowing real wage differentials, especially at the lower end of the wage scale. Indexation, combined with the growing concentration of wage bargaining upon disposable income, caused increases in income taxes or social security contributions to generate persistent upward movements of nominal wages.[43]

---

[41] Albeda (1971).

[42] In 1968 the Government invalidated three wage agreements and proposed a statutory freeze on wages. It was subsequently forced to allow the agreements to stand and to abandon the freeze. In 1969 the Government introduced the new Wage Formation Law without consulting the social partners and decreed a six-month wage freeze in 1970, which led to a nationwide protest strike. A new government elected in 1971 agreed not to use the power to invalidate bargaining agreements. Flanagan, Soskice, and Ulman (1983, pp. 119–20).

[43] Marked increases in tax rates or contributions, imposed to restrain the expansion of nominal demand and hold down inflation, therefore tended to have the perverse effect of heightening cost inflation and intensifying the impact of restrictive financial policies upon profits, investment, and employment, especially in the sectors catering to home demand.

Lasting Consequences of Incompatible Goals in the 1960s

Given the low levels of Dutch wages relative to those of most EEC countries in the mid-1960s, market forces at close to full employment were virtually certain to cause wages in the industrial sector to go up faster than those in competing countries during the boom of the late 1960s. Because of the tradition of uniform wage increases throughout the economy, the faster wage increases in the open sector were more likely to be disseminated to the lower-productivity sheltered sectors than in most other countries[44] and hence were liable to exert greater pressure on sheltered sector prices and the domestic price level in general. Superimpose on this situation almost universal indexation of wages in the Netherlands against little—or much less—indexation in most other countries and it becomes evident that the general level of wages in the Netherlands was prone to go up faster than the average during and after the boom of the late 1960s and to continue to do so even after industrial wages were no longer out of line with those in competing countries.

In the heightened world inflation of the late 1960s, the upward adjustment of wage levels in the open sector, combined with strong union and official support for the principle of uniform wage increases throughout the economy, was incompatible with the goal of price stability.[45] Fiscal and monetary policies framed with the object of maintaining near price stability within the economy were liable to squeeze profits and limit investment in the sectors catering to the home market and to exacerbate conflicts over income distribution and wage differentials. The effort to secure price stability and maintain a fixed exchange rate imposed great strains on the social fabric and political system in the Netherlands. Militant wage bargaining in turn reinforced the authorities' inclination to adopt a conservative policy in financing social security[46] and to permit a steep rise in income tax receipts to be brought about by rising real incomes.[47] Both of these

---

[44] In the Federal Republic of Germany, the rise of low-level wages was mitigated by the huge inflow of foreign workers; there, as in Italy, Japan, and the United States, the low productivity sectors were largely nonunionized.

[45] Kervyn de Lettenhove (1965).

[46] Increases in social security contributions were an important factor in raising the general level of Dutch wage costs during the late 1960s and the first half of the 1970s, and they exerted a contractionary influence on domestic demand when the funds were in substantial surplus from 1968 to 1971 and in 1973. The effect in stiffening collective bargaining was especially marked because the Dutch system relied on contributions from the insured to a much greater extent than was the case in most OECD countries.

[47] Although fiscal drag had been largely offset by periodic adjustment of tax rates or brackets up to 1972, the average tax rate payable at the income corresponding to the average industrial wage more than doubled between 1956 and 1972. Tax and social

strategies had the effect of strengthening wage pressure by focusing collective bargaining on real disposable incomes.

The authorities could influence the level of domestic demand and prices by restrictive fiscal and credit policies and price controls, but while such policies would tend to make manpower more readily available to the open sector, they would not appreciably weaken the power of the unions to secure large wage increases from highly profitable export enterprises. Nor would they insulate smaller businesses catering to the home market from union pressures for similar increases and from the need to raise wages in order to retain labor. Consequently, restrictive demand management would squeeze profits in the small business sector. The possibility of raising productivity there to offset higher unit labor costs tended to be limited by low profits and restricted availability of credit,[48] whereas investment by large export-oriented concerns was favored both by high profits and their ready access to foreign financing in the late 1960s and early 1970s.

Intermittent Recourse to Statutory Incomes Policies

Setting for Incomes Policies After 1970

The refusal of the authorities to accede to the automatic pressures for the adjustment of the external surplus either via a rise in the level of wages and prices at the going exchange rate, or via an adjustment of the rate, caused the Netherlands to enter the 1970s with highly profitable export industries, intensely strained industrial relations, and widespread indexation of wages. Widening income disparities and the evident contravention of the accepted principles on which incomes policies had been based for two decades had created an explosive wage bargaining context and political unrest. Efforts to defuse this situation led to the provision of generous social security benefits and the development of an extraordinarily large public sector in the early 1970s.[49]

---

security receipts rose from 36.5 percent of national income in 1961–65 to 42.1 percent in 1966–70 and 48.1 percent in 1971–74. Organization for Economic Cooperation and Development (March 1979, pp. 7–8).

[48] The Scandinavian authorities, influenced by the Odhner-Aukrust model of wage determination, accepted rising costs and prices in the sheltered sectors as inevitable and did not impose such stringent conditions upon them, making it easier than in the Netherlands for enterprises to respond to the need to raise productivity (see Chapter 2).

[49] Total public sector expenditure rose from 41.8 percent of national income in 1965 to 51.4 percent in 1973, while social security expenditure rose from 13.0 percent to 18.4 percent.

Despite large wage increases in 1969–70, conditions making for a rapid rise in wages continued to prevail in 1971.[50] The decision to allow the guilder to float with the deutsche mark in May reinforced the Government's determination to re-establish centralized control over wage developments and strengthened the support of business and the union federations for a coordinated wages policy.

On the employers' side, enterprises exposed to foreign competition could foresee a greater need to limit wage increases in the context of an appreciating exchange rate; thus they now had a greater community of interest with the many small employers catering to the home market. On the union side, similar considerations tended to increase support for a unified wages policy by lessening the independence of the strong industrial unions and the difference of views between them and the centralized union organizations—especially the NVV, which largely comprised unions covering employees of smaller enterprises. However, the shock of finding that the rise in the value of the guilder (like the unprecedented wage increase in 1963) did not lead to rising unemployment stiffened union claims and raised increasing doubts as to whether the rise in productivity had not been seriously understated.[51]

Relying on its powers to regulate wages under the postwar legislation rather than the disputed Wages Formation Law, in May 1971 the Government set ceilings for pay increases by extending all wage contracts expiring before June 1971 for six months with stipulated maximum increases over the period.[52] Similar statutory interventions for periods of six months to a year were repeated in 1974, 1976, and again during 1980–82. Price controls, which had been eliminated in August 1971, were reintroduced in November, and remained in force until they were selectively lifted in 1982.

Policies of 1971–77

In considering the policies implemented after 1970, one must not forget that they were adopted in extraordinary circumstances when it was exceptionally difficult to foresee future developments. During the "awkward interregnum" of 1971–73, the future of the fixed exchange rate system remained unclear.[53] In the Netherlands case, a further

[50] Unit labor costs in industry were lower relative to those in competitor countries in 1971 than at any time in the 1960s (Chart 9). Upward pressures continued after the realignment of exchange rates at the end of the year because German wages were still rising very rapidly.

[51] The annual increase in nominal wages, which had accelerated to 13 percent in 1969 and 1970, remained about the same in 1971–73.

[52] Driscoll (1982, p. 44).

[53] See Chapter 5.

element of uncertainty concerned the prospective effects of natural gas production upon real national income and its exchange rate implications. The slowdown of world demand after 1973 was seen as a temporary consequence of the deflationary impact of increased oil prices and of measures taken by the largest countries to halt rapid inflation. At this time many governments were confident that strong world demand would be restored once inflation was wrung out of the system and inflationary expectations had been overcome and judged that a countercyclical response was appropriate.

The Social Contract of December 1972

The reinstitution of a statutory incomes policy in 1971 constituted the first move to restore control in the uncertain situation created by the freeing of the guilder. Meanwhile, efforts were made to defuse wage bargaining and political conflicts and to establish a consensus-based incomes policy consistent with the medium-term projections for the economy drawn up in 1971. These projections incorporated estimates of the effect which natural gas production would have in raising real national income, assuming that exchange rates and the relative price of energy and natural gas remained unchanged.

In a situation where the wages share in national income had become a burning political issue, the prospective rise in per capita real national income was bound to be seen by wage earners as grounds for large real wage increases, over and above indexation provisions. Since the faster rise in per capita output reflected the extraordinarily high labor productivity in natural gas production involving little labor input, such a guideline necessarily involved a faster rise in real wages than in productivity over the rest of the economy. Such an increase in real wages, protected by full indexation, was almost sure to imply a very marked weakening of cost competitiveness against countries such as the Federal Republic of Germany and the United States. This effect was intensified by the improvement in the terms of trade for gas after the oil price increase.

In May 1972 the union federations stated the conditions under which they would be prepared to moderate wage claims. Most of these conditions, relating to tax and social security provisions in the 1973 budget and undertakings for longer-term improvements in terms of employment, were incorporated in the Social Contract Agreement of December 1972 between the Government and unions and employers, governing collective settlements for 1973. The process of arriving at agreement by trading adjustments of fiscal measures provided for in the medium-term budget plans against concessions by the unions or employers, the nonwage issues raised by the unions, and the form of the agreement were all repeated in subsequent negotiations at the central level during the 1970s.

The Agreement provided that contractual wage increases should not exceed 3.5 percent over and above indexation, assuming a 4–4.5 percent average increase in productivity. It was associated with the reintroduction of price controls[54] and with government assurances that vigorous efforts would be made to combat unemployment. If labor productivity was found to be increasing faster than assumed, new negotiations were to take place.[55] Efforts were to be made to secure the gradual introduction of a 40-hour workweek and a minimum of 20 days paid vacation time by the end of 1975. The timing of the Social Contract was singularly unfortunate. The Agreement was predicated on the maintenance of the newly established exchange rate and did not allow for the conditions to be created by much higher oil prices. Its achievement after prolonged negotiations limited the authorities' subsequent freedom of action.

In the changed circumstances of 1973, the financial authorities' main concern was to curb the threat of an accelerating price/wage spiral and to achieve a restrictive policy stance in line with that adopted in the Federal Republic of Germany. Changes in budget provisions being largely precluded because they formed part of the Social Contract Agreement, the overall balance of central government financing was sharply reversed by an unvoted administrative change in tax schedules[56] and a large increase in social security contributions. The guilder was permitted to appreciate within the snake by 5 percent in September, in order to lessen the inflationary impact of rising import prices and wages indexation and to forestall a further rise in the balance of payments surplus.

As a consequence of these changes, enterprises were faced in 1973 with sharply increased labor costs, a rise in the exchange rate, declining domestic demand, and stiffened price controls. While profits were squeezed, the steep rise in direct taxes and social security

[54] One third (after mid-1974 one half) of wage increases could be passed on in higher prices in the industrial sector. In the services sector, the proportion was 80 percent (later 75 percent). Prior notification of price increases was reintroduced in May 1973, and regulation of distribution margins was instituted in August.

[55] Before the Agreement was reached, the expert group of the Social and Economic Council had suggested that the increase in productivity might be greater than was projected by the Planning Bureau.

[56] A number of flat rates for broader income brackets replaced a more continuously rising curve. As a consequence, for incomes just above the personal exemption level, tax liability was increased to 25 percent instead of 17 percent. Fiscal drag was also important in 1973–74.

premiums paid by employees absorbed the whole gain in average real gross wages per head. The counterpart of the rise in real wage costs was a large surplus on government and social security account. The combined effect of the Social Contract Agreement and the policies of 1973 was to cause a marked rise in the relative level of Dutch wage costs in 1973–74 (Chart 9). The "defusing" purpose of the Agreement was frustrated. Instead, the nonfulfillment of the promised increase in higher real wages provoked a stiffening of wage claims for 1974 and 1975.

Chart 9. Netherlands: Average Hourly Labor Costs in Industry Compared with Trading Partners

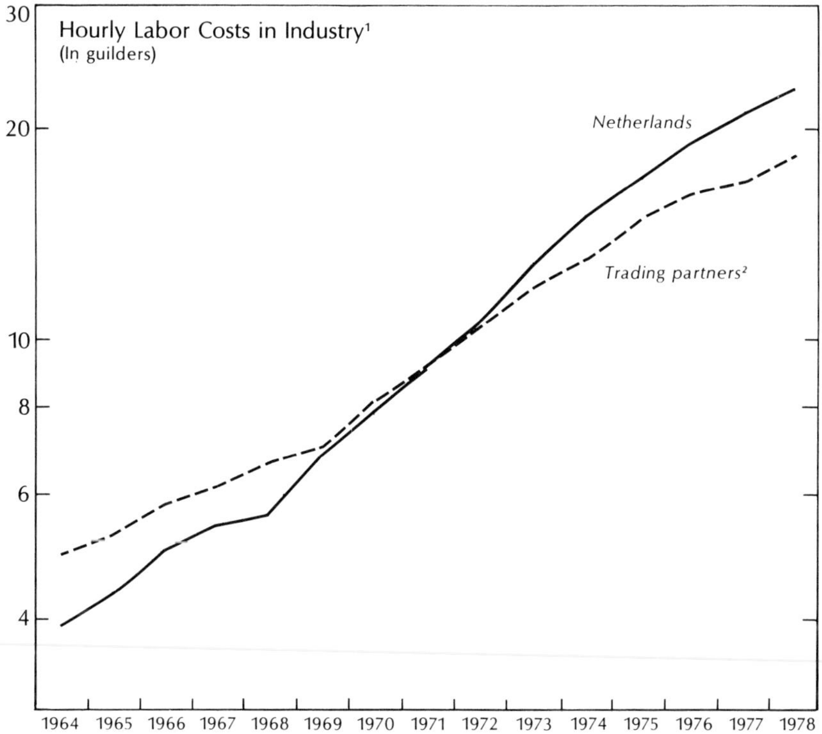

Sources: Swedish Employers' Confederation; OECD Secretariat estimates.

[1]Wages for time worked plus holiday pay, other cash payments, employers' contributions to social security, cost of vocational training, payroll tax, other labor costs.

[2]Trade-weighted average of rates and costs in Federal Republic of Germany, Belgium, France, United Kingdom, Italy, Denmark, United States, Sweden, and Switzerland.

Reproduced from Organization for Economic Cooperation and Development, *OECD Economic Surveys: Netherlands* (Paris, March 1979), p. 11.

Subsequent Developments

Wage negotiations during 1973 took place in a very difficult climate of industrial unrest, union dissatisfaction over widening differentials, and rank and file resentment of increased income tax liability. No central agreement for 1974 could be reached, and industry-by-industry negotiations were suspended when the Government sought special powers to deal with the situation created by the oil price increases. In January 1974, the Government again resorted to a statutory incomes policy, including controls on wages, rents, dividends, and certain professional incomes. The intention was to ensure that much of the deterioration in the terms of trade would be borne by higher-income groups and by profits.[57] The wage regulations permitted a continued rise in real contractual wage rates.[58] The average real wage per employee (before tax) rose by about 5 percent, year over year for the second year in succession (Table 13). However, in contrast to 1973, average real disposable income rose by some 3 percent in 1974. Price increases were kept down by controls and by the effects of the continuing appreciation of the guilder associated with the rising dollar value of the deutsche mark during 1974.[59] The steep rise in wage costs severely squeezed profits and increased the pressure on employers to shed labor.

Income taxes were temporarily reduced in 1975 in an attempt to facilitate a central wage agreement, and it was decided not to raise contributions to cover the recession-related increase in social security costs. The union federations issued guidelines for wage contracts in major industries. The 13 percent rise in nominal wages was a major factor in the continuance of rapid price inflation.

In October 1975, the Social and Economic Council stated that in its view, the increases in taxes and social security charges had been the principal factor underlying the excessive rise in labor costs that had depressed business profits and lowered investment and employment.

---

[57] Organization for Economic Cooperation and Development (March 1976, p. 17).

[58] All employees received holiday bonuses and an immediate increase of f. 15 a month, and there were two further increases of the same amount later in the year. An indexation adjustment of 3 percent was paid three months earlier than usual, and a floor for price compensation was introduced. Further redistribution of real disposable income in favor of lower-paid wage earners was achieved by the introduction of minimum wages for young employees and by a 2.5 percent increase in minimum wages on April 1, 1974.

To counter the 1973 increase in tax liability on lower incomes, the level of exemptions was increased and the range of incomes covered by the first tax bracket was reduced in the 1974 budget, but no adjustment for the impact of inflation was made, with the result that the real tax burden increased, especially for higher-income brackets.

[59] The trade-weighted guilder rate vis-à-vis competitors appreciated by 1.5, 2.5, 5.5, and 6.0 percent, year over year, from 1971 to 1974.

Table 13. Netherlands: Wage Developments and Unemployment, 1972–81

(Percentage changes over preceding year)[1]

	1972	1973	1974	1975	1976	1977	1978	1979	1980	1981
Private Sector										
Wage bill per employee	...	15.4	15.7	13.0	11.2	7.8	7.4	6.4	6.0	4.0
Net of change in employers' social security contributions	*11.6*	*12.9*	*14.8*	*12.8*	*10.9*	*8.3*	*7.6*	*5.8*	*5.7*	*3.7*
Consumer prices	*7.8*	*8.0*	*9.6*	*10.2*	*8.8*	*7.0*	*4.5*	*4.7*	*6.9*	*6.7*
Average real gross wage	*3.8*	*4.9*	*5.2*	*2.6*	*2.1*	*1.3*	*3.1*	*1.1*	*−1.2*	*−3.0*
Average real disposable income[2]	...	...	...	...	...	...	...	*1.5*	*−1.5*	*−3.5*
Sources of change in wage bill per employee in private sector	...	15.4	15.7	13.0	11.2	7.8	7.4	6.4	6.0	4.0
Change in social security contribution	...	*2.5*	*0.9*	*0.2*	*0.3*	*−0.5*	*−0.2*	*0.6*	*0.3*	*0.3*
Indexation provisions	*4.9*	*7.5*	*10.5*	*9.5*	*6.2*	*6.1*	*3.1*	*3.1*	*2.4*	*2.3*
Contractual increases	*5.2*	*3.5*	*3.5*	*3.4*	*2.5*	*2.3*	*1.4*	*0.7*	*0.5–0.0*[3]	*−0.3*[4]
Wage drift	*1.0*	*1.0*	*2.0*	*−0.1*	*2.0*	*1.1*	*1.7*	*1.1*	*1.5–2.0*	*1.0*
Net carry-over effect	*0.5*	*0.9*	*−1.2*	—	*0.2*	*−1.2*	*1.4*	*0.9*	*1.0*	*0.7*
Addendum										
Wage bill per employee in public sector	...	...	...	...	...	7.0	6.7	5.2	3.2	0.6
Unemployment rate	2.7	2.8	3.5	5.0	5.3	5.1	5.0	5.1	5.9	9.1

Sources: Netherlands, Central Planning Bureau, *Centraal Economish Plan* and *Macro Economische Verkenning*, and Central Bureau of Statistics, *Sociale Maandstatistick*, various issues.

[1] Except for unemployment.

[2] Data from Organization for Economic Cooperation and Development, *OECD Economic Surveys: Netherlands*, January 1983, p. 33. The changes in average real disposable income of all wage earners were: for 1979, 1.0; for 1980, −2.5; and for 1981, −4.5.

[3] Includes 0.5 due to effect of increase in the lowest wages under the controls program.

[4] Effect of contractual increases (plus C.5 to 1.0) and of imposed reductions that reduced the wage bill by about 1.0 percent.

The Council recommended that a projected increase in value-added taxes should be canceled, that wage indexation should be discontinued until mid-1976, and that corresponding moderation should be sought as regards incomes not covered by collective agreements.

Acting on this advice, the Government again intervened in the wage settlement process. A six months' wage freeze was imposed from January 1, 1976, and the decision concerning the price compensation due in July was postponed until the summer. No agreement having been reached between the central organizations, the Government prolonged the freeze by one month and then imposed a flat rate increase aimed at limiting the rise in the wage bill per employee in 1976 to 8.5–9 percent, combined with a downward adjustment of various social security premiums. Owing to substantial wage drift, the actual increase was over 11 percent.

Centralized negotiations for 1977 again broke down, and this time the Government indicated its unwillingness to intervene. The employers' resistance to wage claims was strengthened by the continuance of strict price controls during 1977.

Policies of the Late 1970s

In 1978 efforts were again made to moderate union claims by fiscal concessions and measures tending to hold down the inflation rate and indexation.[60] Wage negotiations became increasingly difficult following the tightening of the medium-term financial program by the new Government.

The revised program was designed to relieve the pressure on profit margins and improve competitiveness by containing wage increases and permitting little or no increase in real wages, by stabilizing government revenues and social security charges as a share of national income, and by limiting the public sector deficit. It was expected that these policies would slow the growth of private consumption but enhance the growth of exports and productive investment over the next two or three years, promoting a faster rise in output, higher employment in the private sector, and reduced unemployment.

The revisions lowered the projected growth of aggregate real income from 3.75 percent to 3.0 percent per annum because of a lower forecast for the expansion of world trade and called for a slower rise in taxes

---

[60] Planned increases in rents and the value-added tax on energy were postponed, government contributions to the social security funds were increased, permitting a reduction of employers' and employees' contributions, and additional funds were provided for subsidies to hold down production costs and finance job maintenance.

than previously provided for. The norm for the public sector deficit was reduced to about 4½ percent of national income.[61] To meet this limit, the Government announced that the previously projected increase in public expenditure would be cut by one third by 1981. The reduction was to be achieved mainly by economies in social security payments and cuts in public sector wages. With the lower growth rate assumed, even strict application of the "1 percent norm" for the rise in the collective burden would leave no scope for the desired improvement in business profitability. It was, therefore, proposed to cut back the rate of increase in real social security expenditure automatically every six months, with the object of stabilizing the collective burden by 1981—a rigorous goal should unemployment be increasing rapidly.

The Government also announced that it would seek to secure a reduction of 1 percent per annum in the share of labor income in value added generated in the private sector, in order to stimulate private investment and enhance productivity, growth, and competitiveness. While the Government would contribute to slow the rise in labor costs by containing the growth of social security payments, it counted on the cooperation of the employers' organizations and the unions in realizing this objective. It suggested that there should be no collectively negotiated increases in real wages and salaries before 1981. (Real wage increases would thus come about only through wage drift, forecast at 1–1½ percent per annum.) The proposal implied nominal wage increases of the order of 5.5 percent in 1979 and 4 percent by 1981, when it was hoped to achieve a 2–3 percent rate of inflation. In the event, the target for nominal wage increases was achieved, but consumer prices rose by 6.7 percent in 1981, and unemployment exceeded 9 percent, rising to 12.6 percent in 1982.

A start in cutting government expenditure and social security payments was made in the 1979 budget. However, in order to moderate wage and salary claims, a deviation from the medium-term strategy was accepted and scheduled increases in income tax and rents

---

[61] In the economic program for the next five years, formulated in 1976, the medium-term "norm" for the public sector deficit had been set at 5 percent of national income. This norm was to be attained by 1980: somewhat larger deficits were envisaged for 1977–79 in view of the low level of activity. Initially, the "structural" measures intended to secure the goal of bringing down inflation to 2–3 percent and unemployment to 3 percent by 1981 were a ceiling on the rate at which the "collective burden"—the share of taxes, social security contributions, and nontax revenues to national incomes—was allowed to rise (of not more than 1 percent of national income a year, compared with 1¼ percent during 1960–75); the introduction of more direct subsidies to promote investment than the existing accelerated depreciation and other tax allowances; and substantial provision for labor cost subsidies to employers in 1977–80.

were reduced. Nevertheless, centralized wage negotiations for 1979 broke down over the Government's decisions to cut back the rise in social security benefits as planned and not to allow a recent settlement in the construction industry to raise wages and social security benefits as provided for under the indexation system. Contracts were subsequently negotiated at the sectoral and individual enterprise level.[62] Average real wages rose by 1.1 percent in 1979, compared with 3.1 percent in 1978 (Table 13). The 6.4 percent rise in the wage bill per employee, however, exceeded the 5.5 percent guideline assumption in the budget.

Despite favorable external demand conditions and higher exports in 1979, the slowing of private consumption and the marked reduction of public investment were associated with stagnating private investment and rising unemployment during the year, while import penetration of the home market intensified (Table 14). The oil price increase of 1979 caused the Government to intervene directly in wage settlements in 1980 in order to prevent indexation provisions from causing a reacceleration of nominal wage increases and further erosion of profit margins. The deflationary policies adopted by major countries to limit the effect of the oil price increase faced the Netherlands with an external environment of deepening recession and weak export market growth.

Statutory Incomes Policies in 1980–82

No central agreement having been reached concerning wage increases in 1980, in January 1981 the Government imposed a wage freeze for two months, stating that there was no room for any real wage increases and that the semiannual indexation increases due in mid-1980 should not be made in full. When it became clear that there was no chance of a voluntary agreement being reached along these lines, statutory wage controls were applied until the end of the year. The July indexation adjustment was replaced by a flat rate increase that maintained real wages only at the minimum wage level. Contractual increases were prohibited, and regulations aimed at limiting wage drift at the enterprise level were imposed. Public sector wages were again cut and personal taxes on the lowest incomes were reduced.

[62] Contracts provided for indexation on a revised basis, excluding the effect of changes in indirect taxes and subsidies and giving a reduced weight to medical expenses, for an extra day's paid vacation, and for a lowering of the early retirement age to 62. The settlement for public sector employees called for a reduction in the rate of increase every six months over the next three years and for less complete indexation of the highest salaries—the proceeds to be used to create new public sector jobs or to finance early retirement.

Table 14. Netherlands: Changes in Aggregate Real Demand, 1977–82
(Percentage changes over preceding year at 1977 prices)

	1977[1]	1978	1979	1980	1981	1982[2]
Private consumption	4.4	4.4	2.9	−0.4	−2.6	−2.0
Private investment	17.6	4.1	−1.0	−3.8	−12.2	−5.2
Private nonresidential investment	18.4	5.2	1.8	−6.3	−14.1	−5.2
Public consumption	3.2	3.8	2.8	1.0	1.2	−0.6
Public investment	−11.6	−4.3	−5.6	4.8	−2.3	−0.9
Total domestic demand[3]	5.0	4.1	1.6	−0.1	−5.3	−1.4
	(. . .)	(3.9)	(0.8)	(−0.6)	(−5.8)	(−1.5)
Exports	−1.8	3.4	7.3	1.7	0.9	1.3
Imports	2.9	6.3	6.1	−0.4	−7.4	1.0
Change in external balance[4]	−2.4	−1.3	0.6	1.1	4.1	0.2
GNP	2.4	2.4	2.3	0.9	−1.1	−1.1

Sources: Netherlands, Central Bureau of Statistics, *Nationale Rekeningen*, and Central Planning Bureau, *Centraal Economish Plan*, various issues.

[1]At 1975 prices.

[2]Forecast.

[3]Figures in parentheses show changes in demand for domestic output allowing for rough estimate of effect of import penetration.

[4]As percent of GNP in previous year.

Following the breakdown of the preliminary wage negotiations for 1981, the Government used its statutory powers virtually to eliminate the indexation payments due in January 1981 and to reduce paid vacation time. These measures were accompanied by tax reliefs leaving average take-home pay unchanged. Similar measures were applied in 1982, but indexation adjustments were paid in full on low to average wages. The nominal wage bill per employee in the private sector rose by only 4 percent from 1980 to 1981, while wages in the public sector scarcely increased. Wage increases accelerated in 1982.

Real disposable income per wage earner fell by some 7 percent from 1979 to 1982. Far from creating "room" for the hoped-for shift to profits, the reduction resulted in lower home demand, lower sales, and reduced capacity utilization, since for many smaller enterprises there was no possibility of counteracting the decline in sales to households by selling more abroad, or by supplying demands met by imported products. Despite some improvement in cost competitiveness, import penetration continued and export market shares increased only very slightly. This context was not one to encourage or make possible the financing of higher private investment. Falling investment increased the downward pressure on demand, output, and profits in the economy, and unemployment rose to over 17 percent in 1983 and 1984.

Dutch Experience with Incomes Policy

The Dutch system of centralized wage determination in the 1960s bore some resemblance to the negotiation of "frame" agreements in Sweden and Norway. But in the Netherlands negotiations were not organized and conducted independently by the central federations of the unions and employers' associations, and the Government retained the right to intervene. Each side was aware that the Government could impose a settlement. In effect, the onus of avoiding industrial unrest and stoppages arising from wage disputes was shifted from the bargaining partners to the Government. This context strengthened the Government's inclination to devise policies that limited industrial frictions and avoided relative wage adjustments.

Incomes policy directed at preventing wages from rising faster than average productivity became increasingly difficult to implement when nominal wages began to rise more rapidly in other industrial countries early in the 1960s. Determined efforts to maintain price stability in the Netherlands by restrictive fiscal policy nevertheless served to create a widening gap between the level of wages in the Netherlands and those in neighboring countries and the United States and to strengthen the competitive position of enterprises in the open sector.

The relative decline in wages had the effect of encouraging the development of a highly profitable, capital-intensive export sector of large enterprises. More important for the achievement of the full employment goal, it supported job openings in the small enterprise sector by keeping down the cost of labor relative to the price of tradable goods determined in the world market. This not only served to keep up employment in the smaller import-competing enterprises but also contributed to sustain job openings by keeping down the cost of labor-intensive services such as repair and maintenance work relative to the cost of capital and consumer goods. The effect in sustaining employment in the small enterprise sector was an important element in ensuring the NVV's support for wage moderation.

So long as the Federal Republic of Germany pursued policies strongly oriented toward price stability, the emphasis of Dutch policies was not inappropriate, since maintenance of the competitive position vis-à-vis Germany was important for the profitability and level of activity of a wide range of businesses exposed to competition from across the border. Nevertheless, with the growing undervaluation of the deutsche mark versus the U.S. dollar and several other currencies, maintenance of competitiveness vis-à-vis Germany was liable to cause increasing tensions within the Dutch wage bargaining system since it implied a very strong competitive position in the world market and high profits for the large enterprise export sector. Unions in that sector—mainly the denominational unions—were able to secure substantial increases in wages and benefits. The numerically large and politically influential unions affiliated in the NVV then came under pressure from their membership to obtain similar wage increases.

The Netherlands was perhaps more adversely affected than any other industrial economy by the failure to adjust exchange rates or to abandon fixed exchange rates between major currencies in 1968 or early 1969 (see Chapter 5). Had either course been followed by the German and Dutch authorities, the disastrous buildup of social tensions and spread of wages indexation that so greatly complicated demand management after the mid-1970s could probably have been avoided and the development of the economy during the 1970s and 1980s would almost certainly have been more favorable.

The continued effort of the Dutch authorities to maintain domestic price stability and hold down wage increases by restrictive policies during the export boom of 1968–69, when the new German Government had adopted a highly expansionary fiscal policy and when German wages were rising very rapidly, created an explosive wage bargaining climate and political situation in the Netherlands. Industrial turmoil in 1970–71 coincided with the prospect of a rapid rise in real GNP owing to the development of natural gas production. These circumstances led to the conclusion of the Social Contract between the Government and the unions, the primary purpose of which was to defuse the wage bargaining situation. The effect of the agreement was to commit the economy to substantial contractual wage increases with full indexation against price increases on the eve of the collapse of the fixed exchange rate system and the rise in oil prices.

As a result of the delayed adjustment of exchange rates, the Netherlands was almost simultaneously exposed to three major shocks—the prospective development of natural gas resources, the freeing of exchange rates between the major currencies, and the very large rise in energy prices—while confronting an intensely difficult wage bargaining and political crisis.

In the exchange rate crisis of 1973, the Netherlands had no practical alternative to joining the snake and pegging to the deutsche mark, given its close integration with the German economy and participation in the Common Agricultural Policy of the EEC. However, the 1973 appreciation vis-à-vis the deutsche mark, motivated as a means of checking explosive inflation, compounded the effect of exchange rate adjustment in promoting unemployment in the labor-intensive, small enterprise sector by reversing the protective effects of the previously undervalued exchange rate.

In a less highly charged political climate—and supposing there had been no pre-existing exchange rate disequilibrium—it should have been possible to devise some combination of incomes policy and exchange rate strategy that would have mitigated rather than magnified the impact of natural gas production in raising the level of real wages relative to world market prices for industrial goods.[63] In practice, the options were severely limited. The wage bargaining crisis in 1971–73 almost certainly could not have been resolved without the Government's accepting a strategy that provided for the higher prospective growth of real national income to be distributed largely in the form of contractual wage increases.

It would have been preferable if, as in Norway, the faster rise in real income had been taken as the basis for increases in disposable income via reductions in social security charges and direct taxes. That alternative was not feasible, however, when the unions and their members were convinced that there was scope for negotiating large increases in wages and there was a long tradition of gearing wage increases to the rise in real GNP. Moreover, the unions might with reason have doubted whether such fiscal concessions would be sustained, given the experience of 1973 and the stringent tax policies enforced in earlier years. Acceptance of the principle of increases in real wages reflecting the effect of natural gas production upon the growth of per capita real GNP was almost certain to involve a faster rise in real wages than in non-oil producing industrial countries. Moreover, it implied general indexation and for that reason also meant that Dutch wages would rise relative to those in countries where there was less widespread indexation after the oil price increase. (See Chapter 3, Table 1.) Indexation also rendered the general level of wages highly responsive to price and wage increases brought about by increased demand upon the sheltered sectors, such as construction, that were associated with the natural gas investment boom and the rise in real incomes.[64]

Between 1971 and 1976, the Netherlands changed from being a low-cost to a high-cost industrial producer, in terms of hourly labor costs at the going exchange rate. While it was appropriate and unavoidable for

[63] For a discussion of the issues see Corden (1982).

[64] See the account of developments in Norway.

Dutch wages to be brought more into line with those in competing countries, the excessive increase in relative costs subsequently led to reduced activity and investment and steeply rising unemployment. The inevitable consequence of the income distribution strategy *and* the 1973 appreciation and subsequent pegging of the guilder to the deutsche mark, in the context of the development of natural gas production, was that wages and sheltered sector prices in the Netherlands would rise substantially relative to those in the Federal Republic of Germany. Since the deutsche mark continued to appreciate in real terms against the U.S. dollar and most other currencies, this involved a still more marked weakening of the Netherlands competitive position versus many countries other than Germany.

The effects on employment of the weakened competitive position of small, labor-intensive, import-competing enterprises and of demand shifts away from labor-intensive outputs that had become much more expensive in relation to tradable goods were mitigated and concealed for several years by the high level of domestic demand and private investment connected with the development of natural gas resources and by increasing public expenditures. The rising value of natural gas exports permitted the Government to pursue an expansionary fiscal policy without encountering a balance of payments constraint. After 1976 those consequences began to be apparent in declining profitability, weak private investment, rising unemployment, and a tendency to increasing current account deficits (excluding natural gas receipts). Rising unemployment not only caused an automatic increase in social security expenditure but also led to heightened pressure for early retirement pensions, improvements in unemployment benefits, disability allowances, and job protection. Increasing budget deficits and high public sector financing requirements, combined with monetary policies dictated by the pegged exchange rate, were then associated with the apparent phenomenon of the "crowding out" of private borrowers holding down private investment. In a more fundamental sense, however, this sequence followed from the authorities' decision to implement policies enforcing a considerable degree of price stability when no corresponding degree of stability in enterprises' costs could realistically be foreseen.

Norway: Centralized Wage Bargaining and Combined Income Settlements, 1970–85

The Norwegian economy was more favorably placed than most other industrial countries after 1973 because of its prospective oil production. Output continued to expand quite rapidly during the recession, and investment reached a peak share of GDP in 1976. Nevertheless, unemployment rose during 1975 and the traditional export sectors, especially shipping, were severely depressed. The authorities regarded the "hard currency" option of participation in the snake[65] (which at times involved a significant real appreciation of the exchange rate) as a means of providing a desirable element of stability and discipline. However, cost developments became of increasing concern by the late 1970s.

Institutional Setting

Highly centralized collective bargaining is made possible in Norway by the wide powers that the central union and employers' federations (Landsorganisasjonen i Norge—LO and Norsk Arbeidsgiverforening—NAF) wield over their constituent members.[66] Direct negotiations between the central federations establish a central "frame" agreement; individual unions then negotiate contractual increases for particular industries that fall within defined limits. Actual wage increases also reflect wage drift. Since World War II the system has resulted in legally enforceable agreements on two occasions out of three, and centralized wage determination is generally regarded as a fair and rational feature of the economic system. Frame agreements, usually for two years, customarily incorporate indexation clauses.

Since 1962, the Government has taken part in discussions with the LO and the NAF within the Contact Committee (Kontaktutvalget) at the same time as it negotiates with farmers and fishermen concerning incomes and government support. During the 1960s, various price subsidies were used to influence the outcome of wage negotiations and to avoid or delay the triggering of index clauses. Budgetary measures were increasingly directed to influencing income settlements during the 1970s. After a shift to decentralized wage bargaining was associated with very large wage settlements in 1974, a system of combined "tripartite" settlements negotiated during the early months of each year was implemented until 1978.

The Contact Committee, which is chaired by the Prime Minister, comprises representatives of the Government, the Federation of Trade Unions, the Employers' Confederation, and the Farmers', Fishermen's, and Smallholders' Unions. Political questions are negotiated within a group comprising ministers, top management, and union leaders.

---

[65] See Chapter 3, pp. 39–45.

[66] Korsnes (1979); Organization for Economic Cooperation and Development (March 1982); and Flanagan, Soskice, and Ulman (1983, especially pp. 166–89).

A basis for discussion is provided by the Annual Report on issues relevant to the settlements, presented in February by the Technical Expert Group, a permanent representative body reporting to the Contact Committee.[67] A key role, both in the preparation of the report and in the subsequent discussions, is played by computations from the econometric planning model of the effects of alternative sets of wage and income increases and tax and subsidy proposals. These calculations enable the parties to study various consistent combinations of changes in real disposable incomes of households, tax reductions, and probable rates of inflation. One advantage of the system is that the range of disagreement can be narrowed to substantive issues; unlike the situation in many other countries, it has generally been possible to reach broad agreement concerning the probable impact and costs of alternative income and tax proposals. Acceptance of the model as realistic, and its use to assess the impact of alternative proposals, to some extent helped to restrain excessive claims and to reinforce pressures for compromises between the various parties in the 1960s and early 1970s.

Skånland Committee Proposals

Norway experienced a marked inflation of costs during 1969–72 as the result of booming export markets and export profitability. Wage pressures were heightened by resistance to tax increases following a relaxation of fiscal restraint at the time of the U.S. slowdown in 1969. A committee, under the chairmanship of the Deputy Governor of the Bank of Norway, H. Skånland, was set up to study the sources of the inflationary problems. Its report, published in June 1973, emphasized the conflict between the objectives of the public authorities and those of the private economic interest groups concerning income distribution, in addition to conflicts between the private interest groups. The need to establish a consensus on both sets of issues, it was argued, called for an institution in which the distributional goals of the public authorities and private interest organizations could be reconciled. The report proposed the establishment of a Council for Prices and Incomes Policy, somewhat larger than the Contact Committee (because of the inclusion of three more business organizations), to be charged with negotiating guidelines for wages, prices, price supports, tax rates and subsidies, and social security payments. Its member organizations would be obliged to honor the guidelines.[68]

---

[67] For a description of the procedures in arriving at a tripartite agreement, see Economic Research Institute of the Commercial Banks of Norway (1976).

[68] Flanagan, Soskice, and Ulman (1983, pp. 181–85). See also Norges Bank (1973).

It would seem that the authors of the report were seeking to promote the establishment of an institution resembling the Austrian Parity Commission, in the hope of simplifying decision making by conferring authority on a similar small group of representatives of organized groups outside the parliamentary forum. Possibly, it was also hoped that a moderating influence on wage settlements might be secured by reducing the wage negotiating role of the more radical unions.

The fact that the report implied a considerable strengthening of the powers of the NAF and the LO and left little scope for decentralized bargaining caused the constituent unions of the LO to oppose the recommendations and led to open disagreement between the unions and the LO over the appropriate level for bargaining. As a result, it was decided that negotiations in 1974 should take place at the industry level.

Although both the LO and the Social Democrat Government eventually rejected the committee's recommendations, its analysis of the causes of inflation with the implication "that income determination should move into a multilateral forum" greatly influenced developments after 1973. "Some would say that the committee's fundamental ideas slipped in by the back door."[69]

Government's Policy Strategy

The Government's aim in 1973 was to use the opportunity provided by the prospective increase in real national income and tax revenues from the oil sector to raise personal income and consumption and to maintain full employment until the recession abroad ended. Tax reductions, subsidies, and other budgetary measures granted as part of the coordinated income settlements were to be used to secure an egalitarian redistribution of income and to moderate the scale of wage increases under centralized wage bargaining. In this way, it was hoped to limit domestic cost pressures and protect the competitive position of the export industries while maintaining the pegged exchange rate within the snake as a means of restraining price inflation. However, the Government also undertook to provide direct support to employment in existing export industries and to prevent heavy localized unemployment. A fundamental objective of its policies was to protect the traditional structure of the economy from disruption as a consequence of the development of oil production.

The difficulty of achieving noninflationary coordinated income settlements was greatly increased by the consequences of the extraor-

[69] Flanagan, Soskice, and Ulman (1983, p. 184).

dinarily strong external demand conditions of the late 1960s and early 1970s in promoting a very marked rise of industrial earnings relative to farm incomes (which are maintained by a comprehensive support system and strict import controls). A subsequent decision to give disproportionate increases in income to the farmers and fishermen was in direct conflict with the economic objective of moderating cost pressure.

Even before the Skånland Committee recommendations were published, the Government set up in 1973 a working party of representatives of the main interest organizations to develop a combined settlement of wages, farm product prices, and government policies. Following discussion of the issues within this body, the Government broke with the tradition of noninterference in wage bargaining and intervened to secure less complete compensation for price increases in return for food subsidies and a postponement of increases in public service charges. As a result of these measures and the appreciation of the krone, the rise in consumer prices was slowed during 1973 and real hourly earnings rose less than productivity.

The Episode of Decentralized Bargaining

In 1974, however, under the agreement between the LO and the unions, no centralized wage bargaining took place for the first time in more than a decade, and two-year contracts for 1974–75 were negotiated by individual unions. The budget was aimed at stimulating private consumption by permitting an appreciable rise in real disposable income of households (especially in the lower-income brackets), while holding down company profits by an increase in corporate income tax intended to curb private investment. Close contacts between the central organizations of trade unions and employers and the Government continued and, in an effort to moderate the unions' wage claims, employees' contributions to social security were reduced and social security benefits, food subsidies, and children's allowances were increased.

Although the fiscal measures served as a moderating influence, decentralized negotiations were conducive to large settlements in the prevailing circumstances of tight labor market conditions and sharply increased corporate profits. The settlements provided for roughly 80 percent price compensation during the first year. Hourly earnings increased by more than 20 percent from 1974 to 1975, and disposable incomes rose even faster as a result of reductions in personal taxes in the 1975 budget.

Combined Settlements and Subsequent Developments

Fiscal policy in 1975 was aimed at restraining the rapid expansion of demand. Nevertheless, the further improvement in real disposable incomes of households remained a key objective of policy. When the indexation clause was renegotiated in the fall, weak labor demand and strong cost-push provided a generally favorable setting for "a combined incomes and demand management policy approach consisting of expansionary tax and subsidy measures to support private real income growth and serving. . . to moderate [increases in] wages and prices."[70] The unions' support for combined settlements was strengthened because it was clear that under the prevailing demand conditions, government tax concessions afforded greater possibility of increases in real income than nominal wage settlements.[71] A major complicating factor, however, was the effect of the 1974 wage settlements in precipitating political pressures for a large increase in farm incomes.

Price compensation was reduced to 30 percent in return for a substantial further reduction in direct taxes, increases in family allowances, and measures to hold down consumer prices. As some of these measures could take effect only from the beginning of the fiscal year, a temporary price freeze was imposed from September 1 to the end of 1975. The Government also proposed a number of expansionary measures that facilitated the unions' acceptance of the wage settlements.[72] The March 1976 budget eased the progressivity of direct taxes on lower and middle incomes, partially offsetting fiscal drag. Social security contributions were reduced and subsidies and transfers were increased.

The one-year combined income settlement of April 1976 provided for moderate nominal wage increases (of 3.7 percent in manufacturing and 6.8 percent in central government employment) with no indexation. Normal working hours were cut from 42½ to 40 a week. Farm incomes were, however, increased by almost 50 percent, Parliament having decreed in 1975 that they should be brought up to a level equivalent to average wage earnings in manufacturing by 1982. Pensions were raised by 5–7 percent after tax.

---

[70] Organization for Economic Cooperation and Development (January 1977, p. 6).

[71] Indeed, reductions in nominal tax rates were almost prerequisite for increases in real disposable wages under rapid inflation given the strong fiscal drag resulting from the progressivity of the tax structure.

[72] The measures included extraordinary appropriations for public works projects, an increase in state banks' loan commitment budgets, additional liquidity loans to industry, and a scheme for subsidizing interest costs on loans for financing inventory accumulation.

The aim of reversing accelerating inflation and rising unemployment was broadly achieved in 1976 (Table 15) but the deficit on current account increased to 12 percent of GNP, mainly owing to an unexpectedly large rise in private expenditure. Real consumption rose by almost 6 percent, and, partly because of easy credit conditions, spending on durable goods was particularly strong. Heavy wage drift accounted for almost half of the increase in wages. "Normal" unit labor costs in manufacturing, allowing for 4 percent trend productivity growth, rose by 12.3 percent, compared with 15 percent in 1975. Once again, the rise was substantially greater than the average in competing countries.

To create a favorable setting for the renegotiation of wage contracts in 1977, in January the Government reduced nominal taxes by raising tax rate brackets and increasing exemptions. Indirect taxes on alcohol, tobacco, gasoline, and automobiles and certain public service charges were, however, increased. It was also announced that, providing wage settlements were not such as to raise real income by more than 0.5 percent, further tax reductions would be made so as to guarantee a 2.5 percent increase in real disposable wage income.

Before the combined incomes settlement was reached in April, the worsening balance of payments forced a depreciation of the krone. The additional tax reliefs were granted and the temporary food subsidies were retained until the end of 1977. The settlement resulted in a 3 percent average increase in contractual weekly wages. Real wages before tax rose by 1.5 percent, against 4 percent a year from 1970 to 1976, but the disposable real income of wage earners rose somewhat more than the 2.5 percent envisaged, owing to larger-than-expected wage drift. This compared with a 30 percent increase in the real after-tax income of farmers and a 6–7 percent increase for those on small pensions.

Income Developments, 1978–81

By 1977, the need to slow the expansion of domestic demand and improve the relative cost position was evident. In a decisive policy shift, the Government announced that there was little scope for any increase in real disposable income in the 1978 budget other than a continued rise in minimum pensions. The basis for the unions' cooperation in centralized wage regulation had therefore disappeared. Bilateral negotiations between the LO and the NAF broke down after the depreciation of the krone in February 1978, and for only the third time in almost 30 years, the frame settlement had to be secured by compulsory arbitration. Not unnaturally, the idea that farmers were

Table 15. Norway: Labor Market Developments, Labor Costs, Productivity, and Prices, 1975–84
(Percentage changes or ratios)

	1975	1976	1977	1978	1979	1980	1981	1982	1983	1984
Labor force (year-to-year change)	3.0	4.2	1.6	2.0	1.2	1.9	1.3	1.4	1.3	0.3
Employment (year-to-year change)	2.1	2.4	2.0	1.6	1.0	2.2	1.0	0.7	0.6	0.5
Unemployment rate[1]	2.3	1.8	1.5	1.8	2.0	1.7	2.0	2.6	3.3	3.1
Persons affected by labor market measures[2]	1.1	0.6	0.6	0.6	0.7	0.8	0.9	0.9	1.3	1.8
Total[2]	3.4	2.4	2.1	2.4	2.7	2.5	2.9	3.5	4.6	4.9
Labor costs per man-year (year-to-year change)[3]										
Non-oil economy	18.3	13.6	10.0	8.4	3.6	9.9	11.7	12.0	8.3	...
Manufacturing	20.4	12.4	10.4	8.1	4.0	10.0	11.5	11.3	8.4	...
Productivity per man-year (year-to-year change)[3]										
Non-oil economy	2.4	3.7	1.7	0.3	3.0	0.8	1.3	1.4	1.3	...
Manufacturing	−1.5	0.6	−1.7	−0.1	3.8	−0.8	0.3	1.8	4.5	...
Consumer prices (year-to-year change)	11.7	9.0	9.6	7.5	4.8	10.9	13.6	11.3	8.4	6.3
Relative unit labor costs (change from 1973)[4]	10.8	17.3	24.1	16.7	11.9	15.2	17.9	22.3	23.2	24.4

Sources: Norway, Central Bureau of Statistics, *Statistisk Månedshefte* and *Statistisk Ukehefte*, various issues; Norges Offentlige Utredninger, *Om Grunnlaget for Inntektsoppgjørene, 1984*; and International Monetary Fund, *International Financial Statistics*, various issues.

[1] Survey data: percent of labor force.

[2] Percent of labor force.

[3] Includes the effect of changes in hours worked.

[4] Change in index of relative labor costs, excluding cyclical variations. See International Monetary Fund, *International Financial Statistics*, Table on Cost and Price Comparisons for Manufacturing, Item 2. Method of calculation is described in the notes to the table.

entitled to the average manufacturing wage was used by the LO as grounds for larger-than-average increases to the lower paid. The ruling, covering contracts for 1978 and 1979, provided for a general contractual increase of 1.3 percent, plus a subsequent increase, varying between 0.3 and 2 percent, for those employees earning less than 90 percent of the average wage in the industry. With an expected 5.5–6.0 percent wage drift, it was foreseen that hourly wages would, on average, rise by about 8 percent from 1977 to 1978.

Consumer prices rose substantially following two further depreciations in 1977, and price increases again accelerated after the February 1978 depreciation. To prevent the competitive gain from depreciation being dissipated by inflation, the Government imposed a freeze on incomes and prices in September 1978 to last until the end of 1979. Wage increases, including drift or bonuses, were prohibited, but exceptions were allowed in the case of certain wage agreements expiring just after the freeze was imposed. The announced intention was to hold prices at their February 1978 level, subject to adjustment for higher raw material prices. The freeze kept the rate of price increase below 5 percent. It was extended through the first quarter of 1980.

Wage negotiations in April 1980 took place in a tense atmosphere,[73] following two years of declining real disposable earnings and in the context of a recent surge in prices due to the lifting of controls and increases in the world price of oil and other commodities. The frame agreement provided for a general 5.2 percent increase in weekly wages, again with larger increases for the lower paid, and incorporated an understanding that wage drift would not exceed 3 percent. It also included a provision for the payment of supplementary increases in 1981 to individuals and groups whose earnings remained below 85 percent of the average wage in industry. The average increase in wages in 1980 was to be just over 9 percent, slightly less than the increase in consumer prices forecast for the year. Wages actually rose by 10 percent. The Government again conceded reductions in nominal income tax rates and increases in child allowances (equivalent to 0.5 percent of GDP), in order to contribute toward moderate nominal income settlements.

Wage bargaining in 1981 was extraordinarily difficult. At the beginning of the year the Government reduced income tax rates but increased indirect taxes. No agreement could be reached between the

[73] Early in 1980 there had been local claims for wage awards, and an unofficial strike of bus drivers in Oslo, which continued even after it was ruled illegal by the Labor Court and despite calls by the LO for a return to work. See Dean (1980, p. 185).

NAF and the LO, and mediation also failed. At the Government's insistence, a settlement was obtained in June through compulsory arbitration by the State Wages Council. This essentially repeated the egalitarian provisions of the 1980 settlement. Wage increases were to be limited to 9.65 percent on average from 1980 to 1981, with a ceiling set for wage drift over the 12 months from April 1, 1981. Employees in enterprises where wages were below 85 percent of the average wage in the industry were to receive double the general increase in hourly wage rates and those in firms paying 85–90 percent of the average were to get a third more than the general increase. A supplementary increase was to be paid in October to individuals and groups whose earnings were still below 85 percent of the average wage in industry. Half the cost of this measure was to be borne by the employer, half by all wage and salary earners.

The settlement also included a semiautomatic indexation clause, providing the possibility of reopening wage negotiations if the consumer price index exceeded 126.5 (1979 = 100) by mid-September 1981. In August, the Government again imposed a price freeze in order to secure the unions' agreement not to reopen wage negotiations on the basis of the clause.

Income Developments Since 1981

The new Government that came to power in September 1981 sought to reorient policies toward greater restraint in order to ease labor market pressures and to reduce the growth of public expenditure so as to allow a reduction of the tax burden. It declared its intention of allowing greater scope for market forces in the determination of prices and incomes. Since 1981 the Government has not interfered in negotiations between the employers and unions but has sought to moderate wage settlements by real tax reliefs. Real take-home pay has been maintained, while average real gross wages have fallen by about 3½ percent since 1981. The Government has pursued an active industrial policy.

The arbitration decisions of 1978 and 1981 had a major influence in reinforcing the egalitarian emphasis of the central wage settlements. The 85 percent rule was subsequently incorporated in the two-year settlement of 1982 and in a different form in the 1984 settlement (which called for the average pay in each branch to be at least 85 percent of the average industrial wage). Resistance to egalitarian wage policies in the central negotiations has led to local negotiations aimed at maintaining initial wage differentials and to heavy wage drift. As a result, wage differentials between firms and between branches of industry have moved increasingly out of line with differing productivity trends and product market conditions. Increasing subsidies to industries and enterprises have acted as a substitute for real and relative wage flexibility.[74]

Partly owing to a highly unfavorable development of productivity, Norwegian unit labor costs rose some 11 percent faster than the average for its major trading partners from 1980 to 1984 when measured in local currency terms, and exchange rate adjustments offset little of the discrepancy.[75] A tendency for locally negotiated increases to account for more of the rise in wages has been reinforced. While about two thirds of total wage increases were derived from centrally negotiated increases and one third from wage drift during the 1970s, the proportions were reversed in 1980–84. Centrally negotiated increases declined to 1–1½ percent in 1983 and 1984, but wage drift has remained constant at about 6 percent since 1980 despite sharply rising unemployment.

Lessons of Norwegian Experience Since 1973

Clearly it would have been difficult, if not impossible, to realize all the Government's objectives after 1973 even under the most favorable circumstances. The inherent conflict between greatly raising real per capita incomes and hence consumption demand and at the same time seeking to maintain the pattern of employment associated with a previously greater dependence on foreign demand was obscured by the complex character of the tripartite settlements, and also by the fact that measures aimed at maintaining employment in individual enterprises did not form part of the coordinated income settlements and so did not enter into the Contact Committee's simulations. If the Government had explicitly undertaken to raise disposable incomes and home demand substantially *and* to maintain the existing scale of export industries, the conflict would have been obvious.

In practice, the policy strategy ran into increasing balance of payments problems, and the combined income settlements depended upon the maintenance of the exchange rate within the snake by heavy external borrowing. The main reason why serious problems were encountered was the nonfulfillment of two key assumptions of the Government's program. First, forecasts of oil production proved to be

[74] Organization for Economic Cooperation and Development (January 1985, p. 21, and pp. 41–42).

[75] Organization for Economic Cooperation and Development (January 1985, pp. 18–21). In 1984 the relative level of costs in manufacturing adjusted for exchange rate movement was almost 25 percent higher than in 1973 (Table 15).

overoptimistic and production in 1979 was less than half as large as had been expected. Second, the recession in export markets turned out to be far more prolonged than had been foreseen. These factors were largely responsible for the emergence of a far larger budget deficit than intended and for the deterioration of the balance of payments.

Before 1973, when a conservative budgetary stance was maintained in order to protect the external balance, the Norwegian authorities treated the rate of inflation as externally determined, considering the rate of wage increase to be governed by the movement of world market prices and by the unions' consciousness of the need to compete in world markets and of the balance of payments constraint. The authorities had no experience of how wages and prices would respond in a situation of a rapidly expanding domestic demand, when the balance of payments and budgetary constraints were suddenly eliminated. Nor did they foresee the rapid credit expansion that rising real incomes and the favorable prospects for the economy would induce under a continued accommodative credit policy.

The Norwegian experience with combined income settlements does not enable one to judge whether it is feasible to moderate wage increases by tax reduction "trade-offs," since moderation of wage increases was not in practice a dominant objective. Egalitarian income redistribution to lower-income groups with considerable electoral power and measures to sustain employment in, and support the finances of, enterprises faced with weak foreign demand actually had greater priority. Nor was the Government greatly concerned to ensure budgetary and monetary outcomes supportive of wage restraint in the easy balance of payments and stimulus-justifying environment of the mid-1970s.

Effect of the Policy Strategy on Costs

Norwegian experience illustrates why it is difficult to avoid cost inflation in the context of a marked rise in real national income occasioned by a sudden favorable export development and how this difficulty is likely to be manifest in an economy with strong labor market organizations.

Suppose that a tax reduction substantially raising real disposable personal incomes is granted, at a time of weak foreign demand for traditional exports, as part of an incomes policy settlement that stipulates that there shall be no negotiated increases in wage rates through collective bargaining.[76] The economy has previously been

[76] Effects similar to those described would also arise in the case of an increase in real income distributed via higher public spending, or a rise in average real income associated with localized very high earnings from a new export industry.

close to full employment, with a lower level of real per capita disposable income than now obtains and a higher level of foreign demand for traditional exports. Higher real income implies increased personal spending on "sheltered" and "open" sector outputs, the increases depending on the income elasticities of demand and the availabilities of supply. Thus, the initial effect on the real economy of the country will be a marked increase in demand for income-elastic sheltered sector outputs (which cannot be imported) and a smaller increase in home demand for open sector output, demand for which can be met by imports. (Any marked tightening of home supply availabilities in the open sector, or any rise in prices relative to those abroad, will tend to cause an increase in the share of expenditure going to imports rather than to home-produced open sector outputs.)

In a world characterized by atomistic competition in labor, capital, and product markets and mobility of labor and capital, a slight relative rise in wages and prices in the sheltered sector would suffice to draw labor and capital away from the open sector to meet increased demand in the sheltered sector. Lower world market prices associated with weaker demand abroad would imply such a relative rise, because under competitive conditions enterprises could only remain in business and their employees retain their jobs if prices and wages were reduced. Freely available imports at reduced world market prices and lower export prices would therefore soon bring down the level of earnings in the open sector.

In reality, there may be little tendency for this to occur for a period of years, owing to imperfect competition in product and labor markets, factor immobility, and political forces. Consequently, a marked rise in after-tax income is liable to occasion cost pressures in the sheltered sector and in open sector industries mainly supplying the home market even if there is no increase in collectively negotiated wage rates. A major reason for this is that similar competitive conditions do not apply in the sheltered sector and the open sector—or to be more precise—between the enterprises mainly supplying the home market and those selling largely in the world market; and that difference is reflected both in the existing structure of relative earnings and in the process of wage determination.

Large enterprises selling in the world market typically are able to take advantage of economies of scale and of the restricted entry associated with the difficulty of setting up in large-scale production to maintain markups that permit a continuing high rate of investment and technical progress. At the same time, the greater scope for organization of employees in large enterprises and the restricted entry of new producers to the industry enables the labor force to secure and maintain relatively high earnings compared with most employees and self-employed persons.[77] In a small economy, enterprises predominantly dependent on home demand typically cannot profit fully from large-scale production and must rely on a comparative advantage in localized markets if they supply tradable goods. Thus, the open sector needs to be thought of as comprising (1) specialized, generally large-scale, export industries selling almost exclusively abroad; (2) large-scale enterprises selling a substantial proportion of output abroad; and (3) smaller enterprises subject to import competition but shielded by particular advantages in local markets, and perhaps also by protective measures granted for political reasons.

In the situation outlined above, the initial effect of the tax reductions in the home economy is to increase demand for products of sheltered sector enterprises and of small, open sector enterprises serving localized markets, and to offset, in part or entirely, the weakening of foreign demand for output of large sector enterprises other than the specialized export industries. Stronger demands on the former are reflected in higher sales, increased profits, and local scarcities. Wages tend to rise with increased overtime, the increased ability of wage earners to secure promotions and bonuses, and the bidding up of wages in local labor markets where demand is strong. Rational behavior on the part of enterprises may suggest raising prices rather than expanding output and hiring more employees if it is uncertain whether the higher demand will continue, especially if employees are protected from dismissal. If they do so the likelihood that the existing employees will secure higher earnings through upgrading of jobs and bonuses is increased.

In general, a considerable strengthening of demand for residential construction and locally produced goods and services is likely—and this will be reflected in consumer price indices. These effects will be greatly reinforced if, as in Norway, an accommodative credit policy allows consumers and enterprises to increase their borrowing substantially to finance housing and other durable goods purchases or operating expenses, as they may be inclined to do under the influence of higher incomes and the favorable outlook for the economy.

In the large enterprise sector, where price increases are constrained by foreign competition, pressures for nominal wage increases are generated by increases in the cost of living and in earnings of other

[77] See Chapter 6, "An Alternative View: Discontinuous Adjustment Under Imperfect Competition," for an account of the interdependence of market power in product and labor markets. See Chapter 11 for discussion of a system of open economies comprising large and small enterprise sectors.

wage earners (especially of higher-paid groups such as construction workers and public sector employees). Wage drift may occur because employers fear to lose skilled or reliable workers or because the enterprise has traditionally compensated for price increases through drift in the course of the two-year settlement and seeks to maintain good industrial relations. Moreover, a situation of weak demand and low profits does not invariably reduce the power of the work force to secure wage increases on the shop floor. Under more intense competition for international markets, the enterprise may be especially anxious to avoid an interference with deliveries on time. Similarly, the financially weak enterprise may be dependent on fulfillment of an important contract, or maintenance of a profitable line of production, in order to maintain its creditworthiness. In general, however, resistance to wage claims and upward adjustments of wages at the enterprise level is strengthened by a tight financial position during a slowdown. Wage subsidies to maintain employment and accommodative credit policies may therefore have a considerable effect in sustaining wage drift in the open sector industries.

Price constraint does not impose such a strict limit on wage increases in the large enterprise sector in the short run as it does in the small enterprise sector. Because markups for capital depreciation are high, the large enterprise can raise wages without raising prices by reducing its provision for capital replacement or by actually cutting investment. (In a cyclically sensitive industry, "normal" markups may be set to cover capital costs over the course of the cycle, with the expectation that they will not be realized during slowdowns.) Pressures for wage drift can be acceded to without necessarily endangering the firm's survival.

A decline in activity in the large enterprise sector does not automatically tend to ease cost pressures from the supply side in the sectors mainly supplying the home market. Employees in large enterprises naturally use their bargaining power to secure protection from dismissal or loss of income from unemployment. The reluctance of labor to leave the large enterprise sector is rational, bearing in mind the higher level of earnings than in the small enterprise sector and the expectation of an eventual recovery in foreign demand. This problem has been exacerbated in Norway by labor market policies tending to support the extreme geographical immobility of the labor force. The upward pressure on prices in other sectors would, of course, be eased if heavy unemployment were to involve a marked relative reduction of incomes in the large enterprise sector. But that outcome is unlikely to occur under a system of centralized bargaining. Instead, the unions and employers are likely to exert political pressure to improve their lot.

Implications of Tripartite Income Settlements and Centralized Wage Bargaining

Conditions in Norway were especially favorable for the implementation of a coordinated incomes policy because of the existence of cohesive social groupings, strongly centralized wage bargaining, and the tolerance of market participants for a considerable sacrifice of their independence. The Norwegian experience, however, demonstrates certain adverse features of such a system. The weaknesses of Norwegian policy after 1973--in particular, the inherent conflict between the various policy objectives that has been described—and the continuance of rapid wage increases via wage drift cannot be regarded as accidental features of the implementation of combined income settlements. They were not extraneous to the system but were characteristic of it since they essentially reflected the way in which the comprehensive agreements were secured.

Despite the close coordination of wage settlements and budgetary changes, and "testing" of likely outcomes with the macroeconomic supply-side model of the economy, in the final analysis the system amounted to tripartite bargaining, with the Government entering as one of the three parties involved. The Government, therefore, sacrificed much of its authority as the body responsible for the outcome of overall economic policy.[78] In the process of negotiation, the LO was representing the interests of its constituent unions, the NAF the interests of employers, particularly of large enterprises, while the Government in effect represented the interests of other constituents, especially the politically powerful groups such as farmers and pensioners. A basic constraint of the system was that the outcome had to satisfy the constituent unions of the LO, especially the powerful unions of the large-enterprise open sector, if centralized bargaining was to continue. The Government, the LO, and the NAF were all determined to resist a repetition of independent bargaining by the unions after the experience of extraordinarily large wage increases in 1974. The need to satisfy the industrial unions necessitated measures to support employment in large enterprises selling in the world

[78] The sacrifice of authority had been foreshadowed in the 1973 Skånland Report. "As viewed by the commission, a successful incomes policy would demand that the government give up its total control over its economic-political instruments. In the words of the L.O. representative: Through negotiations the organisations will gain influence over these matters—at the same time the political authorities will gain influence over the outcome of the negotiations. This is also the fundamental philosophy behind the combined settlements. . . . This is basically what we should be discussing: What influence should the organisations have on the economic policy? And what influence should the political authorities have on the negotiations?" Korsnes (1979, p. 369).

market. It also meant that wage drift, which tended to restore wage differentials between wage earners in the large enterprise and other sectors and to compensate for increases in sheltered sector prices, served as an essential "safety valve" to reduce explosive tensions within the system.

These considerations suggest that, on purely economic grounds, there may be reasons to prefer a less formal involvement of the Government in a system of centralized wage bargaining and income settlements of the kind practiced in Sweden and the Federal Republic of Germany. This does not obviate consultation with, and informing the negotiating parties of, the Government's budgetary proposals, as was done in Sweden in the preparation of the semiannual forecasts for the economy before the annual wage negotiations and in Germany through the process of "concerted action."

By its nature, the Scandinavian system of centralized wage bargaining and general frame agreements governing basic wage settlements is likely to generate conflict between those capable of securing drift and those whose earnings are effectively set by the frame agreements. This in turn produces a need for subsequent realignments and for preferential treatment of particular groups in the frame agreements; otherwise, wage drift that produces marked changes in relative incomes, especially when combined with the effects of progressive taxation in holding down the disposable income of higher-paid, salaried employees, may cause the breakdown of coordinated settlements.

The Scandinavian system of coordinated wage bargaining was a favorable factor in containing cost inflation so long as the strongest unions were under constraint of world market prices, effectively enforced by the employers' confederations, and so long as other unions were not favorably placed to secure larger wage increases than those granted in the open sector. The system came under pressure when other sectors became the wage leaders, as for example, in Sweden when construction was booming in the mid-1960s or in Norway when the public sector became the wage leader in the 1970s. Problems inevitably arise when economic conditions are particularly unfavorable for the most strongly organized industries and the power of the unions within the centralized federation is not matched by their economic position.

Policy Options

The Norwegian electorate has chosen to use its oil wealth to raise the average level of personal income and ensure a more egalitarian distribution of income and to maintain full employment. The authorities have sought to sustain a "hard currency" approach of pegging the exchange rate vis-à-vis strong currencies as a constraint on price inflation.[79]

Full employment has been maintained by budgetary supports to the highly protected agricultural sector and to industrial enterprises. Under a system of ambitious production targets and variable subsidies, farm incomes have been raised to a level comparable to the average earnings in industry, even on the least-favored farms.[80] The fact that per capita output in agriculture is worth far less at world market prices than per capita output in industry and services is compensated by price subsidies, but the level of food prices is considerably higher than in most industrial countries in relation to industrial prices.

The effort to attain a more egalitarian distribution of wage income and avoid unemployment requires a support system like that applied in agriculture, under which the less favorably placed businesses receive large subsidies. The need for subsidization of individual enterprises, if heavy unemployment in some areas is to be avoided, is particularly acute because of the geographical dispersion of major enterprises, promoted by dependence on hydroelectric power and natural resources.[81]

Since 1978 centrally negotiated frame agreements providing for small general wage increases combined with supplementary increases to raise lower-than-average wages have been associated with strong local wage bargaining tending to restore differentials. The combination of central and locally negotiated wage settlements and the indexation of farm incomes means that a favorable export situation or a depreciation of the effective exchange rate is likely to precipitate a strong upward movement of the general level of wages and prices and a subsequent deterioration of the balance of payments. The authorities are therefore naturally predisposed to follow a "hard currency" approach.

The tensions within the wage bargaining system, budgetary support to enterprises to avoid unemployment, and the maintenance of a hard

---

[79] Norway maintained a pegged rate within the snake from 1972 until December 1978, and thereafter it maintained the currency against a basket of currencies in which the U.S. dollar had a large weight.

[80] Actual costs and revenues (including subsidies) are estimated for a series of model farms and from these estimates an average net income per man-year is derived. Farm prices and subsidies are automatically determined when farm incomes are tied to industrial wage developments. Organization for Economic Cooperation and Development (January 1985, pp. 28–32).

[81] Organization for Economic Cooperation and Development (January 1985, p. 11).

currency regime together promote industrial stagnation. The prospect of budgetary support lessens the constraint on wage settlements arising from the threat of unemployment or the risk of the enterprise going out of business and reduces the enterprise's incentives for efficiency, especially in the use of manpower. (At the same time, however, the exchange rate policy, combined with technical advances and strong competition in the international capital goods market, tends to bring down the cost of capital relative to labor, making increasing use of capital cost effective.) Existing enterprises have a weaker incentive than those in other countries to risk making major changes in their production, while it is more difficult for new enterprises to attract skilled labor and managers than in countries with stronger incentives to labor mobility. It is not surprising therefore that the Norwegian economy has been marked by reliance on traditional products, stagnating industrial output, and poor productivity performance in recent years.

In criticizing the broad direction of Norwegian policies,[82] one should however bear in mind that Norway's economic situation differs greatly from that of other industrial countries such as the United Kingdom and the Netherlands, with their much larger populations and greater need for industrial employment openings and a competitive industrial sector (Table 9). As an isolated country with a very small population and limited resources other than oil Norway does not possess a comparative advantage for industrial production. In fact, its industrial development has been largely due to deliberate government policies to promote the exploitation of resources such as hydroelectric power. With its isolated position and very small home market, Norway is exceptionally dependent on favorable world demand conditions for an expansion of its industrial sector.

It would clearly be advantageous for the development of the economy if less emphasis was placed on securing an egalitarian distribution of incomes through centralized wage bargaining settlements and the system of agriculture price supports and if the authorities were less prepared to prevent unemployment by supporting enterprises in industries such as shipbuilding, for which demand has contracted. There is a need to assess the full impact of the present agricultural support system and of the ad hoc subsidies to enterprises. However, it is not clear that a sweeping abandonment of agricultural protection and the elimination of industrial supports, even if it was

[82] As is done, for example, in the Organization for Economic Cooperation and Development Economic Survey of January 1985 (pp. 41–43).

politically feasible, would promote rapid industrial development in Norway under present conditions.

The electorate has chosen to enjoy a favorable standard of living as a result of oil wealth without suffering the present social costs and possible reduction of aggregate welfare arising from a more uneven distribution of income and the probably greater risks of unemployment and poverty for the individual over the medium term that would be associated with the unfettered operation of market forces. While the maintenance of real incomes under the present system is highly dependent on what happens in the world oil market, it is not certain that the electorate as a whole, as opposed to particular groups, would benefit from exposing the economy to world market forces and permitting the structure of production and the distribution of income, other than oil revenues, to be freely determined by those forces.

Some Concluding Observations

It may be useful to close with some general observations on European countries' experience with incomes policies in the 1970s as revealed in these studies. The brief recourse to incomes policy in Canada in a very different institutional setting had less lasting impact on that economy and is not considered here.

In many European countries, macroeconomic policy in the years after the abandonment of the fixed exchange rate system consisted of a restrictive monetary policy combined with palliative fiscal measures and legal provisions serving both to protect employees from loss of income as a result of rising unemployment and to increase employment in the public sector. The broad outcome of these policies was a slowing down of inflation by 1978 associated with a large rise in the share of public expenditure in GNP and a marked rise in the nonwage labor costs of enterprises. A move toward easier policies in the Federal Republic of Germany and other European countries in 1978 was cut short by the second round of oil price increases and a renewed intensification of efforts to control inflation.

Labor-supported governments typically resorted to social contract-type policies in the 1970s, bargaining with the union federations, or with the union and employers' organizations, to secure moderate wage settlements in return for improved social security and welfare provisions and protection against redundancy. When adopted in crisis situations, such policies yielded important immediate benefits. In the Netherlands and the United Kingdom where social contracts were initiated in an explosive wage bargaining situation, they served to avert the risk of a severe disruption of the economy. In Germany and

Austria, such policies shielded the strongly organized labor force of the large enterprise sector from the effects of rising unemployment, and served to strengthen the control of union leaders over wage bargaining and to promote a more receptive attitude to the need for moderate wage settlements.

These benefits were however secured at some cost both in terms of adverse effects upon the microeconomic workings of these economies and lessened scope for an active fiscal policy. While the former have received most attention in the current framework of economic analysis, the latter consequences may actually have been at least as important in contributing to the unfavorable development of the European economies in the 1980s, which is examined briefly in the next chapter.

Such microeconomic developments as compression of the wage scale by "solidaristic" wage settlements; anomalies in the relation between wages and nonwage incomes such as unemployment benefits and disability and retirement pensions; and redundancy provisions, guaranteed work weeks, and union supervision of hiring and firing had the effect of reducing the flexibility of the labor market and imparting increased rigidity in the employment of labor at the enterprise level. Where there was a marked compression of the wage scale—as in the Netherlands and the United Kingdom—it led to mounting dissatisfaction among skilled workers, and tended to cause increased pressures for fringe benefits, inflexibility in applying work rules, and mounting disputes over working conditions. Anomalies between wage and nonwage incomes were important not only for their direct disincentive effects but perhaps even more as an irritant to individual employees, damaging industrial relations and eventually undermining the incomes policy. Redundancy provisions served to protect existing employees from unemployment but reduced the willingness of enterprises to take on more employees when demand strengthened.

Discretionary fiscal policy was impeded by the increased provision for public expenditures varying inversely with activity and by the great increase in total public expenditure. On the one hand, a restrictive fiscal policy was hampered by "automatic stabilizer" effects. Deflationary monetary policy was therefore liable to be associated with a rising budget deficit,[83] which reinforced the tendency for an appreciation of the exchange rate in the near to medium term, at

[83] The alternative of a deflationary monetary policy associated with provisions for automatic reductions in the public sector deficits and self-financing of the unemployment insurance system, of the kind adopted in the Netherlands, necessitated higher charges, with the effect of raising employers' nonwage costs and strengthening pressures for wage increases. The impact of deflationary monetary policy in increasing unemployment was thereby heightened, with vicious circle effects.

the same time as it weakened the effect of monetary policy in holding down nominal incomes and expenditure. On the other hand, the high level of public expenditure in relation to GNP, secularly rising commitments for social spending, and concern over the size and servicing of the public debt tended to rule out fiscal expansion by increasing expenditure or lowering taxes.

Two differences stand out in the incomes policy experience of the countries studied here. The first concerns the bodies involved in shaping the national policy. In Austria and Norway, the implementation of social contract-type policies involved bargaining between the Government, the strongly coordinated employers' organizations, and the unions. Other interest groups were also involved in both economies. In the United Kingdom and the Netherlands, however, decisions affecting wages and social programs were arrived at primarily in bargaining between the Government and the central union organizations, and the employers had a much smaller role than in Austria and Norway. This situation provided less scope for a constructive dialogue that aimed at a compromise between the interests of the two sides of industry.

The second, far more important difference separates the three countries with newly developed resources of North Sea oil and gas from the other European countries. The advent of oil income created an exceptional context for incomes policy.[84] In the Netherlands, Norway, and the United Kingdom, social contract policies were not devised solely as incomes policy measures aimed at moderating wage increases; they also met the need to reach a politically agreed allocation of the increased government revenue accruing from the developing oil and gas sector. It is not possible to disentangle the consequences of the "incomes policy" and the "oil economy" aspects of the policies. Nor is it justifiable to present the development of relative incomes and costs in these economies as an inevitable consequence of the development of the oil sector, setting off the so-called Dutch disease. The form and strength of the effects of rising oil income, and the speed with which the effects were felt, were intensified by the political tensions occasioned by the inflationary crisis of the early 1970s and also by the subsequent increase in oil prices. In these three countries, increasing government revenue from the oil sector caused

[84] It is worth noting incidentally that the Australian incomes policy initiated in 1983 was adopted in a similar context of rapid growth in the minerals sector (see Chapter 8). The context for the Canadian Anti-Inflation Program was also influenced, to a lesser extent, by the rapid rise in some provincial governments' revenues and borrowing power associated with the greatly increased value of oil production after 1973.

the potential for increases in government social expenditures to be divorced from the "capacity to pay" of the non-oil private sector. This tended to cause social benefits such as unemployment and sick pay, early retirement and old age pensions, and family welfare assistance to be set at relatively high levels compared with the lower end of the wage scale. Anomalies in the relation between tax-free social benefits and wage earnings from employment were increased by high marginal tax rates on wages.

The experience of the 1970s once again demonstrated that in practice the alternatives for curbing a rapid inflation may be *either* a policy of moderate demand restraint, implemented by a labor or coalition government, supplemented by a union-supported incomes policy and aiming at a gradual slowing of inflation in order to avoid a sharp increase in unemployment; *or* a strongly restrictive policy implemented by a right-wing government, aiming at a rapid restoration of price stability and relying on increasing unemployment to enforce wage moderation. The latter alternative is of course likely to be more successful in an economy without pervasive labor organization.

Many factors, including dissatisfaction with reaccelerating inflation, high taxes to support heavy government spending, and the irritation provoked by anomalous developments in relative incomes, deteriorating industrial relations, and weakened employer control in the workplace, together precipitated a decisive political shift to the right at the end of the 1970s. In a backlash against the consequences of social contracts and of policies of monetary restraint with palliative fiscal measures in Europe and against the inflationary consequences of the expansionist policies of the Carter Administration in the United States, conservative governments came to power promising to restore price stability, to cut government spending and lower taxes, and to promote the free working of the market system. Governments and their supporters looked to higher unemployment under strong monetary restraint to ensure greater flexibility in the labor market, stronger managerial control within the enterprise, and a lowering of wage costs as labor "priced itself back" into employment. In the event, however, it proved difficult to reduce real public spending radically over the next four years or to lower public expenditure in relation to GNP, since the enforcement of strongly deflationary policies almost throughout the industrial countries led to a general decline in levels of activity and employment in the early 1980s, and existing social security and welfare provisions were needed to make rising unemployment politically tolerable.

Part IV
Conclusions

11

On the Nature of Price and Wage Determination in Open Industrial Economies

It may be appropriate to close with a personal view of the general conclusions suggested by the studies in this volume concerning the factors influencing the price/output performance and level of employment in industrial countries, the nature of wage and price determination, and the scope for improving the performance of the economy by incomes policy measures.[1]

Three Main Conclusions

Since the studies were written over a span of two decades, they afford an insight into the dynamic process of the development of industrial economies over time. Three main conclusions stand out: first, the need for a historical perspective that takes into account the general evolution of the international system since World War II in order to understand the development of the individual economies over the last four decades; second, the need to relate the price/output performance of each economy over any particular period to the general development of the industrial economies within the international system over that period; and third, the need—if one is to understand the consequences of changes in the international system—for a model of the individual economy which incorporates crucial features of price and wage determination that are ignored in the neoclassical model. The simplifying assumptions of that model provide a logically

[1] The opinions expressed here are intended to stimulate discussion of the issues. They should not be interpreted as representing the views of the International Monetary Fund.

consistent framework for analyzing the responses of the economy to policy changes and autonomous shocks. However, the analysis is apt to be misleading as a guide in predicting developments or in formulating policies over the medium term because the assumptions are not sufficiently realistic to account for the workings of an industrial economy over a period of years. Later in this chapter, a tentative sketch is presented of the features of price and wage determination that need to be incorporated in order to capture more adequately the workings of an open industrial economy.

Need for Historical Perspective

The economic history of the industrial world since 1945 has to be seen as a long swing from the fragmented system of isolated national economies left by World War II and the autarkic policies of the Great Depression, through a process of gradual reintegration and the overcoming of extreme distortions in some economies, to a situation of close integration during the second half of the 1960s and the early 1970s.[2] There followed a sudden reversal of the pendulum with the breakup of fixed exchange rates permitting greater policy independence, at least for the largest economies. Since 1973 the industrial world has been in the throes of a protracted resolution of the conflict between independent national policymaking and the requirements of an integrated international economy. Those requirements impose a need both for national policies that are consistent with a considerable degree of exchange rate stability under whatever exchange rate system prevails and for a reasonably steady and noninflationary aggregate rate of monetary expansion in the industrial countries.[3]

For much of the 1950s and early 1960s, inflation under the fixed exchange rate system was limited in three ways. (1) The U.S. authorities were emphasizing domestic price stability rather than full employment. (2) Countries in which abnormal conditions of excess labor supply *and* disorganized labor unions prevailed after the war, such as the Federal Republic of Germany, Italy, and Japan, were favorably placed, at prevailing exchange rates, to pursue export-led growth. (3) So long as capital movements were restricted, any country that implemented a highly expansionary policy alone faced a swift deterioration of the balance of payments and this deterred governments from seeking to promote a very rapid expansion of activity. If incomes policy was employed, it was called upon to lessen domestic

[2]See Chapter 5 and Lindbeck (1983).

[3]For proposals along these lines see McKinnon (1984) and Marris (1985).

cost pressures in a situation where the conjuncture of national policies and operation of the payments system generally worked to prevent price inflation.[4]

The reintegration of the industrial economies, rapid industrial growth, and successful operation of the fixed exchange rate system over this period were not the result of purely economic factors, but depended in large measure on the actions of successive U.S. Administrations, who sought to restore a strong Europe and Japan. This political context created a quite exceptional correspondence between the U.S. and other Governments' policy objectives during the 1950s and early 1960s.

By the mid-1960s, the industrial countries approximated a unified economy with integrated product and capital markets. However, the difficulty of achieving the policy coordination now required for the operation of the fixed exchange rate system had increased with the freeing of capital movements and with the weakening of the paramount position of the United States within the system following the emergence of the European Economic Community (EEC) and Japan as major economic powers. Before governments were fully aware of the change, the scope for independent policies had narrowed, while differences in policy objectives widened.

National policies had hitherto been conditioned by marked differences between countries in labor market and wage bargaining conditions, and in industrial wages at prevailing exchange rates (the latter being offset to a varying extent by differences in capital intensity and productivity). Countries faced with structural underemployment and totally inadequate export earnings to pay for imports were naturally disposed to seek export-led growth. As the expansion of their export industries proceeded, the authorities were inclined to buttress the favorable wage-cost position by tight financial policies. The initial high wage-cost countries, on the other hand, tended to encounter increasing difficulty in maintaining output and investment in the open sector, and in sustaining high postwar levels of employment as technology and productivity elsewhere improved. Thus some countries, notably the Federal Republic of Germany, the Netherlands, Italy during the 1950s, and Japan, were inclined to follow strict policies. Others, such as the United Kingdom, Belgium, France during the 1950s, and the United States during the 1960s, were predisposed to deficit spending.

[4] This paragraph and the remainder of this subsection are reproduced with little change from Braun (1985).

By the mid-1960s, the first group and neighboring European countries were at, or close to, full employment and began to experience wage pressures under the influence of tighter labor markets and high export profits at prevailing exchange rates. A growing tendency for wage increases to exceed overall productivity growth was part of an equilibrating process by which, in the absence of exchange rate adjustments, domestic cost levels tended to be brought into line within the fixed exchange rate area under full employment conditions. Rapid industrial development within the EEC, under the stimulus of integration behind the common tariff barrier and of heavy direct investment from outside the area, was also important in raising the general level of wages in some EEC countries. The forces tending to bring about an upward adjustment of wage costs strengthened with the development of international capital markets and the effects of inflationary U.S. policies at the time of the Viet Nam war.

Sudden and unpredictable shifts of the U.S. policy stance increased the difficulty of arriving at a compatible set of national policies and an appropriate adjustment of exchange rates after the mid-1960s. A sharp deceleration of demand, following a shift in U.S. policies in 1969, led to a marked rise in unemployment with little change in inflation in North America and the United Kingdom, and the reverse in most other industrial countries. This difference provoked a still greater divergence of policy objectives between the two groups. Efforts to maintain the fixed exchange rate system under these conditions finally collapsed in 1973, when the control of inflation became of overriding concern in Japan and Germany, where the rate of inflation was accelerating dramatically.

To understand the problems encountered after 1973, one must appreciate the consequences—in heightening social tensions and stiffening the wage bargaining attitudes of organized labor—of the prolonged efforts of many European governments to use restrictive *domestic* demand policies to contain wage pressures generated by *external* factors.[5]

Changing Relationship of National Economies

Does the international economy at any period approximate a single economy or is it more like a set of independent closed economies? "Is the international economy more like the economy of the Midwest, in which Iowa City and Madison and Champaign all face given prices for

[5] See Chapter 5 and Chapter 10, "Netherlands: Incomes Policies of the 1970s and 1980s."

goods; or is it more like the solar system, in which each planet's economy is properly thought of in isolation?"[6] The answer would seem to be that neither metaphor is appropriate because national economies do not remain the same "distance" apart, or maintain constant orbits. In effect, the industrial countries resembled isolated "planets" under the trade and exchange restrictions of the late 1940s and early 1950s. By the mid-1960s they had come to resemble "cities" within a single economy under the fixed exchange rate system. Are they now in the process of spinning apart?

A more appropriate metaphor might be "floating islands." McKinnon rightly comments that accepted theories of macroeconomic policy have lagged behind the internationalization process as Western industrial economies have become more open to foreign trade in assets as well as goods. "Widespread adherence to the concept of national autonomy in monetary matters . . . is more in keeping with an *insular economy*: one with limited financial and commodity arbitrage . . . but not one fully closed to foreign trade."[7] Nevertheless, as long as national economies are politically independent and labor mobility between countries is limited, national economies must retain characteristics of "insular economies."

A system of open economies with closely integrated product and capital markets but limited international labor mobility, in which governments pursue independent and divergent policies, must be prone to increasing protectionism and fragmentation if individual economies are exposed to persisting strains and disequilibrium in the labor market. So long as governments in major countries direct macroeconomic policies primarily toward domestic objectives (such as reducing the tax burden or stabilizing the domestic price level) without regard for the effects on the level of world interest rates and activity, the case for an "insular" adherence to autonomy in economic policymaking elsewhere remains valid. Democratically elected governments inevitably will come under pressure to reinsulate the economy by trade or exchange restrictions or subsidies when faced with external policy shocks inducing destabilizing capital flows or severe unemployment.

Need for a More Realistic Model of the National Economy

To understand the effects of changes in the international system upon the performance of individual economies, it is necessary to relax

[6] McCloskey (1983, p. 495). "If the Iowa City view is correct, then all closed models of economies, whether Keynesian or monetarist or rationally expecting, are wrong" (p. 496).

[7] McKinnon (1984, p. 13).

the simplifying assumptions of the neoclassical model that the national economy is characterized by the general prevalence of competition and rapid adjustment across all markets for products and factor services. If those conditions held, under fixed exchange rates, free trade, and unrestricted capital movements, the world economy would approximate a single economy but one with restricted mobility of labor. Under freely floating exchange rates the workings of competitive national and international markets for assets, goods, and labor would ensure price and wage flexibility and stability of *real* exchange rates except in the very short run, and governments would be able to pursue independent monetary and fiscal policies without adverse effects on the real economy. Unless the properties ascribed to the system in the neoclassical model very largely apply, it is impossible to suppose that marked and persisting changes in real exchange rates and in the structure and level of real output within countries can be avoided under freely floating exchange rates when major countries are pursuing independent and erratically shifting fiscal and monetary policies.

Open Economies with Sectors of Easy and Difficult Entry

In practice, the strength of competitive forces at any time tends to differ widely in different fields of activity, because there are marked differences in the ease with which new producers can enter into various kinds of production. In order to understand the responses of the economy to changes in economic policies and external influences over the medium term, it is necessary to allow for the existence of both auction markets that clear—in which prices are freely determined by supply and demand—and administered price markets in which suppliers are able, for varying periods, to set prices and supply the quantities demanded at that price. The economy is characterized by a range of variable market conditions between the extremes of perfect competition and price rigidity, and this is a major reason for the uncertainty of economic agents concerning prospective developments.

The following view of the characteristics of industrial economies has developed from the work of preparing the studies in this book.[8] It is presented somewhat schematically in order to focus attention on issues that need more rigorous analysis or empirical investigation. The difficulty of establishing the propositions put forward here by empir-

[8] It derives from Kalecki's model of price determination in an economy with an oligopolistic and a competitive sector. Kalecki (1954). See Osiatynski (1986).

ical work should not be underestimated, however, since that requires disaggregated data of output, exports, wages, prices and employment, etc., distinguishing between sectors of easy and difficult entry, i.e., of large-scale and small-scale production. (The need for disaggregated data, it should be noted, arises even in the case of manufacturing, which is commonly treated as a homogenous sector in empirical work.) Such data problems are not encountered in studies based on the neoclassical model, because the assumptions concerning the nature of markets and of price and wage determination are precisely those needed to permit testable propositions to be derived concerning the behavior of macroeconomic aggregates.

For the purpose of this exploratory exposition it will suffice to distinguish sectors to which, in the absence of regulation, entry is relatively easy and in which prices and wages are likely to be more or less continuously determined by competitive forces, and those to which entry is relatively difficult, in which administered prices are set by producers. The former typically comprise sectors of small labor-intensive enterprises, casual labor markets, and self-employment. The latter include sectors of large-scale and capital-intensive production, including natural monopolies (notably public utilities that are generally regulated or owned by the state), and also sectors of small-scale enterprises exploiting advanced techniques or exceptional skills, and professions characterized by heavy investment in human capital (owing to lengthy or costly training), or by licensing requirements. Government services also constitute a sector of restricted entry in that the scale of employment is not determined by cost and profitability: entrants do not compete to supply government services at lower cost.[9]

In the large enterprise sector, market power of the single enterprise or of firms within an industry persists because in a dynamic world of changing technique the ability to charge relatively high markups over costs often confers scope to perpetuate that situation in various ways. The fact that the adoption of advanced techniques or capital-intensive methods lessens the risk of competition from new entrants, in practice constitutes a powerful inducement for technical progress and the realization of economies of scale, under a high rate of investment and rapid replacement of capital.[10] Limited entry is not an extraneous, or an exclusively harmful "rigidity" of the system.

[9] The existence of a large public sector, in which employees are able to maintain their wages in the face of declining demand in the market economy, tends to reinforce the power of business and labor in the large enterprise sector to maintain prices and nominal wages. See the discussion in Chapter 9, United Kingdom, "Incomes Policy and Control of Public Expenditure."

[10] See Chapter 6, "Influence of 'Ephemeral' Monopoly in a Dynamic World."

In the capital-intensive large enterprise sector obsolescence is more important than age in dictating capital replacement, though depreciation "lives" that govern the writing off of capital for tax purposes often exercise an important influence on the timing of capital purchases. The incentive to replace capital is usually related to the rate at which other firms in the industry are acquiring up-to-date equipment[11] and the technical advances embodied in the latest technology. This fact tends to perpetuate high profit markups in particular industries.

IMPLICATIONS OF THIS DIVISION

The division between the two sectors is of profound importance to the workings of the open industrial economy for two reasons. First, there is an association between the large scale of the enterprise and the scope for exploiting opportunities of increasing returns to scale and techniques of mass production, by spreading overheads and sales costs over sales in an extensive market. Large enterprise production provides the incentive and scope to develop worldwide markets. Second, as has been described in Chapter 6, there is an association between the scale of enterprises, the difficulty of entry for new producers, and the ease of organizing the dependent labor force.[12] This association can be presented schematically as follows:

Large-scale enterprises	difficulty of entry for new enterprises	considerable power to set and maintain prices
	ease of organizing labor	considerable power to maintain or raise nominal wages, not mainly conditioned by demand and supply in the domestic labor market

In analyzing open economies it is customary to distinguish between the open sector exposed to foreign competition and the sheltered sector[13] protected from foreign competition, and to ignore the

[11] If all the firms in a depressed industry are driven to hold down the rate of replacement, the aging of equipment beyond its "normal" life (for depreciation purposes) will have little effect in inducing increased investment. The substitution of increased servicing and repairs to older equipment for purchases of new equipment produced by capital-intensive industries of course represents a substitution of labor for capital within the economy.

[12] See the discussion of the nature of wage determination in the large enterprise sector in Chapter 6.

[13] Sheltered output generally includes construction, public utilities, government services, and personal services, as well as output such as agricultural production which is commonly protected to ensure self-sufficiency in food and for political reasons. Without doing too

differences between large enterprise and small enterprise sectors outlined here. The open sector of the economy producing tradable goods and services, however, comprises both large enterprises employing capital-intensive and advanced techniques to supply mass-produced or technically advanced outputs, and small enterprises employing more labor-intensive production methods. The latter typically sell in localized markets and satisfy domestic demands.[14] Generally speaking, only large enterprises can mount the sales effort and organization needed to export successfully in the world market. Thus the great bulk of exports from industrial countries of goods and of services such as banking, insurance, communications, and transportation is supplied by the large enterprise sector. In effect, in each national market, large enterprises face some competition from alternative, but not very similar, outputs of small-scale local enterprises.

The world market for large enterprise output does not comprise a single market in which atomistic competition between a great number of enterprises prevails. At any given period it consists of a set of markets for the specific outputs of particular industries employing specific productive capacity.[15] Each such large enterprise world market comprises a relatively few firms or a single firm in each of a small number of producer countries. Because of international specialization even a small country may supply a large part of the market for some industry's output.

The favorable development of an industrial economy over the medium to long term depends to an important degree on securing and maintaining an adequate base in the large enterprise sector serving the international market for goods and services. This represents both the major source of international purchasing power and the means to attain faster productivity growth and technological advances promoted by the greater scope for capital-intensive techniques and organization to benefit from economies of scale.

---

much violence to the facts, one may consider that agriculture is a sheltered sector in all industrial countries, and that trade in agricultural products *between industrial countries* consists simply of agreed sales at sheltered sector prices (mainly within the EEC; the agricultural exports of the United States and Canada go largely to nonindustrial countries).

[14]The extent to which small enterprises are confined to selling in the home market will of course be influenced by the proximity of production centers to major foreign markets. The constraint will be rather less important in the case of small, strategically located economies such as Belgium and the Netherlands than of large or isolated economies such as the United States, Japan, and Norway.

[15]The characteristic feature of large enterprise output is that it requires the use of advanced or specialized techniques of production, and (generally) that it is only efficiently produced or marketed on a large scale.

Two Subeconomies of the Open National Economy

What is the best way to model "insular" open economies with these characteristics in order to bring out the differences from the neoclassical model?

Since at any particular time there are relatively limited possibilities over the medium term (1) for new producers to enter the large enterprise sector; (2) for small-scale enterprises to sell abroad; (3) for labor outside the large enterprise sector to compete for existing jobs with labor employed in the sector; and (4) for labor to shift from one national labor market to another, it seems natural to consider the national economy as comprising two subeconomies—the large enterprise tradables economy (LETE) and the rest of the economy, which one may call the general labor market economy (GLME).

For a preliminary account of the relation between the LETE and GLME economies, bearing on how price, wage, and output developments in the industrial countries are related under fixed and flexible exchange rates, it may not be inappropriate to suppose that the world comprises only the 14 industrial countries[16] and that all international trade consists of goods and services supplied by LETEs.[17] When free trade prevails, each GLME "exports" only to the national LETE but "imports" freely from all the LETEs. Each LETE "exports" its largely capital-intensive outputs to the rest of the world, including the home GLME, and imports LETE outputs from foreign LETEs. It "imports" sheltered sector outputs, small enterprise outputs of tradables,[18] and additional labor only from the home GLME. Such "imports" of labor services and of small enterprise outputs for use in LETE production processes are limited to a greater or lesser extent in different national economies. In some cases purchases of the LETE from the home

---

[16]This assumption abstracts from the effects of the greater prevalence of competitive supply conditions and of the different export composition of developing countries, certain implications of which were touched upon in Chapter 7. It also unfortunately prevents consideration of the growing competition from LETE enterprises established with foreign capital in developing countries with very low wage levels, such as Korea, Singapore, or Brazil.

[17]This is not to say that there are no possibilities for large exports of small enterprise, labor-intensive products such as textiles, if very low wage costs create evident opportunities for trade. Such exports are important for developing countries with very low wage levels. But in industrial countries, the differential between wages in small enterprises and in the LETE is unlikely to be so large as to create such opportunities for large-scale exports.

[18]Strictly speaking in this model small enterprise outputs that compete with large enterprise tradable outputs are not "tradable" in the world market but it seems simplest to retain the term. See also footnote 13 concerning trade in agricultural products.

GLME may consist mainly of sheltered sector outputs and certain traditional consumer goods.[19]

In the system described here, prices and wages are likely to move differently in the two national subeconomies. Prices of LETE output will reflect demand/supply conditions for LETE outputs in the world market. Prices and incomes in each GLME will be influenced, in varying degree, by national labor market conditions, by the scale of demand for goods and services from the national LETE, and by government policies influencing the level of home demand and the degree of protection and subsidization accorded to sheltered sectors. In the LETE both prices and nominal wages are set rather than continuously determined by supply and demand in product and labor markets.[20] Even when enterprises are competing strongly for markets, prices are relatively inflexible over the short term, since many goods are sold on contract for delivery at a later date and costs are involved in revising widely disseminated price lists, and since wage settlements generally apply for at least one year and reductions in nominal wages are almost always strongly resisted.

Clearly the workings of the international economy and of the national economies will be decisively influenced by the nature of price determination for LETE output in the international market, by the extent to which wages in each national LETE are influenced by or insulated from the influence of demand/supply conditions for labor in the national GLME market, and by the extent to which prices and wages are freely determined by demand/supply conditions for labor in the national GLME market. The system is characterized by changes in the terms of trade between the GLMEs and the worldwide LETE economy. Its workings are complicated by the fact that the changes that tend to occur under different world economic conditions differ between countries and alter over time.

By ignoring the "natural barriers" within the economy and the divisions of the world market for tradables described above, neoclassical theory is able to postulate that prices, wages, and profits are competitively determined throughout the national economy and the world economy, and that each national economy faces a highly elastic demand for its products in the world market at the going level

[19] The distribution of demand between home GLME output and world LETE output in the two subeconomies will of course be influenced by the measure of protection accorded to sheltered sectors such as agriculture.

[20] See Gordon (1981).

of prices.[21] The neoclassical model of an open economy[22] does not take account of the fact that, in competing with large enterprises, small enterprises are limited in the products they can produce, the techniques they can employ, and the markets to which they have access. In the model, labor-intensive or capital-intensive products are largely substitutable, and labor/capital substitution is possible over the whole range of output. There is a unified national labor market and labor competes freely for jobs in meeting home and foreign demand.

Pricing in the Large Enterprise Sector

At any point in time, the capital stock and potential world output of each LETE industry at the "normal" level of capacity utilization is given for the medium term by existing capacity and investments underway.[23] The maximum potential output and the maximum potential demand for labor in each LETE industry and in the LETE economy as a whole is rather closely determined by the labor requirements at normal capacity utilization.[24]

When demand for output, at prices in excess of marginal costs and normal allowance for capital depreciation, consistently exceeds "normal" capacity output and a few large enterprises account for a major share of the world market, those producers will set their prices at the level at which they judge they can sell their normal capacity output. A high profit markup on the cost of variable factors may be realized at that price, sufficient to permit self-financing of a high rate of capital investment and technical improvement.[25] The firm does not hire labor to produce more than it judges the market will absorb at the target price. Lesser enterprises, which because of their limited capacity can supply only a small fraction of the market in the near term even if they

---

[21] See, for example, Sachs (1979 and 1983).

[22] See Malinvaud (1977 and 1982), Bruno (1982), Giersch and Wolter (1983), Sachs (1979 and 1983), Artus (1984), and Lipschitz and Schadler (1984).

[23] Unless marked changes in demand or supply induce exceptional scrapping of capacity, the capital stock will either increase in capacity and technical efficiency over the medium term, or remain more or less unchanged.

[24] In continuous production processes it is difficult to raise output by employing more labor. In other capital-intensive production, it is usually only feasible to raise output slightly by working longer hours, or greatly, by increasing the number of daily shifts, thus requiring a large increase in the work force. The incentive for the firm to make such a radical change is not strong if it can see an alternative of realizing much the same profits by raising prices for its normal capacity output.

[25] Such a price setting context will enable strong unions to raise wages relative to those in the rest of the economy. It may also predispose firms to use wage increases as a means to secure union agreement to changes in production methods and reduced manning, or to avoid stoppages.

maximize their output, charge what the market will bear given the prices set by major producers. If they are low-cost producers—such as enterprises employing similar equipment to that of major producers in countries with low wages at prevailing exchange rates and weak trade unions—very high profit margins will promote a rapid rate of investment.

In time the expansion in overall capacity and the shift in the distribution of capacity will increase the incentive and the scope for other enterprises to compete aggressively with the price leaders for the increasing share of the world market. When capacity has grown to the point that demand no longer exceeds the normal output capacity of the industry, at prices covering the marginal costs of most producers, the level of employment ceases to be determined mainly by capacity, and may be constrained by the need to ensure that the real product wages do not exceed the marginal product of labor. There is reason to believe that in many industries such a change occurred between the 1960s—when the price leaders were large U.S. producers paying high wages, and when producers in lower-wage countries such as Japan, the Federal Republic of Germany, Italy, and the Netherlands generally set their prices not far below those of U.S. producers—and the mid-1970s when world industrial prices were determined by low-cost producers. The change, however, coincided with a weakening of world demand for LETE output occasioned by the oil price increases and the implementation of deflationary monetary policies.

The worldwide average markup in each LETE industry, and in the LETE economy or in manufacturing as a whole, over any period will be influenced by such factors as whether technological leadership and the distribution of up-to-date capacity are concentrated in high-wage or low-cost economies and on how aggressively low-cost producers are competing to increase their share of the market. The lowering of profit margins brought about by stiffer competition in a slower growing world market of course constitutes a rise in real product wages compared with the earlier period. But one cannot attribute such a decline in profits or the corresponding rise in the share of value added going to wages entirely or almost exclusively to increased rigidity in the functioning of national labor markets or to an exogenous rise in oil prices and real wages as recent neoclassical empirical studies do.[26] The reduction in the profit share may actually be largely due to a

[26] For an early and highly influential exposition of the "supply-side" view that the principal reason for the slower growth of output and employment in the 1970s was the decline in the profit share brought about by exogenous wage explosions and increases in oil prices, see Sachs (1979).

reduction in the degree of price rigidity, causing prices to be brought closer into line with marginal costs of lower-cost producers.

The price setting policies and wage bargaining attitudes of large enterprises are conditioned by their expectations concerning the development of the market for their products and the willingness of governments to accommodate price increases. Hopkin has shown that in a closed economy consisting of price setting enterprises, it is difficult to conceive of pure "classical" unemployment resulting from the unwillingness of entrepreneurs to hire labor *because real* product wages have risen. Real wages are determined by wage bargaining, monetary policy, and the output decisions of the enterprises themselves. Nominal wage increases exceeding productivity growth do not involve a rise in real product wages if firms insist on maintaining their profit margins, or if the monetary authority is prepared to validate whatever rate of price increase is required to maintain profit margins.

> Wage settlements reached in collective bargaining may set up situations from which unemployment may follow, but the essential cause of the trouble is the relation between the [prior] money wage settlement and the [subsequent] rate of growth of monetary demand. If in such a situation there is in fact a rise in the outturn real wage, this will result from some or all of the producers manifesting a "compulsion"—not an unwillingness—to supply, and there is a strong presumption that the level of production and employment will actually be higher—in the short (to medium) run at least—than if there had been no such compulsion at work [and enterprises had insisted on maintaining their markups].[27]

An analogous situation will apply in the world LETE under restrictive or accommodative world monetary conditions. So long as some major countries were seeking to promote a rapid reduction in unemployment and others would not allow their nominal exchange rates to appreciate in the early 1970s, monetary expansion tended to mitigate the effect of large nominal wage increases in causing a *general* rise in LETE real product wages. Real product wages were liable to increase however when major countries enforced restrictive policies to curb accelerating inflation.

Implications for Neoclassical Empirical Studies

The preceding account undermines the logical basis for estimating the "warranted" level of real wages or the profit share in value added that is *needed* to ensure full utilization of capacity, as is done in recent production function studies. In such neoclassical empirical work it is assumed that the manufacturing sector, or even the entire economy, can be treated as a homogenous whole and that prices are set

[27] Hopkin (1984, p. 31), words in brackets added.

competitively. That is, profit-maximizing entrepreneurs choose "the amounts of output they supply and inputs they use by employing all variable factors of production up to the point where the marginal product of each is equal to its product price. Output prices, in turn, adjust to ensure that any level of output is absorbed by consumers."[28] It is then assumed that the demand for labor can be derived from the condition that the marginal product of labor equals the real wage. But the marginal product of labor curve is not the demand for labor function in a monetary economy, where the actual level of employment is determined by the level of effective demand for consumption and investment at the existing level of nominal wages.[29]

Empirical studies based on constant elasticity of substitution production functions also assume that throughout lengthy periods it remains equally possible to satisfy demand for "manufactures" by applying more labor to the existing capital stock, and by substituting more labor-intensive goods for capital-intensive outputs when capital is scarce. But suppose that, because of war damage and years of low investment, world capacity for the production of certain goods that can only be produced with *specific* industrial capacity is unusually scarce and abnormally distributed among countries. This was the case in the early 1960s, notably for durables, for which there existed a secular backlog of demand, and for the products of recently introduced technology. Can it be assumed that the marginal product of labor in manufacturing will not exceed the real product wage in some, perhaps most, countries in these circumstances? Or is it reasonable to suppose

---

[28]Lipschitz and Schadler (1984, p. 305). The assumptions imply that value added cannot remain persistently higher in relation to the cost of labor and other variable factors in one industry than in another unless there is greater technical scope for the employment of capital. Persisting differences in the rate of investment must reflect technical differences in the efficiency of capital versus labor in different industrial applications, not a higher degree of monopoly and easier self-financing of investment in some industries than others. The secular rate of technical progress must also be technically determined.

The assumption of competitive price determination ignores the problem of price determination in a LETE industry comprising a small number of major producers who cannot treat the market price as given irrespective of their output decisions, and who do not have to assume that the price will automatically adjust to the competitively determined market clearing level for a number of years, if not indefinitely. It implies that firms are continuously driven to profit-maximizing levels of output, because if they do not utilize labor and raw materials when it is profitable to do so, some other enterprise probably will. That may be true to only a limited extent if much of the capacity of the industry is held by a few enterprises practicing "target" pricing, if entry to the industry is difficult, and if the investment required takes time. See the discussion of price and wage determination under oligopoly in Chapters 4 and 6.

[29]"The marginal product-labor demand approach (which underlies the aggregate supply-side of goods in all *neoclassical models*) is simply incompatible with Keynes' analysis of the aggregate demand for goods in a monetary, entrepreneurial economy." Davidson (1983, p. 56); see also Davidson (1967).

that the actual level of real product wages over some period when the capital capacity of a very *rapidly expanding* LETE (or manufacturing) sector is fully utilized is indicative of the market equilibrium real wage?

In an industrial economy with the characteristics described here, it seems unlikely that the elasticity of substitution between labor and capital would be the same in a secular demand situation characterized by capital scarcity and easy labor supply to the LETE sector as in the opposite situation, where effective world demand for LETE output was persistently held down in relation to the capacity output at existing wage levels, resulting in unemployment of labor and capital in the LETE and requiring the absorption of an increasing proportion of the labor force in less capital-intensive employment in the GLMEs.

Relative Price Movements in the World LETE and the National GLMEs

In the GLME—in the absence of pervasive labor organization throughout the national economy—the tendency for prices to rise and for value added to rise faster than the volume of capital and labor employed is conditioned, not by a capital constraint, but by the elasticity of the national labor supply. In economies where real incomes are low over much of the GLME, additional labor is likely to be readily elicited to meet increased demand (through longer hours of work, "moonlighting," and the entry into the labor force of inactive persons). Additional labor can be employed to meet increased demand in labor-intensive production (notably services) without marginal labor productivity declining. Therefore, provided home demand shifts to labor-intensive GLME output in place of LETE products when world prices rise, a rise in LETE prices may be associated with an increase in output and employment in the labor-intensive sectors of the GLME rather than a rise in prices and wages there. If real product wages are maintained in both subeconomies in these circumstances, the real wage in terms of purchasing power over LETE and GLME consumer goods will rise for labor in the LETE subeconomy, and will fall for labor in the GLME. The two effects will not necessarily be offsetting within the national economy[30] since LETE prices are

[30] The effects of changes in various sectors or industries will not be offsetting as is postulated by Sachs and others (see Sachs (1979, pp. 288–89)). This assumption illustrates that the standard model of the small open economy is actually nearer to being a model of a closed economy because the simplifying assumptions suppress the essential characteristics of an open economy.

determined in the world market and GLME prices within the national economy.

Under deflationary world conditions, the LETE subeconomies are characterized by sticky wages and narrowed profit margins, reduced capacity utilization, and lower employment, particularly in the high wage-cost economies. The absorption of an increasing proportion of the labor supply in the GLME tends to lower productivity and real incomes there, and to increase the labor intensiveness of production. While the lowering of wages and incomes in the GLME has a limited effect in keeping down wage costs in the LETE, it has an effect in reducing demand for LETE output in the world economy. In the aggregate, the reduced purchasing power of the GLMEs tends to compound the reduction of profit margins, and encourages substitution of labor for capital within the industrial economies by reducing net investment and the rate of replacement of existing capital. Over the longer term, the effect of these changes is to increase the scarcity of capital relative to labor.

Since entry into the GLME supplying only the home market is comparatively easy, there are likely to be marked differences between industrial countries in the relative scale of employment and in the relative level of productivity and real wages in the two subeconomies, depending on the past population growth and expansion of employment in the LETE.[31] These differences influence the way the national economy responds to external conditions or domestic policies.

A country which has experienced pressures of a growing labor supply with limited expansion of the large enterprise sector will be one in which much home demand is met by labor-intensive outputs supplied by small enterprises and family businesses under competitive conditions. In such an economy, the level of consumer prices is likely to be more responsive to the level of aggregate demand, and restraint of domestic demand or a weakening of export demand for large enterprise production will be associated with a stronger effect in lowering consumer prices than will tend to occur in other industrial economies. This in turn serves to ease wage pressures in the large enterprise sector. A country with a large peasant agriculture and handicrafts production and weak unionization of the small business sector will show a comparatively slight rise in recorded unemployment when the growth of demand weakens relative to supply in the labor market. Governments in such countries may come under less pressure

[31] Also the expansion of employment connected with the opening up of newly settled areas in the United States and Canada (and Australia).

to adopt expansionary demand policies than those in other industrial countries, and will encounter less powerful political pressure for the provision of unemployment benefits, retirement pensions, protection from redundancy, and other provisions tending to support incomes when unemployment rises. However, they may be under pressure to regulate competition between small businesses, to maintain agricultural prices and limit agricultural imports, and to provide favorable tax treatment and subsidies to groups whose incomes are tending to decline.

Where a large proportion of the labor force is dependent on the large enterprise sector, and much household spending is met by LETE output, the capacity of the GLME to absorb large numbers of new entrants over the medium term will be limited even if wages there fall to very low levels.[32] In these circumstances, increasing unemployment is bound to create powerful political pressures both for social security provisions to maintain the incomes of the unemployed at levels not drastically lower than industrial wages and for the expansion of public sector employment and provision of subsidies to support employment in declining industries.

Differences in the scale of the two subeconomies would be important in themselves, but in practice their effect is greatly compounded since, as will be seen, they are generally associated with major differences in the pervasiveness and strength of labor organization and in the system of wage determination.

Wage Bargaining Characteristics of Industrial Economies

To complete this brief account of the salient features of the industrial economies, it is necessary to consider the actual organization of the labor market in the 14 countries, and how this affects the workings of the economy. The dimensions of the wage bargaining system that are important in this connection include the pervasiveness of labor organization throughout the economy, the wage bargaining strength of unions in the LETE, the organizational basis of collective bargaining, and the degree of centralization of wage decisions.[33]

---

[32] Short of totalitarian repression, there may be no way for the highly industrialized economy with a strongly organized labor force to recapture the flexibility of an economy with a large small enterprise sector, without sacrificing the gains of industrialization and "killing the goose that lays the golden eggs."

[33] For further description of the wage bargaining systems in particular industrial countries, see Chapters 4, 9, and 10.

Pervasive or Limited Labor Organization

Since it is difficult to organize labor successfully under the pressures of a growing labor supply or when heavy immigration is occurring, widespread labor organization typically does not develop until expansion of the large enterprise sector, perhaps combined with slower population growth, begins to strengthen the wage bargaining position of labor in the small enterprise sector. Pervasive unionization is facilitated by geographical concentration of small enterprises in small densely populated countries.

At the present time, labor organization for wage bargaining purposes is weak outside the large enterprise sector both in Japan and Italy, where a considerable part of the population is still dependent on low-income peasant agriculture and small enterprises in the rural economy,[34] and in the largest countries, the United States and Canada. In Japan and Italy isolated regional labor markets and the disbandment of the unions by totalitarian governments during World War II reinforced the influence of the reserve of labor in rural employment in limiting the spread of union influence over wage bargaining. Regional labor markets and large-scale immigration have served to limit the pervasiveness of labor organization in the United States and Canada. These four economies, and to a lesser extent, Switzerland and Germany,[35] display greater divergence of wage movements than the smaller industrial countries characterized by more pervasive unionization.

Nature of Collective Bargaining System

Where capital-intensive enterprises are widely dispersed, unions tend to originate for collective bargaining within separate enterprises,

---

[34] As one indication of the structural differences between the 14 countries, rough estimates based on Table 9 suggest that employment in agriculture and other nonmanufacturing sectors outside the industrial centers may account for more than one fourth of all employment in Italy, for more than one fifth in Japan and Norway, and slightly less in Denmark, France, and Austria. At the other end of the scale such employment probably accounts for less than one tenth of all employment in the United Kingdom and Belgium and only slightly more in the Federal Republic of Germany and the United States.

[35] Switzerland is exceptional in its dependence on temporary recruitment of non-unionized foreign workers. In the Federal Republic of Germany the newly re-established union movement was in no position to organize workers in the small enterprise sector in the face of the heavy inflow of refugees in the early postwar period. Low-paid work was taken over by foreign workers under full employment conditions in the 1960s. The unions have not organized these groups. In France, there were also substantial inflows—of settlers and unskilled workers from the former colonial territories—into the labor market. There, however, the divergence between income movements in the two sectors was lessened by widespread indexation of wages on the minimum wage and the high proportion of wage earner's income derived from social security provisions such as family allowances.

as in the United States and Canada. When industrialization takes place in thickly settled areas, small craft unions of skilled workers who are in relatively short supply generally develop first, followed by larger unions of less skilled workers within industries or cutting across industry lines. In Japan, however, this sequence was inhibited by the establishment of the *nenko*-system of lifetime employment, leading to wage bargaining within the enterprise.[36] In Belgium, the Netherlands, and the United Kingdom, the concentration of large and small enterprises within a limited area facilitated the organization of labor outside the large enterprise sector and the establishment of unions cutting across industry lines.

Wage bargaining by several unions within a plant or industry tends to focus attention on the maintenance of relative wage levels and to intensify wage rigidity both within enterprises and across the economy. Wage bargaining between a single union and the individual enterprise affords greater scope than industry-wide bargaining for wages to be set according to conditions affecting the enterprise, and may provide flexibility of wages in response to fluctuations in demand conditions.[37] Bargaining at the enterprise level is likely to be a favorable feature of the economy where the large enterprise sector faces strong competition. Where enterprises possess a commanding technological advantage, it may result in the joint exercise of market power by management and labor.[38]

Unions originate to represent particular groups of employees. They generally do not develop a coordinated wage bargaining structure unless compelled to do so by the need to bargain effectively with strongly organized employers.[39] In other circumstances, divisions within the union movement are highly resistant to change.[40]

---

[36] Rapid industrialization and technical change obliged Japanese industry to hire inexperienced workers and train them within the enterprise. The *nenko*-system of wages graduated by length of service provided a means of preventing employees from changing jobs and led to the development of enterprise unions. The important consequences of this type of organization are described in Chapter 9.

[37] See Chapter 9, Japan.

[38] The price/wage inflation in the U.S. steel industry at the beginning of the 1960s and price/wage developments in the U.S. automobile industry during the 1950s and 1960s are conspicuous examples of this process. High unit labor costs and profit margins in the United States strengthened the incentives for widespread establishment of the new steel and automobile production facilities in Europe, Japan, and developing countries, and the high level of U.S. wages in these industries caused increasing problems when they faced competition from new, technologically advanced production facilities abroad.

[39] The re-establishment of the unions after World War II under the aegis of the Occupation Forces in Austria, Germany, and Japan constituted an exceptional opportunity for securing major changes in the organizational structure of the unions (see Chapters 9 and 10).

[40] Where unions are organized by occupational groups, the interests of members of craft

Coordinated wage bargaining by employers has usually been initiated as strong industrial unions were appearing, when a few very large enterprises, or a cohesive group of employers, became concerned to protect the scope for profitable export expansion and combined to resist wage claims. (This occurred in Sweden and Norway early in this century and in Austria and the Federal Republic of Germany after World War II.)[41]

Splintered unions and collective bargaining for partial groups of employees do not pose the clear challenge needed to induce employers to coordinate their resistance to wage claims. Pervasive union movements may become politically powerful while the wage bargaining power and legal prerogatives of the individual unions remain limited. In these circumstances, the labor movement is likely to turn to political means to achieve improvements in wages and working conditions.[42] This situation tends to weaken the incentive to develop a more strongly coordinated union structure in order to strengthen wage bargaining power.

Whereas the larger issues are scarcely apparent in uncoordinated and fragmented wage bargaining, under coordinated wage bargaining the broader macroeconomic issues must receive some attention in settlements thrashed out between the employers and union leaders. Each side has to consider the interests of its member organizations, covering a wide area of the economy; some compromise between their

---

unions often diverge from those of members of the general unions. Union leaders also have a vested interest in the survival of their unions. Special factors have been important in perpetuating an uncoordinated union movement in Belgium, the Netherlands, and the United Kingdom. Divisions between French- and Flemish-speaking populations in Belgium and between Protestants and Catholics in the Netherlands are reflected in the wage bargaining system of those countries, and, as in other European countries, such as France, Italy, and pre-World War II Germany and Austria, socialist (or Communist) unions coexist with denominational unions. Such divisions of the labor movement do not exist in the United Kingdom, but there the pressures on employers to combine in resisting wage claims, as well as their incentive to insist on more orderly industrial relations procedures, were weakened by protection of the relatively large home market and the favored position of British exporters in Commonwealth markets (see Chapter 9).

[41] In Austria and Germany the integration of enterprises for war production, especially in the key metalworking industries, and wartime wage controls that established an accepted scale of national and regional wage levels in each industry provided a setting conducive to coordinated wage bargaining by employers after World War II, when unions were re-established with a structure of fewer and larger industrial unions. Similar factors played a part in promoting a unified response by large enterprises to union claims in Japan, though there was less explicit coordination of wage bargaining there. The central employers' federation also wields considerable influence over wage bargaining in France.

[42] Governments may intervene by measures such as setting minimum wages, extension of wage agreements to nonunionized enterprises or industries (Netherlands), or establishment of wage councils (United Kingdom) or of arbitration tribunals (Australia) for setting wages.

competing interests has to be evolved if the coordinated structure is to survive. In favorable circumstances, a strongly centralized wage bargaining system may provide scope for skillful management of wages policy by leaders of the two sides, promoting wage developments appropriate for the economic conjuncture and macroeconomic policies of the government. This is illustrated by the experience of Sweden in the 1930s and 1950s, of Austria since World War II, and of the Federal Republic of Germany following the 1973 appreciation of the deutsche mark.

Pervasive unionization with divided or uncoordinated bargaining by employers represents a difficult environment for the implementation of government economic policies and provides a strong inducement for the application of a statutory or government-sponsored incomes policy. The repeated recourse to incomes policy in the Netherlands and the United Kingdom, and at times in Denmark, since World War II essentially illustrates the use of incomes policy as a substitute for coordinated wage bargaining in strongly unionized national labor markets. The purpose of incomes policy in these countries was not simply to keep down the average rate of increase in nominal wages, but was also to lessen the tensions and economic costs associated with a fragmented and disorganized wage bargaining system in a small country with a strong demand for "equity" in the development of wages and salaries.[43]

Policy Implications of Structural Differences Between National Economies

It is evident that the economic structure and the characteristics of the wage determination system impose severe constraints upon the design of economic policies in some countries. The same prescription will not do for one and all.

As an illustration of the influence of these factors, one may distinguish two polar cases: on the one hand, countries with weak LETE unions and little labor organization in the GLME; on the other, countries with strong labor organizations extending throughout both subeconomies. In the former, if prices and wages in the GLME are freely determined by demand and supply, weakening labor demand or an increasing supply of labor will cause wages and incomes in the

[43] In Belgium, France, and Italy widespread indexation has played a rather similar role in lessening the industrial conflict and social tensions provoked by a fragmented wage bargaining system by promoting a generalized upward movement of wages and salaries. In Australia, reliance on wage decisions by arbitration tribunals has had a similar effect.

GLME to decline to the level at which available manpower is absorbed to meet home demand or participation in the labor market is discouraged even in the absence of unemployment benefits. The decline in wages and prices in the GLME relative to world market LETE prices promotes substitution of GLME for LETE output in meeting home consumer demand, and to some extent in LETE production (by encouraging subcontracting and use of components produced by small enterprises, and employment of supplementary nonunion labor hired in the GLME).[44] The level of costs in the GLME, and to a lesser extent the level of costs in the LETE, is sensitive to demand/supply conditions in the national labor market.

This is not so in the opposite case, where the level of wages throughout the economy tends to respond to rising prices for LETE output in the world market and to be inflexible in the face of declining world prices or rising unemployment in the GLME. Pervasive unionization tends to generalize wage increases across the LETE and the GLME, as unions resist widening wage differentials and declines in real wages when world market prices rise.[45] Under pervasive unionization, wage increases in sectors such as public service, utilities, and construction may influence the movement of wages in general.

Broad macroeconomic policies aimed at bringing down and holding down price inflation are likely to be most effective in the larger or the less urbanized of the 14 countries studied here—the United States, Canada, Japan, and Italy—and in Switzerland and Germany. By reason of the greater flexibility of relative incomes under less pervasive unionization, and the greater influence of flexible prices and wages in the GLME upon wages and costs in the LETE, these countries are better placed to moderate inflation and maintain employment growth under deflationary policies. Similar policies are liable to have greater effects in slowing output growth and increasing unemployment in the other European industrial countries.

This account of the structural and institutional characteristics of the industrial economies would imply that export-led growth will be associated with the expansion in capacity and technical efficiency of the capital stock and rising per capita productivity. An economy which is in a position to secure an increasing share of the world market is likely to secure favorable productivity performance. Conversely, the size and technical efficiency of the capital stock and overall per capita productivity will be highly sensitive to adverse changes in the relative

[44]See Chapter 9, "Wage Bargaining in Japan," p. 233.
[45]See the discussion of the Aukrust model in Chapter 2.

level of costs in the LETE compared with other countries. Restrictive demand management is of limited effectiveness in lowering LETE wage costs in the short to medium term. It follows that, in the interest of the development of the economy over the longer term, the authorities must be concerned to resist cost or demand pressures in the economy that would cause the level of wages in terms of world market prices for industrial products to rise above the level compatible with the desired scale of LETE production. Deflationary policy that promotes a rapid deceleration of price inflation and a marked appreciation of the exchange rate can be expected to have damaging consequences in economies characterized by strong unions and marked inflexibility of wages in the LETE.

The moral would seem to be that countries need to avoid a marked appreciation of the exchange rate except when low real product wages and high profit markups in the LETE under full employment conditions pose the threat of "wage explosions." There are usually severe limitations on the extent to which individual countries can pursue an independent monetary or fiscal policy. If the authorities implement a highly restrictive monetary policy or an expansive increase in the budget deficit promoting capital inflows and causing the exchange rate to appreciate, real product wages go up, the profitability of the manufacturing sector declines, and employment is reduced. Do these effects come about because wages are inflexible? Or do they arise because the authorities insist on achieving price stability or on forcing up the external value of the currency more rapidly than nominal wage increases or wage levels can be brought down, given existing wage contracts and wage bargaining practices?[46]

The integrated international LETE economy will be subject to inflation or to Keynesian unemployment if the aggregate rate of expansion in nominal demand in the industrial countries is too high or too low, or is allowed to accelerate or decelerate sharply. It is not

---

[46]It would seem foolish to suggest that it was to be expected that strongly deflationary policies would not raise the level of unemployment when such policies were expressly intended by some governments to have such an effect, in order to increase flexibility in the labor market and weaken the position of the unions. (See Chapter 9, United Kingdom, p. 227).

As Atkinson points out in commenting on Malinvaud (1982), in the supply-side approach, "the government is viewed as seeking to discover the pattern of factor returns which will ensure its policy objectives with regard to employment and growth. . . . We could turn the analysis on its head, and represent the objectives of the government in terms of a desired pattern of factor rewards, with the level of unemployment being manipulated to achieve this pattern. . . . Rising real wages for the employed accompanied by higher unemployment may not be electorally disastrous." This may be particularly true if the electorate has come to believe that "unemployment imposes little financial hardship because of the existence of generous unemployment insurance." Atkinson (1982, pp. 46–47 and 45).

possible to distinguish Keynesian from classical unemployment if LETE prices are not freely determined by available capacity and demand in the world market, if profit margins are variable, and if the real product wage is affected by changeable pricing policies of large enterprises. Classical unemployment will appear to apply in the large enterprise sector in countries that implement an exceptionally deflationary monetary policy, forcing up the exchange rate and raising the level of real product wages by causing the nominal level of wages to rise in relation to world market prices in home currency. Keynesian unemployment will appear in countries that respond by tightening monetary policy and raising interest rates in order to prevent devaluation.

In a deflationary world environment, the economy with a flexible labor market will experience little rise in unemployment, but a shift of employment toward lower-income, labor-intensive production, and an associated reduction in average productivity growth. The country with strong LETE unions and pervasive unionization will experience a marked rise in unemployment, a consequently smaller shift in the distribution of employment and change in relative incomes in the two subeconomies, and a less marked reduction in average productivity growth. The difference is illustrated by the contrasting experience of the United States and Japan and of Europe since 1973 shown in Table 16 below. The contrast between the experience of the United States and Europe is heightened by the rapid growth of the U.S. labor force and the slow growth of the European labor force during this period.

Recent Development of Employment and Productivity

Constraints of time and space do not permit an empirical investigation of the ideas put forward in this chapter. However, in this connection, it is tempting to glance briefly at developments in the United States, Europe, and Japan during the 1970s and 1980s.

Attention has been focused recently on the contrast between the United States, where, since 1973, output has apparently kept up with the growth needed to maintain employment, and Europe, where it has not. It is generally suggested that the fundamental causes of slower growth and high unemployment in Europe lie in rigidities of the labor market, inflation, and a lack of incentives to enterprise and effort in the private sector of the economy.

> Over the whole period since 1973 the number of jobs in both Canada and the United States has risen by around one-quarter. In Europe there has, on average, been no increase at all. . . .
>
> In the United States an average growth rate of the labour force of something over 2 per cent. per annum has been combined with an average rate of

Table 16. Growth of Labor Supply and Demand in United States, Europe, and Japan, 1960–84

(Geometric average rates of growth in percent per annum)

	Years	Total Labor Force (1)	Total Employment[1] (2)	Unemployment[2] (Increase −) (3)	Productivity (4)	Total Output (5)	Export Volume (6)
United States	1960–68	1.6	1.8	0.2	2.7	4.6	9.6
	1968–73	2.4	2.1	−0.3	1.4	3.5	7.3
	1973–82	2.3	1.8	−0.5	0.1	1.9	2.2
	1982–84[3]	1.5	2.7	1.2	2.5	5.3	0.9
Europe	1960–68	0.3	0.2	−0.1	4.5	4.7	7.9
	1968–73	0.7	0.6	−0.1	4.3	4.9	10.6
	1973–82	0.8	0.0	−0.8	1.9	1.9	3.4
	1982–84[3]	0.4	−0.4	−0.9	2.3	1.7	5.6
Japan	1960–68	1.4	1.5	0.1	8.9	10.5	17.7
	1968–73	1.0	1.0	—	8.1	8.8	12.5
	1973–82	0.9	0.8	−0.1	3.0	3.8	8.4
	1982–84[3]	1.2	1.1	−0.1	3.4	4.6	11.5

Sources: Bank for International Settlements, *Fifty-Fifth Annual Report*, April 1, 1984–March 31, 1985, p. 30; data in Column 6 derived from series published in International Monetary Fund, *World Economic Outlook, April 1985*, Statistical Appendix, Table 21, p. 227; and *International Financial Statistics*, Annual Supplement, May 1977.

[1] Including armed forces.

[2] As indicated by difference between growth of labor force and growth of employment. See footnote 5, Table 17.

[3] Data for 1984 are preliminary.

> productivity growth of only ½ per cent. per annum. Hence, the rate of growth of output needed to keep the growth of employment in line with that of the labour force was about 2½ per cent. per annum, virtually identical—for the period as a whole—to the recorded result.
>
> In Europe labour force growth has averaged only ¾ per cent. per annum, with productivity growth at nearly 2 per cent., the required rate of output growth was over 2½ per cent. per annum—that is, only slightly higher than that in the United States. The difference is that the rate achieved in Europe fell short of this required rate by a little over ¾ per cent. per annum.[47]

As in the passage cited, the rate of productivity growth is usually taken to be independent of the rate of growth of the labor force. However, it has been suggested in this chapter that growth of the labor force, not matched by rising demand for labor over the economy as a whole, is likely to be reflected in a rising share of employment in the easy entry sectors of lower per capita productivity and hence in a reduced average rate of productivity growth. This implies that the reduced growth of productivity in the United States and its better maintenance in Europe is directly connected with rapid growth of the labor force in the one, and slower growth in the other.

Another reason, however, for the more rapid productivity growth in Europe and Japan, which was particularly important in 1983–84, is the influence of the faster growth of exports than of output in general, which arises from the higher-than-average real value added per capita in the LETE subeconomy supplying exports. One may therefore expect a faster growth in average productivity and a smaller increase in employment to be associated with a given rise in output when exports are rising much more rapidly than other output (as was the case in all three areas in 1960–68 and in Europe and Japan in 1968–73 and in 1982–84. In the United States exports rose much less than other output in 1982–84 (see Table 16).

By making an arbitrary assumption about the scale of this effect, it is possible to arrive at a hypothesis concerning the "expected" rate of productivity growth associated with the effect of the changing share of exports in output and, hence, of the growth of output required to maintain the initial volume of employment (see Table 17, footnote 1). Though arbitrary, the assumption made there meshes well with the changes in other variables to provide a consistent and plausible account of changes in productivity in the three areas at different periods. It suggests that under export-led growth, "expected" productivity would be about 1¼ percentage points higher in Europe and Japan than in the United States in 1982–84 (Table 17).

---

[47] Bank for International Settlements (1985, pp. 30–31).

Table 17. Employment and Productivity Developments in United States, Europe, and Japan, 1960–84

	Years	Percentage Growth of: Labor Force (1)	Expected Productivity[1] (2)	Required Output[2] (3)	Actual Output[3] (4)	Difference (3)–(4) (5)	Productivity Excess or Shortfall[4] (6)	Change in Unemployment[5] (Increase −) (7)
United States	1960–68	1.6	2.8	4.4	4.6	0.2	—	0.2
	1968–73	2.4	2.8	5.2	3.5	−1.7	−1.4	−0.3
	1973–82	2.3	2.5	4.8	1.9 (−0.6)	−2.9	−2.4	−0.5
	1982–84[6]	1.5	2.4	3.9	5.3	1.4	0.1	1.2
Europe	1960–68	0.3	3.3	3.6	4.7	1.1	1.2[7]	−0.1
	1968–73	0.7	4.0	4.7	4.9	0.2	0.3	−0.1
	1973–82	0.8	3.0	3.8	1.9 (−1.1)	−1.9	−1.1	−0.8
	1982–84[6]	0.4	3.7	4.1	1.7 (−2.0)	−2.4	−1.4	−0.9
Japan	1960–68	1.4	3.1	4.5	10.5	6.0	5.8[7]	0.2
	1968–73	1.0	2.9	3.9	8.8	4.9	5.2[7]	—
	1973–82	0.9	3.0	3.9	3.8	−0.1	—	−0.1
	1982–84[6]	1.2	3.7	4.9	4.6	−0.3	−0.3	−0.1

Source: Data based on Table 16.

[1]Expected productivity growth abstracting from effects of the growth of the labor force. The figures show assumed normal productivity growth of 2.5 percent per annum plus an adjustment equal to the increase in total output attributable to the faster rise of export volume than of other output (shown in Table 16), taking into account the weight of exports in total output. The assumed effect of export growth in raising productivity is as follows:

	United States	*Europe*	*Japan*
1960–68	0.3	0.8	0.6
1968–73	0.3	1.5	0.4
1973–82	—	0.5	0.5
1982–84	−0.1	1.2	1.2

[2]Growth of output required to avoid increase in unemployment of the initial labor force, allowing for expected effect of export-led growth in raising productivity growth described in footnote 1.

[3]Figures in parentheses show cases where the rate of growth of output fell short of the expected growth in productivity shown in Column 2.

[4]Difference between expected productivity growth in Column 2 and actual productivity growth shown in Table 16.

[5]As indicated by difference between percentage growth of labor force and growth of employment. When unemployment is heavy, the difference may not indicate exactly the increase in unemployment as a percentage of the labor force. The figure for Europe in 1982–84 has been raised to allow for this effect. Slight discrepancies between figures in Column 5 and the sum of Columns 6 and 7 may also be due to rounding of data in Table 16.

[6]Data for 1984 are preliminary.

[7]Abnormal productivity growth associated with structural change and unusual opportunities for raising productivity and reducing underemployment in the GLME(s). See pp. 318–20 above and footnote 49.

In seeking to understand the incidence of lower productivity growth and of increased unemployment in the three areas, it is helpful to distinguish between the growth of output needed to maintain employment of the initial labor force with "expected productivity growth" and the influence of the growth of the labor force. The presentation in Table 17 suggests that the contrast between a fairly rapid expansion of employment in the United States and no employment growth in Europe during 1973–82, when the growth of output was about the same in the two areas, was largely a reflection of the rapid growth in the labor force in the United States, but was also influenced by the higher output growth needed to sustain employment among existing employees in Europe, owing to the higher expected rate of productivity growth associated with export-led growth.[48]

In the United States, the rapid growth of the labor force contributed a marked element of labor market "flexibility," facilitating an increase of employment in the easy entry, lower productivity sectors (since new entrants are more inclined and more obliged to take whatever jobs are available—being more mobile and less tied by acquired skills and often having less unemployment protection). In Europe this element of flexibility was smaller because of the smaller number of new entrants—but in most European countries, it would probably have been much less important than in the United States, even had this not been the case.

The analysis in Table 17 suggests that far from being the consequence of an exogenous "wage boom" squeezing profits, the slower growth of productivity and output after the late 1960s was associated with identifiable structural factors, namely (1) the more rapid growth of the labor force in the United States, (2) the ending of the rapid structural change and abnormally high productivity growth in Japan and Europe associated with the absorption of underemployment during the 1960s, and (3) the disappearance of the productivity-raising effects of rapid export expansion in Europe resulting from the integration of world trade, the establishment of the European Economic Community, and the efforts to avoid revaluation of "strong" currencies during 1968–73. These effects would also be important in

[48]According to the estimates in Table 17, the shortfall of output growth below that required to maintain the 1973 volume of employment with the expected rate of productivity growth, but abstracting from the effects of growth of the labor force, was 1.1 percent per annum in Europe compared with 0.6 percent in the United States. The difference reflected the 0.5 percent higher expected productivity growth in Europe associated with export-led growth. Employment rose 0.8 percent per annum less than the labor force in Europe and 0.5 percent less in the United States (Column 7).

the manufacturing sector, which is usually studied in supply-side empirical work.[49]

Current Problems of Industrial Countries

It is the generally accepted view of governments and economists in the mid-1980s that the industrial economies are not performing as well as they did in the 1960s. The deterioration has been ascribed to increased rigidities in the functioning of markets—more especially of labor markets—coupled in some countries with increasing subsidization or protection of weaker sectors. The first need is therefore held to be a supply-side attack on rigidities rather than an expansion of demand to combat unemployment. Unemployment is regarded as

[49] It is worth remarking that the marked differences in the rate of "disembodied productivity growth" between countries and over time, found in Artus (1984), which suggest that something has been left out of the system of equations, seem to be susceptible to explanation in terms of changes in the proportion of manufacturing employment accounted for by small, labor-intensive enterprises. (Artus describes the effect as arising because "as new products and new production techniques appear, there is often an opportunity for further economies of scale. Such changes, however, occur gradually over time and are unrelated to the levels of capital and labor in the manufacturing sector" (p. 253).) The estimated trend rates of disembodied productivity growth in percent per annum from his Table 3 (p. 270) are as follows:

	1961–73	*1974–82*
United States	2.74	0.89
United Kingdom	3.05	1.04
Canada	3.63	1.15
Germany, Fed. Rep. of	3.05 (1961–82)	
Italy	4.69	2.85
France	5.33 (1965–70)	2.29 (1971–82)
Japan	6.35 (1967–70)	3.68 (1971–82)

These figures suggest that output rises about 3 percent faster than might be expected from the growth of the capital stock and the employment of labor when both are rising and there is no marked change in the share of employment accounted for by large and small enterprises (as in the United States, the United Kingdom, and Canada in the earlier period). Substantially faster productivity growth is experienced when growth of capital and employment is associated with a declining share of manufacturing employment in labor-intensive small enterprise production, as was probably the case in Japan in both periods, and in France and Italy in the earlier period. Substantially lower "disembodied productivity growth" occurs when employment is in manufacturing contracts (as in the United States, the United Kingdom, Canada, and to a lesser extent France, during the later period) probably because the capital stock in the large enterprise sector is less than fully utilized, and possibly also because employment tends to increase in very small enterprises and family businesses employing little capital, where wages are more flexible in the face of rising unemployment. If this interpretation is correct, it is quite misleading to suggest that in Japan "manufacturing production *had* to grow by more than 4 percent a year. . . to lead to an increase in the demand for labor and capital services in manufacturing" whereas in the United States, Canada, and the United Kingdom, an increase in the demand for labor and capital services "could be achieved with an increase in production of only slightly more than 1 percent." (Artus, 1984, p. 272, italics added.)

classical rather than Keynesian in character, being attributed to the effect of real wage increases in conjunction with higher energy prices in reducing the profit-maximizing levels of output.

The Annual Report of the Bank for International Settlements of June 1985 stated this view:

> Macro-economic anti-inflationary policies have now been in place in most western countries for almost five years without having succeeded in eradicating inflation . . . recovery has progressed far without having done more than halt the rise in unemployment in Europe and bring only partial and unevenly distributed relief in the United States. Worse still, in Europe there is little prospect of any really substantial reduction in unemployment even if growth were to continue at a moderate pace for some years to come.
>
> These . . . facts combined suggest, quite bluntly, that something has gone basically wrong in the way prices are set in many western industrial countries, first and foremost in the labour market but also elsewhere: they do not perform their market-clearing function in the face of excess supply, while they react quite quickly and asymmetrically to excess demand. . . .
>
> It would be unwise to claim to know the answers . . . [as to why this has come about], but one major conclusion from the policy point of view nevertheless seems warranted: unless we can restore a greater degree of two-way flexibility to price and wage formation, it would be vain to expect our industrial economies to achieve a growth performance fast enough to absorb unemployment in the foreseeable future. Any marked acceleration of growth achieved solely through a relaxation of macro-economic policies would be very likely to rekindle inflation, and this would soon put an end to the growth process itself. On the other hand, growth rates which are sufficiently modest to allow inflation to be kept under control would be likely to go hand in hand with productivity increases rather than expanding employment—especially in Europe, where labour-market rigidities could well continue to steer capital formation towards labour-saving investment. The sad conclusion is that, given the existing characteristics of labour and product markets, there is no *macro*-economic policy of any shape or combination capable, by itself, of leading simultaneously to full employment and price stability. Or, to put it more positively: the precondition for restoring the effectiveness of macro-economic policies is a much greater flexibility of markets.[50]

This diagnosis raises two questions hinted at in a similar analysis in a study published by the Organization for Economic Cooperation and Development in 1983.[51] First, has performance worsened since the

---

[50] Bank for International Settlements (1985, pp. 4–5).

[51] A Special Group of the Economic Policy Committee concluded that "it is difficult to believe that the oil shock of 1973, the wage-price spiral hereafter and the subsequent energy price increase in 1979 can entirely explain the persistence of poor overall economic performance. Even if other factors bringing about structural adjustment pressures such as shifts in demand, changes in the size and composition of the labour force, introduction of new technologies, more stringent environment standards and new patterns in international trade and capital flows are also taken into account, it appears that a well functioning market economy should normally be able to cope with such challenges.

"The presumption is, therefore, that it is not only the adjustment requirements which have been too great or which came too abruptly, but also a diminished capacity and/or willingness of the economy and society in the industrialised countries to respond positively

1960s because of a change in the functioning of the system or has the deterioration occurred because the industrial economies typically are prone to perform worse in certain circumstances and under certain policies than others? Second, are the structural and institutional characteristics described in this chapter to be regarded as susceptible to change, or as persistent, and in many respects inherent, characteristics of these economies as has been suggested here?

The alternative diagnosis presented here is that the less favorable performance of the industrial economies during the 1970s and early 1980s than during the 1960s has been largely the consequence of (1) the historical process of development in the industrial countries since World War II and (2) the implementation of macroeconomic demand management policies less appropriate for an integrated international system than those of the 1960s owing to the more single-minded pursuit of national policy goals in major countries. That is to say, the pursuit first of very low unemployment regardless of accelerating inflation and then of a rapid deceleration of inflation aimed at securing a radical change in price expectations regardless of the effects in increasing unemployment.

The studies in this volume—in particular the account of wage and price determination in Chapters 4 and 6 and the account of the historical development of the international system in Part I and Chapter 5—suggest that the slower growth of output and employment since the 1960s was in part a result of the ending of a situation abnormally favorable to high profits and rapid growth of the open industrial sector, and was in part brought about by the efforts to bring down the rapid price inflation induced by the highly inflationary policies of the early 1970s. During the 1960s, high profits and rapid growth in manufacturing were made possible in a number of industrial countries by an easy supply of labor and a still limited capital stock, a low level of wages in relation to world market prices of manufactures, and the still relatively weak bargaining position of unions that had been disbanded during World War II.[52] The growth of the industrial

---

to them, which makes present economic difficulties so troublesome to resolve. . . .

". . . it is obvious that, to re-establish sustained non-inflationary growth, appropriate demand management needs to be supplemented by effective supply-side policies. Governments therefore need to pursue conscious policies for positive adjustment, enhancing the flexibility and resilience of markets in the face of change." Organization for Economic Cooperation and Development (1983, paras. 3, 4, and 7, pp. 7–8).

[52] Was it to be expected that widely divergent profit rates during the 1960s (of almost 50 percent in Japan, 38 percent in Germany, and 25 percent in the United States) would continue to exist in manufacturing sectors largely supplying an integrated international market as Sachs assumes in his 1979 study? Or was it to be expected that profit rates would converge? By 1975–78 the range of the corresponding figures had narrowed to 38, 29, and

sector in those countries was likely to slow down with the absorption of the labor reserve in other sectors. The expansion of large enterprise capacity had tended to strengthen competition in the international market and to promote stricter price setting in the late 1960s, at the same time as tightening labor markets tended to improve the wage bargaining power of the unions, causing a tendency for low wage costs in some countries to be brought more into line with those in other manufacturing centers.

Inflationary full employment-motivated policies in high wage-cost countries, such as the United States, the United Kingdom, and Canada, reinforced tendencies for wages in the most cost-competitive countries to be brought closer into line with theirs and hence to rise in relation to world market prices. Chapter 5 has described how booming export profits, rapid wage increases in export industries, faster increases in consumer prices, and the restraints imposed upon the sheltered sector created conditions ripe for "wage explosions" in European countries.

Neither the wage explosions and greatly increased indexation of wages nor the oil price increase of 1973 were exogenous developments: they were endogenous shocks, like earthquakes resulting from accumulating pressures within the system. As such they need to be seen as typical but extreme examples of the discontinuous process of adjustment in economies naturally subject to a changeable incidence of market power, particularly when subjected to sharp changes in macroeconomic demand conditions. Their treatment as "exogenous" developments in the supply-side literature is symptomatic both of a failure to consider the workings of the integrated international system as a whole, and of the failure of the neoclassical model to capture characteristic features of price and wage behavior in the individual open economy.

To conclude, the studies in this volume suggest that several constraints on national policies apply if the price-output-employment performance of the industrial economies is not to be impaired and if an integrated international system is to survive. First, the industrial economy responds poorly to policies involving a sharp acceleration or deceleration of demand or to very sharp changes in the composition of demand. Such policies tend to promote increased exploitation of market power in price and wage setting, and increased rigidities

21. (Figures derived from data given in Sachs (1979, Table 3, p. 276).) This example perhaps illustrates that something is fundamentally wrong with the way that open economies are presented in the neoclassical supply-side model.

serving to protect particular interests (Chapters 6 and 7). Second, there is an upper and a lower limit on the rate of expansion of aggregate nominal demand in the integrated industrial countries as a group if policy-induced inflation or Keynesian unemployment is to be avoided in the world LETE. Third, because of the characteristics of price and wage determination in the LETE, flexible exchange rates can permit only limited policy independence for individual countries if the economic performance of the group—and more especially the performance of certain countries within the group—is not to worsen substantially. Productivity growth within the economy or the industrial sector and the growth in size and technical efficiency of the LETE capital stock are likely to be adversely affected by a marked and persisting rise of the real exchange rate (in terms of LETE wage levels). Marked changes in real exchange rates quickly promote large shifts of LETE production between countries, lessening the possibility for countries to avoid adverse shifts by gradual price and wage adjustments over time or to reduce the impact of the contraction of certain industries by the development of other forms of production. Large shifts in exchange rates are liable to disrupt the integration of the international market by inducing increasing protectionism and autarky.

In sum, an integrated international economy imposes the need for a considerable degree of policy coordination and for compromises between conflicting national policy objectives, whether fixed or flexible exchange rates apply. The widely differing structural and institutional characteristics and political preferences of the industrial countries, however, call for an exchange rate system which provides some latitude for divergent rates of expansion to be accommodated at times by deliberate exchange rate intervention or intergovernmental financial arrangements to mitigate sharp changes in exchange rates.

BIBLIOGRAPHY

Aaron, Henry J., ed., *Inflation and the Income Tax: A Report of a Conference Sponsored by the Fund for Public Policy Research and the Brookings Institution* (Washington: The Brookings Institution, 1976).

Ackley, Gardner (1972a), "The Future of Wage and Price Controls," *Atlanta Economic Review* (Atlanta, Georgia), Vol. 22 (April 1972), pp. 24–33.

——(1972b), "An Incomes Policy for the 1970's," *Review of Economics and Statistics* (Cambridge, Massachusetts), Vol. 54 (August 1972), pp. 218–23.

Addison, John T., *Wage Policies and Collective Bargaining Developments in Finland, Ireland and Norway* (Paris: Organization for Economic Cooperation and Development, 1979).

——, "Incomes Policy: The Recent European Experience," Chap. 8 in *Incomes Policies, Inflation and Relative Pay*, ed. by J.L. Fallick and R.F. Elliott (London: Allen & Unwin, 1981).

Albeda, W., "Recent Trends in Collective Bargaining in the Netherlands," *International Labour Review*, International Labor Office (Geneva), Vol. 103 (March 1971), pp. 247–68.

Alchian, Armen A., "Information Costs, Pricing, and Resource Unemployment," in *Microeconomic Foundations of Employment and Inflation Theory*, by Edmund S. Phelps and others (New York: W.W. Norton, 1970).

Allen, Julius W., *"Wage and Price Policy in Canada,"* in *Wage and Price Policies in Australia, Austria, Canada, Japan, the Netherlands, and West Germany*, a study prepared for the Joint Economic Committee, 97th Cong., 2nd Sess., June 24, 1982 (Washington: Government Printing Office, 1982).

Anderman, Steven D., "Central Wage Negotiation in Sweden: Recent Problems and Developments," *British Journal of Industrial Relations* (London), Vol. 5 (November 1967), pp. 322–37.

Archibald, G.C., "The Structure of Excess Demand for Labor," in *Microeconomic Foundations of Employment and Inflation Theory*, by Edmund S. Phelps and others (New York: W.W. Norton, 1970).

Argy, Victor, "The Design of Monetary and Fiscal Policy: Monetarism and Supply-Side Economics," in *Inflation and Unemployment: Theory, Experience and Policy-Making*, ed. by V.E. Argy and J.W. Nevile (London: Allen & Unwin, 1985), pp. 60–77.

——, and J.W. Nevile, eds., *Inflation and Unemployment: Theory, Experience and Policy-Making* (London: Allen & Unwin, 1985).

Arndt, Sven W., ed., *The Political Economy of Austria* (Washington and London: American Enterprise Institute for Public Policy Research, 1982).

Arrow, Kenneth J., "Toward a Theory of Price Adjustment," in *The Allocation of Economic Resources*, Essays in Honor of Bernard Francis Haley, by Moses Abramovitz and others (Stanford, California: Stanford University Press, 1959).

Artis, Michael, "Some Aspects of the Present Inflation and the National Institute Model," Chap. 1 in *The Current Inflation: Proceedings of a Conference Held at the London School of Economics on 22 February 1971*, ed. by Harry G. Johnson and A.R. Nobay (London: Macmillan, 1971).

——, "Incomes Policies: Some Rationales," Chap. 1 in *Incomes Policy, Inflation and Relative Pay*, ed. by J.L. Fallick and R.F. Elliott (London: Allen & Unwin, 1981).

Artus, Jacques R., "Measures of Potential Output in Manufacturing for Eight Industrial Countries, 1955–78," *Staff Papers*, International Monetary Fund (Washington), Vol. 24 (March 1977), pp. 1–35.

——, "The Disequilibrium Real Wage Rate Hypothesis: An Empirical Evaluation," *Staff Papers*, International Monetary Fund (Washington), Vol. 31 (June 1984), pp. 249–302.

——, and John H. Young, "Fixed and Flexible Exchange Rates: A Renewal of the Debate," *Staff Papers*, International Monetary Fund (Washington), Vol. 26 (December 1979), pp. 654–98.

Atkinson, A.B., "Unemployment, Wages and Government Policy," *Economic Journal* (Cambridge), Vol. 92 (March 1982), pp. 45–50.

Aukrust, Odd, *Prim I: A Model of the Price and Income Distribution Mechanism of an Open Economy*, Article 35, Statistisk Sentralbyrå (Oslo, 1970).

——, "Inflation in the Open Economy: A Norwegian Model," in *Worldwide Inflation: Theory and Recent Experience*, ed. by Lawrence B. Krause and Walter S. Salant (Washington: The Brookings Institution, 1977).

Auld, D.A.L., L.N. Christofides, R. Swidinsky, and D.A. Wilton, "The Impact of the Anti-Inflation Board on Negotiated Wage Settlements," *Canadian Journal of Economics* (Toronto), Vol. 12 (May 1979), pp. 195–213.

Australia, Department of Labour, *Wage Indexation for Australia? A Discussion Paper* (Canberra: Government Publishing Service, 1974).

Australian Conciliation and Arbitration Commission, "National Wage Case, April 1975, Reasons for Decision" (unpublished, Melbourne, April 30, 1975).

Azariadis, Costas, "Implicit Contracts and Underemployment Equilibria," *Journal of Political Economy* (Chicago), Vol. 83 (December 1975), pp. 1183–1202.

Balfour, Campbell, *Incomes Policy and the Public Sector* (London and Boston: Routledge and Kegan Paul, 1972).

Ball, R.J., "Inflation and the London Business School Model," Chap. 3 in *The Current Inflation: Proceedings of a Conference Held at the London School of Economics on 22 February 1971*, ed. by Harry G. Johnson and A.R. Nobay (London: Macmillan, 1971).

Bank for International Settlements, *Fifty-Fifth Annual Report* (Basle, June 10, 1985).

Bank of Canada, *Annual Report of the Governor to the Minister of Finance and Statement of Accounts for the Year 1975* (Ottawa, 1976).

——, *Annual Report of the Governor to the Minister of Finance and Statement of Accounts for the Year 1976* (Ottawa, 1977).

Banque Nationale de Belgique, "Recherche sur les causes des disparités des taux d'information en Belgique, en République fédérale d'Allemagne et aux Pays-Bas," *Bulletin de la Banque Nationale de Belgique* (Brussels, May 1975), pp. 3–62.

Barbash, Jack, *Trade Unions and National Economic Policy* (Baltimore: Johns Hopkins, 1972).

Berger, G.A., *Canada's Experience with Incomes Policy, 1969–70* (Ottawa: Prices and Incomes Commission, 1973).

Bernstein, Edward M., "Wage-Price Links in a Prolonged Inflation," *Staff Papers*, International Monetary Fund (Washington), Vol. 6 (November 1958), pp. 323–68.

——, "Indexing Money Payments in a Large and Prolonged Inflation," in *Essays on Inflation and Indexation* (Washington: American Enterprise Institute for Public Policy Research, 1974).

Bhatia, Rattan J., "Unemployment and the Rate of Change of Money Earnings in the United States, 1900–1958," *Economica* (London), New Series, Vol. 28 (August 1961), pp. 286–302.

——, and Arie C. Bouter, "A System of Governmental Wage Control: Experience of the Netherlands," *Staff Papers*, International Monetary Fund (Washington), Vol. 8 (December 1961), pp. 353–79.

Bilson, John F.O., "The 'Vicious Circle' Hypothesis," *Staff Papers*, International Monetary Fund (Washington), Vol. 26 (March 1979), pp. 1–37.

Blackaby, Frank, "Incomes Policies and Inflation," *National Institute Economic Review*, National Institute of Economic and Social Research (London), No. 58 (November 1971), pp. 34–53.

——, "British Economic Policy, 1960–74: A General Appraisal," *National Institute Economic Review*, National Institute of Economic and Social Research (London), No. 80 (May 1977), pp. 38–57.

—— (1978a), "Incomes Policy" and "General Appraisal," in *British Economic Policy, 1960–74*, ed. by F.T. Blackaby (London: Cambridge University Press, 1978).

—— (1978b), "The Reform of the Wage Bargaining System," *National Institute Economic Review*, National Institute of Economic and Social Research (London), No. 85 (August 1978), pp. 49–54.

——, ed., *An Incomes Policy for Britain: Policy Proposals and Research Needs* (London: Heinemann, 1972).

——, ed., *The Future of Pay Bargaining* (London: Heinemann, 1980).

Blanpain, Roger, "Recent Trends in Collective Bargaining in Belgium," *International Labour Review*, International Labor Office (Geneva), Vol. 104 (July–August 1971), pp. 111–29.

Blinder, Alan S., *Economic Policy and the Great Stagflation* (New York: Academic Press, 1979).

——, "Inventories and Sticky Prices: More on the Microfoundations of Macroeconomics," *American Economic Review* (Nashville, Tennessee), Vol. 72 (June 1982), pp. 334–48.

Bosworth, Barry, "Phase II: The U.S. Experiment with an Incomes Policy," *Brookings Papers on Economic Activity: 2* (1972), The Brookings Institution (Washington), pp. 343–83.

——, "The Inflation Problem During Phase III," *American Economic Review, Papers and Proceedings of the Eighty-Sixth Annual Meeting of the American Economic Association* (Nashville, Tennessee), Vol. 64 (May 1974), pp. 93–99.

Bouey, Gerald K., "Remarks," *Bank of Canada Review* (Ottawa), June 1975, pp. 13–19.

Braun, Anne Romanis (1971a), "The Phillips Curve," *Finance & Development*, International Monetary Fund and World Bank (Washington), Vol. 8 (December 1971), pp. 58–65.

——(1971b), "Wages in the United Kingdom: Has There Been a Shift in the Phillips Curve?" *Staff Papers*, International Monetary Fund (Washington), Vol. 18 (March 1971), pp. 136–82.

——, "Compulsory Arbitration as a Form of Incomes Policy: The Australian Case," *Staff Papers*, International Monetary Fund (Washington), Vol. 21 (March 1974), pp. 170–216.

——, "The Role of Incomes Policy in Industrial Countries Since World War II," *Staff Papers*, International Monetary Fund (Washington), Vol. 22 (March 1975), pp. 1–36.

——(1976a), "Indexation of Wages and Salaries in Developed Economies," *Staff Papers*, International Monetary Fund (Washington), Vol. 23 (March 1976), pp. 226–71.

——(1976b), "Inflation and Stagflation in the International Economy," *Finance & Development*, International Monetary Fund and World Bank (Washington), Vol. 13 (September 1976), pp. 29–32.

——, "Incomes Policies in Industrial Countries Since 1973" (unpublished, Washington: International Monetary Fund, January 31, 1978).

——, *Some Reflections on Incomes Policy and the International Payments System*, Discussion Paper No. 132 (Ottawa: Economic Council of Canada, September 1979).

——, *Inflation and Unemployment in Canada and Other Industrial Countries*, Discussion Paper No. 184 (Ottawa: Economic Council of Canada, January 1981).

——, "Some Conclusions from Incomes Policy Experience in Industrial Countries," in *Inflation and Unemployment: Theory, Experience and Policy-Making*, ed. by V.E. Argy and J.W. Nevile (London: Allen & Unwin, 1985), pp. 134–52.

See also Romanis, Anne.

Brehmer, Ekhard, and Maxwell R. Bradford, "Incomes and Labor Market Policies in Sweden, 1945–70," *Staff Papers*, International Monetary Fund (Washington), Vol. 21 (March 1974), pp. 101–26.

Brenner, Reuven, "Unemployment, Justice, and Keynes's 'General Theory,'" *Journal of Political Economy* (Chicago), Vol. 87 (August 1979), pp. 837–50.

——, and Don Patinkin, "Indexation in Israel," in *Inflation Theory and Anti-Inflation Policy*, Proceedings of a Conference Held by the International Economic Association, ed. by Erik Lundberg (Boulder, Colorado: Westview Press, 1977).

Brown, William, "Central Co-Ordination," *Oxford Bulletin of Economics and Statistics* (Oxford), Vol. 45 (February 1983), pp. 51–62.

Browne, M.H., "Industrial Labour and Incomes Policy in the Republic of Ireland," *British Journal of Industrial Relations* (London), Vol. 3 (March 1965), pp. 46–66.

Bruno, M., "World Shocks, Macroeconomic Response and the Productivity Puzzle," in *Slower Growth in the Western World*, ed. by R.C.O. Matthews (London: Heinemann, 1982).

Brunot, Max, "Les régimes de prix concertés," *Droit Social* (Paris, March 1974), pp. 69–84.

Buiter, Willem H., and Marcus H. Miller, "Changing the Rules: Economic Consequences of the Thatcher Regime," *Brookings Papers on Economic Activity: 2* (1983), The Brookings Institution (Washington), pp. 305–65.

——, "Costs and Benefits of an Anti-Inflationary Policy: Questions and Issues," in *Inflation and Unemployment: Theory, Experience and Policy-Making*, ed. by V.E. Argy and J.W. Nevile (London: Allen & Unwin, 1985), pp. 11–38.

Cagan, Phillip, "Controls and Monetary Policy, 1969–1973," in *A New Look at Inflation: Economic Policy in the Early 1970s*, by Phillip Cagan and others (Washington: American Enterprise Institute for Public Policy Research, 1973).

——, and others, *A New Look at Inflation: Economic Policy in the Early 1970s* (Washington: American Enterprise Institute for Public Policy Research, 1973).

Cairncross, Alec, *Years of Recovery: British Economic Policy, 1945–51* (London and New York: Methuen, 1985).

Calmfors, Lars, "Inflation in Sweden," in *Worldwide Inflation: Theory and Recent Experience*, ed. by Lawrence B. Krause and Walter S. Salant (Washington: The Brookings Institution, 1977).

——, "Real Wages, Inflation and Unemployment in the Open Economy," Chap. 2 in *Inflation and Employment in Open Economies*, ed. by Assar Lindbeck (New York: North-Holland, 1979).

——, and Jan Herin, "Domestic and Foreign Price Influences: A Disaggregated Study of Sweden," Chap. 11 in *Inflation and Employment in Open Economies*, ed. by Assar Lindbeck (New York: North-Holland, 1979).

Canada, Anti-Inflation Board, *First Year Report* (Ottawa: Supply and Services, 1976).

——, *Second Year Report* (Ottawa: Supply and Services, 1977).

——, *Third Year Report* (Ottawa: Supply and Services, 1978).

——, *Final Report* (Ottawa: Supply and Services, 1979).

———, "Attack on Inflation: A Program of National Action," Policy Statement tabled in the House of Commons by the Honourable Donald S. Macdonald, Minister of Finance, on October 14, 1975 (Ottawa).

———, Budget Speech by the Honourable Donald S. Macdonald, Minister of Finance (Ottawa, May 1976).

———, Department of Finance, *Budget Document* issued by the Honourable Donald S. Macdonald, Minister of Finance (Ottawa, March 31, 1977).

Carew, Anthony, *Democracy and Government in European Trade Unions* (London: Allen & Unwin, 1976).

Carlton, Dennis W., "Market Behavior with Demand Uncertainty and Price Inflexibility," *American Economic Review* (Nashville, Tennessee), Vol. 68 (September 1978), pp. 571–87.

———, "Contracts, Price Rigidity, and Market Equilibrium," *Journal of Political Economy* (Chicago), Vol. 87 (October 1979), pp. 1034– 62.

Caves, Richard E. and Associates, *Britain's Economic Prospects* (Washington: The Brookings Institution, 1968).

Chamberlain, Neil W., *Forces of Change in Western Europe* (London and New York: McGraw-Hill, 1980).

Chamberlin, Edward H., "Labour Union Power and Cost-Inflation," in *Inflation: Proceedings of a Conference Held by the International Economic Association*, ed. by D.C. Hague (New York: St. Martin's Press, 1962), pp. 221–32.

Chater, Robin E.J., Andrew Dean, and Robert F. Elliott, eds., *Incomes Policy* (Oxford: Clarendon Press; New York: Oxford University Press, 1981).

Christofides, L.N., and D.A. Wilton, *Wage Controls in Canada (1975:3–1978:2): A Study of Their Impact on Negotiated Wage Rates* (Ottawa: Anti-Inflation Board, 1979).

Claassen, Emil-Maria, "World Inflation Under Flexible Exchange Rates," in *Flexible Exchange Rates and Stabilization Policy*, ed. by Jan Herin, Assar Lindbeck, and Johan Myhrman (Boulder, Colorado: Westview Press, 1977).

———, and Pascal Salin, eds., *Stabilization Policies in Interdependent Economies: Proceedings of a Conference Held at the University of Paris-Dauphine, March 25–27, 1971* (Amsterdam and London: North-Holland, 1972).

Clegg, Hugh, *How to Run an Incomes Policy and Why We Made Such a Mess of the Last One* (London: Heinemann, 1971).

———, "A Workable Incomes Policy for Britain," in *An Incomes Policy for Britain: Policy Proposals and Research Needs*, ed. by Frank Blackaby (London: Heinemann, 1972).

Cooper, Richard N., "Monetary Theory and Policy in an Open Economy," in *Flexible Exchange Rates and Stabilization Policy*, ed. by Jan Herin, Assar Lindbeck, and Johan Myhrman (Boulder, Colorado: Westview Press, 1977).

Corden, W.M., "Exchange Rate Policy and the Resources Boom," *The Economic Record* (Melbourne), Vol. 58 (March 1982), pp. 18–31.

Corina, John, "Trade Unions and Wage Restraint" (unpublished doctoral dissertation, Oxford: Nuffield College, 1962).

———, *Incomes Policy: Problems and Prospects* (London: Institute of Personnel Management, 1966).

Courchene, Thomas J. (1976a), *Monetarism and Controls: The Inflation Fighters* (Montreal: C.D. Howe Research Institute, 1976).

——— (1976b), *Money, Inflation, and the Bank of Canada: An Analysis of Canadian Monetary Policy from 1970 to Early 1975* (Montreal: C.D. Howe Research Institute, 1976).

Cousineau, Jean-Michel, and Robert Lacroix, *Wage Determination in Major Collective Agreements in the Private and Public Sectors* (Ottawa: Economic Council of Canada, 1977).

———, "L'impact de la politique canadienne de contrôle des prix et des revenus sur les ententes salariales," *Canadian Public Policy—Analyse de Politique* (Guelph, Ontario), Vol. 4 (Winter 1978), pp. 88–100.

Crockett, A.D., and Morris Goldstein, "Inflation Under Fixed and Flexible Exchange Rates," *Staff Papers*, International Monetary Fund (Washington), Vol. 23 (November 1976), pp. 509–44.

Crouch, Colin, "Inflation and the Political Organization of Economic Interests," Chap. 9 in *The Political Economy of Inflation*, ed. by Fred Hirsch and John W. Goldthorpe (Cambridge, Massachusetts: Harvard University Press, 1978).

Cunningham, Francis S., "Use of Price Indexes in Escalator Contracts," *Monthly Labor Review*, U.S. Department of Labor (Washington), Vol. 86 (August 1963), pp. 948–52.

Dabscheck, Braham, "The 1975 National Wage Case: Now We Have an Incomes Policy," *Journal of Industrial Relations* (Sydney), Vol. 17 (September 1975), pp. 298–309.

David, Lily Mary, "Cost-of-Living Escalation in Collective Bargaining," *Price and Wage Control: An Evaluation of Current Policies*, Hearings Before the Joint Economic Committee, 92nd Cong., 2nd Sess., November 13–15, 1972 (Washington: Government Printing Office, 1973), Part 2, pp. 332–41.

Davidson, Paul, "A Keynesian View of Patinkin's Theory of Employment," *Economic Journal* (Cambridge), Vol. 77 (September 1967), pp. 559–78.

———, "The Dubious Labor Market Analysis in Meltzer's Restatement of Keynes' Theory," *Journal of Economic Literature* (Nashville, Tennessee), Vol. 21 (March 1983), pp. 52–56.

Dawkins, Peter J., "Incomes Policy," in *The British Economy in the 1970s*, ed. by W.P.J. Maunder (London: Heinemann, 1980).

———, and Richard Blandy, "Labour Costs and the Future of the Accord," *Australian Economic Review* (Melbourne), No. 70 (Second Quarter 1985), pp. 37–50.

Day, William H.L., "Monetary Policy Coordination in Areas of Internally Fixed Exchange Rates: A Simple Expository Model" (unpublished, International Monetary Fund, March 29, 1978).

———, "Domestic Credit and Money Ceilings Under Alternative Exchange Rate Regimes," *Staff Papers*, International Monetary Fund (Washington), Vol. 26 (September 1979), pp. 490–512.

Dean, A.J.H., "Roles of Governments and Institutions in OECD Countries," in *The Future of Pay Bargaining*, ed. by F.T. Blackaby (London: Heinemann, 1980).

———, "Public and Private Sector Pay and the Economy," Chap. 3 in *Incomes Policies, Inflation and Relative Pay*, ed. by J.L. Fallick and R.F. Elliott (London: Allen & Unwin, 1981).

Delamotte, Yves, "Recent Collective Bargaining Trends in France," *International Labour Review*, International Labor Office (Geneva), Vol. 103 (April 1971), pp. 351–77.

Delors, J., "Politique des revenus et stratégie du développement," *Revue d'Economie Politique* (Paris), Vol. 75 (May–June 1965), pp. 559–92.

Dernberg, Thomas F., "Inflation Indexing of the Personal Income Tax: The Case from the Perspective of Stabilization Policy" (unpublished, International Monetary Fund, February 14, 1975).

Dessau, Jan, "Planning and Incomes Policy in France," *British Journal of Industrial Relations* (London), Vol. 1 (October 1963), pp. 310–17.

———, "Recent Discussions on Incomes Policy in France," *British Journal of Industrial Relations* (London), Vol. 2 (November 1964), pp. 356–59.

de Wolff, Piet, "The Netherlands," in *On Incomes Policy: Papers and Proceedings from a Conference in Honour of Erik Lundberg* (Stockholm: Industrial Council for Social and Economic Studies, 1969).

———, "Incomes Policies," in *Inflation Theory and Anti-Inflation Policy*, Proceedings of a Conference Held by the International Economic Association, ed. by Erik Lundberg (Boulder, Colorado: Westview Press, 1977).

———, and Wim Driehuis, "Postwar Economic Development in the Netherlands, with Special Reference to Inflation," in *The Economy and Politics of the Netherlands Since 1945*, ed. by Richard T. Griffiths (The Hague: Martinus Nijhoff, 1981).

Dicks-Mireaux, L.A., and J.C.R. Dow, "The Determinants of Wage Inflation: United Kingdom, 1946–56," *Journal of the Royal Statistical Society* (London), Series A, Vol. 122, Part 2 (1959), pp. 145–84.

Doeringer, Peter B., "Pay Policy in the United States—1971: A Speculative View," in *An Incomes Policy for Britain: Policy Proposals and Research Needs*, ed. by Frank Blackaby (London: Heinemann, 1972).

Dornbusch, Rudiger, in "General Discussion: What Have We Learned? Where Are the Fundamental Conflicts of Opinion?" in *Flexible Exchange Rates and Stabilization Policy*, ed. by Jan Herin, Assar Lindbeck, and Johan Myhrman (Boulder, Colorado: Westview Press, 1977).

———, "The Theory of Flexible Exchange Rate Regimes and Macroeconomic Policy," in *Flexible Exchange Rates and Stabilization Policy*, ed. by Jan Herin, Assar Lindbeck, and Johan Myhrman (Boulder, Colorado: Westview Press, 1977).

Douty, H.M., *Cost-of-Living Escalator Clauses and Inflation*, Staff Report, Executive Office of the President, Council on Wage and Price Stability (Washington: Government Printing Office, August 1975).

Dow, J.C.R., *The Management of the British Economy, 1945–60* (London: Cambridge University Press, 1964).

Downie, Jack, "What Can We Learn from European Experience?" in *Unemployment and the American Economy* (First Conference on Unemployment and the American Economy, Berkeley, California, 1963), ed. by Arthur M. Ross (New York: Wiley, 1964).

Driscoll, David D., "Wage and Price Policy in Austria," Chap. II in *Wage and Price Policies in Australia, Austria, Canada, Japan, the Netherlands, and West Germany*, a study prepared for the Joint Economic Committee, 97th Cong., 2nd Sess., June 24, 1982 (Washington: Government Printing Office, 1982).

——, "Wage and Price Policy in the Netherlands," Chap. V in *Wage and Price Policies in Australia, Austria, Canada, Japan, the Netherlands, and West Germany*, a study prepared for the Joint Economic Committee, 97th Cong., 2nd Sess., June 24, 1982 (Washington: Government Printing Office, 1982).

Duesenberry, James, "Domestic Policy Objectives and the Balance of Payments," *The Journal of Finance: Papers and Proceedings of the Twenty-Fourth Annual Meeting of the American Finance Association* (New York), Vol. 21 (May 1966), pp. 345–53.

Dunlop, John Thomas, *Wage Determination Under Trade Unions* (original edition, 1944; reprinted New York: Augustus M. Kelley, 1966).

——, "Guideposts, Wages, and Collective Bargaining," in *Guidelines, Informal Controls, and the Market Place: Policy Choices in a Full Employment Economy*, ed. by George P. Shultz and Robert Z. Aliber (Chicago: University of Chicago Press, 1966).

—— (1974a), "Inflation and Incomes Policies: The Political Economy of Recent U.S. Experience," *Eighth Monash Economics Lecture, 1974* (Clayton, Victoria, Australia: Monash University, 1974).

—— (1974b), "Statement," in *Oversight on Economic Stabilization*, Hearings Before the Subcommittee on Production and Stabilization of the Senate Committee on Banking, Housing, and Urban Affairs, 93rd Cong., 2nd Sess., February 6, 1974 (Washington: Government Printing Office, 1974), pp. 445–667.

——, and Walter Galenson, eds., *Labor in the Twentieth Century* (New York: Academic Press, 1978).

Eckstein, Otto, and Roger Brinner, *The Inflation Process in the United States*, a study prepared for the use of the Joint Economic Committee, 92nd Cong., 2nd Sess., February 22, 1972 (Washington: Government Printing Office, 1972).

Economic Commission for Europe, *Incomes in Postwar Europe: A Study of Policies, Growth and Distribution (Economic Survey of Europe in 1965: Part 2*, Geneva, 1967).

Economic Research Institute of the Commercial Banks of Norway, "Prices and Incomes Policy in Norway," *Norwegian Commercial Banks Financial Review* (Oslo), Vol. 50 (June 1976), pp. 1–5.

Edelman, Murray, *National Economic Planning by Collective Bargaining: The Formation of Austrian Wage, Price, and Tax Policy After World War II* (Urbana, Illinois: University of Illinois, Institute of Labor and Industrial Relations, 1954).

——, and R.W. Fleming, *The Politics of Wage-Price Decisions: A Four-Country Analysis* (Urbana, Illinois: University of Illinois Press, 1965).

Edgren, Gösta, Karl-Olof Faxén, and Clas-Erik Odhner, "Wages, Growth and the Distribution of Income," *Swedish Journal of Economics* (Stockholm), Vol. 71 (September 1969), pp. 133–60.

——, *Wage Formation and the Economy* (London: Allen & Unwin, 1973).

Elbaum, Bernard, "The Internalization of Labor Markets: Causes and Consequences," *American Economic Review, Papers and Proceedings of the Ninety-Fifth Annual Meeting of the American Economic Association* (Nashville, Tennessee), Vol. 73 (May 1983), pp. 260–65.

Elliott, R., "Industrial Relations and Manpower Policy," Chap. 13 in *British Economic Policy, 1960–74*, ed. by F.T. Blackaby (London: Cambridge University Press, 1978).

Estey, Marten, "Wage Stabilization Policy and the Nixon Administration," in *A New Look at Inflation: Economic Policy in the Early 1970s*, by Phillip Cagan and others (Washington: American Enterprise Institute for Public Policy Research, 1973).

Fallick, J.L., and R.F. Elliott, eds., *Incomes Policies, Inflation and Relative Pay* (London: Allen & Unwin, 1981).

Fane, C.G., "Index-Linking and Inflation," *National Institute Economic Review*, National Institute of Economic and Social Research (London), No. 70 (November 1974), pp. 40–45.

Farnleitner, Johann, and Erich Schmidt, "The Social Partnership," in *The Political Economy of Austria*, ed. by Sven W. Arndt (Washington and London: American Enterprise Institute for Public Policy Research, 1982).

Faxén, Karl-Olof, "Incomes Policy in Sweden: Problems and Developments," *British Journal of Industrial Relations* (London), Vol. 2 (November 1964), pp. 340–48.

Fellner, William, and others, *The Problem of Rising Prices* (Paris: Organization for European Economic Cooperation, 1961).

Fels, Allan, *The British Prices and Incomes Board* (London: Cambridge University Press, 1972).

Fels, Gerhard, "Inflation in Germany," in *Worldwide Inflation: Theory and Recent Experience*, ed. by Lawrence B. Krause and Walter S. Salant (Washington: The Brookings Institution, 1977).

Fischer, Stanley, "Wage Indexation and Macroeconomic Stability," *Journal of Monetary Economics* (Amsterdam), Vol. 5, Supplementary Series (1977), pp. 107–47.

Fishlow, Albert, "Indexing Brazilian Style: Inflation Without Tears?" *Brookings Papers on Economic Activity: 1* (1974), The Brookings Institution (Washington), pp. 261–82.

Flanagan, Robert J., David W. Soskice, and Lloyd Ulman, *Unionism, Economic Stabilization, and Incomes Policies: European Experience* (Washington: The Brookings Institution, 1983).

Fleming, J. Marcus, "International Aspects of Inflation," in *Inflation Theory and Anti-Inflation Policy*, Proceedings of a Conference Held by the International Economic Association, ed. by Erik Lundberg (Boulder, Colorado: Westview Press, 1977).

Flemming, John Stanton, *Inflation* (London: Oxford University Press, 1976).

———, "The Economic Explanation of Inflation," Chap. 1 in *The Political Economy of Inflation*, ed. by Fred Hirsch and John W. Goldthorpe (Cambridge, Massachusetts: Harvard University Press, 1978).

Friedman, Milton, "The Role of Monetary Policy," *American Economic Review* (Nashville, Tennessee), Vol. 58 (March 1968), pp. 1–17.

———, "A Theoretical Framework for Monetary Analysis," *Journal of Political Economy* (Chicago), Vol. 78 (March–April 1970), pp. 193–238.

———, "Monetary Correction," in *Essays on Inflation and Indexation* (Washington: American Enterprise Institute for Public Policy Research, 1974).

Galenson, Walter, ed., *Incomes Policy: What Can We Learn from Europe?* (Ithaca, New York: Cornell University, 1973).

———, with the collaboration of Konosuke Odaka, "The Japanese labor market," in *Asia's New Giant: How the Japanese Economy Works*, ed. by Hugh Patrick and Henry Rosovsky (Washington: The Brookings Institution, 1976).

Garbarino, Joseph W., "The Economic Significance of Automatic Wage Adjustments," in *New Dimensions in Collective Bargaining*, ed. by Harold W. Davey, Howard S. Kaltenborn, and Stanley H. Ruttenberg (New York: Harper and Row, 1959).

———, *Wage Escalation and Wage Inflation* (Washington: The Brookings Institution, 1960).

Geluck, Jan, "Wage Indexation," in *Wage Determination: Papers Presented at an International Conference, Paris, 3–6 July 1973* (Paris: Organization for Economic Cooperation and Development, 1974).

Genberg, Hans, and Alexander K. Swoboda, "Causes and Origins of the Current Worldwide Inflation," in *Inflation Theory and Anti-Inflation Policy*, Proceedings of a Conference Held by the International Economic Association, ed. by Erik Lundberg (Boulder, Colorado: Westview Press, 1977).

Giersch, Herbert, "Macroeconomic Policy in West Germany," in *Economic Planning and Macroeconomic Policy: Papers and Proceedings of a Conference held by the Japan Economic Research Center in September 1970*, Vol. I (Tokyo: Japan Economic Research Center, 1971).

———, "Index Clauses and the Fight Against Inflation," in *Essays on Inflation and Indexation* (Washington: American Enterprise Institute for Public Policy Research, 1974).

———, *A Discussion with Herbert Giersch: Current Problems of the West German Economy, 1976–77* (Washington: American Enterprise Institute for Public Policy Research, 1977).

———, and Frank Wolter, "Towards an Explanation of the Productivity Slowdown: An Acceleration-Deceleration Hypothesis," *Economic Journal* (Cambridge), Vol. 93 (March 1983), pp. 35–55.

Giugni, Gino, "Recent Developments in Collective Bargaining in Italy," *International Labour Review*, International Labor Office (Geneva), Vol. 91 (April 1965), pp. 273–91.

———, "Recent Trends in Collective Bargaining in Italy," *International Labour Review*, International Labor Office (Geneva), Vol. 104 (October 1971), pp. 307–28.

Godley, Wynne A.H., "Inflation in the United Kingdom," in *Worldwide Inflation: Theory and Recent Experience*, ed. by Lawrence B. Krause and Walter S. Salant (Washington: The Brookings Institution, 1977).

Goldstein, Morris, "Wage Indexation, Inflation, and the Labor Market," *Staff Papers*, International Monetary Fund (Washington), Vol. 22 (November 1975), pp. 680–713.

Goldthorpe, John W., "The Current Inflation: Towards a Sociological Account," Chap. 8 in *The Political Economy of Inflation*, ed. by Fred Hirsch and John W. Goldthorpe (Cambridge, Massachusetts: Harvard University Press, 1978).

Goodman, J.F.B., and G.M. Thomson, "'Cost of Living' Indexation Agreements in Post-War British Collective Bargaining," *British Journal of Industrial Relations* (London), Vol. II (July 1973), pp. 181–210.

Goodwin, Craufurd D., ed., *Exhortation and Controls: The Search for a Wage-Price Policy, 1945–1971* (Washington: The Brookings Institution, 1975).

Gordon, Donald F., and Allan Hynes, "Diffusion Processes and Optimal Advertising Policy on the Theory of Price Dynamics," in *Microeconomic Foundations of Employment and Inflation Theory*, by Edmund S. Phelps and others (New York: W.W. Norton, 1970).

Gordon, Robert J., "Wage-Price Controls and the Shifting Phillips Curve," *Brookings Papers on Economic Activity: 2* (1972), The Brookings Institution (Washington), pp. 385–430.

———, "The Response of Wages and Prices to the First Two Years of Controls," *Brookings Papers on Economic Activity: 3* (1973), The Brookings Institution (Washington), pp. 765–79.

——— (1977a), "Recent Developments in the Theory of Inflation and Unemployment," in *Inflation Theory and Anti-Inflation Policy*, Proceedings of a Conference Held by the International Economic Association, ed. by Erik Lundberg (Boulder, Colorado: Westview Press, 1977).

——— (1977b), "World Inflation and Monetary Accommodation in Eight Countries," *Brookings Papers on Economic Activity: 2* (1977), The Brookings Institution (Washington), pp. 409–68.

———, "Output Fluctuations and Gradual Price Adjustment," *Journal of Economic Literature* (Nashville, Tennessee), Vol. 19 (June 1981), pp. 493–530.

Gregory, R.G., and Ralph E. Smith, "Unemployment, Inflation and Job Creation Policies in Australia," in *Inflation and Unemployment: Theory, Experience and Policy-Making*, ed. by V.E. Argy and J.W. Nevile (London: Allen & Unwin, 1985), pp. 325–45.

Grey, Jo Anna, "Wage Indexation: A Macroeconomic Approach," *Journal of Monetary Economics* (Amsterdam), Vol. 2 (April 1976), pp. 220–35.

Griffin, Keith B., "A Note on Wages, Price and Unemployment," *Bulletin of the Oxford University Institute of Statistics* (Oxford), Vol. 24 (August 1962), pp. 379–85.

Guglielmi, J.-L., "'Echelle mobile' ou 'indexation' des salaires en France?" *Revue Economique* (Paris), March 1955, pp. 218–35.

Guitton, Henri, "Le problème économique de l'indexation," *Revue Economique* (Paris), March 1955, pp. 218–35.

Günter, Hans, and Gerhard Leminsky, "The Federal Republic of Germany," in *Labor in the Twentieth Century*, ed. by John T. Dunlop and Walter Galenson (New York: Academic Press, 1978).

Gylfason, Thorvaldur, and Assar Lindbeck, *Competing Wage Claims, Cost Inflation, and Capacity Utilization*, Institute for International Economic Studies, Seminar Paper No. 224, University of Stockholm (Stockholm, October 1982).

——, "The Political Economy of Cost Inflation," *Kyklos* (Basle), Vol. 35 (Fasc. 3, 1982), pp. 430–55.

Hackett, John W., and Anne-Marie Hackett, *Economic Planning in France* (London: Allen & Unwin, 1963).

Hall, Robert E., "Employment Fluctuations and Wage Rigidity," *Brookings Papers on Economic Activity: 1* (1980), The Brookings Institution (Washington), pp. 91–123.

Hague, D.C., ed., *Inflation: Proceedings of a Conference Held by the International Economic Association* (New York: St. Martin's Press, 1962).

Hamada, Kōichi, "Lessons from the Macroeconomic Performance of the Japanese Economy," in *Inflation and Unemployment: Theory, Experience and Policy-Making*, ed. by V.E. Argy and J.W. Nevile (London: Allen & Unwin, 1985), pp. 181–99.

Hamilton, Mary T., "Price Controls in 1973: Strategies and Problems," *American Economic Review, Papers and Proceedings of the Eighty-Sixth Annual Meeting of the American Economic Association* (Nashville, Tennessee), Vol. 64 (May 1974), pp. 100–104.

Hansen, Bent, and Gösta Rehn, "On Wage-Drift: A Problem of Money-Wage Dynamics," in *25 Economic Essays in Honour of Erik Lindahl* (Stockholm, 1956).

Harberger, Arnold C., "Monopoly and Resource Allocation," *American Economic Review, Papers and Proceedings of the Sixty-Sixth Annual Meeting of the American Economic Association* (Nashville, Tennessee), Vol. 44 (May 1954), pp. 77–87.

Hardy, Charles O., "Prospects of Inflation in the Transition Period," in *Prices, Wages, and Employment*, Postwar Economic Studies, No. 4 (Washington: Board of Governors of the Federal Reserve System, 1946).

Hauge, Gabriel, and Erik Hoffmeyer, *The International Capital Market and the International Monetary System*, The 1978 Per Jacobsson Lecture (Washington: The Per Jacobsson Foundation, 1978).

Haythorne, George V., "Prices and Incomes Policy: The Canadian Experience, 1969–72," *International Labour Review*, International Labor Office (Geneva), Vol. 108 (December 1973), pp. 485–503.

Hayward, J.E.S., "Interest Groups and Incomes Policy in France," *British Journal of Industrial Relations* (London), Vol. 4 (July 1966), pp. 165–200.

Heller, Walter W., "Has the Time Come for Indexing?" *Wall Street Journal* (New York), June 20, 1974.

Henry, S.G.B., "Incomes Policy and Aggregate Pay," Chap. 2 in *Incomes Policies, Inflation and Relative Pay*, ed. by J.L. Fallick and R.F. Elliott (London: Allen & Unwin, 1981).

Herin, Jan, Assar Lindbeck, and Johan Myhrman, eds., *Flexible Exchange Rates and Stabilization Policy* (Boulder, Colorado: Westview Press, 1977).

Hicks, J.R., "Mr. Keynes and the 'Classics'; Suggested Interpretation," *Econometrica* (Chicago, Illinois), Vol. 5 (1937), pp. 147–59.

———, *Value and Capital* (Oxford: Clarendon Press, 2nd ed., 1946).

———, *A Contribution to the Theory of the Trade Cycle* (Oxford: Clarendon Press, 1950).

———, "The Instability of Wages," *The Three Banks Review* (Edinburgh), No. 31 (September 1956), pp. 3–19.

———, *The Crisis in Keynesian Economics* (Oxford: Basil Blackwell, 1974).

———, "What is Wrong with Monetarism," *Lloyds Bank Review* (London), No. 118 (October 1975), pp. 1–13.

Hill, T.P., and K.G.J.C. Knowles, "The Variability of Engineering Earnings," *Bulletin of the Oxford Institute of Statistics* (Oxford), Vol. 18 (May 1956), pp. 97–139.

Hoffmeyer, Erik, "Incomes Policy in Denmark: Recent Developments," *British Journal of Industrial Relations* (London), Vol. 2 (November 1964), pp. 349–55.

Högberg, Gunnar, "Recent Trends in Collective Bargaining in Sweden," *International Labour Review*, International Labor Office (Geneva), Vol. 107 (March 1973), pp. 223–38.

Holtrop, M.V., "Method of Monetary Analysis Used by De Nederlandsche Bank," *Staff Papers*, International Monetary Fund (Washington), Vol. 5 (February 1957), pp. 303–16.

———, "The Relative Responsibilities of Governments and Central Banks in Controlling Aggregate Demand," Chap. 13 in *Inflation*, Proceedings of a Conference Held by the International Economic Association, ed. by D.C. Hague (New York: St. Martin's, 1962).

———, "On the Effectiveness of Monetary Policy: The Experience of the Netherlands in the Years 1954–69," *Journal of Money, Credit and Banking* (Columbus, Ohio), May 1972, pp. 283–311.

Hopkin, Sir Bryan, "Real Wages and Unemployment," Panel Paper No. 24 presented at the Twenty-Fourth Meeting of the Panel of Academic Consultants (London: Bank of England, October 1984), pp. 21–32.

Hughes, James J., "Cost of Living, Threshold Bargaining and Incomes Policy," *Industrial Relations Journal* (Nottingham, England), Vol. 4 (Winter 1973/74), pp. 23–33.

Hunter, Laurence C., "Some Lessons from the Failure of British Incomes Policies," in *Incomes Policy: What Can We Learn from Europe?* ed. by Walter Galenson (Ithaca, New York: Cornell University, 1973).

Ingham, M., "Appendix—Incomes Policies: A Short History," in *Incomes Policies, Inflation and Relative Pay*, ed. by J.L. Fallick and R.F. Elliott (London: Allen & Unwin, 1981).

Institute of Applied Economic and Social Research, "The Economic Situation," *Australian Economic Review* (Melbourne), No. 31 (3rd Quarter 1975), pp. 4–13.

International Monetary Fund, *Annual Report of the Executive Directors for the Fiscal Year Ended April 30, 1964* (Washington, 1964).

——, Fiscal Affairs Department, "Adjustment of Taxation for Inflation" (unpublished, International Monetary Fund, May 23, 1975).

Irwin, J.A., "Inflation and Taxation," *International Tax News*, Price Waterhouse International (London), December 1976.

Isaac, John E., "Australian Compulsory Arbitration and Incomes Policy," in *An Incomes Policy for Britain: Policy Proposals and Research Needs*, ed. by Frank Blackaby (London: Heinemann, 1972).

——, "Incomes Policy: Unnecessary? Undesirable? Impracticable?" *Journal of Industrial Relations* (Sydney), Vol. 15 (September 1973), pp. 237–58.

——, "Economics and Industrial Relations," *Journal of Industrial Relations* (Sydney), Vol. 24 (December 1982), pp. 495–516.

Isard, Peter, "Exchange-Rate Determination: A Survey of Popular Views and Recent Models," Studies in International Finance, No. 42 (Princeton, New Jersey: Princeton University Press, May 1978).

Izzo, Lucio, and Luigi Spaventa, "Macroeconomic Policies in Western European Countries: 1973–1977," in *Macroeconomic Policies for Growth and Stability: A European Perspective*, ed. by Herbert Giersch (Tübingen: J.C.B. Mohr, 1981).

Johnson, Harry G., *Essays in Monetary Economics* (Cambridge, Massachusetts: Harvard University Press, 1967).

——, "The Case for Flexible Exchange Rates, 1969," *Review*, Federal Reserve Bank of St. Louis (St. Louis, Missouri), Vol. 51 (June 1969), pp. 12–24.

—— (1971a), "The Inflation Crisis," *International Currency Review* (London), Vol. 3 (August 1971), pp. 5–11.

—— (1971b), "The Keynesian Revolution and the Monetarist Counter-Revolution," *American Economic Review, Papers and Proceedings of the Eighty-Third Annual Meeting of the American Economic Association* (Nashville, Tennessee), Vol. 61 (May 1971), pp. 1–14.

—— (1972a), Contribution to the panel discussion, "World Inflation," in *Stabilization Policies in Interdependent Economies, Proceedings of a Conference Held at the University of Paris-Dauphine, March 25–27, 1971*, ed. by Emil Claassen and Pascal Salin (Amsterdam and London: North-Holland, 1972).

——(1972b), *Inflation and the Monetarist Controversy* (Amsterdam and London: North-Holland, 1972).

——(1972c), "Notes on Incomes Policy and the Balance of Payments," in *Incomes Policy and Inflation*, ed. by Michael Parkin and Michael T. Sumner (Manchester: Manchester University Press, 1972).

——, "Comment on Mayer on Monetarism," in *The Structure of Monetarism*, by Thomas Mayer (New York and London: W.W. Norton, 1978).

——, and A.R. Nobay, eds., *The Current Inflation: Proceedings of a Conference Held at the London School of Economics on 22 February 1971* (London: Macmillan, 1971).

Johnston, T.L., *Collective Bargaining in Sweden: A Study of the Labour Market and Its Institutions* (Cambridge, Massachusetts: Harvard University Press, 1962).

——, ed., *Economic Expansion and Structural Change: A Trade Union Manifesto*, report submitted to the Swedish Confederation of Trade Unions (London: Allen & Unwin, 1963).

Jones, Aubrey, *The New Inflation: The Politics of Prices and Incomes* (London: André Deutsch, 1973).

Kafka, Alexandre, "Indexing for Inflation in Brazil," in *Essays on Inflation and Indexation* (Washington: American Enterprise Institute for Public Policy Research, 1974).

Kahn, R.F., evidence before the Committee on the Working of the Monetary System (Radcliffe Committee), *Principal Memoranda of Evidence*, Vol. 3 (London: H.M. Stationery Office, 1960).

Kaldor, Nicholas, *Causes of the Slow Rate of Economic Growth of the United Kingdom* (London: Cambridge University Press, 1966).

——, "Inflation and Recession in the World Economy," *Economic Journal* (London), Vol. 86 (December 1976), pp. 703–14.

Kalecki, M., "Three Ways to Full Employment," in *The Economics of Full Employment* (Oxford: Basil Blackwell, 1944).

——, *Theory of Economic Dynamics: An Essay on Cyclical and Long-Run Changes in Capitalist Economy* (London: Allen & Unwin, 1954).

——, *Studies in the Theory of Business Cycles, 1933–1939* (Oxford: Basil Blackwell, 1966).

——, "Class Struggle and the Distribution of National Income," *Kyklos* (Basle), Vol. 24 (Fasc. 1, 1971), pp. 1–8.

Kaliski, S.F., and D.C. Smith, "Inflation, Unemployment and Incomes Policy," *Canadian Journal of Economics* (Toronto), Vol. 6 (November 1973), pp. 574–91.

Kasper, Wolfgang, "Stabilization Policies in a Dependent Economy: Some Lessons from the West German Experience of the 1960s," Chap. 10 in *Stabilization Policies in Interdependent Economies: Proceedings of a Conference Held at the University of Paris-Dauphine, March 25–27, 1971*, ed. by Emil Claassen and Pascal Salin (Amsterdam and London: North-Holland, 1972).

Katzenstein, Peter J., "Commentary," in *The Political Economy of Austria*, ed. by Sven W. Arndt (Washington and London: American Enterprise Institute for Public Policy Research, 1982).

Kervyn de Lettenhove, A., "Politique des revenus: l'expérience hollandaise," *Revue d'Economie Politique* (Paris), Vol. 75 (May–June 1965), pp. 608–38.

Keynes, John Maynard, *A Tract on Monetary Reform* (London: Macmillan, 1923).

——, *The General Theory of Employment, Interest and Money* (London: Macmillan, 1936).

Kienzel, H., "Prices Policy and Incomes Policy in Austria," in *Supplement to the Report, Non-Wage Incomes and Prices Policy* (Paris: Organization for Economic Cooperation and Development, 1966).

Klein, L.R., and R.J. Ball, "Some Econometrics of the Determination of Absolute Prices and Wages," *Economic Journal* (London), Vol. 69 (September 1959), pp. 465–82.

Klein, L.R., and A.S. Goldberger, *An Econometric Model of the United States, 1929–1955* (Amsterdam: North-Holland, 1955).

Knowles, K.G.J.C., "Wages and Productivity," Chap. 14 in *The British Economy in the Nineteen-Fifties*, ed. by G.D.N. Worswick and P.M. Ady (Oxford: Clarendon Press, 1962).

——, and D.J. Robertson, "Earnings in Engineering, 1926–1948," *Bulletin of the Oxford University Institute of Statistics* (Oxford), Vol. 13 (June 1951), pp. 179–200.

——, and C.B. Winsten, "Can the Level of Unemployment Explain Changes in Wages?" *Bulletin of the Oxford University Institute of Statistics* (Oxford), Vol. 21 (May 1959), pp. 113–20.

Koren, Stephan, "Austrian Monetary and Exchange Rate Policies," in *The Political Economy of Austria*, ed. by Sven W. Arndt (Washington and London: American Enterprise Institute for Public Policy Research, 1982).

Korsnes, O., "Duality in the Role of Unions and Unionists: The Case of Norway," *British Journal of Industrial Relations* (London), Vol. 17 (November 1979), pp. 363–75.

Kouri, Pentti, "Profitability and Growth in a Small Open Economy," Chap. 5 in *Inflation and Employment in Open Economies*, ed. by Assar Lindbeck (New York: North-Holland, 1979).

Krause, Lawrence B., and Walter S. Salant, eds., *Worldwide Inflation: Theory and Recent Experience* (Washington: The Brookings Institution, 1977).

Kredietbank, "Index-Linking of Wages," *Weekly Bulletin* (Brussels), April 14, 1972, pp. 157–62.

Laffer, Kingsley, "Cost-of-Living Adjustments in Australian Wage Determination," *Industrial and Labor Relations Review* (Ithaca, New York), Vol. 7 (January 1954), pp. 278–87.

Laidler, David, "The Current Inflation—The Problem of Explanation and the Problem of Policy," in *After Keynes: Papers Presented to Section F (Economics) at the 1972 Annual Meeting of the British Association for the Advancement of Science*, ed. by Joan Robinson (Oxford: Basil Blackwell, 1973).

———, "Expectations and the Phillips Trade Off: A Commentary," *Scottish Journal of Political Economy* (Edinburgh), Vol. 23 (February 1976), pp. 55–72.

———, "Monetarism: An Interpretation and an Assessment," *Economic Journal* (London), Vol. 91 (March 1981), pp. 1–28.

Lanzillotti, Robert F., and Blaine Roberts, "The Legacy of Phase II Price Controls," *American Economic Review, Papers and Proceedings of the Eighty-Sixth Annual Meeting of the American Economic Association* (Nashville, Tennessee), Vol. 64 (May 1974), pp. 82–87.

———, Mary T. Hamilton, and R. Blaine Roberts, *Phase II in Review: The Price Commission Experience* (Washington: The Brookings Institution, 1975).

Lecaillon, Jacques, "La politique des revenus," *Revue d'Economie Politique* (Paris), Vol. 75 (May–June 1965), pp. 517–58.

Lent, George E., "Adjustment of Taxable Profits for Inflation," *Staff Papers*, International Monetary Fund (Washington), Vol. 12 (November 1975), pp. 641–79.

Lerner, Abba P., "The Essential Properties of Interest and Money," *Quarterly Journal of Economics* (Cambridge, Massachusetts), Vol. 66 (May 1952), pp. 172–93.

Lerner, Shirley W., "Wage Drift, Wage Fixing and Drift Statistics," *The Manchester School of Economic and Social Studies* (Manchester), Vol. 33 (May 1965), pp. 155–77.

Levine, Solomon B., "Changing Strategies of Unions and Management: Evaluation of Four Industrialised Countries," *British Journal of Industrial Relations* (London), Vol. 28 (March 1980), pp. 70–81.

Liefmann-Keil, Elizabeth, "Index-Based Adjustments for Social Security Benefits," *International Labour Review*, International Labor Office (Geneva), Vol. 79 (May 1959), pp. 487–510.

Lindbeck, Assar (1972a), "Stabilization Policy in an Open High-Employment Economy: Swedish Experiences," Chap. 9 in *Stabilization Policies in Interdependent Economies: Proceedings of a Conference Held at the University of Paris-Dauphine, March 25–27, 1971*, ed. by Emil Claassen and Pascal Salin (Amsterdam and London: North-Holland, 1972).

——— (1972b), Contribution to the panel discussion, "World Inflation," in *Stabilization Policies in Interdependent Economies: Proceedings of a Conference Held at the University of Paris-Dauphine, March 25–27, 1971*, ed. by Emil Claassen and Pascal Salin (Amsterdam and London: North-Holland, 1972).

———, "Imported and Structural Inflation and Aggregate Demand: The Scandinavian Model Reconstructed," Chap. 1 in *Inflation and Employment in Open Economies*, ed. by Assar Lindbeck (New York: North-Holland, 1979).

———, "The Recent Slowdown of Productivity Growth," *Economic Journal* (Cambridge), Vol. 93 (March 1983), pp. 13–34.

Lippman, Steven A., and John J. McCall (1976a), "The Economics of Job Search: A Survey," *Part I, Economic Inquiry* (Long Beach, California), Vol. 14 (June 1976), pp. 155–89.

——, (1976b), "The Economics of Job Search: A Survey," *Part II, Economic Inquiry* (Long Beach, California), Vol. 14 (September 1976), pp. 347–68.

Lipschitz, Leslie, and Susan M. Schadler, "Relative Prices, Real Wages, and Macroeconomic Policies: Some Evidence from Manufacturing in Japan and the United Kingdom," *Staff Papers*, International Monetary Fund (Washington), Vol. 31 (June 1984), pp. 303–38.

Lipsey, Richard G., "The Relation Between Unemployment and the Rate of Change of Money Wage Rates in the United Kingdom, 1862–1957: A Further Analysis," *Economica* (London), New Series, Vol. 27 (February 1960), pp. 1–31.

——, and J.M. Parkin, "Incomes Policy: A Re-appraisal," *Economica* (London), New Series, Vol. 37 (May 1970), pp. 115–38.

Lowenstern, Henry, "Adjusting Wages to Living Costs: A Historical Note," *Monthly Labor Review*, U.S. Department of Labor (Washington), Vol. 97 (July 1974), pp. 21–26.

Lucas, Robert E., Jr., "Tobin and Monetarism: A Review Article," *Journal of Economic Literature* (Nashville, Tennessee), Vol. 19 (June 1981), pp. 558–67.

——, and Leonard A. Rapping, "Real Wages, Employment, and Inflation," in *Microeconomic Foundations of Employment and Inflation Theory*, by Edmund S. Phelps and others (New York: W.W. Norton, 1970).

Lundberg, Erik, "Incomes Policy Issues in Sweden," in *Incomes Policy: What Can We Learn from Europe*? ed. by Walter Galenson (Ithaca, New York: Cornell University, 1973).

——, *Inflation Theory and Anti-Inflation Policy*, Proceedings of a Conference Held by the International Economic Association (Boulder, Colorado: Westview Press, 1977).

McCloskey, Donald N. "The Rhetoric of Economics," *Journal of Economic Literature* (Nashville, Tennessee), Vol. 21 (June 1983), pp. 481–517.

McCracken, Paul, and others, *Towards Full Employment and Price Stability*, a report to the OECD by a group of independent experts (Paris: Organization for Economic Cooperation and Development, 1977).

MacDougall, Sir Donald, "Inflation in the United Kingdom," *The Economic Record* (Melbourne), Vol. 35 (December 1959), pp. 371–88.

McKinnon, Ronald I., *An International Standard for Monetary Stabilization*, Institute for International Economics, Policy Analyses in International Economics: 8 (Washington, March 1984), pp. 481–517.

McMahon, C.W., "Is There an International Monetary System?" *Quarterly Bulletin*, Bank of England (London), Vol. 18 (June 1978), pp. 240–43.

Malinvaud, Edmond, *The Theory of Unemployment Reconsidered* (New York: John Wiley, 1977).

——, "Wages and Unemployment," *Economic Journal* (Cambridge), Vol. 92 (March 1982), pp. 1–12.

Marchal, Jean, "Les conditions de l'équilibre macroéconomique dans la stabilité des prix," *Revue Economique* (Paris), No. 6 (November 1964), pp. 853–67.

Markmann, Heinz, "Incomes Policy in Germany: A Trade Union View," *British Journal of Industrial Relations* (London), Vol. 2 (November 1964), pp. 322–39.

Marris, Stephen, "Wage Determination in Selected Countries," Appendix 4 in *The Problem of Rising Prices*, by William Fellner and others (Paris: Organization for European Economic Cooperation, 1961).

——, Contribution to the panel discussion, "World Inflation," in *Stabilization Policies in Interdependent Economies: Proceedings of a Conference Held at the University of Paris-Dauphine, March 25–27, 1971*, ed. by Emil Claassen and Pascal Salin (Amsterdam and London: North-Holland, 1972).

——, *Deficits and the Dollar: The World Economy at Risk*, Institute for International Economics, Policy Analyses in International Economics (Washington, 1985).

Maslove, Allan M., and Gene Swimmer, *Wage Controls in Canada, 1975–78: A Study of Public Decision Making* (Montreal: Institute for Research on Public Policy, 1980).

Massé, Pierre, *Rapport sur la politique des revenus établi à la suite de la Conférence des revenus, Octobre 1963–Janvier 1964*, La Documentation Française (Paris, 1964).

Maunder, W.P.J., ed., *The British Economy in the 1970s* (London: Heinemann, 1980).

Mayer, Thomas, "The Structure of Monetarism (I)" and "The Structure of Monetarism (II)" in *The Structure of Monetarism* (New York and London: W.W. Norton, 1978).

Mire, Joseph, "Incomes Policy in Austria Under a Voluntary Partnership," *Monthly Labor Review*, U.S. Department of Labor (Washington), Vol. 100 (August 1977), pp. 13–17.

Mitchell, Daniel J.B., "Phase II Wage Controls," *Industrial and Labor Relations Review* (Ithaca, New York), Vol. 27 (April 1974), pp. 351–75.

——, and Arnold R. Weber, "Wages and the Pay Board," *American Economic Review, Papers and Proceedings of the Eighty-Sixth Annual Meeting of the American Economic Association* (Nashville, Tennessee), Vol. 64 (May 1974), pp. 88–92.

Mitchell, Joan, *The National Board for Prices and Incomes* (London: Secker & Warburg, 1972).

Mortensen, Dale T., "A Theory of Wage and Employment Dynamics," in *Microeconomic Foundations of Employment and Inflation Theory*, by Edmund S. Phelps and others (New York: W.W. Norton, 1970).

Mouly, Jean, "Wages Policy in Sweden," *International Labour Review*, International Labor Office (Geneva), Vol. 95 (March 1967), pp. 166–201.

Mundell, Robert A., "A Theory of Optimum Currency Areas," *American Economic Review* (Nashville, Tennessee), Vol. 51 (September 1961), pp. 657–65.

Munthe, Preben, "Norway," in *On Incomes Policy: Papers and Proceedings from a Conference in Honour of Erik Lundberg* (Stockholm: Industrial Council for Social and Economic Studies, 1969).

Mussa, Michael, "The Exchange Rate, the Balance of Payments and Monetary and Fiscal Policy Under a Regime of Controlled Floating," in *Flexible Exchange Rates and Stabilization Policy*, ed. by Jan Herin, Assar Lindbeck, and Johan Myhrman (Boulder, Colorado: Westview Press, 1977).

Myhrman, Johan, "The Determinants of Inflation and Economic Activity in Sweden," Chap. 12 in *Inflation and Employment in Open Economies*, ed. by Assar Lindbeck (New York: North-Holland, 1979).

National Institute of Economic and Social Research, "Summary and Appraisal," *National Institute Economic Review* (London), No. 65 (August 1973), pp. 3–6.

——, "Appraisal," *National Institute Economic Review* (London), No. 67 (February 1974), pp. 3–7.

——, "Chapter I. The Economy in 1976," *National Institute Economic Review* (London), No. 79 (February 1977).

——, "Chapter I. The Economy in 1977," *National Institute Economic Review* (London), No. 84 (May 1978).

New Zealand Monetary and Economic Council, *Inflation and the Labour Market—December 1971*, Report No. 22 (Wellington: Government Printer, 1971).

Niehans, Jürg, "Some Doubts About the Efficacy of Monetary Policy Under Flexible Exchange Rates," *Journal of International Economics* (Amsterdam), Vol. 5 (August 1975), pp. 275–81.

Nordhaus, William D., "Inflation Theory and Policy," *American Economic Review, Papers and Proceedings of the Eighty-Eighth Annual Meeting of the American Economic Association* (Nashville, Tennessee), Vol. 66 (May 1976), pp. 59–71.

Norges Bank, "Fresh Approach to Prices and Incomes Policy," *Economic Bulletin* (Oslo), Vol. 44 (September 1973), pp. 116–26.

Oettinger, Martin P., "Nation-Wide Job Evaluation in the Netherlands," *Industrial Relations: A Journal of Economy and Society* (Berkeley, California), Vol. 4 (October 1964), pp. 45–59.

Okun, Arthur M., "The Great Stagflation Swamp," *Challenge* (White Plains, New York), Vol. 20 (November–December 1977), pp. 6–13.

——, *Prices and Quantities: A Macroeconomic Analysis* (Washington: The Brookings Institution, 1981).

——, and George L. Perry, "Innovative Policies to Slow Inflation," *Brookings Papers on Economic Activity: 2* (Special Issue, 1978), The Brookings Institution (Washington).

On Incomes Policy: Papers and Proceedings from a Conference in Honour of Erik Lundberg (Stockholm: Swedish Industrial Council for Social and Economic Studies, 1969).

Organization for Economic Cooperation and Development, *Policies for Prices, Profits and Other Non-Wage Incomes* (Paris, 1964).

——, *Wages and Labour Mobility* (Paris, 1965).

——, *Non-Wage Incomes and Prices Policy: Trade Union Policy and Experience*, Background Report for a Trade Union Seminar (Paris, 1966).

____, *Inflation: The Present Problem* (Paris, 1970).

____(1971a), *OECD Economic Surveys: Norway* (Paris, January 1971).

____(1971b), *Present Policies Against Inflation* (Paris, June 1971).

____, *The Adjustment of Personal Income Tax Systems for Inflation: A Report by the Committee on Fiscal Affairs* (Paris, 1976).

____, *OECD Economic Surveys: Austria* (Paris, July 1976).

____, *OECD Economic Surveys: Netherlands* (Paris, March 1976).

____, *The Development of Industrial Relations Systems: Some Implications of Japanese Experience* (Paris, 1977).

____, *OECD Economic Surveys: Norway* (Paris, January 1977).

____, *OECD Economic Surveys: Netherlands* (Paris, March 1979).

____, *OECD Economic Surveys: Norway* (Paris, March 1982).

____, *OECD Economic Surveys: Norway* (Paris, February 1983).

____, *Positive Adjustment Policies: Managing Structural Change* (Paris, 1983).

____, *OECD Economic Surveys: Australia* (Paris, June 1984).

____, *OECD Economic Surveys: Norway* (Paris, January 1985).

____, *OECD Economic Surveys: Australia* (Paris, June 1985).

Osiatynski, Jerzy, *Kalecki's Theory of Economic Dynamics After Thirty Years*, Discussion Paper 214, Institute of Development Studies, University of Sussex (Brighton: IDS Publications, 1986).

Page, S.A.B., and Sandra Trollope, "An International Survey of Indexing and Its Effects," *National Institute Economic Review*, National Institute of Economic and Social Research (London), No. 70 (November 1974), pp. 46–60.

Paish, F.W., *Studies in an Inflationary Economy: The United Kingdom, 1948–1961* (London: Macmillan, 1962).

____, "The Limits of Incomes Policies," in *Policy for Incomes?* by F.W. Paish and Jossleyn Hennessy, Hobart Paper No. 29 (London: Institute of Economic Affairs, 1st ed., 1964).

____, *Rise and Fall of Incomes Policy*, Hobart Paper No. 47 (London: Institute of Economic Affairs, 1969).

Parkin, Michael, "Incomes Policy: Some Further Results on the Determination of the Rate of Change of Money Wages," *Economica* (London), New Series, Vol. 37 (November 1970), pp. 386–401.

____, "Comment," in *Flexible Exchange Rates and Stabilization Policy*, ed. by Jan Herin, Assar Lindbeck, and Johan Myhrman (Boulder, Colorado: Westview Press, 1977).

____, and Alexander K. Swoboda, "Inflation: A Review of the Issues," in *Inflation Theory and Anti-Inflation Policy*, Proceedings of a Conference Held by the International Economic Association, ed. by Erik Lundberg (Boulder, Colorado: Westview Press, 1977).

Peacock, A.T., and W.J.L. Ryan, "Wage Claims and the Pace of Inflation (1948–51)," *Economic Journal* (London), Vol. 63 (June 1953), pp. 385–92.

Pedersen, Jørgen, "The Control of Wages and the Value of Money: The Dutch Experience," *Quarterly Review*, Banca Nazionale del Lavoro (Rome), No. 40 (March 1957), pp. 3–25.

——, "Incomes Policy—Danish Style," *Quarterly Review*, Banca Nazionale del Lavoro (Rome), No. 69 (June 1964), pp. 160–82.

Pels, P.S., "The 'Labour Foundation' in the Netherlands," *International Labour Review*, International Labor Office (Geneva), Vol. 75 (May 1957), pp. 437–49.

Pen, Jan, "The Strange Adventures of Dutch Wage Policy," *British Journal of Industrial Relations* (London), Vol. 1 (October 1963), pp. 318–30.

——, "Income Policy in the Netherlands, 1959–1963," *Scottish Journal of Political Economy* (Edinburgh), Vol. 11 (November 1964), pp. 179–93.

Pencavel, John H., "The American Experience with Incomes Policies," Chap. 7 in *Incomes Policies, Inflation and Relative Pay*, ed. by J.L. Fallick and R.F. Elliott (London: Allen & Unwin, 1981).

Perry, George L., "The Success of Anti-Inflation Policies in the United States," *Journal of Money, Credit and Banking* (Columbus, Ohio), Vol. 5, No. 1, Part 2 (February 1973), pp. 569–93.

Peston, Maurice, "The Integration of Monetary, Fiscal and Incomes Policy," *Lloyds Bank Review* (London), No. 141 (July 1981), pp. 1–13.

Phelps, Edmund S., "Phillips Curves, Expectations of Inflation and Optimal Unemployment over Time," *Economica* (London), New Series, Vol. 34 (August 1967), pp. 254–81.

——, *Inflation Policy and Unemployment Theory: The Cost-Benefit Approach to Monetary Planning* (New York: W.W. Norton, 1972).

——, and others, *Microeconomic Foundations of Employment and Inflation Theory* (New York: W.W. Norton, 1970).

Phelps Brown, E.H. (1962a), *The Economics of Labor* (New Haven and London: Yale University Press, 1962).

—— (1962b), "Wage Drift," *Economica* (London), New Series, Vol. 29 (November 1962), pp. 339–56.

——, "Guidelines for Growth and for Incomes in the United Kingdom: Some Possible Lessons for the United States," in *Guidelines, Informal Controls, and the Market Place: Policy Choices in a Full Employment Economy*, ed. by George P. Shultz and Robert Z. Aliber (Chicago: University of Chicago Press, 1966).

——, *Pay and Profits* (Manchester: Manchester University Press, 1968).

—— (1971a), *Collective Bargaining Reconsidered*, Stamp Memorial Lecture, 1971 (London: Athlone Press, 1971).

—— (1971b), "Industrial Relations and the Law: Lessons of Australian Experience," *Three Banks Review* (Edinburgh), No. 89 (March 1971), pp. 3–29.

——, "A Workable Incomes Policy for Britain," in *An Incomes Policy for Britain: Policy Proposals and Research Needs*, ed. by Frank Blackaby (London: Heinemann, 1972).

——, and Margaret H. Browne, *A Century of Pay* (London: Macmillan, 1968).

Phillips, A.W., "The Relation Between Unemployment and the Rate of Change of Money Wage Rates in the United Kingdom, 1861–1957," *Economica* (London), New Series, Vol. 25 (November 1958), pp. 283–99.

———, "Employment, Inflation and Growth," *Economica* (London), New Series, Vol. 29 (February 1962), pp. 1–16.

Piore, Michael J., "Unemployment and Inflation: An Alternative View," *Challenge* (Armonk, New York, May–June 1978), pp. 24–32.

Polak, J.J., and Victor Argy, "Credit Policy and the Balance of Payments," *Staff Papers*, International Monetary Fund (Washington), Vol. 18 (March 1971), pp. 1–24.

Poole, William, "Wage-Price Controls: Where Do We Go from Here?" *Brookings Papers on Economic Activity: 1* (1973), The Brookings Institution (Washington), pp. 285–99.

Popkin, Joel, "Prices in 1972: An Analysis of Changes During Phase 2," *Monthly Labor Review*, U.S. Department of Labor (Washington), Vol. 96 (February 1973), pp. 16–23.

Porter, Michael G., and Victor Argy, "The Forward Exchange Market and the Effects of Domestic and External Disturbances Under Alternative Exchange Rate Systems," *Staff Papers*, International Monetary Fund (Washington), Vol. 19 (November 1972), pp. 503–32.

Prais, S.J., "Some Mathematical Notes on the Quantity Theory of Money in an Open Economy," *Staff Papers*, International Monetary Fund (Washington), Vol. 8 (May 1961), pp. 212–26.

Purvis, Douglas D., "Wage Responsiveness and the Insulation Properties of a Flexible Exchange Rate," Chap. 9 in *Inflation and Employment in Open Economies*, ed. by Assar Lindbeck (New York: North-Holland, 1979).

Pym, Denis, "Is There a Future for Wage Incentive Schemes?" *British Journal of Industrial Relations* (London), Vol. 2 (1964), pp. 379–97.

Reddaway, W.B., "Australian Wage Policy, 1929–1937," *International Labour Review*, International Labor Office (Geneva), Vol. 37 (March 1938), pp. 314–37.

Reder, M.W., "The Theory of Occupational Wage Differentials," *American Economic Review* (Nashville, Tennessee), Vol. 45 (December 1955), pp. 833–52.

———, "Chicago Economics: Permanence and Change," *Journal of Economic Literature* (Nashville, Tennessee), Vol. 20 (March 1982), pp. 1–38.

Rees, Albert, "The Construction Industry Stabilization Committee: Implications for Phase II," *Brookings Papers on Economic Activity: 3* (1971), The Brookings Institution (Washington), pp. 760–68.

———, *The Economics of Work and Pay* (New York: Harper and Row, 1979).

———, *Striking a Balance: Making National Economic Policy* (Chicago: University of Chicago Press, 1984).

Rehn, G., *Wage Drift in Sweden*, Trade Union Research Department, European Productivity Agency (Paris, 1959). This is an English summary of *Löneglidning; Rapport från expertgrupp tillsall at SAF och LO* (Stockholm, 1957).

Reichel, Hans, "Recent Trends in Collective Bargaining in the Federal Republic of Germany," *International Labour Review*, International Labor Office (Geneva), Vol. 104 (December 1971), pp. 469–87.

Reid, Frank, "The Effect of Controls on the Rate of Wage Change in Canada," *The Canadian Journal of Economics* (Toronto), Vol. 12 (May 1979), pp. 214–27.

Roberts, Benjamin Charles, *National Wages Policy in War and Peace* (London: Allen & Unwin, 1958).

——, and Sheila Rothwell, "Recent Trends in Collective Bargaining in the United Kingdom," *International Labour Review*, International Labor Office (Geneva), Vol. 106 (December 1972), pp. 543–71.

——, Hideaki Okamoto, and George C. Lodge, *Collective Bargaining and Employee Participation in Western Europe, North America and Japan*, Report of the Trilateral Task Force on Industrial Relations to the Trilateral Commission (New York, Tokyo, and Paris: The Trilateral Commission, 1979).

Robinson, Derek, *Incomes Policy and Capital Sharing in Europe* (New York: Harper and Row, 1973).

——, and Ken Mayhew, eds., *Pay Policies for the Future* (Oxford and New York: Oxford University Press, 1983).

Robinson, Joan, *Essays in the Theory of Employment* (London: Macmillan, 1937; 2nd ed., Oxford: Basil Blackwell, 1947).

——, ed., *After Keynes: Papers Presented to Section F (Economics) at the 1972 Annual Meeting of the British Association for the Advancement of Science* (Oxford: Basil Blackwell, 1973).

Romanis, Anne, "Relative Growth of Exports of Manufactures of United States and Other Industrial Countries," *Staff Papers*, International Monetary Fund (Washington), Vol. 8 (May 1961), pp. 241–73.

——, "Balance of Payments Adjustment Among Developed Countries," *Staff Papers*, International Monetary Fund (Washington), Vol. 12 (March 1965), pp. 17–36.

——, "Towards an Incomes Policy: A Survey of Recent Institutional Developments in the United Kingdom" (unpublished, International Monetary Fund, July 28, 1966).

——, "Cost Inflation and Incomes Policy in Industrial Countries," *Staff Papers*, International Monetary Fund (Washington), Vol. 14 (March 1967), pp. 169–209.

Ross, Arthur M., "The Dynamics of Wage Determination Under Collective Bargaining," *American Economic Review* (Nashville, Tennessee), Vol. 37 (December 1947), pp. 793–822.

——, "Guideline Policy—Where We Are and How We Got There," in *Guidelines, Informal Controls, and the Market Place: Policy Choices in a Full Employment Economy*, ed. by George P. Shultz and Robert Z. Aliber (Chicago: University of Chicago Press, 1966).

Rothschild, Kurt W., "The Phillips Curve and All That," *Scottish Journal of Political Economy* (Edinburgh), Vol. 18 (November 1971), pp. 245–80.

Routh, Guy, "The Relation Between Unemployment and the Rate of Change of Money Wage Rates: A Comment," *Economica* (London), New Series, Vol. 26 (November 1959), pp. 299–315.

Ruben, George, "Major Collective Bargaining Developments—A Quarter-Century Review," *Current Wage Developments*, U.S. Department of Labor (Washington), Vol. 26 (February 1974), pp. 42–54.

Sachs, Jeffrey D., "Wages, Profits, and Macroeconomic Adjustment: A Comparative Study," *Brookings Papers on Economic Activity: 2* (1979), The Brookings Institution (Washington), pp. 269–319.

———, "Real Wages and Unemployment in the OECD Countries," *Brookings Papers on Economic Activity: 1* (1983), The Brookings Institution (Washington), pp. 255–89.

Salin, Pascal, and Georges Lane, "Inflation in France," in *Worldwide Inflation: Theory and Recent Experience*, ed. by Lawrence B. Krause and Walter S. Salant (Washington: The Brookings Institution, 1977).

Sargan, J.D., "A Study of Wages and Prices in the U.K., 1949–1968," Chap. 4 in *The Current Inflation: Proceedings of a Conference Held at the London School of Economics on 22 February 1971*, ed. by Harry G. Johnson and A.R. Nobay (London: Macmillan, 1971).

Saunders, C.T., "Incomes Policies—What Are They an Instrument For?" *Economic Planning and Macroeconomic Policy: Papers and Proceedings of a Conference held by the Japan Economic Research Center in September 1970*, Vol. II (Tokyo: Japan Economic Research Center, 1971).

———, "Lessons for Britain from European Experience," in *An Incomes Policy for Britain: Policy Proposals and Research Needs*, ed. by Frank Blackaby (London: Heinemann, 1972).

Schackle, G.L.S., "Keynes and Today's Establishment in Economic Theory: A View," *Journal of Economic Literature* (Nashville, Tennessee), Vol. 11 (June 1973), pp. 516–19.

Schultze, Charles L., *Recent Inflation in the United States*, Study Paper No. 1, prepared for consideration by the Joint Economic Committee, 86th Cong., 1st Sess. (Washington: Government Printing Office, September 1959).

Seidel, Bernhard, *Wage Policy and European Integration* (Hampshire, England: Gower, 1983).

Seidel, Hans, "The Austrian Economy: An Overview," in *The Political Economy of Austria*, ed. by Sven W. Arndt (Washington and London: American Enterprise Institute for Public Policy Research, 1982).

Seki, Hideo, "Employment Problems and Policies in an Ageing Society: The Japanese Experience," *International Labour Review*, International Labor Office (Geneva), Vol. 119 (May–June 1980), pp. 351–65.

Sellier, François, "Les transformations de la négociation collective et de l'organisation syndicale en Italie," *Sociologie du Travail* (Paris), April–June 1971, pp. 141–58.

Sen Gupta, A.K., "Appendix II: Survey of Wage-Price Links in Various Countries," *Staff Papers*, International Monetary Fund (Washington), Vol. 6 (November 1958), pp. 343–68.

Sheahan, John, *The Wage-Price Guideposts* (Washington: The Brookings Institution, 1967).

Shirai, Taishiro, and Haruo Shimada, "Japan," in *Labor in the Twentieth Century*, ed. by John T. Dunlop and Walter Galenson (New York: Academic Press, 1978).

Shiskin, Julius, "Updating the Consumer Price Index—An Overview," *Monthly Labour Review*, International Labor Office (Geneva), Vol. 97 (July 1974), pp. 3–20.

Shultz, George P., and Robert Z. Aliber, eds., *Guidelines, Informal Controls, and the Market Place: Policy Choices in a Full Employment Economy* (Chicago: University of Chicago Press, 1966).

Sims, Christopher A., "Money, Income, and Causality," *American Economic Review* (Nashville, Tennessee), Vol. 62 (September 1972), pp. 540–52.

Skånland, Hermod, "Incomes Policy: Norwegian Experience," *British Journal of Industrial Relations* (London), Vol. 2 (November 1964), pp. 309–21.

Slichter, Sumner H., "Do the Wage-Fixing Arrangements in the American Labor Market Have an Inflationary Bias?" *American Economic Review, Papers and Proceedings of the Sixty-Sixth Annual Meeting of the American Economic Association* (Nashville, Tennessee), Vol. 64 (May 1954), pp. 322–46.

Smith, Anthony D., ed., *The Labour Market and Inflation* (London: Macmillan, 1968).

Smith, David C., *Incomes Policies: Some Foreign Experiences and Their Relevance for Canada* (Ottawa: Economic Council of Canada, 1966).

——, (1968a), "Incomes Policy," in *Britain's Economic Prospects*, Richard E. Caves and Associates (Washington: The Brookings Institution; London: Allen & Unwin, 1968).

——, (1968b), "Some Issues in the Incomes Policy Debate," in *Wages, Prices, Profits and Economic Policy: Proceedings of a Conference Held by the Centre for Industrial Relations*, ed. by John H.G. Crispo (Toronto: University of Toronto Press, 1968).

Smith, Eric Owen, "Collective Bargaining," in *The British Economy in the 1970s*, ed. by W.P.J. Maunder (London: Heinemann, 1980.)

Soffer, Benson, "Cost-of-Living Wage Policy," *Industrial and Labor Relations Review* (Ithaca, New York), Vol. 7 (January 1954), pp. 192–99.

——, (1959a), "The Effects of Recent Long-Term Wage Agreements on General Wage Level Movements: 1950–1956," *Quarterly Journal of Economics* (Cambridge, Massachusetts), Vol. 73 (February 1959), pp. 36–60.

——, (1959b), "On Union Rivalries and the Minimum Differentiation of Wage Patterns," *Review of Economics and Statistics* (Cambridge, Massachusetts), Vol. 41 (February 1959), pp. 53–60.

Spitäller, Erich, "Incomes Policy in Austria," *Staff Papers*, International Monetary Fund (Washington), Vol. 20 (March 1973), pp. 170–202.

——, "Commentary," in *The Political Economy of Austria*, ed. by Sven W. Arndt (Washington and London: American Enterprise Institute for Public Policy Research, 1982).

Sraffa, Piero, "The Laws of Returns Under Competitive Conditions," *Economic Journal* (London), Vol. 36 (December 1926), pp. 535–50.

Staller, Jerome M., and Loren M. Solnick, "Effect of Escalators on Wages in Major Contracts Expiring in 1974," *Monthly Labor Review*, U.S. Department of Labor (Washington), Vol. 97 (July 1974), pp. 27–32.

Streeten, Paul, "Wages, Prices and Productivity," *Kyklos* (Basle), Vol. 15 (Fasc. 4, 1962), pp. 723–31.

Sturmthal, Adolf, ed., *Contemporary Collective Bargaining in Seven Countries* (Ithaca, New York: Cornell University, 1957).

Suzuki, H., "Age, Seniority and Wages," *International Labour Review*, International Labor Office (Geneva), Vol. 113 (January–February 1976), pp. 67–84.

Swoboda, Alexander K., "Monetary Approaches to Worldwide Inflation," in *Worldwide Inflation: Theory and Recent Experience*, ed. by Lawrence B. Krause and Walter S. Salant (Washington: The Brookings Institution, 1977).

Tanzi, Vito, "Adjusting Personal Income Taxes for Inflation: The Foreign Experience," Chap. 8 in *Inflation and the Income Tax: A Report of a Conference Sponsored by the Fund for Public Policy Research and the Brookings Institution*, ed. by Henry J. Aaron (Washington: The Brookings Institution, 1976).

Tinbergen, Jan, "An Economic Policy for 1936," in *Selected Papers*, ed. by L.H. Klaassen, L.M. Koyck, and H.J. Witteveen (Amsterdam: North-Holland, 1959).

Tobin, James, *Asset Accumulation and Economic Activity: Reflections on Contemporary Macroeconomic Theory* (Oxford: Basil Blackwell, 1980).

Townshend, Hugh, "Liquidity-Premium and the Theory of Value," *Economic Journal* (London), Vol. 47 (March 1937), pp. 157–69.

Trevithick, James A., "Keynes, Inflation and Money Illusion," *Economic Journal* (London), Vol. 85 (March 1975), pp. 101–13.

Turner, M.A., and H. Zoeteweij, *Prices, Wages, and Incomes Policies in Industrialised Market Economies* (Geneva: International Labor Office, 1966).

Ulman, Lloyd, "Under Severe Restraint: British Incomes Policy," *Industrial Relations: A Journal of Economy and Society* (Berkeley, California), Vol. 6 (May 1967), pp. 213–66.

——, and Robert J. Flanagan, *Wage Restraint: A Study of Incomes Policies in Western Europe* (Berkeley, California: University of California Press, 1971).

United Kingdom, Council on Prices, Productivity and Incomes, *First Report* (London: H.M. Stationery Office, 1958).

——, *Second Report* (London: H.M. Stationery Office, 1958).

——, *Third Report* (London: H.M. Stationery Office, 1959).

——, *Fourth Report* (London: H.M. Stationery Office, 1961).

——, Department of Employment [and Productivity], *In Place of Strife: A Policy for Industrial Relations*, Cmnd. No. 3888 (London: H.M. Stationery Office, 1969).

——, National Board for Prices and Incomes, *General Report, April 1965 to July 1966*, Cmnd. No. 3087 (London: H.M. Stationery Office, 1966).

——, *Second General Report, July 1966 to August 1967*, Cmnd. No. 3394 (London: H.M. Stationery Office, 1967).

———, *Third General Report, August 1967 to July 1968*, Cmnd. No. 3751 (London: H.M. Stationery Office, 1968).

———, *Fourth General Report, July 1968 to July 1969*, Cmnd. No. 4130 (London: H.M. Stationery Office, 1969).

———, *Fifth and Final General Report, July 1969 to March 1971*, Cmnd. No. 4649 (London: H.M. Stationery Office, 1971).

———, National Incomes Commission, *Report No. 4: Agreements of November–December 1963 in the Engineering and Shipbuilding Industries*, Cmnd. No. 2583 (London: H.M. Stationery Office, 1965).

———, Royal Commission on Trade Unions and Employers' Associations, *Report*, Cmnd. No. 3623 (London: H.M. Stationery Office, 1968).

———, *Research Paper No. 1: The Role of Shop Stewards in British Industrial Relations* (London: H.M. Stationery Office, 1966).

———, Trades Union Congress, *Cost of Living Threshold Agreements* (London, 1972).

———, Treasury, *Economic Report on 1964* (London: H.M. Stationery Office, 1965; issued as a Supplement to *Economic Trends*, No. 137, March 1965).

———, *Incomes Policy: The Next Step*, Cmnd. No. 1626 (London: H.M. Stationery Office, 1962).

———, *Economic Progress Report* (London, September 1977).

United States, *Economic Report of the President*, January 1962 (Washington: Government Printing Office, 1962).

———, Cost of Living Council, *Economic Stabilization Program Quarterly Report Covering the Period ...* (Washington: Government Printing Office, 1971–74).

———, *Economic Report of the President*, January 1973 (Washington: Government Printing Office, 1973).

———, *Economic Report of the President*, February 1974 (Washington: Government Printing Office, 1974).

Wachter, Michael L., "Phase II, Cost-Push Inflation, and Relative Wages," *American Economic Review* (Nashville, Tennessee), Vol. 64 (June 1974), pp. 482–91.

———, "The Changing Cyclical Responsiveness of Wage Inflation," *Brookings Papers on Economic Activity: 1* (1976), The Brookings Institution (Washington), pp. 115–67.

Weber, Arnold R., *In Pursuit of Price Stability: The Wage-Price Freeze of 1971* (Washington: The Brookings Institution, 1973).

Weinberg, Nat, "The Death of the United States Guideposts," Chap. 3 in *The Labour Market and Inflation*, ed. by Anthony D. Smith (London: Macmillan, 1968).

White, William H., "House Depreciation and Interest Costs and the Reliability of Recent Measured Increases in the Cost of Living (unpublished, International Monetary Fund, April 28, 1967).

———, "Anti-Inflationary Advantages of Financial Indexation" (unpublished, International Monetary Fund, February 13, 1976).

——, "The Case for Moderate Use of Monetary Policy to Reduce Lags and Capital Flows" (unpublished, International Monetary Fund, August 27, 1976).

Whitman, Marina v. N., "The Payments Adjustment Process and the Exchange Rate Regime: What Have We Learned?" *American Economic Review, Papers and Proceedings of the Eighty-Seventh Annual Meeting of the American Economic Association* (Nashville, Tennessee), Vol. 65 (May 1975), pp. 133–46.

Wilkinson, Frank, "The Outlook for Wages in the Short Run," *Economic Policy Review* (Cambridge, England), No. 1 (February 1975), pp. 26–28.

Willey, Richard J., "Trade Unions and Political Parties in the Federal Republic of Germany," *Industrial and Labor Relations Review* (Ithaca, New York), Vol. 28 (October 1974), pp. 38–59.

Wilson, Thomas A., and Gregory V. Jump, *The Influence of the Anti-Inflation Program on Aggregate Wages and Prices: A Simulation Analysis* (Toronto: Institute for Policy Analysis, University of Toronto, 1979).

Wilton, D.A., *Wage Inflation in Canada, 1955–75* (Ottawa: Economic Council of Canada, 1980).

Windmuller, John P., *Labor Relations in the Netherlands* (Ithaca, New York: Cornell University Press, 1969).

Worswick, G.D.N., "The Stability and Flexibility of Full Employment," in *The Economics of Full Employment* (Oxford: Basil Blackwell, 1944).

——, "The End of Demand Management?" *Lloyds Bank Review*, Lloyds Bank Ltd. (London), No. 123 (January 1977), pp. 1–18.

——, and P.H. Ady, ed., *The British Economy in the Nineteen-Fifties* (Oxford: Clarendon Press, 1962).

Zoeteweij, Bert, "The Adjustment of Wages to Changes in the Cost of Living," *International Labour Review*, International Labor Office (Geneva), Vol. 66 (August 1952), pp. 89–112.

——, "National Wage Policy: The Experience of the Netherlands," *International Labour Review*, International Labor Office (Geneva), Vol. 71 (February 1955), pp. 148–79.